THE HERITAGE GUIDEBOOK

LANDMARKS AND HISTORICAL SITES IN SOUTHEASTERN WISCONSIN

historically and/or
architecturally
significant buildings,
monuments and sites
in five southeastern
wisconsin counties

by
H. RUSSELL ZIMMERMANN

SECOND EDITION
WITH INDEX

HARRY W. SCHWARTZ, MILWAUKEE, WISCONSIN

1989

Library of Congress Catalog Card Number 88-51951

ISBN 0-96220-300-9

First Edition — 1st printing — 1975
2nd printing —1976
3rd printing — 1978
Second edition, with index —— 1989

Dust Cover: Henry Collins residence, 6419 Nicholson Road, Racine, in February, 1975. Page 395, No. 948

End Sheets: Birdseye view of Juneau Park and Yankee Hill area, Milwaukee from *A Souvenir of the 24th Sängerfest of the N.A. Sängerbund July 21-25, 1886* Caspar & Zahn (publishers).

Frontispiece: Central Mansard tower of the Mitchell Building, 207 E. Michigan St., Milwaukee. Page 46, No. 22

ACKNOWLEDGEMENT

The index was prepared in 1980
by Carol Hackenbruch of the Milwaukee Public Library.

FOREWORD

by

JOHN O. NORQUIST

MAYOR OF MILWAUKEE

I hope that as you page through this book, the buildings described will still be standing.

Thanks to a strong anti-freeway movement in the 1960s and 1970s, and to a dedicated band of historic preservationists, Milwaukee is one of the few cities in America that hasn't yet torn itself down. Buildings that bustled with human activity before the turn of the century are still in service as places for Milwaukeeans to live, work and play. Many fine old structures remain to remind us of Milwaukee's rich cultural heritage.

But threats to historically significant buildings continue and this book serves a purpose beyond historical record keeping. It should be viewed as an appeal for the preservation of the very buildings it describes.

The rich and diverse ethnic background of those who made Milwaukee their home for the past 143 years has given our city its unique character and sense of community. The mosaic of Milwaukee's colorful past is reflected in the character of those peoples' homes and places of commerce and government. Our historic buildings are a treasure to be enjoyed by the people and respected by the government and developers.

Historic preservation not only saves and enhances works of architecture for their artistic qualities, it also serves to shape and enrich the environment in which Milwaukeeans live and work. Renovated historic buildings serve as reminders of the proud accomplishments of past generations while contributing to the renewed life of the city.

During the past 10 years, Milwaukee has witnessed the rescue and preservation of many old structures which housed the business, industry and government that built this city. Three notable examples are the Plankinton Arcade, the former Schlitz Brewing Co. complex and the former Valentine Blatz Brewing Co. buildings.

As we build for Milwaukee's future, we must make it a priority to preserve the city's historically rich architecture. Where we can, we must find new uses for our legacy of stately structures whose intricate designs and fine craftsmanship would be impossible to reproduce today. We must find alternatives to development plans that consider only the wrecking ball as a tool for progress. An even if time has eroded the structural soundness of historic buildings, the facades can still be preserved to grace the front of new construction. Historic buildings are a valuable resource that contribute significantly to the quality of life for which Milwaukee is famous. Unfortunately, old buildings are not a renewable resource, and we must be careful not to deplete our precious supply.

It's also my hope that architects building new landmarks for our city will have an eye for architectural design that will be revered by generations to come. I am pleased that several recently built landmarks gracing the city's skyline reflect the architectural themes of some of the older buildings around them.

For example, City Hall's towering Flemish Renaissance architectural style is echoed in the soaring design of its next door neighbor, the Milwaukee Center. The home of the new theater district also incorporates the majestic Pabst Theater and the restored and adapted former Wisconsin Electric Power Company generating plant, which now adds to the creative vitality of Downtown as the home of the Milwaukee Repertory Theater. The distinctive copper roofs of a bygone era grace not only the Milwaukee Center but also the scrolled gables and cupola-capped peak of the new 100 East Wisconsin Avenue Building, whose design recalls the historic Pabst Building that once stood on the site.

I commend H. Russell Zimmermann, noted Milwaukee architectural design consultant and architectural historian, for his dedication and contributions to the preservation of Milwaukee's great architectural treasures. His photographic record of our city's past will increase awareness among residents and visitors alike of the wealth of history that built Milwaukee into a great city.

I also salute the Harry W. Schwartz Bookshops, an historic institution in its own right since 1927, which recognized the value of republishing Zimmermann's original book.

May this book act as a catalyst to further the appreciation and preservation of Milwaukee's historic buildings for generations to come.

John O. Norquist

TABLE OF CONTENTS

Page

Preface 5
Table of Contents 7
Introduction 9
How to Use Guide 12
Cream City Brick 14
Glossary 23
Milwaukee County 33
   Juneautown 37
   Old Third Ward 42
   Yankee Hill 51
   Prospect Avenue Area 67
   Prospect Hill 79
   North Point 83
   Shorewood/Whitefish Bay 93
   Old Milwaukee Township 97
   Near East Side 100
   Kilbourntown 103
   Old City of Milwaukee 123
   Grand Avenue Area 129
   Sauerkraut Blvd. 138
   Old Wauwatosa Township 142
   Walker's Point & Southwest 155
   Bay View/St. Francis 170
   Oak Creek/Franklin/Greenfield 176
Ozaukee County 183
   General 185
      Little Kohler (*367, 368*)
      Ulao (*356*)
   Cedarburg 190
   Grafton 207
   Hamilton 210
   Mequon 213
   Port Washington 216
   Saukville 226
   Thiensville 229
   Waubeka 232
Washington County 235
   General 237
      Addison (*519*)
      Boltonville (*524, 525, 526, 527*)
      Fillmore (*528*)
      Nenno (*520, 521*)
      Richfield (*514*)
      St. Lawrence (*515, 516*)
      Wayne (*522, 523*)
   Germantown 247
   Hartford 250
   Kewaskum 254
   Newburg 257

Page

Slinger 260
West Bend 263
West Bend (Barton) 270
Waukesha County 273
  General 276
    Brookfield (*619, 620, 621*)
    Dousman (*613, 614*)
    Genessee (*623*)
    Genessee Depot (*624, 625*)
    Lannon (*608, 609, 610*)
    Mapleton (*603*)
    Nashotah (*611, 612*)
    New Berlin (*627, 628, 629, 630*)
    North Lake (*606*)
    Okauchee (*604*)
    Ottowa (*622*)
    Tess Corners (*641*)
  Delafield 288
  Eagle 292
  Hartland 293
  Menomonee Falls 295
  Merton 298
  Mukwonago 300
  Oconomowoc 303
  Pewaukee 315
  Saylesville 317
  Sussex 319
  Waterville 321
  Waukesha 324
Racine County 343
  General 346
    Franksville (*807*)
    Sturtevant (*804*)
    Union Grove (*805, 806*)
  Burlington 354
  Caldwell 363
  Racine 367
  Rochester 396
  Waterford 400
Ackowledgments 405
Index 407

INTRODUCTION

With the exception of man's interpersonal relationships, scarcely anything is more thoroughly interwoven in our daily lives than architecture. We are born under a man-made roof, and we spend the greater part of our lives working, playing, worshiping, loving and suffering in buildings. Architecture's omnipresent influence on us cannot be underrated. As Winston Churchill once said, "First we shape our buildings and then they shape us." But the buildings around us are more than just utilitarian constructions or artistic designs; they create tangible links with the past — an encyclopedia of history.

In a single building we may study the tastes of a bygone era, enjoy the artistic and engineering achievement of a master architect, observe the materials and craftmanship of forgotten trades or feel the presence of people and significant events. In subsequent remodelings we might observe the fads and foibles of many generations. Architecture may reveal, in its design and construction, the influences of social etiquette, economic pressure, technology, superstition, religious beliefs or the nationality of its builder.

It is hoped that this book will increase the reader's awareness and appreciation of the architectural/historical environment. Since we all must continually circulate in this environment, it stands to reason that those who can see more along the way will have richer lives.

The area covered in the book includes Milwaukee County and the four surrounding counties (Ozaukee, Washington, Waukesha and Racine). Within these boundaries, buildings, monuments, historical and archeological sites have been selected on the basis of their architectural and/or historical significance. In addition to residences, churches, factories, civic and commercial buildings, a number of parks and three nature centers have been included. The guidebook does not pretend to be an exhaustive or all-inclusive encyclopedia for southeastern Wisconsin, but it is rather a broad selection of buildings and sites which, hopefully, will promote wider exploration and serious future research.

The earliest structures in the book date from the 1830's and a few were built as recently as 1975. Within this area many Indian names will be found on towns and cities, streets and waterways and many of the major roads were made to follow Indian trails. A large percentage of the earliest settlers were foreign immigrants and their influence can still be seen in the names and architecture of the region. In a few cases, the present owners of a house were found to be descendants of the original settler who first claimed the land.

Originally conceived as a brochure with a small number of obvious and well-known landmarks, this project grew to become a listing of 968 buildings and sites with 58 maps, a glossary, and a guide for its use. The few official listings that were available, at the outset, did not begin to adequately represent the variety and depth of southeastern Wisconsin's wealth. It was decided, therefore, that a new inventory had to be made. This was accomplished by purchasing city and county maps and methodically driving the thousands of miles necessary to cover all crossroads, settlements and cities in the five county area. In the beginning, an attempt was made to faithfully cover every county trunk road and alleyway, but this soon proved to be far beyond the scope of the project.

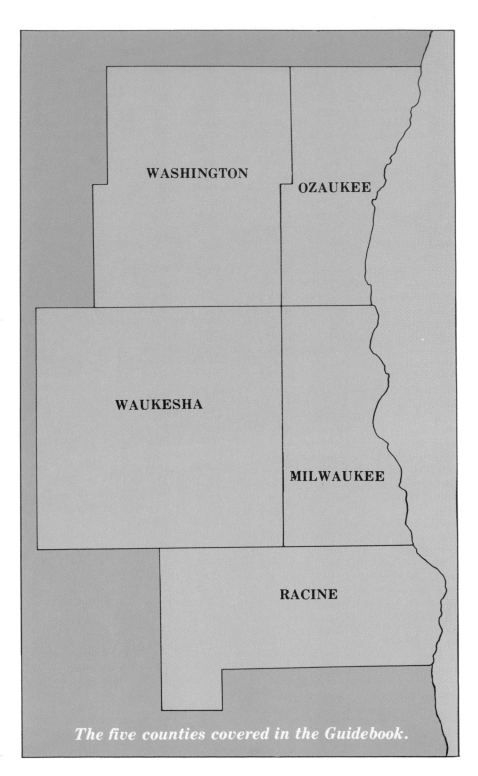

The five counties covered in the Guidebook.

Over a year passed between the beginning of the raw inventory and the final proofreading. After the first lists were compiled, a second trip was made to each site to take photographs. With the photographs, and specially-designed information forms, the final selections were made. Research was relatively easy in Milwaukee County where many well-organized records survive, but in the adjacent counties central sources of information proved to be rare if non-existent. There it was necessary to make additional return trips to read property abstracts, seek out official records, and interview building owners.

In most cases, the present owners knew almost nothing about their buildings and the time-honored expedient of ringing doorbells and interviewing older residents had to be employed. To clear up the many ambiguities in early location descriptions, it was often necessary to return to the site and record odometer readings. These measurements made it possible to compare current maps with 19th century property atlases.

Because of the restless, and ever-changing nature of the country today, it was difficult to keep the manuscript current. At least two of the landmarks have been razed since their inclusion on this list and one was destroyed by fire. One house (Luther Clapp, see #266) was slated for demolition but, at the last minute, it was purchased and will be moved to a new site shortly after this book goes to press. One street name, Dunbar Place (see #243), changed after the type was set.

In all possible cases, the names of the original owners have been used instead of the popular custom of listing the current owner or a previous occupant with a famous name. In a number of instances before and after pictures were used where the present condition of the building would not permit visualizing its original shape (i.e. Van Buren School, see #496 and the Woodlands Hotel, see #711).

A few of the landmarks were of such architectural importance or they had such a rich history that longer paragraphs were written and additional photographs were included. Most of the listings are situated within the appropriate city or county limits; but, for the sake of convenient location, a number of rural entries have been attached to the nearest town or city. In one case (Strang house, see #846) the building is actually outside the book's territory in Walworth County. It is just a few feet over the county line, but importantly related to the old Voree settlement (see #845) which straddled that division. Where possible, official historical marker plaques have been quoted verbatim in their entirety.

While maps are readily available for counties and major cities, finding maps for some of the smaller settlements proved difficult if not impossible. In two cases, a special map had to be drawn on the site. With the 58 maps provided here it should not be necessary to carry or struggle with the usual hard-to-read folding roadmaps. Each county has its rural landmarks and the towns represented in this book shown on a general map. Only the major highways and neccesary connecting roads are shown with the rest being eliminated for simplicity. Towns and cities have their own individual maps.

Most of the houses listed here are private property and their inclusion in this book does not mean that they are open to visitors.

H. Russell Zimmermann
Wauwatosa, Wisconsin — April 1976

11

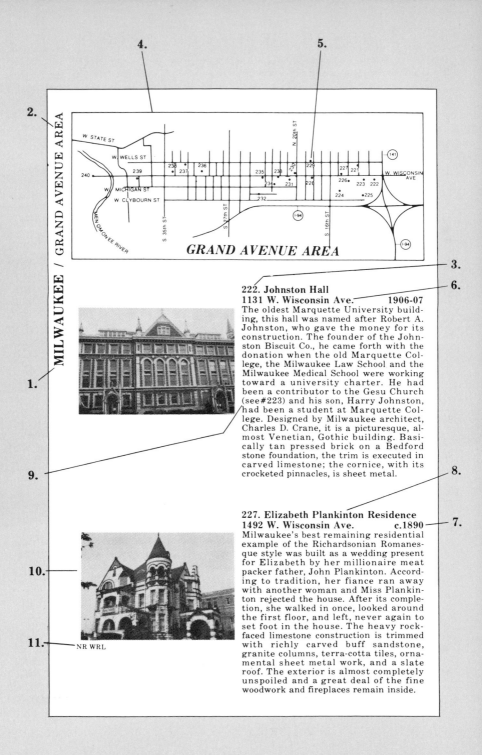

GRAND AVENUE AREA

222. Johnston Hall
1131 W. Wisconsin Ave. 1906-07
The oldest Marquette University building, this hall was named after Robert A. Johnston, who gave the money for its construction. The founder of the Johnston Biscuit Co., he came forth with the donation when the old Marquette College, the Milwaukee Law School and the Milwaukee Medical School were working toward a university charter. He had been a contributor to the Gesu Church (see #223) and his son, Harry Johnston, had been a student at Marquette College. Designed by Milwaukee architect, Charles D. Crane, it is a picturesque, almost Venetian, Gothic building. Basically tan pressed brick on a Bedford stone foundation, the trim is executed in carved limestone; the cornice, with its crocketed pinnacles, is sheet metal.

227. Elizabeth Plankinton Residence
1492 W. Wisconsin Ave. c.1890
Milwaukee's best remaining residential example of the Richardsonian Romanesque style was built as a wedding present for Elizabeth by her millionaire meat packer father, John Plankinton. According to tradition, her fiance ran away with another woman and Miss Plankinton rejected the house. After its completion, she walked in once, looked around the first floor, and left, never again to set foot in the house. The heavy rock-faced limestone construction is trimmed with richly carved buff sandstone, granite columns, terra-cotta tiles, ornamental sheet metal work, and a slate roof. The exterior is almost completely unspoiled and a great deal of the fine woodwork and fireplaces remain inside.

NR WRL

HOW TO USE THE GUIDEBOOK

1. Boldface type indicates one of the five counties covered in this book.
2. Lightface type designates the village, town or city within the county. (Each county chapter begins with a general section where rural listings are grouped with towns too small to deserve a separate section - see table of contents)
3. Each landmark and historical site has its own number which corresponds to a dot on a map. (see #5)
4. The book's 58 maps make it easy to pinpoint all 968 landmarks and historical sites. A five-county map (page 10) shows the geographic relationship of the major divisions in the text. Five individual county maps indicate the principal communities represented in the book and show the location of rural entries. Each major division (city, town, village or important neighborhood) has its own map. All maps are oriented with north being at the top of the page. In many cases all but the most important streets were eliminated for clarity.
5. Dot shows exact location of landmark or historical site and the adjacent number corresponds to a story (see #3).
6. Addresses are by street number except where no address has been assigned or when only a postal route number is used. In these cases a street corner or mileage coordinate is given.
7. Dates:
    1876 — an exact, known date
    1892-93 — First date indicates cornerstone laying; second is date of completion
    c.1874 — Exact date unknown: This is an estimated year based on architectural style, city directory listings, construction details, or word-of-mouth information.
    1924 and later — indicates a starting date and many subsequent additions.
    1890 and 1912 — Built in two sections at two different times.
8. In all possible cases the name of the original, or first, owner has been used. (Numerous important landmarks have become popularly associated with the names of less significant later owners.)
9. (see #   ) refers to another numbered entry in the book. Hundreds of cross-references have been used within cities and between counties to create meaningful links between people, buildings and architectural styles.
10. Most of the photographs were taken in 1975, but a few historical pictures (old photographs or artwork) were inserted for before and after comparisons.
11. Abbreviations:
    HABS   HISTORIC AMERICAN BUILDINGS SURVEY: This landmark has been recorded by the National Park Service and related materials (photographs, historical and architectural information) have been deposited in the Library of Congress in Washington, D.C.
    NR   NATIONAL REGISTER OF HISTORIC PLACES: A list of historical buildings and sites of national, state, regional and local importance.
    *   Asterisk means the nomination is in progress at the time of publication.
    WRL   WISCONSIN REGISTERED LANDMARK: Historic sites and landmarks of local and regional significance designated by the Wisconsin Council for Local History.
    WHM   WISCONSIN OFFICIAL HISTORICAL MARKER: Sites "of special historical, archeological, geological or legendary significance" in the state.
    CCB   CREAM CITY BRICK: (History and importance explained in the following story.)

1870s pressed cream city brick. James S. Peck residence. Page 55 No. 45

MILWAUKEE'S CREAM CITY BRICK

Milwaukee's most important architectural asset is not so much the buildings themselves as their collective color. This comes from the unique and omnipresent yellow brick which is responsible for the longstanding nickname, "the Cream City." With the confusing coincidence that Wisconsin is "America's Dairyland," it is understandable that the original implication of "Cream City" is on the wane. Although less prominent than it was in the 19th century, this epithet survives in the name of 17 businesses listed in the 1975 Milwaukee telephone directory. (The diverse applications include a beer pipe cleaner, a casket manufacturer and an auto body and spring company.)

Milwaukeeans may not fully appreciate this unusual building material which was once so desirable that, while local architects were using it as the common material in everything from homes to factories, buyers across the nation were paying double the price to import it for sparing use in a facade.

For over a century, outsiders have been admiring and praising Milwaukee brick. The well-traveled Capt. Willard Glazier made this observation in his 1884 book, *Peculiarities of American Cities*, ...(the cream colored brick) "gives the streets a peculiar light and cheerful aspect. The whole architectural appearance of the city is one of primness rather than of grandeur, which might not inappropriately suggest for it the name of the 'Quaker City of the West.' "

Praise from outsiders began as far back as 1846, the year Milwaukee was incorporated as a city. A correspondent from the New York *Courier and Enquirer*, after spending a fortnight here, wrote, "This brick is one of the remarkable features, and certainly a very ornamental one, of Milwaukee. Its color, which is permanent and unchangeable by exposure to the elements, is light yellow — resembling very much that of the famous building material of England, the Portland stone." A year later a different set of superlatives was penned by a reporter for the Buffalo *Commercial Advertiser*, "There (in Milwaukee) are made the best bricks I ever met with. They are very hard and durable, and stand fire and the weather better than any I ever saw, unless it be those little yellow bricks which are imported from Holland, by the Dutch of Fort Orange to build their houses with. Their color is yellow, not that glaring glossy yellow, which is so odious in my sight — but a pale and modest color, assorting well with those sober shades nature assumes in our cool northern climes."

The "pale and modest" color, the most sought-after attribute of cream city brick, is a product of the unusual chemical composition of the clay from which it is made. While brickmaking clays are readily available throughout Wisconsin, no two deposits have identical chemical formulae, and the Milwaukee deposit belongs to a group of clays which have a very narrow geographic distribution. To appreciate the uniqueness of its formula, Milwaukee's clay must be compared to those elsewhere in the state.

Wisconsin clays may be divided into two basic types, residual and transported. The former group is created by the disintegration of rock where it stands. Transported clays originate in the decomposition of rock on the slopes and crests of high ground and slowly work their way into the valleys with the assistance of water. Since the number and variety of sources for a single deposit may be great, these clays tend to be more complex. Milwaukee's is a member of the Lacustrine group of water-deposited sedimentary clays and was supposedly formed during the successive advances and recessions of the ice during the glacial epoch.

Although the state's Lacustrine deposits are in a small area (narrow strips along Lake Michigan and the southern banks of Lake Superior), they are unusually deep, reaching in places over 100 feet in depth. The reason for the rarity and unique color of Milwaukee's clay lies in its chemical analysis. Since the composition of clay varies according to the quantity and quality of rock in the zone supplying each respective deposit, only average percentages are quoted for the ingredients in the following list: a typical bed contains 41% silica (silicon oxide), 14.5% lime (calcium oxide), 8.34% magnesia (magnesium oxide), 8% alumina (aluminum oxide), 3% iron (ferric oxide), 3% potash (potassium oxide), 20% combined water, and insignificant amounts of soda, titanic acid and manganese oxide.

Since almost all clays contain this same list of ingredients, it becomes obvious that their proportions are the critical factor. When compared with a sampling of brick clays from across America, Milwaukee's clay reveals many differences. It has approximately 20% less silica and only one-fourth to one-third the amount of alumina. It is a suprise to find that the percentage of iron (the ingredient which gives the bright red color to most of the nation's brick) is close to the average. The answer to the mystery is in the uncommonly large percentages of calcium and magnesium. While these elements normally constitute less than 1% of the total mixture, Milwaukee clays contain 14.5% calcium and 8.34% magnesium. These constituents have the common effect of neutralizing the color resulting from the presence of any iron in the mixture. It is clear that this chemistry was not understood in the early days when the following comments were written:

—*2nd Milwaukee City Directory* (1848-49), "The yellow color is attributable to the absence of iron in the composition of the clay."

—The Chronicles of Milwaukee (A.C. Wheeler — 1861), "The peculiar composition of Milwaukee clay — sulphate of sulphur entering largely into the aluminous compound — gives to the earth when burnt its peculiar straw colored hue."

—History of Milwaukee (Western Historical Co. — 1881), "The clay from which these bricks are made contains a large porportion of lime and some sulphur. The sulphur gives the creamy tint, which no other bricks present."

The earliest brickmakers not only misunderstood the chemistry of their product but underrated the desirability of its off-beat color. Historian James Buck described the reaction of a pioneer brick maker, Benoni W. Finch, to his first batch of cream-colored brick, "He was not a little disgusted when he saw his bricks were not red, thinking they were, of course, worthless."

There seems to be some disagreement as to the establishment of the first brickyard in Milwaukee. Nelson Olin, one of the city's earliest settlers, who died in August of 1895, was asked in February of that year to recall the events surrounding the beginnings of Milwaukee. He wrote that "In September, 1835, my brother and I put up a kiln containing 25,000 brick at the foot of Huron Street, that being the first kiln of brick made in Milwaukee. Nowadays people would laugh to see the way we made brick then. We excavated a large hole in the ground which we filled with sand and clay, and then set our oxen to treading the mixture until it was worked fine enough to mold well."

Howard Louis Conard corroborates this story in 1895 in his *History of Milwaukee County*, adding that Solomon Juneau, who supposedly decided that brick should be manufactured "at home," was responsible for bringing the Canadian brickmaker, Olin, here to open a yard. He says that the original 25,000 brick were used in the construction of the William Sivyer house, the first brick dwelling to be erected in Milwaukee. Buck maintains however, that the first brickyard was opened at the foot of 14th Street by Benoni W. Finch.

A third story is told in an 1895 newspaper interview with Mrs. William Sivyer, mother of the first white child born in Milwaukee. "... In the fall of that year Mr. Sivyer purchased from Mr. Juneau a building lot where 449 Jackson Street is located and which was a portion of the forest. He then started a brickyard, the first to be operated in the place, and which was situated on some of the ground now forming Juneau Park. He manufactured the brick and then built a home on his lot, the first brick house erected in the place".

Neither Benoni Finch nor William Sivyer was ever listed in the City Directories as a brickmaker (Sivyer was always described as a mason-contractor). Since there are so few irrefutable records surviving from the 1830's, we may never know who produced the first brick. There seems to be no question about its application however. All sources agree that the first cream brick home was built in May of 1836 at the rear of 447 Jackson Street (old number) and that it was the home of William Sivyer.

The first brick commercial block was built on the northwest corner of Third and Chestnut (Juneau) Streets in 1840 for Hon. John Hustis. It was 40 x 50 feet, three stories high, and became the first theatre in Milwaukee. In the early days, when most Milwaukee buildings were made of wood, the proud owners of the brick stores called attention to the fact in their advertising. Fred Wardner's dry goods establishment was advertised in the First City Directory as being located in Rogers' Brick Block.

Before the demand for brick was augmented, there were only two yards of any importance here — those of Horace Kaffren (for William Sivyer at the head of Oneida Street) and Benoni W. Finch (in the Menomonee Valley at the foot of 14th Street). As the virtues of yellow brick were recognized, the demand began to grow at a tremendous pace. The 1840 U.S. Census records a total of $500 worth of brick produced in that year; by 1850, when the population was 21,000, there was a capital investment of $22,000 in the industry, with an annual production of twice that figure. Only three years later, when 6,000,000 brick were produced at $12 per thousand, one-third of them were being shipped out of state.

St. Mary's Catholic Church - 1846 – The oldest standing brick church in Milwaukee

This fast-booming business attracted a doctor from Massachusetts, John A. Messenger, who had come here in 1836 only to find that doctors were more numerous than opportunities for medical practice. He opened a brickyard on Chestnut Street above 12th. Another early brickyard, located on Hanover near Virginia Street on the South Side, was operated by the Childs brothers.

In 1844 George and John Burnham entered the business and eventually eclipsed the efforts of all others combined. The Burnham yard became synonymous with cream city brick, and the operation which lost $1,000 in the first year grew to a complex of plants valued at $1,200,000 in 1892.

The fame of Milwaukee brick, which became a prestige building material across the country, was already under way in 1846 when a number of buildings were erected with it in Chicago. In 1847 the Chicago *Tribune* announced that "a handsome building is going up on the corner of Lake and Water Streets ... it is built entirely of Milwaukee brick, which, at a little distance, looks almost as well as marble." Colonel Morris of the Chicago *Journal* visited Milwaukee in 1853 and sent these comments back. "There is one thing undeniable about the buildings here, and we in Chicago may lament that it is so, but there are architects here, and in outside appearance all the buildings far surpass anything we have of like character, that is, their dwelling houses are put up with taste, and their bricks are arranged with good design and present a finished and complete front. We may well envy

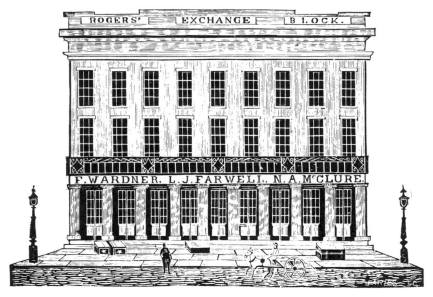

Rogers' Brick Block, the third brick commercial building erected in Milwaukee
Opposite: Lucius S. Blake residence. Page 374 No. 878

our neighbors their quality of brick. In Milwaukee this brick is made and used to perfection and ... it retains its rich color and gives an air of neatness and cleanliness to the place, which is both peculiar and pleasing." Chicagoans were such good customers that there was an almost continuous supply being shipped south. (A record survives that 566,000 were used in one month alone — October, 1853.) After the great fire in 1871, the Chicago *Tribune* specified cream city brick for the rebuilding of its offices.

As the reputation spread, Milwaukee received praise from all parts of the country. A Mr. Starbuck of the Cincinnati *Times* encouraged his readers to place orders, saying, "This quality of brick is only obtained at Milwaukee, and although the cost and transportation is double that of common brick, it is greatly cheaper than the stone fronts would be and much handsomer."

18

The editor of the Albany (N.Y.) *Journal* kept a Milwaukee brick on his desk "which he exhibited to the curious in such matters." From throughout New York State orders poured in ... a contract for 300,000 for the New York deaf and dumb asylum; a shipment for the construction of the Utica city hall; a large order for a mansion in Buffalo. In September of 1853, the N.Y. *Evening Mirror* printed the superlative to end all: "the best article of this kind in the universe. Genuine Milwaukee brick, when contrasted with brown stone, will make as beautiful a building as any material in the world." Bayard Taylor in a letter to the N.Y. *Tribune* (1855) said, "No ice, however, can freeze up the hospitable doors of Milwaukee, and the gentle, social atmosphere within its yellow, Italian-looking houses, makes one fancy himself in a milder latitude." In that year the famous Henry Ward Beecher visited the city and waxed poetic on the "extremely fine effect" of Milwaukee brick.

Michigan, too, was highly impressed and reciprocated with orders and praise. Grace Church, Detroit, was faced with cream brick. A store built in Grand Rapids was described as the "finest and most tasteful" store in the city and was made of "beautiful Milwaukee brick".

In 1858, the St. Louis *Intelligencer* published the opinion that Milwaukee "must also be one of the most beautiful cities in the world so far as brick buildings are concerned." The Cleveland *Herald* said, "To our eye, Milwaukee beats the west in brick." The fine reputation, of what was rapidly becoming Milwaukee's trademark, had extended so far that in his *Chronicles* (1861) A. C. Wheeler said, "Indeed, we believe, in one or two instances Milwaukee bricks have been sent to Europe."

Although color was its most famous attribute, this venerable brick was superior in other ways as well. It was more durable in the face of weather and had a much harder texture which required four times more fuel to "burn" than red brick. It was said that the light color reflected the sun instead of absorbing the heat and allowed the day's temperature buildup to escape rapidly after nightfall. The color was so uniform that visitors often expressed surprise that all Milwaukee buildings should be *painted* the same color.

Since brickmaking techniques differed from yard to yard and fluctuated with the introduction of new methods and equipment, no single statement accurately describes its manufacture. An extensive survey of the industry, made in the late 1890's, serves as the best extant record of the business. According to the survey, the all-important clay deposits, which dictated the location of the brickyards, were scattered generously around Milwaukee County. It was in the Menomonee River valley, just south of the city, that the stratum was most easily worked and the great Burnham yard was located. The average deposit was composed of two layers: an upper clay of reddish color and a lower one of grayish blue, which was worked in some places to a depth of 40 feet.

The clay was excavated by plow in some areas, while the primitive pick and shovel method was used in others. The raw material was then transported, usually by horsecart, to the weathering area where the proper moisture content was adjusted by aging and soaking. A pug mill was then employed to blend the clays in a proportion of one blue to four red. Fine quartz sand or coal screenings were sometimes added during the tempering. From this point the clay was moulded by one of the many methods employed in Milwaukee yards.

Sand molding, a hand process, involved wooden molds which were first dipped in water, filled with sand and then emptied, leaving a sand-lined mold.

Slop Brick, also hand-made, required steel-lined molds which were water dipped. (In the two hand methods the sand or water was used as a lubricant to aid in the release of the tacky clay from the mold.)

Soft mud, stiff mud and dry press brick were three machine methods which required various degrees of dryness in the clay used. An advantage of the dry press system was that, unlike all of the other processes, the raw brick did not have to be dried before stacking in the kiln.

There were so many variables affecting the outcome of a batch of bricks that it is surprising that they could have been classified at all. The individual chemistry of the deposit, the blending of clays, the weathering, grinding and soaking, the two hand and three machine molding methods, drying and burning in updraft, downdraft, scove or

Ornamental title from late 19th century Milwaukee souvenir book

continuous kilns all contributed to the wide variety of cream city bricks. Out of this melange came two more or less rough categories of brick, the "common" or "kiln run" brick and the "pressed" or "preferred."

Common brick were usually sold ungraded and were inconsistent in both size and color. Their position in the kiln could cause colors ranging between white and yellow-green because of the differences in temperature. Whatever their color, it was frequently diminished in effect by the moulding sand which adhered to the surface. Being coarser and sandy, they tended to attract and retain dirt and become black faster. Their porosity, however, became an advantage in insulation; as poor conductors of heat, common brick were superior for this application. The 1848 prices were from $3.50 to $4.00 per thousand and the (not-too-often met) size standard was 8¼" x 4" x2¼".

Steam-pressed brick, on the other hand, were uniform in size and color. Having been subjected to terrific pressure, they emerged with perfectly smooth faces and sharp square corners and had a metallic ring when struck. The absence of sand in the mold left a cleaner, more uniform yellow color than the common variety. What little idiosyncrasies remained after a burn were carefully sorted out to create the "select" or "best" grade which were used on the fronts of buildings and could be laid with close joints for a beautiful precision effect. Being denser and harder, the pressed brick had greater strength and durability and did not attract dirt so readily. As a result there are many select brick buildings which have lasted a century without cleaning and are still recognizably yellow. The two disadvantages of steam-pressed brick were its poor insulating qualities and higher cost, $4-$5 per thousand in 1848. The standard size was 8¾" x 4" x 2⅜".

The "light and cheerful aspect" of Milwaukee's streets, mentioned by Glazier in 1884, has vanished but several thousand buildings of cream-colored brick survive. Some have been temporarily brightened by removing the original surface by sandblasting or hydrofluoric acid. Both of these processes make the brick porous and liable to blacken considerably faster the second time, a fate that would be especially unfortunate for pressed brick with its original hard, resistant finish.

"Milwaukee bricks ... to which the eyes of our citizens have become so accustomed that they scarcely appreciate their beauty, are getting to be well known and much admired abroad," stated a *Sentinel* editorial in 1853. Local apathy is as formidable today as it was then. However, indifference 123 years ago was not destructive, while today it is responsible for chiselling away the single greatest architectural asset in the city. Hundreds of acres of cream brick buildings have been indiscriminately weeded from the cityscape by an uninformed populace. Of those surviving, many have been irretrievably altered or permanently ruined by a coat of paint. The community must become aware of its priceless heritage and rekindle a pride in what remains if we are to salvage the genesis of "Milwaukee Wisconsin, Cream City of the Lakes."

Russell Zimmermann's Cream City Brick article first appeared in the March, 1970 Historical Messenger (Milwaukee County Historical Society) and has been re-printed in Historic Preservation (1970 The National Trust for Historic Preservation) and the Milwaukee Journal (1972).

CCB

This account of "cream city" brick was based in Milwaukee, where that product attained national recognition. It should be noted, however, that there were numerous other brickyards in the southeastern Wisconsin region producing a similar material. As the composition of clays varied from location to location, the brick would take on slightly different colors ranging from near-white to a pinkish yellow. Since it is, in most cases, difficult to determine whether the brick was made in Milwaukee and shipped out or manufactured in a local yard, the abbreviation *CCB* (cream city brick) has been used throughout the book as a generic term. Where a brickyard outside the Cream City could be confirmed, it is so noted in the text.

Opposite: Milwaukee City Hall tower. Page 37 No. 1

PICTORIAL GLOSSARY

ARCHITECTURAL TERMS
USED IN THE GUIDEBOOK

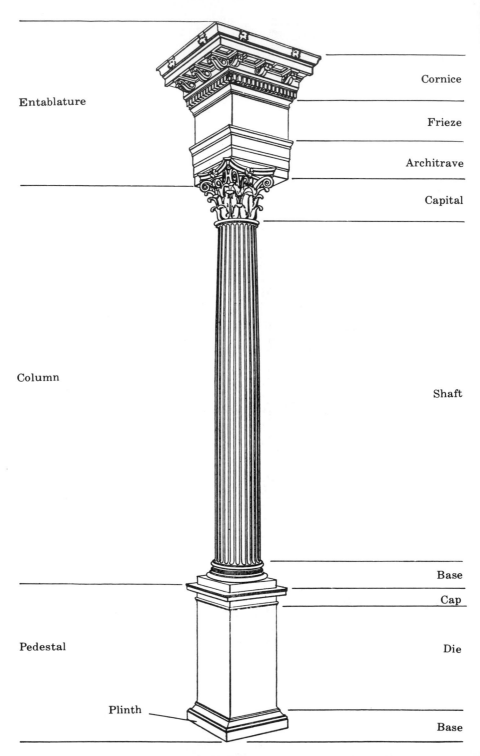

Entablature

Cornice

Frieze

Architrave

Capital

Column

Shaft

Base

Cap

Pedestal

Die

Plinth

Base

24

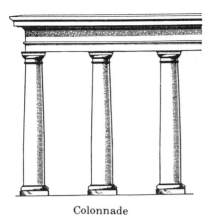

Colonnade

Arcade

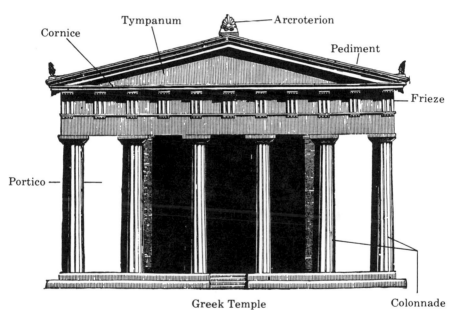

Greek Temple

Cornice

Tympanum

Arcroterion

Pediment

Frieze

Portico

Colonnade

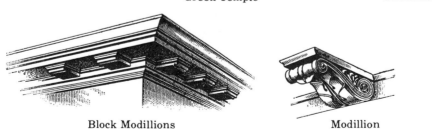

Block Modillions

Modillion

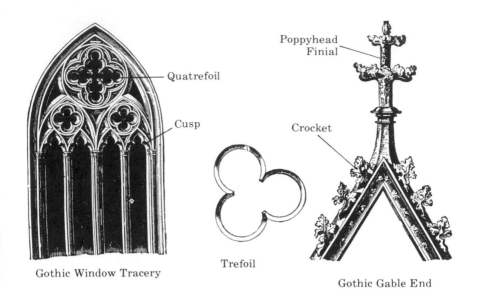

Quatrefoil

Cusp

Gothic Window Tracery

Trefoil

Poppyhead Finial

Crocket

Gothic Gable End

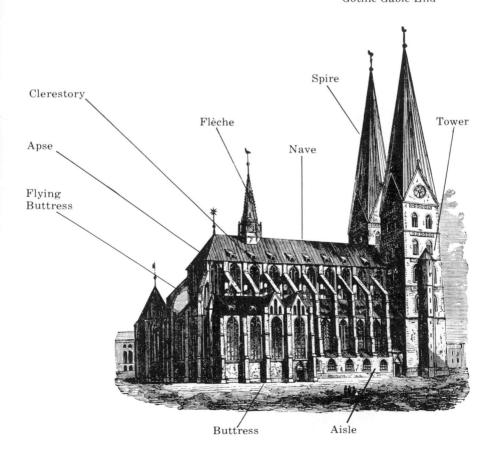

Clerestory

Flèche

Spire

Nave

Tower

Apse

Flying
Buttress

Buttress

Aisle

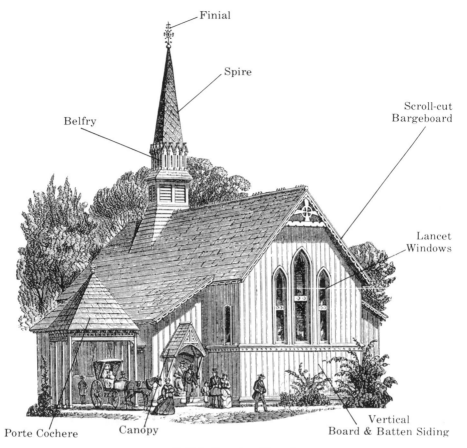

Finial

Spire

Belfry

Scroll-cut
Bargeboard

Lancet
Windows

Porte Cochere   Canopy

Vertical
Board & Batten Siding

Gothic Country Church

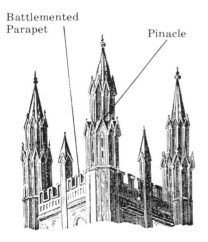

Battlemented
Parapet

Pinacle

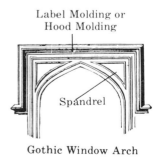

Label Molding or
Hood Molding

Spandrel

Gothic Window Arch

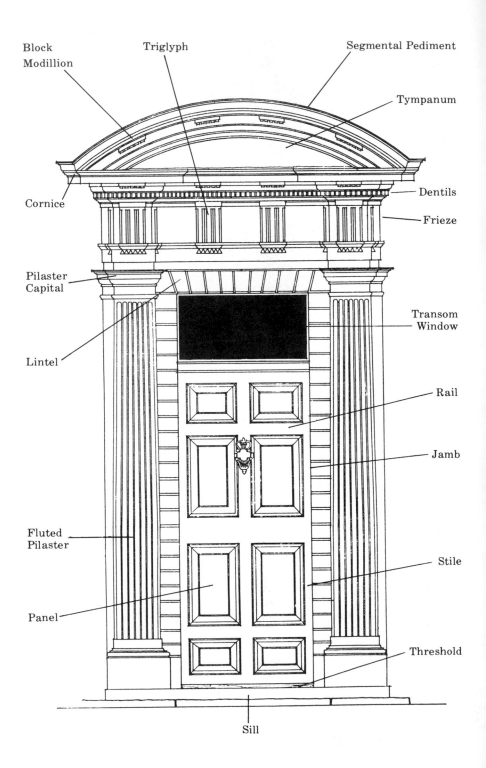

Block
Modillion

Triglyph

Segmental Pediment

Tympanum

Cornice

Dentils

Frieze

Pilaster
Capital

Transom
Window

Lintel

Rail

Jamb

Fluted
Pilaster

Stile

Panel

Threshold

Sill

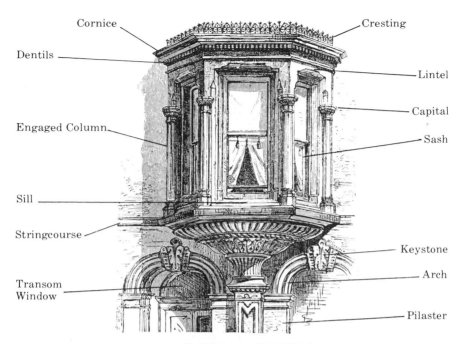

Cornice

Dentils

Engaged Column

Sill

Stringcourse

Transom Window

Cresting

Lintel

Capital

Sash

Keystone

Arch

Pilaster

Half-Octagon Oriel Window

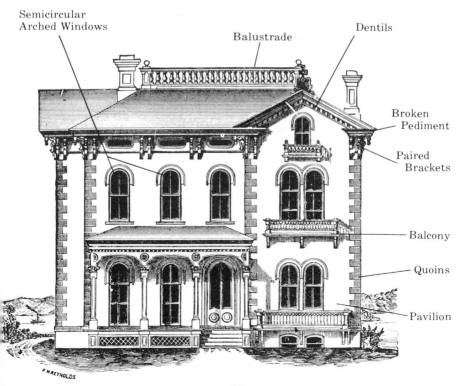

Semicircular Arched Windows

Balustrade

Dentils

Broken Pediment

Paired Brackets

Balcony

Quoins

Pavilion

F.M.REYNOLDS

29

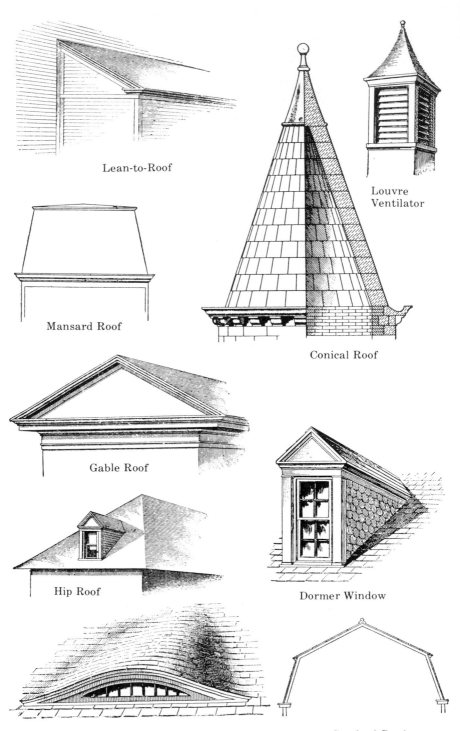

Lean-to-Roof

Louvre
Ventilator

Mansard Roof

Conical Roof

Gable Roof

Dormer Window

Hip Roof

Eyebrow Window

Gambrel Roof

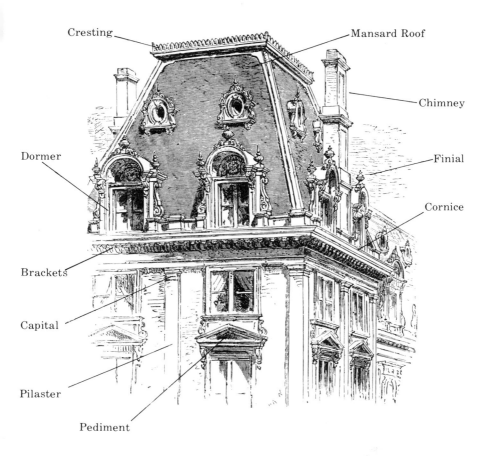

Cresting

Mansard Roof

Chimney

Dormer

Finial

Cornice

Brackets

Capital

Pilaster

Pediment

Purlin

Principal
Rafter

Strut

Collar
Beam

Hammer
Beam

Arched
Brace

Wall Post

Corbel

Hammerbeam
Ceiling

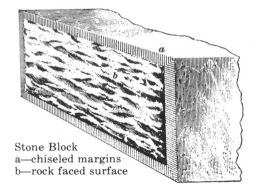

Stone Block
a—chiseled margins
b—rock faced surface

Stretcher Bond

Header Bond

Fieldstone Construction

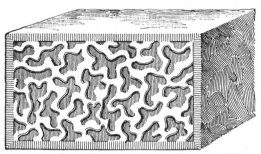

Stone block with vermiculated (worm-eaten)
rustication and chiseled margins

English Bond

Flemish Bond

Chisel

Bush Hammer

Opposite: William O. Goodrich residence Page 78 No. 110

MILWAUKEE COUNTY

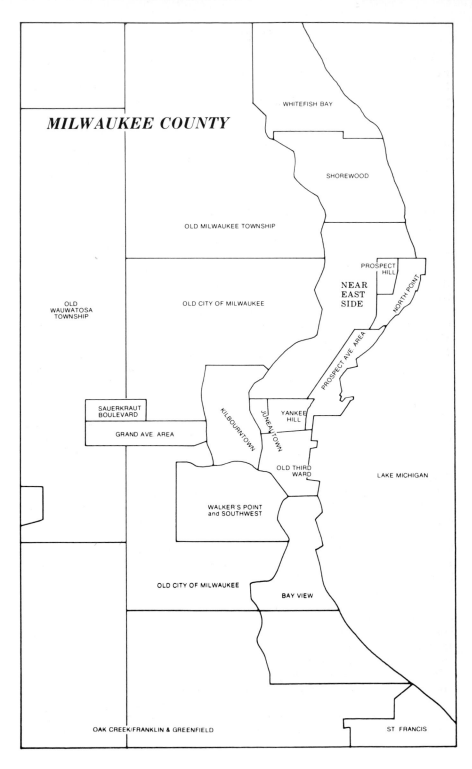

MILWAUKEE COUNTY

WHITEFISH BAY

SHOREWOOD

OLD MILWAUKEE TOWNSHIP

PROSPECT HILL

NEAR EAST SIDE

NORTH POINT

OLD WAUWATOSA TOWNSHIP

OLD CITY OF MILWAUKEE

PROSPECT AVE. AREA

SAUERKRAUT BOULEVARD

GRAND AVE. AREA

KILBOURNTOWN

JUNEAUTOWN

YANKEE HILL

OLD THIRD WARD

LAKE MICHIGAN

WALKER'S POINT and SOUTHWEST

OLD CITY OF MILWAUKEE

BAY VIEW

OAK CREEK/FRANKLIN & GREENFIELD

ST FRANCIS

MILWAUKEE

Most nineteenth century American cities began simply as a group of buildings erected at the intersection of two or more roads or were built around a grist mill on a river. Milwaukee, however, had a complex beginning as three different communities separated by three rivers which joined here to flow into Lake Michigan.

The northeastern sector, roughly framed by the Milwaukee River and the lake, was established by Solomon Juneau and called Juneautown. To the west of the Milwaukee River, and centered around what is now N. 3rd Street and W. Juneau Avenue, was another settlement, promoted by Byron Kilbourn, which was called Kilbourntown. George Walker led the third community, Walker's Point, in the area just south of the Menomonee River and near the lake.

Before the white men discovered the advantages of this confluence of rivers at a natural bay on the lake, Milwaukee had been a meeting place for Indians. The original landscape included a steep bluff along the lakefront, a sizeable amount of swampland and a high·plateau to the west near what is now N. 8th Street.

Although there had been explorers through the area, and a few fur traders had set up temporary quarters here, it was not until 1818 that Milwaukee's first permanent white settler arrived. He was Solomon Juneau, a French Canadian, who had been appointed an agent of the American Fur Company for this location. Juneau built his log house and two other buildings on the northeast corner of N. Water Street and E. Wisconsin Avenue.

In the beginning an intense rivalry existed between the three pioneer settlements as each competed for the steady flow of immigrants, and at least two (Kilbourntown and Juneautown) sought to become the location of government. In 1846 the competition ended; and the City of Milwaukee was incorporated, with Solomon Juneau as its first mayor.

But the early incompatibilities left a never-to-be-forgotten permanent scar on the city. Since they had no intention of merging, each community had laid out its streets without any regard for each other. In fact, Kilbourn is said to have purposely surveyed his streets so that they would not line up with those on the east side. Later, when it came to connecting these thoroughfares over the river, the bridges had to be set on the diagonals which survive today.

There was another important early activity which changed the landscape permanently. What were originally wild rice and tamarack swamps in the low areas were filled by grading down the substantial bluffs and using them as landfill. There are locations in the downtown area that were over 60 feet higher in the beginning, and some that were covered by brackish water.

Milwaukee grew to become one of the favorite American destinations for European immigrants. By the turn of the century, it was the most German city in the country and had German newspapers, German language theaters, German food and beer, and many other ethnic carry-overs to make strangers from the old country feel at home.

With the Germans, and the many other immigrants who eventually settled here, came a generous number of artists, architects and craftsmen who have left the unmistakeable mark of their national backgrounds on the city's buildings. Milwaukee is fortunate to have a relatively large number of surviving examples of the stylistic tastes and fine craftsmanship preferred by this broad ethnic background.

The following divisions of the city are related to specific areas of development which have historical significance. Juneautown, for instance, is one of the three original settlements that later combined to become the City of Milwaukee. However, within its boundaries are two other important, but distinctly different areas, which deserve separate mention. These are Yankee Hill, which was basically a wealthy residential neighborhood, and the old Third Ward, which was partly commercial and partly low-income residential.

JUNEAUTOWN

Of the three pioneer settlements, which later became Milwaukee, Juneautown was the first to be organized. The area between the Milwaukee River, Lake Michigan, E. Wisconsin Avenue and E. Juneau Avenue was a part of Solomon Juneau's original 160-acre claim. First called "Juneau's Side", this district had more high and dry land than its rivals; and it quickly became the most important community. When Juneau had the streets surveyed, he guessed that 12 city blocks would remain the maximum size of the town. A part of Juneautown later became the richest and most prestigious of early residential neighborhoods (see *Yankee Hill*).

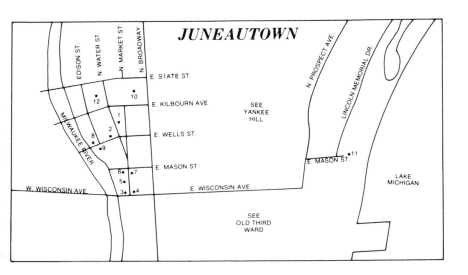

JUNEAUTOWN

EDISON ST.
N. WATER ST.
N. MARKET ST.
N. BROADWAY
N. PROSPECT AVE.
LINCOLN MEMORIAL DR.
MILWAUKEE RIVER

E. STATE ST.
E. KILBOURN AVE.
E. WELLS ST.
E. MASON ST.
E. MASON ST.
E. WISCONSIN AVE.
W. WISCONSIN AVE.

SEE YANKEE HILL

LAKE MICHIGAN

SEE OLD THIRD WARD

1. City Hall
200 E. Wells St.   1893-96

Milwaukee's most spectacular and important landmark has been virtually the symbol of the city since it was built. This unique structure, designed by H.C. Koch and Co., cost over a million dollars in a day when that figure was a rarity. Contractor Paul Riesen set a 20-foot band of Berea sandstone on a base of black granite. The rest of the construction, including the 393-foot tower, is St. Louis pressed brick trimmed with ornamental terra-cotta of a matching color. The roof is slate and sheet copper. Although an eclectic design, it bears a strong resemblance to the late 19th century "New Renaissance" style so popular in Germany and the low countries. A 10-ton bell, once the third largest in the world, hangs in the tower, but is rarely rung because its vibrations weaken the structure.

HABS NR WRL

2. Pabst Theater
144 E. Wells St. **1893-95**
Designed by architect Otto Strack, this is actually the second theater on the lot. The first, Nunnemacher's Grand Opera House (1871), was remodeled in 1890 and renamed the Stadt Theater, but it was short-lived and in 1893 the western two-thirds burned to the ground. When Captain Frederick Pabst (who was then the owner) built the present theater to replace it, the remaining east end of the old building was grafted on to become the Pabst Theater Cafe. Still another fire destroyed the last of Nunnemacher's and until the recent restoration project the unfinished scar where they once joined was visible. The Renaissance Revival design is richly ornamented with wrought iron, sheet metal and orange terra-cotta.

3. Pabst Building
110 E. Wisconsin Ave. **1891-92**
Once the most spectacular skyscraper among Milwaukee's commercial buildings, this imposing late Victorian structure was built for Frederick Pabst (see #230). It was designed by S.S. Beman of Chicago (see #25) and originally sported a 4-story tower. The tower with its octagonal cupola and Renaissance gables, and the 3-story mansard roof on the lower blocks with their gables and ornamental cresting were removed in 1948 in a major rebuilding. When the original picturesque roof was intact, this building was rivaled only by City Hall which has many of the same Flemish and Romanesque features. Occupied for years by the First National Bank, the building's principal attraction is the immense semi-circular stone arch over the main entrance with its richly carved spandrels.

4. Bankers Building
710 N. Water St. **1928**
This 14-story office building was designed by the architectural firm Eschweiler and Eschweiler. The orange-brown brick of the facade is relieved by darker brick of a similar color and sculptured ornament in low relief made with a light orange terra-cotta. The ornamental masonry, mostly at the roof line, is still intact but the original first three floors were remodeled in 1971-72. Milwaukee architect, Kenneth Kurtz, carried out the design in such a way as to create a new look for the lower floors without destroying the basic "1928 modern" character of the upper floors.

5. Marshall & Ilsley Bank
721 N. Water St. 1911

One of Milwaukee's most distinguished neo-classical structures, this handsome limestone bank was designed by the architectural firm of Brust, Phillip & Heimerl. The massive entablature is supported by two square pilasters and a monumental pair of 3-story high Greek Ionic fluted columns. In 1930 Richard Phillip was called back to design the 2-story stone addition on the roof. By extending the pilasters up to the new cornice, which matches the angle and shape of the original, and giving the new floors a setback, he was able to preserve the effectiveness of the original design. The interior, also neo-classical in character, is mostly done in Botticino marble.

6. First National Bank Building
735 N. Water St. 1912-14

Once the home office of Wisconsin's largest bank, this 16-story "skyscraper" was abandoned when the First Wisconsin Center was completed (see #21). When it was completed, this impressive structure was a spectacular addition to Milwaukee's skyline. Its architects, D.H. Burnham & Co. of Chicago, used granite facing on the first four floors; pressed buff brick on the upper stories. The huge 4,732,184 cubic foot building was erected by Sterling Engineering Co. Classical ornament, including fluted pilasters, cornucopias and leaves, is carved in high relief at the second floor level. All corridors in the building are wainscoted in marble.

7. First Wisconsin Garage Building
746 N. Water St. 1928-29

In a day when parking structures are among the ugliest things on a cityscape, it is pleasant to remember this finely disguised facility. When new it was called "one of the most efficient multi-floor garages in the country." Milwaukee architects, Martin Tullgren & Son Co., designed the 8½-story building which has office space only on the Water Street side of the first floor. It was claimed that the new d'Humy automobile ramps were so well designed that ladies would not hesitate to drive all the way to the top. The 400-car capacity garage is not only well disguised, but a well proportioned example of the "moderne" style of the day executed in brick and ornamental terra-cotta.

WHM

8. Oneida Street Station
108 E. Wells St. **1898**

Built as a power station for the Milwaukee Electric Railway and Light Co., this orange, pressed brick structure was designed by architect Herman J. Esser. In this station pulverized coal was first successfully burned continuously and at high efficiency in furnaces of stationary steam boilers November 11-15, 1919. This radical departure from conventional firing methods of the period was vigorously opposed by some engineers during its early stages. It soon met with local, national and international acceptance, and has resulted in great benefits to mankind through reduced cost of electric power and conservation of fuel resources. In 1909 the rich terra-cotta cornices on the building were removed and the scars were filled with brick.

9. The Meinecke Toy Co. Building
125 E. Wells St. **1891**

Adolph Meinecke, a pioneer manufacturer of bamboo and punjab furniture novelties and willow ware, had warerooms and factories on Mason and E. Water Streets. As his business in wooden toys grew he formed the Meinecke Toy Co. and in 1891 built this imposing 6-story building for that company. He became an importer and jobber of toys, fancy goods and notions, including everything from willow carriages to bird cages. The now-painted CCB facade is trimmed with red sandstone which includes carved capitals on the ground floor with the initials A.M. entwined in a monogram. With sheet metal 3-story bay and cornice it resembles the Italianate style so popular 20 years earlier.

10. MGIC Plaza
250 E. Kilbourn Ave. **1971-72**

Erected on a 2½ acre site, this two-building urban complex consists of the headquarters building for the MGIC Investment Corporation and a ten-story office building. Between them is a landscaped plaza common to both structures, an underground garage, and an area to the east which is reserved for a future building to complete the project. The concrete shell of the MGIC Building is sheathed in Italian travertine marble and each floor is cantilevered 15 feet over the floor below. The total overhang reaches 45 feet beyond the main entrance and gives the mass a shape like an inverted pyramid. Architects and engineers on the project were Skidmore, Owings and Merrill of Chicago who worked in cooperation with Fitzhugh Scott Architects, Inc., of Milwaukee.

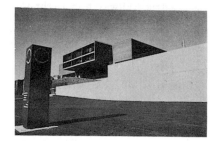

11. Milwaukee County War Memorial Center
750 N. Lincoln Memorial Dr.   1957

Conceived as a tribute to those who gave their lives in World War II and the Korean conflict, this versatile building serves as an art gallery, meeting facility and for offices. It was designed by Detroit architect Eero Saarinen who elevated the large cruciform-shaped building on steel and concrete supports to avoid interrupting the broad expanse of lake view. The western facade was designed to accept a large mosaic by Milwaukee artist, Edmund D. Lewandowski. When it was installed, this Italian tessera mural was considered to be the largest outdoor mosaic in America. Its semi-abstract design incorporates the Roman numerals which, when read correctly, spell out the beginning and end dates of the two wars. (1941-1945, World War II) and (1950-1953, Korea).

12. The Performing Arts Center
929 N. Water St.   1966-69

This spacious and versatile facility was orignally intended to be a part of the War Memorial Center complex at the lakefront (see #11). In 1961 the present site on the east bank of the Milwaukee River was selected. Architect Harry Weese & Associates of Chicago, drew the plans with consultation on the theater by George Izenour. This strongly rectilinear composition is a steel skeleton sheathed in Italian travertine marble. The building is set in a spacious area and surrounded by a grove of chestnut trees, sculpture, a large modern bronze fountain, and a river promenade with a boat dock.

OLD THIRD WARD

Peter Juneau, Solomon's brother, once owned the 156-acre tract which later became the Third Ward. He first lived about 200 feet south of his brother's log house (northwest corner of N. Water Street and E. Wisconsin Avenue), but later built what was described as "one of the finest buildings in the city" where the Federal Building now stands (see #20). Water Street (the first to be graded in the city) became the principal business thoroughfare and was lined with the buildings of wholesale merchants and hotels. Almost the entire Third Ward was destroyed in a disastrous fire which levelled 440 buildings in October of 1892. Among the few survivors of this conflagration is the Cross Keys Hotel (see #29).

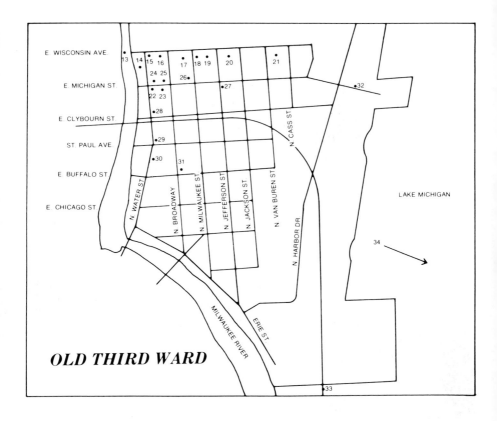

OLD THIRD WARD

13. Wisconsin Avenue Lift Bridge
Wisconsin Ave. at Milwaukee River
1975

This award-winning bridge design was created by the Milwaukee Bureau of Bridges and Public Buildings. The first one to be built on this plan was the St. Paul Avenue structure in 1967. That 61-foot lift span received an award for its design, and a clean unobstructed roadway, from the American Institute of Steel Construction. When the second to last swing bridge, at Pleasant Street was destroyed in 1972 it was also replaced by this type of bridge. Working with numerous pulleys, and counterweights, this hydraulic-operated bridge rises parallel with the water.

14. Marine Plaza
111 E. Wisconsin Ave. **1960-61**

The Marine Plaza was an important pioneer investment in the redevelopment of the Milwaukee River and a general indication of faith in the renewal of the downtown area. Designed by New York architects, Harrison and Abramovitz, it was the first major glass curtain wall skyscraper in the city. The 288-foot, 22-story bank and office building is set on its lot in such a way as to create a much needed public open space. A large 3-story glass-enclosed entrance pavilion, supported by concrete columns and vaulting, is a separate, but connected structure. The building's glass skin, with both transparent and opaque panels, is vertically accented by stainless steel mullions which extend to the roofline.

HABS NR WRL

15. Excelsior Block
205 E. Wisconsin Ave. **1860-61**

Milwaukee's only cast iron building, this historic structure is one of a rapidly vanishing breed across America. When it was built, by James B. Martin, the novelty was so irresistible that Milwaukeeans nicknamed it "The Iron Block" and that name has remained with the building until today. It was designed by George H. Johnson, who was the manager of the architectural department of Daniel Badger's Architectural Iron Works in New York City. The design of the exterior, inspired by Venetian Renaissance buildings, was cast in hundreds of small pieces and assembled on the spot. While custom designing was possible, these buildings could be purchased out of catalogs and this one has an almost identical twin in New York City. Located on Chambers and Reade Streets, The Cary Building is also illustrated in Plate VII of Badger's 1865 catalog.

16. Railway Exchange Building
233 E. Wisconsin Ave. 1901

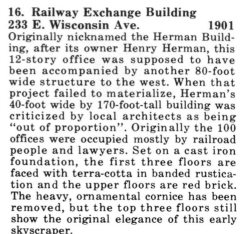

Originally nicknamed the Herman Building, after its owner Henry Herman, this 12-story office was supposed to have been accompanied by another 80-foot wide structure to the west. When that project failed to materialize, Herman's 40-foot wide by 170-foot-tall building was criticized by local architects as being "out of proportion". Originally the 100 offices were occupied mostly by railroad people and lawyers. Set on a cast iron foundation, the first three floors are faced with terra-cotta in banded rustication and the upper floors are red brick. The heavy, ornamental cornice has been removed, but the top three floors still show the original elegance of this early skyscraper.

17. Birchard's and Follansbee's Block
323-331 E. Wisconsin Ave. 1867

One of Milwaukee's oldest commercial buildings, this half-block-long structure was built as a joint venture by three men. John F. Birchard built the large segment on the corner of Milwaukee St. A pioneer furniture manufacturer from New York, he used the first floor for salesrooms and the rest for manufacturing. Samuel A. Field, a dealer in real estate, built a small section in the middle. Alanson Follansbee, a very wealthy baker, owned the remainder but died before it was completed. Originally a 4-story CCB Italianate design with a mansard roof, it has been all but destroyed by remodelings and additions.

18. T.A. Chapman Co. Store
407 E. Wisconsin Ave. 1884

Only the Milwaukee Street facade of the old Chapman's dry goods store remains to indicate the former elegance of this pioneer retail establishment. The first Chapman store on this lot burned to the ground in an 1884 fire and the present building was immediately erected to replace it. An eclectic four-story brick edifice , its Wisconsin Avenue front was highly ornamental, but was removed in a 1930 remodeling. Inside, a spectacular 3-sided fireplace and four large murals by Vergilio Tojetti provide luxurious touches. The murals, in rooftop skylights, could once be seen from the main floor, but the large open well has been built over to increase square footage.

19. Goldsmith Building
425 E. Wisconsin Ave.   1892

One of the largest firms of its kind in the northwest, Goldsmith & Co. was a wholesale and retail carpet, house furnishing goods, and bedding dealer. The business was founded in 1867 by Joseph Goldsmith and his son Bernard. In 1892, the surviving partner, Bernard, engaged Milwaukee architect, W.D. Kimball, to design this 8-story office building and store. The red pressed brick walls are relieved with limestone, sheet metal, and terra-cotta trim. Basically Romanesque in character, there are five projecting pavilions with large arches under which three-faceted bays project. The cornerstone is actually a limestone plinth for the northeastern corner pilaster and its date is flanked by delicate incised scroll ornaments.

20. Federal Building
517 E. Wisconsin Ave.   1892-99

This is Milwaukee's finest and most monumental example of the 19th century Romanesque style which now carries the name of its chief proponent, Henry Hobson Richardson, an architect from Boston. The plans were drawn by James Knox Taylor who was an architect attached to the Treasury Department in Washington, D.C. The building's gray Maine granite facing is relieved with richly carved Romanesque leaf ornaments and occasional faces and gargoyles. A large wing, almost doubling the size of the structure, was added on the rear in 1930.

21. First Wisconsin Center
777 E. Wisconsin Ave.   1973

The tallest building in the state of Wisconsin stands 42 stories and rises 601 feet. Architects were Skidmore, Owings & Merrill, Chicago, and Fitzhugh Scott, Milwaukee. The steel-framed skyscraper is sheathed in white-painted aluminum and bronze heat-absorbing, glare-reducing glass. With the Galleria, an enclosed mall with shops and restaurants, and the parking structure, it covers two city blocks. The works of three widely known artists, Helen Frankenthaler, Jack Youngerman, and Edmund Lewandowski are a part of the interior. Seven million pounds of travertine marble were used for trim.

22. Mitchell Building
207 E. Michigan St. 1876

One of the finest Second Empire mansard style commercial buildings in the country, this richly ornamented structure was erected by Alexander Mitchell. The architect, Edward Townsend Mix, created a compositon with projecting pavilions, high-relief moldings, and carved ornaments which ranks among the most elegant Victorian buildings in the state. The 6-story office building, originally a bank, is set on a heavily rusticated granite foundation. Lion head keystones, winged horses, caryatid figures, and rusticated quoins combine to give richness to the facade. The iron-framed mansard roof is covered with slate shingles and an unusual pair of cast metal griffins still guard the main entrance.

23. Chamber of Commerce Building
225 E. Michigan St. 1879-80

One of Milwaukee's most important Victorian commercial buildings, the old Chamber of Commerce, was promoted by Alexander Mitchell (see #178) and designed by Edward Townsend Mix, the architect of the Mitchell building next door. The cornerstone, laid by the Grand Lodge of Free Accepted Masons, is dated October 30, 5879 (1879). The design of the gray Ohio sandstone building was described as "simple Italian" when it was new, but by today's standards it is one of the most ornate and elaborate buildings in the city. The entrance is flanked by massive granite pillars and the foundation is band-rusticated granite. Over the doors are two deeply carved spandrels, with a steam locomotive and a fishing boat. Other carved symbolism includes the traditional bull and bear, higher on the tower, and the great seal of the State of Wisconsin. A large figure, "Commerce", once stood immediately above the entrance but has since been taken down and moved to a park (see #342). The Chamber served as a marketplace where the crops of midwestern farms were bought and sold.

24. Bank of Milwaukee Building
210 E. Michigan St. 1856-58

The oldest bank structure in Milwaukee, this 4-story Italian Renaissance facade is one of the most elegant commercial buildings ever built here in the 19th century. Its finely proportioned limestone facade is decorated with rich deep-relief carving, elaborate window lintels, rusticated quoins, and a pair of spiral ropetwist columns. The Bank of Milwaukee eventually, through merger, became a part of the Marine National Exchange Bank. Carlisle D. Cooke was the builder and first proprieter.

HABS NR WRL

25. Northwestern Mutual Life Insurance Building
611 N. Broadway   **1885**

S.S. Beman, the Chicago architect who designed the city of Pullman, Illinois, was retained to design this distinguished office building. It replaced the Newhall House Hotel which only two years earlier burned to the ground killing 71 persons in one of the worst hotel disasters in history. A good example of the Richardsonian Romanesque style, it has characteristic massive arches and heavy stone masonry. Fox Island granite was used for the first story, Halowell granite for the second, and Bedford limestone for the remaining facade. Inside is one of the best preserved and most spectacular 19th century commercial interiors in the state. An open, rectangular staircase rises in a lightwell to a large ornamental iron skylight. Marble wainscoting and the original tile floors add warmth and color.

26. McGeoch Building
322 E. Michigan St.   **1894-95**

Milwaukee has long been one of the nation's important printing and lithographing centers and this building was originally the home of five printing firms. Built by Peter McGeoch, president of the Milwaukee City Railway Company, the six-story structure is made of tan pressed brick and is trimmed with terra-cotta and a sheet metal cornice. Plans were drawn by Milwaukee architect, Eugene R. Liebert. Among the first printer-tenants were Burdick & Allen, Dawe Bros., Meyer Rotier, Standard Printing & Stationery and the 20th Century Press. This historic printing intersection also had the *Evening Wisconsin* newspaper office on the northeast corner and the *Milwaukee Journal* on the southeast.

27. Johnson Service Co. Building
507 E. Michigan St.   **1902 & 1924**

The first reinforced concrete building in Milwaukee, this seven-story structure was built in two stages. 4700 man hours of labor had been expended on the first half when it collapsed. There were no injuries, but the project had to be started again. This section, which contains the limestone entrance on Michigan St. and the entire Jefferson St. side, was designed by architect H.J. Esser. In 1924 the building was extended to the east by architects Buemming & Guth. Faced with a smooth red pressed brick, the most attractive features of the building are the carved limestone corbels, with keystoned arches, that support the cornice.

28. Button Block
500 N. Water St. 1892

Dr. Henry Harrison Button was a pioneer druggist who, with his lifelong business partner Thomas Greene, built one of the largest and most successful drug businesses in this part of the country. In the early days, before they built the mansion on State Street (see #44), the Buttons lived in the historic United States Hotel which once occupied this lot. One of their sons, Charles Pearson Button, was born in that hotel and after his father's death, in 1890, promoted the erection of this building as a lasting monument to them. Richardsonian design is built with dark red pressed brick on two stories of rock-faced red sandstone. A spectacular 7-story cylindrical bartizan decorates the corner of the building and is partially supported by a large granite column. The red terra-cotta ornamental trim includes a plaque at the roofline which reads, "Button Block 1892".

29. Cross Keys Hotel
402 N. Water St. 1853

The oldest building on Milwaukee's oldest street is the last of the historic Water Street inns. Before the Civil War, when immigrants arrived by boat through the Milwaukee River, Bailey Stimson operated the Cross Keys Hotel. Note the curved limestone lintel over the 3rd floor corner window which has the clearly chiseled inscription, "B. Stimson July 4, 1853". Since it is built over what used to be a swamp, the building has sunk through the years. That plus the great number of resurfacings on Water Street has put the lobby floor 3 feet below grade. (Actually the floor was once raised 2 feet so that the total difference from the present sidewalk would be 5 feet.) In the 1870's the original top (fourth) floor leaned so much that it was removed.

30. J.P. Kissinger Block
330-32 N. Water St. 1893

The J.P. Kissinger Company was a wholesale dealer in wines and liquors and a "rectifier of spirits". Mr. Kissinger, who was raised in the wine trade in Germany, came to Milwaukee and established the business in 1856. Eleven years later he moved to this location and in 1893 had grown large enough to require this new building. Milwaukee architects, Schnetzky & Liebert, drew the plans for this 5-story iron beam and column structure. It is faced with red pressed brick and decorated with ornamental terra-cotta of a similar color. Although the elaborate cornice has been removed, the name "Kissinger", flanked by two cherubs, can still be seen in the terra-cotta pediment at the roof line.

31. Baumbach Building
302 N. Broadway   1899-1900

Designed by Milwaukee architect, Eugene R. Liebert, this handsome commercial block was once a part of the Phoenix Hosiery Co. which also occupied the large concrete building immediately to the east. Here they had a dining room on the ground floor, stock on the second, and knitting machines on the 3rd, 4th, and 5th floors. The owner was Ernst von Baumbach, eldest son of Ludwig (see #273) and brother to one of the most important German families in early Milwaukee. Ernst was consul to the double monarchy of Austria-Hungary for 20 years and before the family moved here his father had been president of the Landtag of Hesse Cassel.

32. 1st Milwaukee Cargo Pier Marker
Clybourn St. at Lake Michigan   1963

"Near here, at the foot of Huron (now Clybourn) Street, the first cargo pier in Milwaukee harbor was built by Horatio Stevens, Richard Owens, Amos Tufts and J.G. Kendall during the winter of 1842-43. The first vessel to dock at North Pier was the CLEVELAND, under command of Captain M. Hazard on June 1, 1843. The pier, 1,200 feet long and 44 feet wide, with a freight shed at the end and a warehouse and tollgate at the entrance, permitted the unloading of freight and passengers from large vessels which could not enter the original mouth of the Milwaukee River, south of Jones Island. Near this pier was the first Milwaukee brewery, founded in 1840. In the following years, three more lake shore piers were built which created lively business activity on Milwaukee's east side, known as Juneautown. The first pier was destroyed during the winter of 1846 by strong winds and ice. The same fate later overtook the other piers. A new straight cut, opened in 1857, provided access to the Milwaukee River and to the downtown inner harbor which then developed."

33. Harbor Entrance Bridge
Milwaukee River at Lake Michigan
                               1974

As far back as 1946, the Department of Public Works envisioned a southern extension for Lincoln Memorial Drive and an arched suspension bridge which resembles the one finally built. This design, by Howard Needles, Tammen & Bergendoff of Milwaukee, is a "through tied-arch structure" and one of eleven designs submitted by consultants for the project. Fabricated by the Pittsburg-DesMoines Steel Company, the cost was approximately $25,000,000. It was given the 1975 Long Span Bridge Award by the American Institute of Steel Construction. Clearance over the water channel is 120 feet.

34. Breakwater Light
Milwaukee Harbor   1926

The principal navigational light in the Milwaukee harbor, this steel sheet pile and concrete structure rises five stories above the water. It is operated by the United States Coast Guard and has a fog horn and a radio beacon. Its light, which is 61 feet above the water, has a range of 14 miles. Until 1963 the building was operated by rotating four man crews which lived under the light for 21 days and were off duty for seven days. Since then the operation has been automated and is now controlled from a panel at the beach station at 2420 S. Lincoln Memorial Drive.

YANKEE HILL

The high ground east of the river was destined, from the beginning, to become Milwaukee's choicest residential district. It was the location of the first two courthouses and the home of the city's founder and first mayor, Solomon Juneau. The area acquired its nickname in the 1840's when hundreds of "Yankees" from New England and New York State settled here. Although a few prominent Germans infiltrated the area later in the century (see #58), it was always predominantly "Eastern". The Juneau Village project destroyed hundreds of the finest mansions ever built in Milwaukee. In addition to their buildings we are reminded of the Easterners in the street names which survive in this district...Astor, Marshall, Van Buren, Franklin, Jackson and Jefferson.

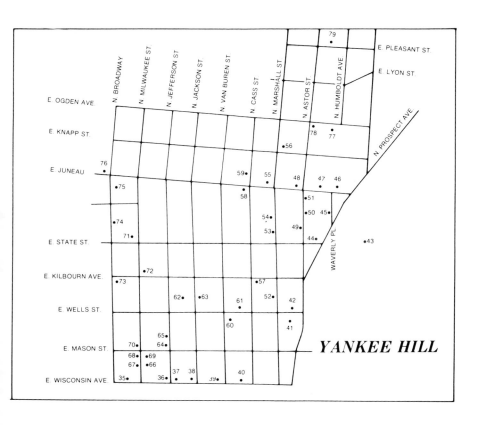

35. Wells Building
324 E. Wisconsin Ave.   1901

When Daniel Wells, Jr. erected this 15-story office building, it replaced an historic Federal Court and Post Office which had occupied this lot since 1856. The new structure, according to Wells, was "his monument." At that time he reminisced about hunting quail in this location when he was a pioneer settler and the area was covered with hazel brush. Architects H.C. Koch & Co. faced the 200-foot tall building with an off-white pressed brick and glazed terra-cotta of a matching color. The first two floors are sheet copper with cast bronze ornament, and the spectacular arched entrance has inset tiles and 3 mosaic domes in the vestibule. The lobby is fully paneled in marble. Much of the building's character was lost when the top 4 floors were stripped of the once rich terra-cotta cornice and the richly sculptured ornament.

HABS

36. Pfister Hotel
424 E. Wisconsin Ave.   1892-1893

One of only a few hotels in the country which have survived with a good percentage of their original Victorian elegance inside and out. Conceived by Guido Pfister, one of Milwaukee's pioneer tanners, the project of building a great hotel for the city was finally executed by son Charles. Architects Henry C. Koch and Hermann J. Esser created a Richardsonian Romanesque building where the first three floors were rock-faced limestone and the rest were CCB trimmed with buff terra-cotta and stained glass. A good part of the richly ornamented lobby survives along with an important collection of 19th century paintings. Rasche, Schroeder, Spransy & Associates designed the 1965 tower addition.

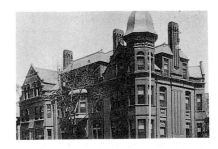

37. The Milwaukee Club
706 N. Jefferson St.   1883

It is quite an exception that such a fine, old clubhouse in such a prime downtown location should have survived in virtually unchanged condition for so many years. Organized in February of 1882, this men's club still occupies its original building. Alexander Mitchell was the first president (see #178) and the building was designed by Milwaukee architect, Edward Townsend Mix. In 1893, as club requirements demanded more space, Chicago architect W.A. Holbrook doubled the size of the north bay on Jefferson St. and extended the building 18 feet. Three red materials, sandstone, brick and terra-cotta, are blended with wrought iron and a slate roof in this eclectic Victorian design.

38. Northwestern National Insurance Company
526 E. Wisconsin Ave.   **1904-06**

Architects George Bowman Ferry and Alfred C. Clas made the drawings for this dignified French Renaissance-styled office building. The design refinements and detailing are especially interesting and they were executed in only the finest and most durable of materials. The limestone ashlar walls are broken into window bays by pairs of fluted Ionic columns with ornamental stone carving in the bottom third of each flute. Wrought bronze was used for entrance gates, lanterns, and balcony railings. Behind the stone roof balustrade is a terra-cotta tiled mansard roof trimmed in sheet copper.

39. Milwaukee Gas Light Company
626 E. Wisconsin Ave.   **1929-30**

This fine specimen of the rectilinear skyscraper style of architecture was designed by Eschweiler and Eschweiler. With the various setbacks at different levels, an interesting composition was created. The foundation and 2½ stories are faced in granite. The brick of the upper floors is graduated in color from a purplish brown at the bottom to a light buff at the top which has the effect of increasing the apparent height of the building. The carved trim and cornices are executed in kasota stone. Between the first and second floors are cast metal panels which show this building surrounded by a sunburst. Unfortunately a similar openwork metal sunburst, which once decorated the huge space above the main entrance, has been removed.

40. Northwestern Mutual Life Insurance Company
720 E. Wisconsin Ave.   **1912**

Northwestern Mutual has built three buildings of landmark quality to serve as headquarters and home offices in Milwaukee. The first, erected in 1870, was a distinguished 5-story Victorian Gothic structure with a mansard roof. (razed in 1965). The second, built in 1885, was of Richardsonian Romanesque design and is still standing (see #25). This imposing neo-classical edifice, with its 10 monumental Corinthian columns, is faced with granite and serves as the company's present home office. It was designed by Marshall & Fox of Chicago, and has been impeccably maintained. Holabird & Root (Chicago) drew plans for the 8-story addition to the rear in 1930.

41. Cudahy Tower and Apartment Building

925 E. Wells St.   1908-09 & 1928-29

The original southern half of this huge lakefront complex was called "Buena Vista Flats". Built by Patrick Cudahy, the meat packer after whom Cudahy, Wisconsin, is named, this first segment was the work of Milwaukee architects, Ferry & Clas. The 6-story plus basement structure is faced with white glazed brick and terra-cotta. Especially interesting are the five loggias on the Mason St. facade and the terra-cotta ornament. In 1928, Chicago architects Holabird & Root designed the 231-foot high northern half in more of a skyscraper style, but faced in compatible white glazed masonry. This 16-story, 155-unit building was equipped with apartments and hotel transient rooms.

42. University Club

924 E. Wells St.   1926

Architect John Russell Pope designed this distinguished Georgian clubhouse to replace the previous structure which is still standing on Jefferson St. looking into Cathredral Square. The club, founded in 1898, had as a prerequisite for membership a college degree. The semicircular, copper-sheathed cocktail lounge on the roof was added in the 1950's in spite of strong aesthetic objections. When a second addition was built over the parking lot in 1973, Milwaukee architect George Schneider carefully selected materials and designed the facade to match the Georgian character of the original building.

43. Juneau Park

Lake bluff from E. Wisconsin Ave. to E. Juneau Ave.

There was once a short street running along the lake bluff called Juneau Place. The residents, in those days, objected to the planting of trees in the park as it would have obstructed their view of the lake. Eventually, in the 1920's, the houses and the street disappeared and this half-mile-long park grew wider and began to grow trees. A bronze statue of Milwaukee's founder and first mayor stands atop a pink granite monument on the bluff. It was a gift to the city by Charles T. Bradley and William H. Metcalf (see #59) in 1887. Further north is a bronze statue of Leif Ericson which is a replica of one in Boston. Although the park is now greener it has lost some of its earlier features, such as a life-sized elk monument, a Spanish-American War cannon and an iron footbridge over a ravine.

44. Dr. Henry Harrison Button Residence
1024 E. State St. **1875**

One of Milwaukee's finest Italianate mansions, this CCB structure was finely proportioned by a long forgotten architect. In a day when wooden details could be ordered from a catalog, at a saving, this house and all its ornament was carefully designed by the same man. The sandstone keystones and window details, as well as the wooden brackets and porch, show the unmistakable touch of a single guiding hand. Although it once had a handsome 3-story tower and an "L"-shaped verandah, it still retains an unusual percentage of its original character. Button, who had practiced medicine in New York before coming here in 1848, found that the wholesale drug business was more lucrative than the labors of a pioneer physician. (see #28).

45. James S. Peck Residence
1105 N. Waverly Place **c. 1870**

One of the most finely detailed and best-preserved Italianate houses in the city, this was the home of the president of the Converse Cattle Company. When the house was built, Peck worked for Angus Smith & Co., storage and commission merchants. The most notable features in this design are the two windows above the porch on the Waverly Pl. facade. The little circular attic window is flanked by high relief wood carvings which are certainly the finest examples of their type in the city. The single window under that has an unusually fine and complicated wooden lintel.

46. George P. Miller Residence
1060 E. Juneau Ave. **c. 1885**

One of the best preserved mansions of its style in the Midwest, this Victorian eclectic structure was built by T.A. Chapman (see #18) for his daughter, Mrs. George P. Miller. Unlike most of the houses built in 19th century Milwaukee, which followed more or less closely a Revival substyle, this is a completely original and pure Victorian. It was built with an unusually wide variety of the very finest materials. The first floor and porch are pink abelman stone with a second floor of Milwaukee pressed brick. The broad cornice consists of three bands; carved stone, small buff terracotta tiles and sheet copper hammered into the shape of acanthus leaves. Other materials include stained glass, wrought iron, wood, brass, and a roof made of gray slate. The unspoiled and nearly original condition of this residence is extremely rare.

47. Hotel Knickbocker
1028 E. Juneau Ave.   1929-30

Before construction began, this project was to be called the "East End Manor-Apartment/Hotel," but by the time it was completed the name had been changed to Knickerbocker. Like its close neighbor to the east, The Astor (see #48), this building is 8-stories tall, has residential as well as transient rooms, and was located purposely near the lake in a quiet neighborhood. Architects Rosman & Wierdsma trimmed the brown brick with buff glazed terracotta which includes ornamental arches, a colonnade, and a decorative frieze at the eighth floor level.

48. Hotel Astor
924 E. Juneau Ave.   1920 & 1925

When it was built, the Astor was considered to be one of the finest hotels in the Midwest. Its location, in a principally residential neighborhood, and its proximity to the bluff gave it the early title, "Astor-At-The-Lake." More residential than transient, this large structure was built with smooth limestone ashlar and brown brick and its well-crafted interior was designed to be the ultimate in luxurious accomodations. One of the early hotels built by Walter Schroeder, the two eastern segments were begun in 1920 and the western addition in 1925. Schroeder's other hotels included the Retlaw (Walter spelled backward) in Fond du Lac, the Loraine in Madison, the Northland in Green Bay, the Wausau in Wausau, the Duluth in Duluth and finally, the Schroeder (see #170).

49. James K. Ilsley Residence
1037 N. Astor St.   1897

Built for the cashier of the Marshall & Ilsley Bank, this residence is one of only a few erected here in this style (see #85). Patterned after French Renaissance chateaux, these houses followed the tradition breaking mansion built in New York by William K. Vanderbilt in 1881. Alexander C. Eschweiler was the architect and John Debbink the builder. Basically pressed brick, the facade derives most of its character from the terra-cotta drip moldings over the windows and porch arches. Ogee in shape, the moldings terminate in fleur-de-lis. The steeply pitched French roof and dormers, with their fleur-de-lis finials, complete the chateau impression.

50. Immanuel Presbyterian Church
1100 N. Astor St. 1873

One of the most important commissions executed by architect Edward Townsend Mix, Immanuel Church was called "Modern Gothic" when it was built. It is distinguished from other Gothic churches of the same period by the imaginative use of different materials and colors. Buff-colored and rock-faced local limestone is trimmed with dark red and gray sandstone. The colorful doorways, windows and belt courses are complemented by polished granite columns, wrought iron grilles and stained glass. The resulting composition is lively and reminiscent of the Gothic buildings in Venice. Although the original interior was destroyed in an 1887 fire and has subsequently been altered many times, the exterior is still in nearly original condition.

51. James S. Brown Residence
1122 N. Astor St. c. 1850

Built on the highest ground between the river and Lake Michigan, this brick double house is one of Yankee Hill's most historic buildings. James S. Brown, one of the city's most prominent pioneer lawyers, served in many civic posts and in 1861 became Milwaukee's 11th mayor. After declining a second mayoral term, he was elected to Congress from the 1st District. Included among the subsequent list of owners were Riverius P. Elmore (first coal dealer in Wisconsin), Henry C. Payne (a Postmaster General of the United States), and Charles Schley (whose illustrious Baltimore family included Maryland's most beautiful woman). Since 1927 the house has been used for business.

52. Francis M. Baumgarten Residence
817-819 N. Marshall St. 1898

The design of this imposing pressed-buff-brick and limestone residence was loosely adapted from English Renaissance forms. It was built for the vice president of the Milwaukee Apron Company by architects, Ferry & Clas. Originally built as a double house, the northern half was occupied by Mr and Mrs. Francis Baumgarten and the southern half by lawyer, Otto C. Baumgarten. Of special interest is the pierced, carved stone balustrade in front of the roof dormers and an unusual limestone molding where the brick walls meet the foundation.

53. George W. Peckham Residence
1029 N. Marshall St.   1855 and later
Begun in 1855, as a relatively modest Italianate house, this large, painted CCB structure has been rebuilt and remodeled seven times. It was originally the home of George W. Peckham, a prominent early attorney and first president of the Bank of Commerce. When new, the house was much smaller and only two stories tall, but later additions included raising the roof six feet to create a third floor. Although neo-classical details dominate, close inspection will reveal eight different window styles, a fact which corroborates its many changes. The original architects were Mygatt & Schmidtner.

HABS

54. Robert Patrick Fitzgerald Residence
1119 N. Marshall St.   1874
A one-time lake captain, Fitzgerald became a wealthy shipowner and manager of a fleet of vessels. When he built this house he retained architect Edward Townsend Mix to create a well constructed Italian villa. The handsome proportions of this house set it apart from most of its contemporaries. The deep wooden cornice, with its attic windows, and the broad overhang of the roof are responsible for a great deal of the building's character. The paired brackets, which support the overhang, are of high quality, with carved rope molding and other details. When the present owners (the College Women's Club) added the south wing in 1965, they used original brackets and keystones and duplicated arches in an effort to relate the new with the old in a proper manner.

HABS NR WRL

55. All Saints' Episcopal Cathedral
828 E. Juneau Ave.   1868
The First Episcopal Cathedral in the United States was built by Congregationalists. This fine Gothic Revival structure was originally the Olivet Congregational Church, but financial problems forced that group to sell their new building in 1872. Attributed to architect E. T. Mix, this handsome church is made of pressed CCB, trimmed with limestone and decorative molded brick. There are brick label moldings over windows, wooden and sheet metal cornices, and a slate roof with fish scale shingles on the spire.

56. St. Paul's Episcopal Church
914 E. Knapp St. 1883-84

Milwaukee's oldest Episcopal parish, St. Paul's, was organized in 1838. The Richardsonian Romanesque edifice, designed by architect Edward Townsend Mix, is the city's finest example of this style as applied to churches. Built of rock-faced Lake Superior sandstone, the massive arches and square towers with their battlemented parapets, give the structure a great feeling of strength and solidity. Many of the stained glass windows were created by the famous Tiffany Studios in New York, and have been celebrated since they were new. It is probably no coincidence that the design of St. Paul's closely resembles one drawn by Henry Hobson Richardson for Trinity Church in Buffalo, N.Y. The plans for that church, which was never built, were published in the *Architectural Sketch Book*, July 1873.

57. Woman's Club of Wisconsin Clubhouse
813 E. Kilbourn Ave. 1887-88

This is the oldest woman's clubhouse in the United States and it was built by the first stock company of women in the world. The Woman's Club of Wisconsin was founded in 1876 at a meeting in Mrs. Alexander Mitchell's house (see #178). The honored guest and speaker for the occasion was Mrs. Julia Ward Howe, of Boston, author of "The Battle Hymn of the Republic". In 1886, after numerous temporary meeting places, the club members decided to form a company and sell stock to erect their own building. Architects Ferry and Clas drew the plans and for $14,000 the CCB clubhouse was built. Its primary purpose was to provide clubrooms; but a ballroom, dressing rooms, and reception halls were included to raise rental money for the upkeep of the building.

58. John Dietrich Inbusch Residence
1135 N. Cass St. 1874

This is a two and one-half story formal Italianate square residence with projecting central pavilion and rear wing. Pressed CCB on limestone foundation trimmed with handsome wooden window casings over molded limestone sills. Most important feature is a 3½-foot high cornice pierced with attic windows and supported by richly carved paired brackets. The central roof block has a convex mansard curve and once supported a cupola. It is one of the most finely proportioned Italianate houses in the state. Inbusch was one of three brothers who came here from Westphalia, Germany, and built one of the Midwest's largest wholesale grocery houses.

59

59. William H. Metcalf Residence
1219 N. Cass St.   1854 and later

This once imposing mansion was moved 50 feet north of its original location in 1902 when Summerfield Methodist Church was built in its front yard. The victim of many additions and remodelings, it has little resemblance to the first Greek Revival block which is now the east wing. The 1854 house was enlarged in 1870 and 1876 and once had a 4-story mansard-roofed tower. Metcalf made his million in the boot and shoe industry here and once had a large art collection in a wing that was once attached to the northeast corner of the house. The CCB structure is trimmed with red sandstone quoins.

60. Wisconsin Consistory
790 N. Van Buren St.   1889 & 1936

This building is two landmarks in one. The original structure was the Plymouth Congregational Church, designed by architect Edward Townsend Mix in 1889. It was a huge brick Romanesque structure with a spacious entrance arch on Van Buren Street. Rev. Judson Titsworth promoted this $100,000 behemoth as an institutional church, and it was open for social, athletic, and educational activities seven days a week. In 1936 the Scottish Rite Masons acquired the building and hired architect H. W. Tullgren to completely remodel it. Both street facades were faced with carved and cut limestone in the modern style popular at that time. The parapet wall is decorated with large robed figures and eagles. The rock-faced stone foundation and the eastern (alley) wall are the only remaining evidence of the original exterior.

61. Francis E. McGovern Residence
718 E. Wells St.   c. 1852

This fine, early example of Italianate design has survived in almost original condition. The only exterior changes involve the entrance which has been rebuilt. Originally a pair of doors, with oddly shaped panels, opened under a segmentally-arched porch canopy which was supported by a pair of columns. Brick quoins give an impression of formalty and solidity to the structure, which is built of painted CCB, trimmed with limestone keystones and a wooden bracketed cornice. In 1921 it became the residence of a former governor of Wisconsin, Francis McGovern.

62. Courthouse Square
Kilbourn, Wells, Jackson
and Jefferson Streets

Milwaukee's first courthouse was built on this square by Solomon Juneau (the city's first mayor) and Morgan L. Martin. The building and the block of property were then given to the city by these men. The courthouse was a 2-story frame building with a columned portico and a wing which housed the jail. In 1870 it was replaced by a large red sandstone structure with a dome. When the new courthouse was completed, in 1929, this building was abandoned and vandalized for ten years. During that time a great controversy raged over its fate. Some said it was ugly and should be torn down, but William H. Schuchardt, an architect and city planner from Los Angeles, drew up a plan to take off the dome and top two floors and convert it into an art museum. The building was finally razed in 1939.

63. St. John's Cathedral
802 N. Jackson St.   1847

One of Milwaukee's oldest and most beautiful churches, St. John's was designed by Victor Schulte. The original structure was much shorter and it had a different tower with a bulbous, baroque roof. By 1880 the substructure had deteriorated to the point where it had to be removed. In 1892 George B. Ferry, of Ferry & Clas, designed the present tower which has such dignity and fine proportions that it ranks among the finest in the country. Old bricks from demolished houses of the period were used to match the original. A disastrous fire, in 1935, destroyed the interior and the roof. At that time it was rebuilt and the nave was extended to Van Buren Street.

64. Watts Building
761 N. Jefferson St.   1925

One of the finest examples of ornamental terra-cotta architecture in the city, this two-story building is still occupied by its builder. George Watts & Son, Inc., has been a purveyor of fine china and glassware for over a century here; the firm erected its own building in 1925. Architect Martin Tullgren & Sons drew the plans for the structure, which was originally described as 3 stores, 4 offices and a tea shop. The entire facade, on both streets, is sheathed in 2 colors of glazed terra-cotta. Trim is sheet copper, polychrome terra-cotta, and leaded glass. The building's design was influenced by the Italian Renaissance and its exterior is almost completely unspoiled.

HABS

65. Matthew Keenan Residence
777 N. Jefferson St. 1860

Milwaukee's finest remaining example of the Italianate-styled townhouse. Matthew Keenan, politician and one-time vice president of Northwestern Mutual Life Insurance Co., engaged the city's most celebrated architect, Edward Townsend Mix, to design this elegant double house. Built with pressed CCB and trimmed with limestone quoins and window casings, this well preserved specimen still has one of its original mahogany staircases, a good proportion of the original ornamental plasterwork, and a few white marble fireplaces.

66. Commercial Buildings
700 Block of N. Milwaukee St.
1865 and later

This row of eight commercial buildings affords an unusual opportunity to visualize the look of downtown Milwaukee in the 19th century. The Pierce Block, on the corner, began as a three-story flat-roofed Italianate building. Later, when the French mansard roof was considered stylish, two additional floors were added. Although it has been seriously altered, there are still evidences of a fine suite of rooms designed in the art nouveau style on the top floor. The other buildings were erected at different times, but most of them share an Italianate inspiration.

67. Commercial Building
727 N. Milwaukee St. 1881

This eclectic Victorian building was one of only two structures in Wisconsin pictured in *L'Architecture Amércaine*. Published in Paris in 1886, this influential survey of American buildings helped the French, who up till then had no respect for what was going on overseas, to reappraise the quality of design here. No one knows why the author was attracted to this building, but the picture of it, when new, makes the selection more understandable. Hidden under layers of paint is a beautiful design in different colored bricks. Today's one-color scheme is also obscuring red sandstone, limestone, terra-cotta, wood and sheet metal trim. A picturesque chimney has been removed and 14 stained glass panels have been removed from the bay windows.

68. Lou Fritzel Store
733 N. Milwaukee St.   **1939**

An excellent, and well-maintained, example of the "moderne" store fronts of the 1930's. The smooth black masonry becomes the background for a metal composition carried out in sheet and cast bronze. An original sheet metal sculpture above the entrance, the cornice trim, casings, and the name are periodically stripped and refinished as this type of metalwork was intended to be. The building itself dates back to the 19th century and was once 3 stories tall. In the last of five major face-lifts (1939) the top two floors were removed.

69. John Mariner Building
411 E. Mason St.   **1937**

The first building in Milwaukee to be equipped with central air conditioning, this "moderne" six-story structure was named after the man who built the Mariner Tower (see #173). The facing is smooth limestone decorated with "speed-line" ribs and a low-relief carved ornament over the corner entrance. Milwaukee architects Eschweiler & Eschweiler drew the plans and their name appears on the bronze name and date tablet near the E. Mason St. entrance.

70. Colby and Abbot Building
759 N. Milwaukee St.   **1881**

This building was originally the general offices of the Wisconsin Central Railroad of which Charles L. Colby was president and Edwin H. Abbot was vice president and secretary. Mason John Roberts, supervised the construction of the red brick building, with its terra-cotta frieze and ornament. Unfortunately much of the polychrome, that gave this building its character, was hidden in 1969, when two coats of white cement were applied and covered with marble chips. Not only the colors, but the crisp outlines of pilasters and the sharp contours of moldings were obscured.

71. North Presbyterian Church
1001 N. Milwaukee St.   **1854**

Organized in 1849, the North Presbyterian Church erected its first small building on this lot the same year at a cost of $720. In 1854 the present CCB structure was built to replace it. The congregation united with the First Presbyterian, in 1870, to form Immanuel (see #50). This building was then taken over by the Welsh Calvinistic Society. Although greatly altered, it still has many fine details of the Gothic Revival. A fine wooden Gothic cornice is applied over the brick and the colored grisaille-type lancet windows have been damaged, but survive. The original entrance on Milwaukee Street was later filled in with an incompatible stained glass window.

72. Fred Loock Engineering Center
432 E. Kilbourn Ave.   **1966**

This modern educational facility, of the Milwaukee School of Engineering, incorporates major laboratories and classrooms in a cleanly sculptured brick building. Architect Fitzhugh Scott emphasized the rectilinear brick and applied tile facing, and recessed the glass, making it of secondary importance. The large shallow dome, on the rooftop, and the test cells on Milwaukee St. are covered with ceramic tiles. The center is named for the former president of Allen Bradley Co. (see #284), Fred Loock, who was elected chairman of the MSOE Board of Regents in 1955. Among the excellent, and up-to-date facilities here is one of the state's most advanced computers and a 25 million electron volt betatron (an electron accelerator type X-ray unit) for nondestructive testing.

73. St. Mary's Church
836 N. Broadway   **1846**

The city's first German Roman Catholic church, this venerable structure was built in the year that Milwaukee became a city. The original building was 4 window-bays deep and 56 feet wide, and it had an octagonal lantern set under a dome. The ground floor was used as a school; and the sanctuary, upstairs, was reached by a 12-foot staircase. In a major 1867 rebuilding, a large block was attached to the front and back; and the present tower with steeple was added. The school was eliminated and the sanctuary floor was lowered to its present level. Victor Schulte, the German-born architect of St. John's Cathedral (see #63) and Holy Trinity Church (see #290), drew the plans. A painting of the Annunciation, over the altar, was a gift from King Ludwig I of Bavaria.

HABS NR WRL

64

HABS NR *

74. German-English Academy
1020 N. Broadway **1890-91**

In 1851 the German-English Academy was founded to provide a quality education in two languages. In 1878 the National German-American Teachers Seminary, which was organized to train instructors according to the principles of German universities, was joined with the Academy. In 1890, Mrs. Elizabeth Pfister and Mrs. Louisa Vogel donated the grounds and the present 3-story school building which was designed by architects Crane & Barkhausen. At that time the normal department of the North American Gymnastic Union was united with the Academy and a gymnasium was built next door (the Turnlehrer Seminar). Both buildings are lavishly decorated with cream-colored terra-cotta. The gym has its arch spandrels filled with athletic equipment, including fencing foils and turners' clubs. A scallop shell cornice, acanthus leaf belt-courses and corbels on the Academy building are in the same material.

75. Val. Blatz Brewing Co. Office Building
1120 N. Broadway **1890**

A Milwaukee architect, Herman P. Schnetzky, designed this general office building for the now defunct Valentine Blatz Brewery. Built by mason Julius Hauboldt, the heavy rock-faced Wauwatosa limestone facade is trimmed with sandstone. The massive Romanesque entrance arch is supported by two pairs of polished granite columns with heavily carved Byzantine capitals. At the top of the entrance pavilion is a carved six-pointed star with a hop bud and the initials, V.B. This was the trademark of the brewery and it can be seen on the other buildings in the complex nearby.

76. Grace Lutheran Church
1209 N. Broadway **1900**

Grace Church was designed by architect H.C. Koch and executed in pressed orange/brown brick with terra-cotta trim in a matching color. The eastern (front) porch, almost entirely terra-cotta, is one of the better examples of that material in the city. Three Gothic arches, with sculptured spandrels, step back in a series of columns to 3 pairs of double doors. Over the entrance and surrounding the great rose window, is a band of terra-cotta with the German inscription ... "1850 Evangelisch-Lutherische Gnaden Kirche 1900." When the timber-framed towers became seriously deteriorated in 1953, both were decapitated and rebuilt without the original ornamental terra-cotta features.

77. Abbot Row
1019-1043 E. Ogden Ave.   1889

Architect Howland Russel drew the plans for this block of ten connected town houses. Unlike New York and Chicago, which spawned literally miles of these structures, Milwaukee never saw the need for many. Of the few remaining here, Ogden Row (which it is now called) is certainly the finest and best preserved example. Edwin Hale Abbot is the name listed on the 1889 building permit, but according to a popular legend, the reason for the Row's existence was the Bielefeld Beer Garden, which once stood on this lot. It is said that Mrs. Abbot, who tired of the nightly revelry immediately behind her Knapp Street house, bought the beer garden to get rid of it and built the "Row" in its place. Posson Brothers built the Row for $30,000.

HABS NR WRL

78. First Unitarian Church
1009 E. Ogden St.   1892

Although technically within the period called Victorian, the Gothic design of this church follows more closely than most the original English forms. Architects Ferry and Clas created a distinguished church of the perpendicular period (the last of the three basic English Gothic styles). Built with rock-faced Bedford limestone, it is relieved with carved bosses and wooden tracery. Inside massive hammerbeams, on carved stone corbels, support the roof. Among the finely carved faces to be seen on the exterior is that of William H. Metcalf (see #59) who donated the organ for the new church.

HABS

79. Herman W. Buemming Residence
1012 E. Pleasant St.   1901

Herman W. Buemming is said to have built this house for his honeymoon, and it was set on the lot which was a gift from his father-in-law, Louis Durr. As the architect (his firm was Buemming & Dick), he took special interest in the project and followed every stage of the construction carefully. Obviously inspired by the Classical Revival, this formal composition resembles a Greek temple with its ionic colonnade and triangular pediment trimmed with acroteria. Buemming designed an almost identical frame home at 3112 W. McKinley Blvd. (see #247). His own house, the more purely Grecian of the two, has an unusual leaded glass transom window, with a fish scale pattern, over the door.

PROSPECT AVENUE AREA

Milwaukee's "Gold Coast" or "Kings Row" began as a muddy lane, part of which followed the Sauk Indian Trail. By 1854 it had been graded and planked, and there were already substantial homes along its southern blocks. They were considered summer homes in the beginning, because Prospect was then beyond the city limits. As the population increased and moved north along the lake, Prospect Avenue grew to become the showplace of Milwaukee. Out-of-town visitors were frequently given a tour of this street and its great mansions. The nearby parallel and intersecting streets attracted similar development.

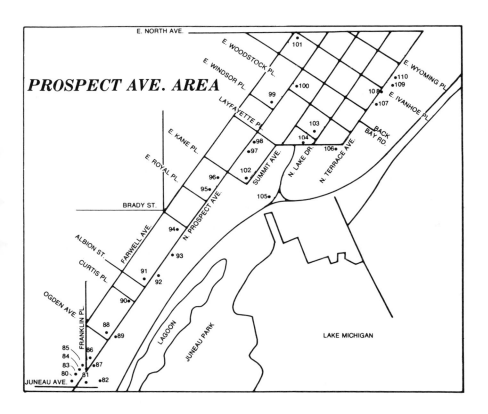

HABS

80. Jason Downer Residence
1201 N. Prospect Ave. 1874
One of Milwaukee's most historic mansions, this Victorian Gothic residence was originally begun as a church. In 1869, Bishop Kemper (see # 649) officiated at the laying of a cornerstone on this property for a Milwaukee Episcopal cathedral. At the same time, coincidentally, the Olivet Congregational Church had fallen into financial difficulties and was offering to sell their newly built Gothic structure for a bargain price. The Episcopalians accepted the offer and moved into that church (see #55). Jason Downer, a prominent early lawyer, former editor of the *Milwaukee Sentinel*, and *Judge*, bought the unfinished foundation. He made a few modifications and then built this handsome house on the original stone. As a strong supporter of women's education, his efforts eventually led to the adoption of his name for Milwaukee-Downer College (see #160) as well as Downer Avenue.

81. Stephen A. Harrison Residence
1216 N. Prospect Ave. 1866
Prospect Avenue's oldest house was erected by master builder, Stephen A. Harrison, who was responsible for the main building at the Soldier's Home (see #255). It had a twin to the north (now gone) and has lost its original entrance, a bay window, and a circular Gothic window on the south gable. The handsome cast iron fence, which runs along two sides of the lot, is probably the longest surviving example in the city. A gentle curve at the eaves, and the pierced bargeboards give distinction to the roof. A blend of Italianate and Gothic styling, it is made of CCB with brick quoins.

82. White Manor Apartments
1228-36 E. Juneau Ave.
1856 and later
Built in many sections, and for many reasons, this fascinating complex has now become one of the lakefront's most desirable apartments. In 1856, David P. Hull built a large Italianate residence to block the northward extension of Juneau Place (a street - now gone - which paralleled the bluff through what is now Juneau Park). Hull's intentions succeeded, but he lost the house, financially, before it was completed. After one family lived in it, the house was sold, in 1869, to the Protestant Orphan Asylum. For twenty years the asylum made major additions and constructed other buildings on the property. Finally, in 1930, a developer connected all of the buildings in a $100,000 remodeling.

83. Francis Hinton Residence
1229-31 N. Prospect Ave.   c. 1877

The house that started a Prospect Avenue feud was built by Francis Hinton, once manager of the Illinois Steel Company in Bay View. According to an early story, Judge Jason Downer could look from his eastern bay window (1201 N. Prospect...see #80) and see both the lake and a fountain splashing in the little park bounded by Prospect, N. Franklin Pl. and E. Knapp Street. When Hinton's 3-story town house was erected right up to the property line, it permanently eliminated the fountain view. It is said that Downer retaliated by building another 3-story brick dwelling (1223 N. Prospect) to block Hinton's view of the lake. The "reply" house is so close to its neighbor that it would be difficult to squeeze a butter knife between them.

HABS

84. Edward Diedrichs Residence
1241 N. Franklin Place   c.1855

This neo-classical mansion was built by a native German, Edward Diedrichs, who came to Milwaukee from Russia. It was designed by the distinguished pioneer architectural firm of Mygatt & Schmidtner. A disastrous fire all but destroyed the house in 1859 and it was rebuilt "exactly as it was". However, it did destroy Diedrichs, whose many investments failed, and he left town by 1863 and subsequently died in the poorhouse in New York. In 1895, Milwaukee banker, John Johnston, added the second story, enlarged the front porch, and put a bay on the south wall. Howland Russel was the architect, and the alterations were done with such good taste that they all look original.

85. Hawley-Bloodgood Residences
1249 N. Franklin Place
& 1139 E. Knapp St.   1896

Actually two dwellings joined by a party wall, this French Chateau-styled structure was designed by one of Milwaukee's first formally educated architects, Howland Russel. It was inspired by the rash of Chateau building in New York which began with William K. Vanderbilt's Fifth Avenue mansion in 1881. Francis Bloodgood built the northern half, and his initial along with that of his wife's maiden name (Hawley), appears in a terra-cotta monogram above the entrance. The south half was built by Mary B. Hawley, after whose family Hawley Road was named. 450 Gothic crockets, made of sheet metal, ornament the gables and pinnacles.

86. Robert Burns Statue
N. Prospect Ave. & E. Knapp St. 1909

James Anderson Bryden, an early Milwaukeean of Scottish descent, gave this bronze statue of poet Burns to the city in 1909. It is a replica of his famous statue in Kilmarnock, Scotland, by Edinburgh sculptor William Grant Stevenson. For many years a group of local curlers, including Alexander Mitchell (see #178) and John Johnston (see #84), planned to donate a statue of their favorite poet. One by one they died and Bryden, the only survivor, decided to take action in his will. He later reconsidered, saying, "Why not have the enjoyment of seeing the monument myself," and he commissioned the project immediately. There were nearly 2,000 people present when Mayor David Rose accepted the statue in behalf of the city.

87. Twelve Sixty Apartment
1260 N. Prospect Ave. 1938

One of Milwaukee's most spectacular and important "moderne" structures of the 1930's, this apartment was built by Harry Grant, former owner and publisher of the *Milwaukee Journal*. There are 32 apartments, 8 on each floor, and two penthouses. Milwaukee architect, Herbert W. Tullgren, designed each suite with two floors connected by a stairway. By having the elevators stop at every other floor (1, 3, 5, 7, 9) the upper level bedrooms in each apartment were isolated from public corridors, thus offering maximum quiet. Each unit has two bay windows, one in its dining room, and a solarium connected to a bedroom. The building is faced with limestone ashlar and steel casement windows. Much of the original art-deco ornament survives.

88. Collins/Elwell Residence
1363 N. Prospect Ave.   1876

Erected by grain broker, Gilbert E. Collins this unusual Victorian mansion was never occupied by its builder. The first listed resident was his daughter, Ella, and her husband Edward F. Elwell, of Beaver Dam, Wisconsin. It was designed by one of Milwaukee's pioneer architects, James Douglas, who had been a carpenter on the old City Hall, Holy Trinity Church (see #290) and the original roof of St. John's Cathedral (see #63). Douglas gained a national reputation for his uniquely styled residences which were described by an early historian as "Termes Mordax, or 'ant hill' style, a term probably suggested from a fancied resemblance between the roofs of the dwellings constructed upon this plan, and the villages of these little pugnacious, cone-building, African termites." This house, representative of the style, has one of the most complex rooflines in the city. Chiseled hip, pitched octagonal, and half octagonal roof segments result in such complexity that one third floor room has 49 wall and ceiling surfaces.

89. Evan and Marion Helfaer
Jewish Federation
Community Service Building
1360 N. Prospect Ave.   1973

Designed by Edward Durrell Stone, one of the world's most distinguished modern architects, this building was the gift of Milwaukee philanthropist, Evan Philip Helfaer. Inside its finely proportioned massing of rectilinear blocks is a large atrium which rises the full height of the building. Installed therein is the only tapestry in the United States designed by Marc Chagall. This celebrated piece was commissioned especially for the building by Helfaer and measures 14 x 19 feet. Originally painted by Chagall as a gouache, it was made into a tapestry at the atelier of Yvette Cauquil-Prince in Paris.

90. First Church of Christ Scientist
1451 N. Prospect Ave.   1907-08

Chicago architect S.S. Beman drew the plans for this Classical edifice and specified Bedford limestone for its construction. On February 5, 1908, a fire destroyed the building while it was under construction. Only the west wall remained standing, but it was ruled unsafe and had to be taken down to the water table and rebuilt. The original building permit was extended to cover reconstruction. Four partially-fluted Doric columns frame the entrance porch.

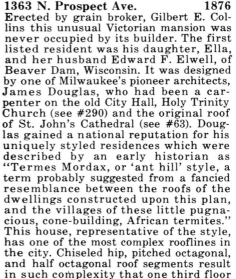

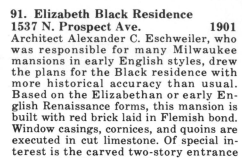

91. Elizabeth Black Residence
1537 N. Prospect Ave.   **1901**

Architect Alexander C. Eschweiler, who was responsible for many Milwaukee mansions in early English styles, drew the plans for the Black residence with more historical accuracy than usual. Based on the Elizabethan or early English Renaissance forms, this mansion is built with red brick laid in Flemish bond. Window casings, cornices, and quoins are executed in cut limestone. Of special interest is the carved two-story entrance panel with its deep-relief, sculptured, doorway arch. Copper downspouts receive rainwater through the parapet wall.

92. Fred T. Goll Residence
1550 N. Prospect Ave.   **1898**

Architects Ferry & Clas created this imposing English-styled mansion long before the great Tudor rage reached its peak in the 1920's. It is an unusual blend of English forms in pressed brick and cut limestone. The street facade is strongly reminiscent of Elizabethan manor houses; the south gable has nogged timber construction and bargeboards on the edge of the roof, a richly carved board forms the base of the triangular gable and is supported by corbels with heads carved on them.

93. Charles L. McIntosh Residence
1584 N. Prospect Ave.   **1904**

Chicago architect, H.R. Wilson, drew the plans for this handsome Classic Resurgence style mansion. McIntosh, a director of the Milwaukee Harvester Co., came here from New York via Racine, where he bought a controlling interest in the J.I. Case Co. Only the finest materials were used throughout. The basic material is Galesburg paving brick, trimmed with Michigan raindrop brown stone. Cornices and balustrade are sheet copper and the roof is covered with tile. Four fluted Corinthian columns support the imposing portico, and the balcony with wrought iron railing is supported on four double brackets over the front door. Inside, the major design feature is a giant 25' x 50' music room and dance hall in the French 18th century style. When the house was new, a newspaper article called it a "veritable paradise".

94. E.D. Adler Residence
1681 N. Prospect Ave. 1888

One of only a few late Victorian mansions remaining on the "Gold Coast", this eclectic design shows the strong influences of Queen Anne and Romanesque styling. It was designed by Milwaukee architect, A.C. Clas, and built by Fred Werner. The first floor is rock-faced limestone laid random ashlar and the second is red pressed brick. Buff sandstone and carved wood are used for trim, and red terra-cotta fish scale shingles cover the gable and third floor of the tower. The roof and two dormers are slate. Wrought iron railing, beveled plate leaded glass, and sheet metal complete the unusually wide variety of materials used here.

HABS

95. Charles Allis Residence
1630 E. Royal Place 1909

This fine Tudor mansion was built by Charles Allis, first president of the Allis Chalmers Manufacturing Co. Architect Alexander Eschweiler used a red/purple brick and trimmed it with Lake Superior sandstone of a similar color. The interior is elegantly finished with Circassian walnut and French polished mahogany panelling. Ornamental plaster, a variety of marbles, leaded glass, and Tiffany fixtures combine to provide a backdrop worthy of Mr. Allis' fine collection of paintings and objets d'art. When his widow died in 1945, the mansion and its contents were willed to the City of Milwaukee. The Charles Allis Art Library is open to the public.

96. Sanford Kane Residence
1841 N. Prospect Ave. 1883

Milwaukee's finest remaining example of the Queen Anne style, This building serves as a reminder of the Kane family which once owned the whole neighborhood and after which nearby Kane Place was named. Sanford's father, Philander, and his four brothers operated the American House Hotel in the 1850's. Then the largest hotel in the city, it stood where the Plankinton Building is today (see #164) until it burned down in 1861. The Kanes later operated a mineral spring (the Siloam) on their 40-acre property which included this area. This is a remarkably well preserved example of a style which has many irregular projections, and bays, gables, dormers, wood framing with carved details, and picturesque chimneys.

97. Park Lane Apartments
1930 N. Prospect Ave.   **1930**

The Park Lane, the Embassy, and the Park View apartment buildings were all built by Evan P. Helfaer. This structure is a good example of art deco styling as applied to a high-rise apartment. Basically scratch-faced, variegated buff brick, it is trimmed in five colors of glazed terra-cotta. The foundation is black and the facing of the two side projections is accomplished with 3 mottled colors (ivory, pink, and rust) up to the fifth floor level. The cornice is black with vertically reeded panels of metallic gold glazed terra-cotta.

98. Shorecrest Hotel
1962 N. Prospect Ave.   **1924 & 1928**

One of the earliest high-rise developments on Milwaukee's lake bluff, the Shorecrest Apartment/Hotel was built in two stages. The first 8-story structure fronted on what was then called Hathaway Place (now Summit Ave.) and replaced the old homestead of Christopher W. LeValley who was the president of Chain Belt Company. Designed by Milwaukee architects, Martin Tullgren & Sons, the building was doubled in capacity in 1928, when a $400,000 western addition extended the new front to N. Prospect Avenue. The lobby was wishfully described as "early Italian style" and the roof included a dining room and a children's playroom. The first floor of the original exterior is relieved with glazed terra-cotta ornament, including spiral twisted columns supporting arches which are decorated with griffins.

99. Bertelson Building
2101-05 N. Prospect Ave.   **1927**

One of the finest examples of terra-cotta construction in the city, this unique complex of five stores and a studio was designed by Martin Tullgren & Sons. The multicolored, glazed terra-cotta blocks were not only used as the basic facing material, but for the rich and decorative ornament. The main entrance arch, with its lavishly decorated spandrels, demonstrates well the features which made this material so popular in the 1920's. It was an inexpensive way to produce ornament and, as can be seen, the material resists the ravages of time and weather. The details are reminiscent of the Italian Renaissance.

100. Northwestern Hannah Fuel Co. Building
2150 N. Prospect Ave. 1934

Architect H.W. Tullgren drew the plans for this very fine example of 1930's moderne/art deco design. Its exterior, which has survived in almost new condition, is built with a well-planned complement of materials and colors. The basic color is two slightly different buff bricks laid to create subtle horizontal lines. The trim is mostly orange terra-cotta with accents of black. Between the vertical buttresses are tan terra-cotta bas-reliefs showing three scenes in man's use of coal. First is a coal miner with a pick, then the transportation of coal in boats, railroad cars, and trucks. The last panel has a man shovelling coal into a boiler. Even the semi-cylindrical bay windows, with their built-in flagpoles, are unspoiled.

101. Oriental Theater
2230 N. Farwell Ave. 1927

Milwaukee's finest remaining "Golden Age" movie palace is the best preserved and most typical in all respects of its breed. Movie houses of this vintage were not intended to become architectural masterpieces, but to create an opulent and imaginative atmosphere in which the public could escape its daily surroundings and enter the dream world on the screen. Styles were therefore chosen to be as foreign to everyday experience as possible. Architects Gustav A. Dick and Alex H. Bauer created an "artistic temple of Oriental art". The spectacular lobby features glazed terra-cotta lions, murals, rich carpets and draperies, majolica tiles, wrought iron, and 16 silver-leafed elephant heads.

102. Hathaway Apartments
1830 E. Kane Place 1931

The ultimate in "moderne" design when it was built, this compact miniature skyscraper is almost completely unspoiled and has many details typical of the art-deco and speed-line era. The square monolith is given a feeling of greater height by the use of dark panels between the windows. Both these stripes and the foundation are black glazed terra-cotta. The buff pressed brick and terra-cotta do not come to sharp corners, but have a radius, which was typical of the period. The entrance mantel, with its multi-faceted arch, is faced with black glass. Illuminated art-deco numbers flank the doorway.

103. Howard Greene Residence
2025 N. Lake Drive   **1907**

Designed by Milwaukee architect William Schuchardt, this Georgian-styled residence was one of many similar projects undertaken by the same man in the same materials. Mason Elias Grunewald, was responsible for the red brick walls with their imitation corner quoins made of the same material. Three handsome dormers are set on the lower slope of the gambrel roof. In 1938 architect R.B. Williamson reworked the interior into a multi-family apartment.

104. William E. Fitzgerald Residence
2022 E. Lafayette Place   **1901**

This red brick house is an unusual blend of the Classical Revival and the Georgian. The formal symmetry of its facade is framed by brick quoins and a wooden modillioned cornice. Architects Ferry & Clas drew the plans for the house in 1901 and a stable with living quarters over it in 1903. In 1939 the residence was restructured on the interior to create a duplex by architect, A.C. Eschweiler. Of special interest are the shapes of the window lintels, made with tapered brick, and their matching keystones. Also note the treatment of the entrance framing and its sidelight windows.

105. Flushing Station
1701 Lincoln Memorial Dr.   **1888**

This CCB building once housed steam pumps which drew water from Lake Michigan and forced it through a long tunnel to the Milwaukee River near the North Ave. dam. The purpose was to cool the river water, make it flow faster, and flush the gathering pollution downstream. The $275,000 project included this building and a 2,534-foot-long tunnel which was 12 feet in diameter and had its inlet at the Yacht Club basin. The cream brick of the pumphouse is decorated with buff sandstone string courses and a decorative sheet metal cupola with ventilating louvers. An unusual matched pair of carved keystones can be seen in the north and south entrance arches with the date "1888" on them. In 1912 the steam pumps were changed to electrical. Today the facility is shut down since the lake is also polluted.

106. Emil H. Ott Residence
2127 E. Lafayette Place　　　**1907**

Plans for this English Tudor mansion were drawn by A.C. Clas of the firm Ferry & Clas. The finely pointed limestone masonry was executed by Charles Gruenewaldt and the carpenter was Louis Clas. Copper gutters and downspouts, wrought bronze, leaded glass, and a red slate roof are among the first-class materials used in this well-built residence. The interior, however, is the most important part of the design. Executed in marble, oak panelling, ornamental plaster and wrought iron, it ranks among the very finest in the city. Especially spectacular is the carved English Renaissance staircase in a vaulted two-story well. Emil Ott was president of Steinmeyer's (see #189).

107. Halbert E. Paine Residence
2214 N. Terrace Ave.

c.1860-65 and later

The oldest house on Terrace Ave., this quasi-Georgian facade hides a Civil War vintage Italianate mansion with a free-standing square tower. One of the city's most remodelled houses, it began as an irregular villa in the 1860's, was streamlined by architect Alexander Eschweiler in 1902, and again completely re-built to its present form by architect Fitzhugh Scott in 1915. Although the name of the builder has not been determined, Halbert Paine was the first to be listed as an occupant. Paine was a prominent attorney who later moved to Washington, D.C., to become commissioner of patents. Herman W. Falk (founder of the Falk Corporation) was the owner who ordered both remodellings.

108. Lloyd Raymond Smith Residence
2220 N. Terrace Ave.　　　**1922**

HABS NR WRL

Milwaukee's finest example of Mediterranean architecture was designed for an A.O. Smith Corporation executive by Chicago architect, David Adler. Its red brick walls are painted white and the "U"-shaped living quarters enclose an open courtyard in the style of an Italian palazzo of the 12th or 13th century. The front of the courtyard is screened from the street by a wall which has a beautiful wrought iron doorway executed by Cyril Colnik. At the rear a wide terrace, flanked by a pair of vaulted porches, overlooks a "view garden" which extends 1,000 feet down the bluff to Lake Michigan. A stone staircase, with a cascading waterfall down the middle, descends to lake level between hedges. Donated to the city in 1966, the building is now called "Villa Terrace" and is a decorative arts museum.

109. Gustav G. Pabst Residence
2230 N. Terrace Ave.   **1906**

Gustav Pabst engaged the architectural firm of Ferry & Clas to draw the plans for his lake bluff mansion. The Wisconsin Avenue residence built by his father, Captain Frederick Pabst, was designed by the same firm. The four fluted Corinthian columns supporting the portico on its classical facade are special. When they were first delivered, Mrs. Pabst was disappointed with their sectioned construction and ordered new ones cut from single blocks of stone. The limestone ashlar facade is trimmed with very costly wrought bronze grilles. Sheet copper dormers project from a green glazed tile mansard roof.

110. William O. Goodrich Residence
2234 N. Terrace Ave.   **1894-95**

This Victorian Gothic house is said to have been built as a wedding gift for Goodrich when he married Marie Pabst. Famous Milwaukee brewer, Capt. Frederick Pabst, engaged architect Otto Strack, who had executed work for the brewery and the Pabst Theater. Pabst's gift inscription, engraved on the brass chandelier hanging in the dining room, reads "All care abandon ye who enter here — Frederick Pabst — Anno Domini — 1892". The building is of pressed brown brick trimmed with buff terracotta and has a slate roof with sheet metal ornament.

PROSPECT HILL

This pioneer neighborhood development was platted in 1893 and included 90 acres bounded by N. Lake Drive, Park Place, Downer Avenue, and Kenwood Boulevard. Originally part of a 265-acre farm, this tract was purchased by E.P. Hackett and S.H. Hoff for $425,000. They organized the Prospect Hill Land Company and immediately laid water, sewer and gas mains and constructed asphalt streets. Newberry Boulevard was planned as the highlight of the development. Two of the earliest houses built here were those of James Sawyer (see #116) and George Douglass (see #117). The B.M. Goldberg residence was the first built on Newberry Boulevard (1896 - see #113).

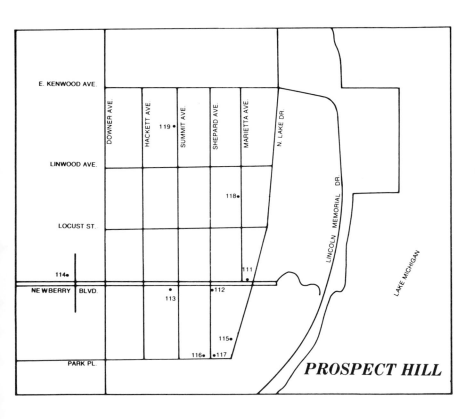

111. A.F. Gallun Residence
3000 E. Newberry Blvd. 1914

Built by the president of the Gallun Tannery, this stone Tudor mansion is one of the city's largest and best constructed. It is trimmed with Bedford limestone, oak timbers, and copper gutters and has a Vermont slate roof. Architect Richard Philipp laid out the ground plan in a "U" shape surrounding a central courtyard with an access passageway under part of the building. The house has three major fronts and is surrounded by one of the finest wrought iron fences in the state. After a major fire, heavy vandalism, and abandonment, it has been restored with great integrity.

112. Carl A. Miller Residence
2909 E. Newberry Blvd. 1917

Carl Miller was the son-in-law of Frederick Miller, who founded the Miller Brewing Company. When he first came to Milwaukee, he worked at the brewery for awhile, but then founded the lumber company which bears his name today. In 1917 he engaged architect Charles W. Valentine to design this large residence, built with Bedford, Indiana, limestone. Wrought iron balconies, a green tile roof and the carved details around the entrance give character to an otherwise bold but severe composition. Of special interest is the two-story passageway at the rear which connects the house with the garage and servant's quarters.

113. B.M. Goldberg Residence
2727 E. Newberry Blvd. 1896

This was the first house to be built on Newberry Boulevard. It is a highly unusual and creative variation on the Victorian Gothic style and was designed by Milwaukee architects, John A. Moller and George C. Ehlers. The pressed light tan brick rests on a limestone foundation and is trimmed with smooth limestone and with copper and galvanized sheet-metal ornament. The most uncommon feature of the design is the cylindrical corner tower which terminates in a parapet with a pierced Gothic railing. Set in the middle is an octagonal room with triangular gables which, graduate into a slate covered spire.

114. Dr. Thomas R. Bours Residence
2430 E. Newberry Blvd. 1921

This house has, for years, been attributed to Frank Lloyd Wright or the "Taliesen School", but it was, in fact, designed by Milwaukee architect, Russell Barr Williamson. There is, however, a strong resemblance between this design and Wright's work. The brick walls are set on a concrete foundation and are decorated with ornamental panels made of pre-cast concrete. The strong horizontals, created by stringcourses and the unusually broad overhang of the eaves, are contrasted with unbroken vertical brick pilasters. The highly geometric leaded glass windows are accented with tiny gold-mirror squares, another design device often associated with Wright.

115. Edward G. Cowdery Residence
2743 N. Lake Drive 1896

Built by the general manager of the Milwaukee Gas Light Company, this imposing residence was designed by architect Alexander C. Eschweiler. Its pleasant coloration comes from the orange/brown pressed brick and the light orange terra-cotta trim. The focal point of the design is the porte cochere under the off-center entrance gable. Originally open so that carriages could pass through, this heavy masonry porch has an openwork Gothic railing and a pair of terra-cotta elves sitting atop the two angle buttresses.

116. James Sawyer Residence
2705 N. Shepard Ave. 1894

This is a three-story frame residence on a brick foundation with four fluted Ionic columns supporting a balustraded balcony and pedimented porch. Sawyer, a member of Milwaukee's Board of Trade, engaged Milwaukee architect, W.D. Kimball, to design this Classical Revival style dwelling in clapboard with rich moldings. The hollow pediment overhanging the front porch is pierced by five "porthole" windows surrounded with classical ornamental trim.

HABS

117. George Douglass Residence
2704 N. Shepard Ave.   **1894**

James Sawyer (see #116) wished to have a close friend as a neighbor when he built in Prospect Hill. An old friend from New York, George Douglass, had just been married to the daughter of R. G. Dunn (president of the mercantile agency which later became Dunn & Bradstreet). Sawyer talked the elder Dunn into buying the lot across the street, and building a house for the newlyweds which would ensconce them in surroundings he thought worthy of their social and financial background. Three-story frame, hip roof, with unusual double, Palladian-style windows on the second floor facade.

118. Otto Zielsdorf Residence
2931 N. Marietta Ave.   **1899**

Built for the president of the C. Hennecke Iron Works, this Classical Revival house is surfaced with stucco and rests on a CCB foundation. It closely resembles, in basic style and proportion, the James Sawyer (see #116) and Fred Pabst Jr. (see #245) houses which were built earlier in the same decade. Architects Mollerus & Lotter used four, fluted, Ionic columns to support the portico and acanthus-leaf brackets to support the eaves. The triangular pediment, contrary to tradition, is faced with shingles.

HABS NR WRL HABS

119. William W. Akin Residence
3043 N. Summit Ave.   **1910**

A fine example of Richard Philipp's early Georgian work, this 2½-story red brick house has a well-proportioned front porch supported by four fluted Ionic columns. The frame dormers and richly constructed chimneys provide a pleasant skyline to finish the formal symmetry of the street facade. The brick is laid Flemish bond, and window lintels are characteristically made with the same brick and limestone keystones. The architectural firm, Brust & Philipp, worked with mason William Winter on the job.

NORTH POINT

The northernmost corner of Milwaukee Bay has, from the earliest times, been a prime location. From its high bluff a fine view can be had of the bay and the city beyond. In 1854, Jefferson W. Glidden and John Lockwood subdivided more than 100 acres of this area and established the prestige residential neighborhood which survives today. A year later Lockwood built a spectacular $20,000 Italianate mansion in what is now a park at the bluff end of Lafayette Place. Before it was torn down that house was enlarged and given a mansard roof and was last operated as a resort-hotel.

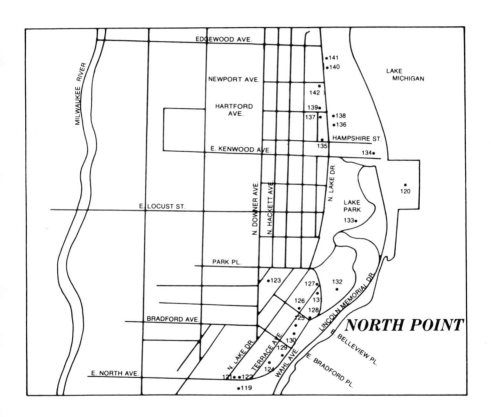

120. North Point Water Tower
East end of North Avenue   1873

One of America's most beautiful remaining water towers, this Victorian Gothic structure was designed by architect Charles A. Gombert. When new, its only neighbor was St. Mary's Hospital and a cow pasture to the south. Directly below the tower, at the bottom of the bluff, was a fine CCB and limestone pumphouse, also Gothic, which was razed in 1963 to be replaced by the present structure. The 175-foot-high Wauwatosa limestone tower is a decorative sheath for a four-foot diameter iron standpipe. Since water is non-compressible, this pipe was necessary to absorb the uneven pulsations of the old steam pumping engines, which otherwise would have broken the mains. A spiral staircase winds around the pipe and leads to the decorative sheet metal top with its central spire, four turrets, and four gables.

121. St. John's Infirmary Marker
N. Lake Drive at North Ave.   1848

WHM

"Founded May 15, 1848, with the Daughters of Charity of St. Vincent de Paul providing direction and nursing, St. John's Infirmary offered Wisconsin's first public hospital care under the supervision of the patient's physician. (Prior institutions merely isolated the sick: no medical care was given.) St. John's original location was the southeast corner of Jackson and Wells Streets. In 1855 it was moved downtown, and, in 1858 was built on this site on three acres given by the city. The name was changed to St. Mary's Hospital. It was also a Marine Hospital for Great Lakes seamen. During the Civil War, the sisters cared for as many as 110 casualties at one time. A famed chief surgeon here was Dr. Erastus B. Wolcott. His achievements included the first recorded kidney removal on June 4, 1861."

122. St. Mary's Hospital
2320 N. Lake Drive   1908-10

Milwaukee's oldest hospital and the state's first public hospital, St. Mary's was founded in 1848 by the Sisters of Charity of St. Joseph. The original structure was erected in 1856 on land donated by the city and stood for years in the middle of pastureland. Large additions were made in 1888 and 1894, but the first building remained until it was replaced by the present one. This five-story giant, 194 feet by 225 feet, was designed by Chicago architect, Richard E. Schmidt. The north wing was added, in 1958, by St. Louis architects, Magulo & Quick.

123. Kenwood Masonic Temple
2648 N. Hackett Ave.   **1915**

Architects Leenouts and Guthrie designed this unique-for-Milwaukee clubhouse in 1915. Now officially the Kenwood Lodge, No. 303 F. & A.M., this clubhouse is reminiscent of the Italian Gothic palazzi along the canals of Venice. Its scratched brown brick walls are decorated with white terra-cotta ornament and leaded glass windows. The principal interest in the composition is the recessed two-story loggia with its openwork Gothic arcades which were obviously inspired by the Palazzo Ducale or Doges Palace in Venice.

124. F.C. Bogk Residence
2420 N. Terrace Ave.   **1916**

This is the only important residential project by Frank Lloyd Wright in Milwaukee. Unlike the Burnham Street houses (see #322) this was surpervised and followed to completion by the architect. Built during his so-called Japanese years, during which he was working on the Imperial Hotel in Tokyo, this house bears some resemblance to that design period in Wright's development. The buff-colored tapestry brick is trimmed with ornamental cast concrete and geometric leaded glass with tiny gold squares. The green-tiled roof, with its wide overhang and the deeply recessed windows, are characteristic of his "prairie" houses. In fine original condition inside and out, this is the city's most important example of Wright's work.

125. Walter Kasten Residence
2550 N. Terrace Ave.   **1908**

This is another of many creative local variations on the Georgian style designed by Richard Philipp of the architectural firm, Brust & Philipp. This semiformal composition is symmetrically arranged around the Ionic-columned wooden entrance. A pair of two-story half-octagon bays repeat the balance on both sides. Red brick, laid Flemish bond, is trimmed with cut limestone stringcourses and keystones. Three dormers, with broken pediments, spring from the pitched gable roof.

85

126. Gustav J.A. Trostel Residence
2611 N. Terrace Ave.   **1899**

An excellent example of the German New Renaissance style, this house was designed by Adolph Finkler (Trostel's brother-in-law) and Hans Liebert. Today its stylistic rarity and nearly mint condition make this an important landmark. Only the finest and most costly materials were used... pressed brown brick on a limestone ashlar foundation, trimmed with cut and carved limestone, stained glass, sheet copper, exposed timber, wood carving, and a red pantile roof. Cyril Colnik created numerous wrought iron furnishings, including a fine front door grille which displays the owner's initial "T."

127. A. Lester Slocum Residence
2675 N. Terrace Ave.   **1930**

A fine and creative variation on the English Tudor style, this distinguished residence was designed by architect Richard Philipp for the president of the Slocum Straw Works. Unlike so many of its contemporaries, which have false timberwork made with thin applied planks, this house was built with genuine structural ash timbers taken from an old barn. Its south bay and entrance pavilion are framed in this manner and are cantilevered on timber corbels. With the coursed rubble limestone construction and the heavy shingle tile roof, a pleasant and quiet effect is obtained. A hand wrought iron fence and gateway complete the fine complement of materials.

128. William F. Luick Residence
2601 N. Wahl Ave.   **c.1922-23**

Designed by Milwaukee architect, Richard Philipp, this stone house is only one variation of the English styles at which he was so successful. He designed the Gallun house (see #111) which was more like a formal Tudor manor house, and the Slocum residence (see #127) which had an earlier feeling with genuine half timber work. Ice cream manufacturer Luick requested, instead, an authentic English Cotswold house complete with a typical stacked stone drywall around the perimeter of the lot.

129. Robert Nunnemacher Residence
2409 N. Wahl Ave. **1906**

Designed by Milwaukee architect, Alexander C. Eschweiler, this spacious mansion resembles the country seats or manor houses of 17th century England. Working with the finest craftsmen (mason Charles Grunewald and carpenter John Debbink) Eschweiler built the walls of red brick, trim with Bedford limestone, roof of slate, and used wrought iron and leaded glass for decoration. When the house was sold in 1928, it lay vacant for a while and then became the rectory for St. Mark's Episcopal Church. Since 1962 it has been divided into apartments.

130. John F. Kern Residence
2569 N. Wahl Ave. **1899**

The first house built on Wahl Ave., the Kern mansion is said to have contained the city's first individual room airconditioning system. Large 2 x 3 foot wooden ducts carried cool air throughout the house where separate thermostats controlled shutters. John Kern followed his father in operating the Eagle Flour Mill (see #206), which became one of the largest in the country. The plan for his house, drawn by architects Crane and Barkhausen, is heavily influenced by the German New Renaissance style. The pressed orange/brown brick is trimmed with red sandstone and wrought iron by Cyril Colnik.

131. Victor L. Brown Residence
2691 N. Wahl Ave. **1915**

Built for Milwaukee attorney, Victor L. Brown, this English Tudor house was designed by Alexander C. Eschweiler. Although not strictly accurate, there are many features about the composition which closely follow the late 15th and early 16th century precedent. Especially interesting are the twin chimney stacks on the north facade, built, in typically English fashion, with brick and in a spiral twist. Some sections of the structure are red brick trimmed with sandstone while others are timber-framed with stucco. Wrought iron, leaded glass, carved wooden bargeboards, and terracotta tiles are used to complement the basic materials.

132. North Point Lighthouse
On the lake bluff at the intersection of N. Terrace Ave. and N. Wahl Ave.
1868, 1879, 1912

The first lighthouse at this location, built in 1855, was 100 feet closer to the lake and had a 28-foot CCB tower. When bluff erosion forced a move, in 1879, a new 35-foot cast iron tower was erected with bolted sections. The lantern, made in Paris by Barbier, Benard, & Turenne, was taken from the old lighthouse and installed in the new tower. By 1912, when the surrounding trees had grown tall enough to interfere with the light, a new 36-foot riveted steel section was built, and the old tower, with its 1868 lantern, was hoisted to the top. The present 1,300,000 candlepower flash can be seen for 25 miles.

WHM

133. Lake Park
Lake bluff south of E. Kenwood Blvd.
1889 and later

One of the first five parks planned by the newly formed Park Board, this was originally part of the Gustavus Lueddemann farm. Later called Lueddemann's- on-the-Lake, it became a picnic spot and pleasure resort until it was purchased by the city. The grounds, which consisted of two large ravines and a sinuous lake bluff, were planned and developed by Frederick Law Olmstead & Co. of Brookline, Massachusetts (famous for the plan of Central Park, New York). The pavilion was designed in 1903 by Milwaukee architects, Ferry & Clas. One of the city's most beautiful and historic areas, Lake Park offers numerous attractions. Two handsome cast iron bridges span the parallel ravines and are decorated with 8 life-sized, carved stone lions by sculptor, P. Kupper. In 1968 the bridges, which were originally used for vehicular traffic, were narrowed and restricted to pedestrian use. Between the ravines, on a peninsula, is the historic North Point Lighthouse. Nearby is the imposing equestrian statue and monument to General Erastus B. Wolcott. The surgeon general of Wisconsin troops during the Civil War, Wolcott performed the first successful operation to remove a kidney in medical history. His widow, also a doctor and said to be the third woman in the United States to be licensed to practice, provided for this monument in her will. A little southwest of the intersection of Locust St. and N. Lake Drive is a prehistoric Indian burial mound. The last of a group of mounds in the vicinity, this earth dome was marked by a bronze tablet in 1910.

134. Myron T. MacLaren Residence
3230 E. Kenwood Blvd. 1920

Milwaukee's finest English Tudor residence sits majestically at the very edge of a high bluff overlooking the lake. Its design and construction details are far more authentic than the hundreds of other Tudor homes still to be found here. The plans were drawn by Fitzhugh Scott Sr. and Mac-Donald Mayer. Plymouth stone (an eastern quartzite) is the basic material and the trim, with its numerous carved details, is done in sandstone. Only the finest materials were employed, including lead for rainwater heads and downspouts, copper flashing, green and purple slate on the roof, and leaded glass windows with extremely fine-painted medallions. The interior woodwork is typically oak-trimmed with hand wrought iron hardware, said to have come from old English castles and manor houses.

135. Dearholt Residence
3201 N. Lake Drive 1897

An unusual variation on the Classical Revival, this imposing house combines a number of normally unrelated forms. Architects Leenhouts and Guthrie framed each block with corner pilasters and supported the front porch canopy with six fluted Ionic columns. Beneath the canopy is a Palladian-influenced bay window above the main entrance. Two additional "Palladian"-style windows, with scallop shell arches, flank the entrance. The theme again appears in an attic dormer over the porch. Also projecting from the tiled hip roof are dormers that have windows with intersected tracery.

136. Orrin W. Robertson Residence
3266 N. Lake Drive 1911

This pretty little French chateau-styled residence was designed by Eschweiler & Eschweiler in 1911. Robertson, president of Western Lime & Cement Company, had an unusually narrow lot for Lake Drive; and the house was designed with a tall, but narrow, facade with the bulk of its space running parallel with the property line to the east. The buff, scratch-faced brick is laid Flemish bond and is trimmed with cut limestone. Principal features in the design are the symmetrically placed pair of corner bartizans with their standing seam conical spires made of sheet copper.

89

137. Armin A. Schlesinger Residence
3270 N. Marietta Ave. c.1912

Mr. Schlesinger founded the Milwaukee Solvay Coke Company in 1905 and was its president. He was also a vice president of Milwaukee Coke & Gas Co., which was founded by his father, Ferdinand, and he had an interest in numerous iron companies. This imposing mansion, which fronts on N. Lake Drive, E. Hartford Ave. and N. Marietta, is an amalgam of English styling from several centuries. The red brick, laid Flemish bond, is complemented by a wine-colored sandstone and red tiles. The southern gable on the Lake Drive side has herringbone brick nogging between its timbers. On the south wall is an interesting 9-sided solarium made of sheet copper.

138. Henry M. Thompson Residence
3288 N. Lake Drive 1913

Now the Sisters of Saint Mary Episcopal Convent and House of Retreats, this imposing stone mansion was once a private residence. Lumberman Henry M. Thompson engaged Milwaukee architect A. C. Eschweiler to design his Lake Drive house in 1913. The basic material for the English Tudor-styled structure is rock-faced limestone laid random ashlar. A fine complement of costly materials contributes to the solidity of this design, including copper flashing and gutters, terra-cotta chimney pots, leaded glass, and a slate roof. Built at a cost of $200,000 by contractor S.J. Brockman, the house remains in nearly original condition except for the removal of four magnificent wrought iron gates which once adorned the stone posts on Lake Drive.

139. Paula & Erwin Uihlein Residence
3319 N. Lake Drive 1913

Said to have been adapted from a 17th century English priory, this imposing mansion was designed by Milwaukee architects, Kirchhoff & Rose. Paula, and her brother Erwin, were children of August Uihlein who, with his five brothers, built the Schlitz Brewery (see #193) after their uncle, Joseph Schlitz, died in 1875. This brick and limestone structure is filled with English woodwork, fireplaces and panelling. The walled garden encloses two greenhouses and a gatehouse. The wrought iron work on gates and doors is by Cyril Colnik.

140. Samuel A. Field Residence
3432 N. Lake Drive 1890-95

Chicago architect, August Fiedler, designed each room of this mansion to contain specific art objects which had been collected in Europe by Mr. and Mrs. Field. The house originally stood at the eastern end of Martin (now E. State Street) in what is now Juneau Park. In 1926, Prospect Ave. was extended south from Juneau Ave., and the house was threatened. Its owner then, George Louis Kuehn, moved it to the present Lake Drive location. Each stone was serial-numbered and disassembled — then moved to the new lot where it was rebuilt to be three instead of four stories tall. The remaining stones were used to create the 4-car garage wing to the west. The English Renaissance design, in Bedford stone, has a sheet copper roof which was added by Mr. Kuehn.

141. J. Stanley Stone Residence
3474 N. Lake Drive 1928

Milwaukee's finest French Provincial residence was designed by architects Whitney & Beck. When this house was built, the city was having a love affair with English Tudor and Mediterranean designs, but the French Provincial, for some reason, never became popular here. An excellent example of its style, the Stone house is connected by a wall to its garage, forming an "L". Additional walls continue around to enclose a typically French courtyard which is paved in stone blocks of two colors, making a geometric design. The buff brick house is trimmed with shutters, copper sheet metal work, and a green Vermont slate roof. A special refinement is made at the cornice with ornamental brickwork and a gentle upturn at the edge of the roof.

142. Randall Austin Ross Residence
2933 E. Newport Ave. 1930

This fine original interpretation of English Georgian architecture was designed by Herman W. Buemming (see #79). The red brick, laid Flemish bond, is trimmed with limestone quoins and keystones. A denticulated wooden cornice, a well-proportioned doorway with scrolled pediment, and an arched window with intersected tracery give the projecting central pavilion great distinction. The house has an unusual cornerstone which displays not only the usual date, but the name of the builder and the architect.

143. Linwood Avenue Filtration Plant
3000 N. Lincoln Memorial Dr. 1935-39
Until 1910 Milwaukee water was pumped
directly from Lake Michigan to the con-
sumers. Thereafter, the only treatment
was the addition of chlorine until this
facility was authorized by the Common
Council in 1933. The Chicago firm of Al-
vord, Burdick & Howson designed this
$5,500,000 filtration plant and construc-
tion began in 1935. Inside the "moderne"
Lannon stone walls are 32 filtration beds
filled with sand. Lake water flows by
gravity through a 7,000-foot intake tunnel and is pumped up 30 feet, after
which it flows by gravity through the
sand beds and down to the North Point
Pumping Station (see #119) and the
Riverside Station on the Milwaukee
River north of Locust Street. Approximately 300 million gallons of water a
day receive chlorine treatment, filtration, and have tastes and odors removed
with activated carbon.

SHOREWOOD-WHITEFISH BAY

In 1834 Dr. Amasa Bigelow built the first sawmill on the Milwaukee River just south of Capitol Drive. Two years later there was another mill; and a village, called Mechanicsville, had been platted. At one time this town was predicted to outstrip "Juneau's and Kilbourn's on the swamp", but it eventually failed. As a mineral spring park, and later as an amusement park, the river area developed into an asset. It was not until the 1920's that Shorewood became the "model twentieth century village". To the north lies Whitefish Bay, which was named for the fish taken in that area by what was once a flourishing commercial fishing business. In the 1880's a subdivision was platted, and then the resort (see#145) was built as the suburb's greatest attraction.

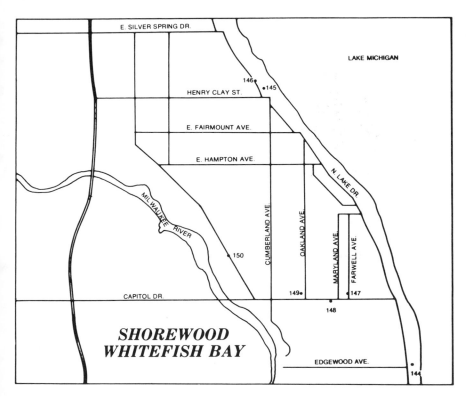

144. Fred Vogel Jr. Residence
3510 N. Lake Drive   1923

This fine Georgian mansion was built by the president of the Pfister & Vogel Leather Co., which was one of the world's largest tanneries in its heyday. The 23-room, 10-fireplace residence was designed by Milwaukee architects, Walter Judell and Harry Bogner. New York decorator, Leonard L. Lock, designed the interiors. The door architraves in the living room are said to have been taken from a 16th century farmhouse in England.

145. Pabst Whitefish Bay Resort Site
Northeast corner N. Lake Dr.
& E. Henry Clay St.   1889

Rivalling the Schlitz Palm Garden as one of the great places to drink beer in the Midwest, this resort was established three years before the village of Whitefish Bay. A narrow 18-acre park, which extended north of Henry Clay along the lake bluff, it was developed by Captain Frederick Pabst (see #230) in 1889. There was a giant, gingerbread encrusted, 250-foot-long pavilion with dining rooms where a planked whitefish dinner could be had, featuring fresh fish caught daily in the bay. There were landscaped walks, a bandstand, a shooting gallery, and a ferris wheel for entertainment. The resort business deteriorated and in 1914 the buildings were razed, the property subdivided, and mansions were built on the land (see #146).

146. Herman Uihlein Residence
5270 N. Lake Drive   1918

This distinguished Italian Renaissance mansion is built with buff Bedford limestone taken from only one level in a single quarry. Architect Thomas L. Rose, of Kirchhoff & Rose, took great pains to make this one of the city's best built and most finely detailed houses. Stone was shipped oversize and carved on the job site to avoid damage. Eight different marbles were used on the interior, as well as Caen stone, walnut doors and panelling, and ornamental plaster. The great sweeping staircase in the main hall has an exquisite wrought iron balustrade by Cyril Colnik. The Matthews brothers did the woodwork, including a panelled dining room which was adapted from England's Forde Abbey.

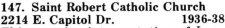

147. Saint Robert Catholic Church
2214 E. Capitol Dr.   **1936-38**

This creative interpretation of Lombardy Romanesque was designed and supervised by Maginnis & Walsh, of Boston, and Milwaukee architects, L.A. Brielmaier & Sons. St. Robert parish, created by Archbishop Messmer in 1912, laid the cornerstone for this well detailed structure on August 12, 1936. The variegated red brick walls are decorated with square and lozenge-shaped insets of different colored marbles. The carved limestone and brick entrance portico is supported by polished Dakota granite columns. The nave and side aisle roofs are tile-covered, and the conical spire atop the campanile has a colored and glazed tile surface. Brass studs enhance the heavily panelled oak doors.

148. Annason Apartment Building
2121 E. Capitol Dr.   **1930**

One of the finest "moderne" structures in Milwaukee, this 60-unit apartment was designed by architect Julius Leiser. A very well proportioned example of the art-deco, or modern style popular in the 1930's, this building is in almost original condition. The buff pressed brick is trimmed with high glaze black terracotta, polished granite, aluminum, and leaded glass. The entrance, with its 7-sided transom window, is sheathed in granite and the address appears between the front door push-bars in cutout aluminum numbers. Black glazed and metallic silver tiles line the vestibule, and the first floor hall has a stepped "speedline" ceiling. Between the steel casement windows are low relief decorative panels with one of the era's favorite motifs, the sunburst.

149. Armory Courts Building
4001-15 N. Oakland Ave.   **1930-31**

Now called the North Shore Apartments and the North Shore Bank, this building took its original name from a National Guard Horse Cavalry Armory which once occupied the site. Designed by Milwaukee architect, Herbert W. Tullgren, this is one of the city's best examples of the "moderne" style of the 1930's. The corner pavilions are smooth limestone ashlar with black glazed terra-cotta and steel casement windows. Low relief art deco ornament decorates the pavilions, the cornice, and the polished-granite bank entrance mantel on the Oakland Avenue side.

HABS NR WRL

150. Benjamin Church Residence
Estabrook Park   **c.1844**

Milwaukee's finest remaining example of the Greek Revival style, this frame house first stood at 1533 N. 4th Street between Cherry and Galena Streets. In 1938, it was cut into four pieces, moved to this site, and restored as a WPA project. Benjamin Church, a pioneer builder and carpenter, built the house out of hewn timbers nogged with CCB and covered it with clapboard. The fluted Doric columns and the finely proportioned moldings and window and door casings give the house true distinction. During the summer it is opened to the public by the Milwaukee County Historical Society.

OLD MILWAUKEE TOWNSHIP

Originally this civil township included the city of Milwaukee. When the city was chartered, in 1846, a large section was removed from its southern end, leaving an 8-mile long and 2½-to 4-mile wide township. Today this once-farm district, which extended north to the Ozaukee County line, includes Glendale, River Hills, Bayside, Fox Point, Whitefish Bay, and Shorewood.

151. Schlitz Audubon Center
1111 E. Brown Deer Rd.   **1971**

Since 1835, when the first deeds were issued on this land, it has remained unspoiled. The 185.7 acres of hill, ravine, and forest land is the largest undeveloped tract of lake shore property in the Milwaukee area. In 1885 the Uihlein brothers (of the Jos. Schlitz Brewing Co.) purchased the acreage and used it for farming. Among their livestock were draft horses, which were bred on this land to pull beer delivery wagons in the city. In 1971 the Schlitz Foundation presented the property to the National Audubon Society for the purpose of creating an educational nature center. Once called the Nine Mile Farm because its location is nine miles from Wisconsin Ave., the area stretches along 2200 feet of Lake Michigan shoreline. The interpretive building (pictured) was designed by Milwaukee architect, Fitzhugh Scott, and was completed in 1974. Its horizontal cedar siding is a pleasant compatible material which blends well with its surroundings.

152. Henry Bergh Monument
4151 N. Humboldt Blvd.   **1891**

Henry Bergh was the founder of the American Society for the Prevention of Cruelty to Animals and this statue is said to be the only one erected to his memory in the United States. When it was dedicated on April 29, 1891, it stood in the square in front of Old City Hall (the one before #1). In the beginning its granite base was twice as tall and it stood in the middle of a huge fountain and watering basin. Until 1941 the basin served dogs and horses, but was then filled with soil and became a flower bed. The bronze statue, paid for by popular subscription, depicts Bergh with his hand on a dog with a splinted paw. When the monument was moved to the Humane Society grounds, only the top half was erected.

153. Adelman Laundry Building
709-33 E. Capitol Drive   **1930**

Built by Benjamin Adelman in 1930, this buff brick and terra-cotta structure is one of the city's better examples of the art-deco or "moderne" style. Ornamental trim, typically geometric, is carried out in cut limestone, leaded glass, and stone bas-relief. The architect, Herman W. Buemming, created an unusual entrance pavilion by stacking progressively smaller octagonal drums. An octagonal lantern, in stainless steel, tops the pavilion and reflects, in its openings, the stepped arch motif which is used as a panel outline over the windows.

154. Radio City
720 E. Capitol Drive   1941

"A building devoted to service so thoroughly modern as radio, seems to demand for itself a truly modern design." This was the way architects Eschweiler & Eschweiler described their commission to design this "functionally correct" radio station and office building. The principal material is a soft pink limestone, quarried in Minnesota, called kasota stone. The facade is accented with groups of incised "speedlines" and a low relief geometric cornice at the roofline. All corners have a radius, and the original "moderne" lanterns and sheet copper canopy surround the main entrance. Television was added to the building's uses and a later addition, with a two-story semicircle of glass, was attached on the west.

155. Garden Homes
Housing Project and Park
N. 25th and N. 26th Sts. between
W. Atkinson & W. Ruby   1921-23

William Schuchardt and other Milwaukee architects designed this historic area believed to be the first municipally sponsored housing project in the United States. A similar federally financed "New Deal" project, Greendale (see #348), was built more than ten years later. This undertaking was financed with city, county and private money and was first envisioned by socialist mayor Dan Hoan in 1918. By 1923, 105 units were constructed on curving streets around a 2-acre neighborhood park. Typical houses sat on 40 x 100-foot lots, were spaced 20 feet apart and consisted of five or six rooms. The project was intended to relieve the post World War I housing shortage and to promote cooperation in planning and construction.

NR*

NEAR EAST SIDE

This area includes the land between the lakefront development and the Milwaukee River and between Yankee Hill on the south and the southern boundary of Shorewood. Geographically the area is made complex by the intersection of two street grids set at different angles and by the meandering river with its occasional high, wooded banks.

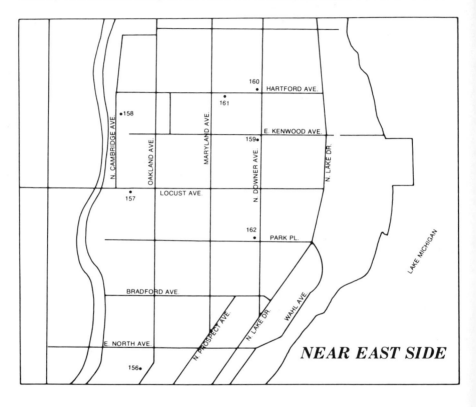

NEAR EAST SIDE

156. Holy Rosary Catholic Church
2011 N. Oakland Ave.   1885-86
Distinguished by its unusual open-timberwork tower, this CCB and frame church is set on a rock-faced limestone foundation. This strange eclectic design includes a "rose" window in a panelled square frame, ornamental chamferring on the belfry beams, and shingle siding on the main gable and the tower. These details and others lean to the Queen Anne style, while the brick lower half has Roman arched windows. The parish was organized in 1885 by Archbishop Heiss who appointed a Canadian-born priest, Father McGill, who had been educated at St. Francis (see #335) and had just completed 7 years as an assistant at St. John's Cathedral (see #63).

157. Riverside High School
1615 E. Locust St.   **1912**

One of Milwaukee's finest English Renaissance school buildings, this imposing structure is reminiscent of the Elizabethan "H" plan manor houses. Built with red scratched-face brick, it is trimmed with cut Bedford limestone, much of which is carved with typical Gothic and Tudor ornamental forms. The entrance doors, transom lights, and their framing are made of sheet copper. Architects Van Ryn & DeGelleke drew the plans for this well-sited and distinguished school on the banks of the Milwaukee River.

158. Edmund B. Gustorf Boat House
3138 N. Cambridge Ave.   **1924**

Certainly the only one of its kind in the county, this unusual boat-shaped house was built by a traveling salesman and marine enthusiast. Gustorf reportedly ordered the wood for his "house" cut at a Green Bay boat works to the standard dimensions of a Great Lakes vessel. Although it has never been on the water, this "boat" looks seaworthy and measures 72 feet long with a 16-foot beam. The picket fence surrounding the corner lot, with its top cut in a wave pattern, and a lighthouse near the boat complete the seafaring imagery. The boat has since been covered with aluminum siding, but its prow still points to the original view of the Milwaukee River.

159. Fourth Church of Christ Scientist
2519 E. Kenwood Blvd.   **1931**

Chicago architect, Charles Draper Faulkner, drew the plans for this Georgian-inspired church. The red brick is trimmed with Bedford limestone, sheet copper, and a slate roof. The semi-elliptical entrance portico, with steps following the curve, is supported by 8 one-piece stone columns. The long rectangular plan, which includes a 1,000 seat-semicircular auditorium, was provided with a landscaped court at each end. The feature which most distinguishes the church, however, is its very narrow, needle-like spire.

HABS NR WRL WHM

160. Milwaukee-Downer College Buildings
NW corner E. Hartford and N. Downer Aves. 1897-1905

A rare and unusual example of a Gothic quadrangle, this group of buildings is also a monument to a pioneering liberal arts college for women. It was the only institution of its kind in the Midwest and its buildings were equally scarce. Architect Alexander C. Eschweiler designed a campus which had the romantic forms and character of universities in England and the eastern United States. They are related in materials (red pressed brick, red sandstone, red terra-cotta and slate roofs) as well as in design. The rich ornamental effect of Gothic gargoyles, waterspouts, poppyhead finials, and battlemented parapets is everywhere. Turrets, towers, and an observatory dome create a picturesque skyline. The complex was purchased by the University of Wisconsin-Milwaukee when Downer merged with Lawrence College at Appleton in 1964.

161. UWM Library Building
2311 E. Hartford Ave. 1966 and 1974

Architect Fitzhugh Scott was responsible for both stages of the library construction, completed in the summers of 1966 and 1974. The design has been described as "clean, functional, undated Classic; feeling of timelessness rather than a particular period." Textured, varicolored and red brick is laid in the pleasant Flemish bond design and the simple rectilinear composition is topped with a pyramidal roof of green tile. It is actually two buildings which connect over a courtyard. The straight linearity is relieved on the interior, with massive arches of the same brick; the woodwork is white oak stained pecan.

162. Spite House
2705 N. Downer Ave. 1925

In 1924 a local developer purchased this lot and announced an $85,000, three-story, 14-unit apartment building. The neighbors complained and the building permit was cancelled. After the developer's appeal was denied, he built this 18-foot high, two-story structure with a flat roof. According to an early newspaper article this "shack" was "thrown together" and painted black to look as ugly as possible. By 1935, it had been covered with shingle siding and painted in horizontal bands to relieve the monotony of the shape. It was then described as a "charming cottage."

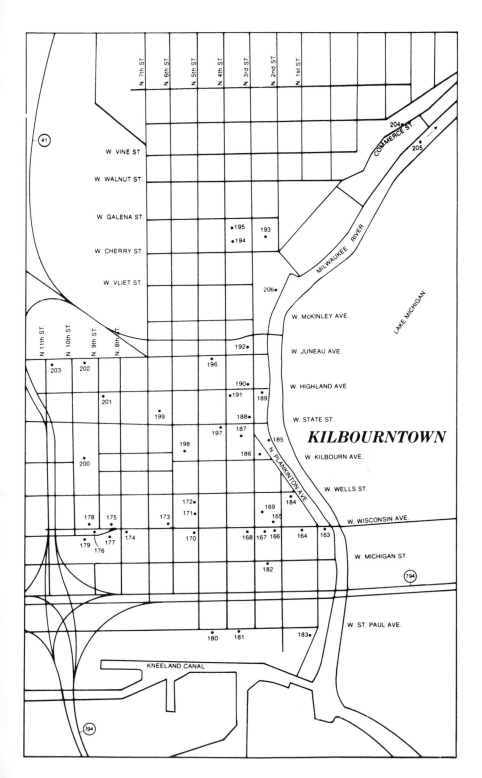

KILBOURNTOWN

According to pioneer historian James S. Buck,"...The west side, or Kilbourn Town, as it was called in 1836-37, did not present a very inviting aspect to the eye whereon to build a city compared with the east, or Juneau's side". In the area roughly bounded by the Milwaukee River, the Menomonee River, 5th Street and W. Wisconsin Avenue was an "impassable" wild rice swamp. It was on the higher ground to the north that Byron Kilbourn laid out his west side settlement. The first buildings appeared near the corner of Chestnut Street (now Juneau Avenue) and N. 3rd Street. Chestnut was the "Main Street" of Kilbourntown. As much as 22 feet of fill was required to dry up the swamps, but as Kilbourn had argued in the beginning, the west side was not confined to a narrow strip of land, and it would eventually become the city. As development spread to the west, Wisconsin Avenue (see *Grand Avenue Area*) became Milwaukee's principal thoroughfare.

163. Gimbels Department Store
101 W. Wisconsin Ave.   **1901-25**
Adam Gimbel's original "Palace of Trade" was in Vincennes, Indiana, a town on the Wabash River which had great potential until railroads put a crimp in the river commerce. His seven sons looked for a new frontier and decided on Milwaukee in 1887. The store they built here grew in stages and the company expanded to become one of the nation's important chains. Beginning with a small Grand Avenue store (now Wisconsin Ave.), the business bought the entire square block piece-by-piece and remodeled, razed, rebuilt, and joined sections until, in 1925, the giant block-long eastern facade was made uniform by the addition of thirteen 4-story high fluted Ionic columns. This monumental feature is executed in white glazed terra-cotta.

164. Plankinton Arcade Building
161 W. Wisconsin Ave. 1916 and 1924

Originally built as a 2-story shopping arcade and office building, this half-square block structure was enlarged for an additional million dollars in 1924. Five stories were added in a different style, but in the same material. The first two floors have Gothic details, while the upper stories are decorated with Renaissance motifs including a cornice of scallop shells which encircles the building. The interior, which was originally a cruciform-shaped shopping mall, has been partially defaced by rental-space oriented remodeling. A good proportion of the 2-story, glass-skylighted open space remains in the unspoiled central rotunda. The centerpiece under this spectacular light well is a bronze statue of John Plankinton that once stood in the old Plankinton House Hotel which previously occupied this site. Around the statue are four segments of a huge circular staircase which leads down to a lower arcade and a fishpond. Both the original building and the addition were designed by Chicago architects Holabird & Roche.

165. Warner Building
212 W. Wisconsin Ave. 1930

One of the city's finest examples of the "moderne" style of skyscraper, popular in the 1930's, this 13-story structure was built by Warner Brothers Theaters, Inc. Chicago architects, C.W. & Geo. L. Rapp, drew the plans for the office structure and the 2,431-seat theater which was almost identical to the Paramount in Portland, Oregon. Polished pink & black granite faces the first 2 floors and climbs to the 5th floor, pyramid style, between the steel-casement windows. Cast metal panels between the windows form 4 vertical lines on the street facade. The entrance and lobby are embellished with nickle-plated radiator shields, balustrades, mailbox, and grilles, all in art deco styling. This structure, now called the Centre Building, replaced the old Butterfly Theatre.

166. Kresge Building
215 W. Wisconsin Ave. 1930

An excellent example of modern architecture in which the modest application of ornament do not overpower the handsome proportions. Although the first-floor has been completely destroyed, the upper stories have managed to survive in original condition. The name "Kresge", incised in a "moderne" typestyle very popular during the period, and the low relief ornament are carved in the smooth finish limestone facade. Darker art-deco ornament panels between the floors are set and colored in such a way as not to interfere with the classically inspired pilasters and the dignified composition. J.E. Sexton, of the construction and store equipment department of the S.S. Kresge Company, drew the plans.

167. Majestic Building
231 W. Wisconsin Ave. 1907-08

The Majestic was once the "center of Milwaukee officedom and the theater of more varied activities than any other structure in Milwaukee." Architects Kirchhoff & Rose, who moved their offices to the new building, designed a 2,000-seat vaudeville theater into the lower floors of this 14-story early skyscraper. Porcelain finish brick and white glazed terra-cotta were used to give the building an easy-cleaning and bright facade. The same architects had designed the Schlitz Palm Garden, which faced Third Street, and a connection was made at the rear so that the vaudeville audiences could visit that establishment without going outside. Now renamed the Universal Building, the once handsome cornice has been removed and most of the theater has been put to other uses.

168. Matthews Building
301 W. Wisconsin Ave. 1892

Architects Ferry & Clas designed this finely proportioned commercial building for the Matthews Brothers, a nationally renowned woodworking firm. The company produced mantels, furniture, and all varieties of fine interior woodwork, such as the panelling and custom-designed furniture in the Pabst mansion (see #230). Originally this pressed brick, Romanesque structure had an elaborately sculptured entrance with highly ornamental columns, but it was destroyed in the remodelling of the first two floors. Tapered brick was used in all the arches and terra-cotta was employed for trim. The Matthews can still be remembered in the decorative cartouche high on the corner of the building, which displays the letter "M."

169. Hotel Wisconsin
720 N. 3rd St.   1912-13

Although originally planned as a 375-room hotel, the developers Arthur and Harold Richards, acquired an adjoining site after the steel frame was already up and expanded the capacity to 500 rooms. By acquiring the 50-foot site which was planned for a new 10-story building for the Philip Gross Hardware Co., they increased the cost of the project to nearly 2 million dollars. Chicago architects, Holabird & Roche, created an unusual design for such a tall building, with pitched roof and gables. The scratch-face dark red brick is trimmed with white brick, buff terra-cotta and an elaborate bracketed cornice of sheet copper. The entire 12-story facade is decorated with white quoins and a regular pattern of white bricks.

170. Schroeder Hotel
509 W. Wisconsin Ave.   1927

Holabird & Roche, a Chicago architectural firm, designed this skyscraper hotel which is still one of the largest in the state. The first three floors are limestone ashlar set on a polished pink and black granite foundation. The remainder is red brick with buff terra-cotta trim. An unusual flagstaff base, at the 5th floor level and above the east entrance, is supported by two modern eagles. Low relief ornament, influenced by the art deco style, is everywhere. A bronze placque on the Wisconsin Avenue side reminds us that in 1833 this was the site of a Potowatomi Indian village at the foot of a steep bluff.

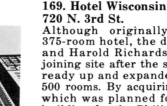

171. Wisconsin Telephone Company Grand Avenue Building
735 N. 5th St. 1905

This handsome 9-story office building was designed by architect A.C. Eschweiler in 1905, and has managed to survive without any exterior modification. It served as Telephone Company headquarters from 1906 until 1917 and was an exchange building for many years. When newly completed, the company served 48,500 phones in Wisconsin, with 18,000 of these in Milwaukee. The first two stories, which are set on a granite foundation, are limestone with banded rustication, while the upper floors are red brick. Trim is executed in carved limestone and buff terra-cotta. A number of the huge carved stone lion heads at the second floor level are attached to a bell. This bell motif is carried throughout the building and appears on such things as cast iron stair risers and the brass escutcheon plates on the doors.

172. Time Insurance Office Building
515 W. Wells St. 1969

"A ten-story,poured-in-place concrete building with strong vertical emphasis to overcome its nearly cube dimensions of 110 feet by 110 feet by 123 feet tall. The exterior motif also includes a dark bronze anodized aluminum curtain wall system employing a five-foot module. The glass panels are all reflective insulating units passing eight percent of incident visible light, which accounts for the lack of drapes, shades or other interior window covering. The new Time Building ties in with most of the old neighboring buildings' floor levels to allow for future growth laterally."

173. Wisconsin Tower Building
606 W. Wisconsin Ave. 1929-30

Once called the Milwaukee Tower and then the Mariner Tower, after its builder, John Mariner, this imposing building on the Milwaukee skyline was designed by Chicago architects, Weary & Alford. It is a typical example of the "moderne" style and is embellished with art-deco ornament at the lower levels. The huge mantel around the main entrance is carved in deep relief and surrounds an ornamental cast iron grille. Low relief decorative panels of cast iron are employed between the windows up to the fifth floor. They are placed in a stepped or set-back composition to reflect the treatment of the building's upper floors. Only the escutcheons remain from the original entrance lanterns.

174. Continental Plaza
735 W. Wisconsin Ave.   1969

Built for the Continental Bank & Trust Company, this bank and office structure was "designed to reflect the open, spacious character of a contemporary bank and the strength and durability expected of a financial institution." Its design was planned to emphasize rather than disguise the structural elements. Architects Miller, Waltz & Diedrich used cast-in-place exposed concrete with the tie holes and joints prominently featured. The 12-story tapering exterior columns resemble Gothic buttresses and serve as wind braces.

HABS NR WRL

175. Milwaukee Public Library
814 W. Wisconsin Ave.   1893-97

Milwaukee's finest and one of the earliest examples of the Classical Revival, this masterpiece was the winning design in a national architectural competition. A local firm, Ferry & Clas, drew the plans and the basic material used is Bedford (Indiana) limestone. The ornamental features, which were strongly influenced by the Italian Renaissance, were carved in stone after the rough blocks were already set in place. Above the sunken entrance loggia are two stone eagles with bronze wings. Inside, the rotunda expands from its mosaic floor all the way up to the elaborately coffered dome at the roof.

176. Court of Honor
W. Wisconsin Ave. between
9th & 10th Sts.

Originally a bluff, nearly 60 feet high, interrupted what is now W. Wisconsin Ave. at the intersection of 8th Street. Before it was cut down, the upper and lower streets were laid out with no thought of their ever connecting. When this improvement finally came, the two sections did not match up; so instead of simply jogging, the streets were made to run parallel for a few blocks and then merge. In one block a green mall, the Court of Honor, was created to display monuments. Elizabeth Plankinton (see #227) gave the first statue, a bronze of George Washington, in 1885. It was created by Florentine sculptor R.H. Park. The second, a bronze soldier with rifle, commemorates those who fought in the war with Spain (1898-1902). A 65-foot column, with a sphere on top, is a reminder of a week-long carnival held in 1900. The most significant monument is the 1898 Civil War grouping of 4 soldiers created by John S. Conway and cast in Rome.

177. St. James Episcopal Church
833 W. Wisconsin Ave. 1867

Architect Edward Townsend Mix drew the plans for this Gothic Revival masterpiece which is believed to be the city's first stone church. A 9-bell carillon, cast in Troy, NY, was installed in the tower in 1871. The next year a fire broke out near the pipe organ and spread quickly through the church. There was a delay in the fire department's arrival and a scarcity of water in the neighborhood: so the church was almost completely destroyed. Only the tower and most of the walls were saved. The Milwaukee County limestone structure was rebuilt in 1872 and an addition was attached to the rear in 1899.

178. Alexander Mitchell Residence
900 W. Wisconsin Ave.
1870/earlier and later

Just when the first part of the large Mitchell house was built seems to be lost in history, but it may have been as much as 20 years before the tower and mansard roof additions were made in 1870 by architect Edward Townsend Mix. Originally a humble house on a small lot, it grew in stages to become an imposing mansion on a square-block estate. It is basically a CCB bracketed Italianate block with an added five-story tower and mansard roof. In 1895 it was purchased by the Deutscher Club and a 500-foot greenhouse was razed to accomodate a club dining room wing on the west. The scroll-cut octagonal summerhouse on the front lawn was built in 1871 and is one of the finest examples of its kind in the country. Sometimes called summerhouses, tea houses, pavilions or gazebos, these decorative lawn structures are usually small in size and simple in construction. This example, however, has little balconies with the initials "A-M" in scrollwork panels, a cupola with superb quality high-relief carving and more gingerbread fretwork than half-a-dozen average gazebos. Inside, the walls are wainscoted with imported English encaustic tiles. There was once a hand-carved wooden chandelier hanging from the domed plaster ceiling where painted and gold-leafed ornament can still be seen.

179. Calvary Presbyterian Church
935 W. Wisconsin Ave.   1870

Milwaukee's third Presbyterian congregation retained the firm of Koch & Hess (H.C. Koch-see #1) to draw the plans for this church. Although the Victorian Gothic structure is built of CCB, it has been painted red for so long that few can remember its original color. When the church was being completed, it is said that one of the congregation's officers questioned the strength of the strikingly tall western spire. He said that a team of horses could pull it over; so the architects called his bluff and arranged for a test. Ropes were rigged around the tower and the team failed to pull it down. The spire is still standing, in spite of a $150,000 fire which nearly destroyed the church in 1947.

HABS

180. Milwaukee Road Passenger Station
433 W. St. Paul Ave.   1965

Both of the city's spectacular Victorian railroad depots have been torn down (Chicago & Northwestern in 1968 and the old Milwaukee Road in 1965.) This structure was erected to replace the old Romanesque depot on Fowler Street between 3rd and 4th Streets. Designed by Donald L. Grieb Associates, the facades are decorated with semicircular arches supported by precast columns. Between the columns are dark tinted glass windows which are surrounded by glazed brown brick. A painted steel tower rises above the 125-foot roof and supports a hanging electronic bell.

181. United States Post Office
341 W. St. Paul Ave.   1966-68

Architects Miller & Waltz designed this huge (950-foot-long) building to "express its main function, that of a vehicle-oriented receiving and distribution center for mail." A 240-foot ramp to N. Plankinton Avenue and a 300-foot bridge to the 6th St. viaduct make the total structure five blocks long. The principal material is concrete, faced with Lannon stone slabs with their natural bed surface exposed. Various thicknesses, sizes and colors were used to create a fine textural and shadow-producing surface. This is accented with the soft rusty texture of weathering steel, a material which was first used in a downtown building on this job. Inside is a sophisticated, computer-controlled, mail handling system. Consulting engineers on the project were Ammann and Whitney, Inc.,of Milwaukee.

182. Public Service Building
231 W. Michigan St.   **1903-05**

Herman J. Esser drew the plans for this distinguished structure which served as general office, central car house, and terminal station for the Milwaukee Electric Railway and Light Company. Set on a granite foundation, the first story consists of limestone with banded rustication, while the upper floors are pressed brick trimmed with cut stone. The 2-story entrance is lined with cast bronze and flanked by a pair of carved stone medallions showing a horse-drawn streetcar in 1890 (National Ave. & Walnut St.) and an electric car in 1905. The elaborate lobby is embellished with 4 varieties of marble and a leaded glass dome over the staircase landing. Originally a 4-story building, it was enlarged in 1926 with the $30,000 addition of another floor. In recent years the streetcar tunnel, which passed through the building, was reclaimed for office space.

183. Pritzlaff Hardware Building
305 N. Plankinton Ave.   **1875**

One of the city's finest remaining examples of the 19th century wholesale house, this handsome CCB Italianate structure has a remarkably well preserved street facade. The original cast iron columns are on the first floor and the sheet metal cornice is still intact with its bracketed support. Note the name, "Pritzlaff", and the date in the pediment. John Pritzlaff, one of the city's pioneer hardware dealers, founded his business in the 1850's and also employed William Frankfurth, Charles Hilgendorf, and Philip Gross, who went on to found their own businesses. The 1876 building has a later addition on the north.

184. Germania Building
135 W. Wells St.   1896

In its prime the Germania Building was called "the world's largest German newspaper building." For George Brumder it marked the culmination of 32 years in the publishing, bookbinding, printing, and bookselling business. He published the *Germania-Abendpost, The Milwaukee Herold,* and the *Sonntagpost* as well as a number of weeklies and quarterlies. His great Classical Revival building was designed by architects Schnetzky and Liebert, who topped it off with four hemispherical domes of sheet copper. During World War I the domes with their spikes were called "Kaiser's helmets" and the sentiment toward Germany prompted the removal of a huge statue, "Germania," which stood over the entrance. Two stories of rusticated limestone rise from the granite foundation and the rest is pressed brick trimmed with terra-cotta. Note the carved limestone cartouche over the entrance with initials "G.B." for George Brumder, whose name now identifies the building.

185. Father Marquette's Camp
Milwaukee River between
Kilbourn Ave. and State St.   1674

"Father Jacques Marquette, the French Jesuit missionary who with Sieur Louis Joliet discovered and first explored the upper Mississippi in 1673, stayed on this site November 23-27, 1674. Marquette, with two French Canadians, Pierre Porteret and Jacques Largillier, was returning south to open a mission requested by the Illinois Indians. They were the first known white men to visit this site."

186. Second Ward Savings Bank
910 N. 3rd St.   1911-13

The last owner of this triangular neo classical building, The First Wisconsin National Bank, donated it to the Milwaukee County Historical Society for use as a museum and library in 1965. Built on a granite foundation, the basic material is Bedford, Indiana, limestone and the windows are framed in cast iron. The rich moldings, fluted Ionic columns, balustrade, and carved cartouches show the influence of the French Renaissance. Architects, Kirchhoff & Rose, designed the main banking floor to have a two-story ceiling, but in later years a second, or mezzanine, level was added around the perimeter. Here is a rare opportunity to see the architects' original drawings in india ink on linen displayed in the building they delineate.

HABS NR WRL

187. The Journal Company Building
333 W. State St.   1924

Chicago architect, Frank D. Chase, designed this distinctive "modern" newspaper office building. Praised by the *American Architect* magazine, the design is more than superficially decorative. The pink limestone facing, which sets on a granite foundation, is relieved by numerous bas relief carvings which are appropriate to the business conducted therein. The third floor window arches display the colophons of early pioneers in the history of printing. Seventy-one feet up, at the roofline, is a low relief carved frieze depicting the history of the dissemination of news from cavemen to high-speed presses. The building's principal focus is an imposing 2-story semicircular arch embellishment with low relief carving and trim of painted cast iron.

188. John Hinkel Saloon
& Restaurant
1001 N. 3rd St.   1877

A native of Gauweinheim, Germany, John Hinkel came to Milwaukee in 1857 and worked at the Best (later Pabst) Brewery. During the Civil War he rose to the rank of foreman there, but soon after decided to open a saloon. This building, his second establishment, cost $30,000 in 1877 and was called "one of the finest in the state." Known in early days as "Central Hall Restaurant," it is a handsome eclectic Victorian design with a lean to the Italianate. Now painted CCB, it still has a cast iron balcony over the State Street entrance, the original sheet metal cornice, and the inscription, "J. Hinkel 1877," at the roofline on its angled corner.

189. Steinmeyer Building
1050 N. 3rd St.   1893
Once the home of the William Steinmeyer Co., wholesale and retail grocers, this imposing building was completed the year after the founder died. Based on a cash-only philosophy, Steinmeyer had built a huge business by sending order solicitors around Milwaukee one day and making deliveries the next day. In the new building his son-in-law, Emil Ott (see #106), and his brother, Charles, continued the reputation for quality, service, and reasonable price until national chains and automobiles forced them to close in 1940. The handsome Richardsonian Romanesque building was designed by architects Ferry & Clas and cost $50,000. The pressed red brick is trimmed with orange terra-cotta and wrought iron. The structure was enlarged in 1898.

190. Lipps Hall
1101 N. 3rd St.   c. 1879
This Victorian eclectic design shows great originality and detailing. Built as a public hall, it is made of CCB and the front (3rd St.) facade is faced with buff sandstone. One unusual feature is the large size of the facing blocks. Rather than being laid like structural pieces, these extremely large slabs are treated as a surface panelling. Another uncommon detail is the large dog-tooth molding under each window lintel. The original stone corbel course and the bracketed sheet metal cornice at the roofline create a rich and pleasant effect. Although the first floor exterior is altered, the original structural columns can still be seen inside.

HABS NR*

191. Turnverein Milwaukee Hall
1034 N. 4th St. 1882-83

The Milwaukee Turners Gymnastic & Fraternal Society was organized in 1853 and this structure, the largest of many built here, was begun in 1882 and cost $80,000. Designed by architect Henry C. Koch, its CCB facade is built on a rock-faced limestone foundation and is trimmed with decorative belt courses of dark red brick. Basically Richardsonian Romanesque, the front is broken into three projecting pavilions; two have triangular gables and the middle one becomes a tower capped with a pyramid. A great ballroom and theater stage on the second floor was designed in "Renaissance style" by the Associated Artists of Milwaukee. A serious fire in the hall in 1933 caused so much damage that it has been unused ever since. Fortunately a 1966 plan to raze the 2nd floor was abandoned and the building is being renovated.

192. Nicholas Senn Block
300 W. Juneau Ave. 1876

One of the most renowned and important surgeons in United States medical history erected and occupied this building. Dr. Nicholas Senn, the 49th president of the American Medical Association, was a native of St. Gall, Switzerland. He was graduated cum laude from Chicago Medical College in 1868, and after internship there went to Ashford, Wisconsin, for 8 years and then came to Milwaukee. He held high offices in and belonged to numerous medical societies throughout the world. He is remembered for his application of bacteriology to surgery and was internationally renowned as "the great master of abdominal surgery." This 4-story CCB Italianate block served as offices and laboratories and had a pharmacy on the street floor. For years it was occupied by the West Side Bank.

193. Jos. Schlitz Brewing Co.
235 W. Galena St.   1870's-present
Founded in 1849 by August Krug, the Schlitz Brewery has grown to become the largest in Milwaukee and the second largest in the nation. While none of the original buildings have survived, there are many in the complex which date from the 19th century and are ornamented with terra-cotta and sheet-metal designs and brewing symbolism. The large building pictured resembles the German New Renaissance style which was popular there in the late 19th century. It has a convex mansard dome trimmed in wrought iron and sheet metal and has a glazed lantern with an onion dome on top. Originally there was an identical tower at the north end of the building.

194. St. John deNepomuc Rectory
N. 4th St., S.E. corner W. Court St.
1869
Originally this building was erected by Father Joseph Gartner to serve as a mission house from which priests of Czechoslovakian origin would travel to serve the Midwest. The dream never materialized and his parish, which had its church to the south (facing Cherry St.), used it as a rectory. A distinguished late Gothic Revival structure, it is made of CCB on a dressed limestone foundation with wooden trim. By alternating red-stained brick with cream brick, a picturesque Venetian Gothic effect was achieved. A fine Gothic-molded limestone water table marks the first floor.

195. Fourth Street School
1542 N. 4th St.   c. 1885
This monumental and picturesque school building, an eclectic blend of the Richardsonian Romanesque and Queen Anne styles, is built in a prominent location looking over the city. Basically CCB on a rock-faced limestone foundation, the school wins its character not only from the design, but the rich combination of building materials. The main pavilion, in the center of both east and west facades, has a giant 22-light stained glass installation which extends over 3 arches. Below are three deep-red terra-cotta panels; one says "Public School" and the other two are owls surrounded by olive branches and acanthus leaves. Buff terra cotta is used for the drip course moldings over the large arches and sheet metal and limestone trim is used throughout.

HABS

196. Gipfel Brewery
423 W. Juneau Ave.   1843
Milwaukee's oldest remaining brewery building, this rare Federal-styled commercial structure was erected by David Gipfel. Originally a 10-barrel operation, the pioneer brewery was continued by his son Charles until 1872, at which time the firm was brewing Weissbier. The building is one of the oldest in Milwaukee County, but has been so rebuilt and abused over the years, that very little remains of the original structure beyond its shape and proportion. Even the street facade, which was CCB like the rest of the building, has been refaced with a newer brick.

WHM

197. Invention of the Typewriter
Historical Marker
"At 318 State Street, approximately 300 feet northeast of here, C. Latham Sholes perfected the first practical typewriter in September, 1869. Here he worked during the summer with Carlos Glidden, Samuel W. Soule and Matthias Schwalbach in the machine shop of C.F. Kleinsteuber. During the next six years, money for the further development of the typewriter was advanced by James Densmore, who later gained the controlling interest and sold it to E. Remington & Sons of Ilion, N.Y."

198. Milwaukee Auditorium
500-590 W. Kilbourn Ave.   1907-09
The originally stated purpose of this 6,600,000 square-foot building was "auditorium, market, music, convention, assembly and banquet hall." This historic site, which has been called "Milwaukee's Amusement Square," began with the West Side Market Hall in 1867. That was replaced, in 1881, with the Exposition Building — a fanciful and festive structure which covered the entire block. Once the city's pride, this picturesque, domed and turreted eclectic Victorian building burned to the ground in 1905. Plans for the present building were drawn by architects Ferry & Clas.

199. Milwaukee Vocational School
1015 N. 6th St. 1918-27

In 1911 the Wisconsin legislature passed the first compulsory continuation school law in the United States. This meant that all boys and girls under the age of 16 who had obtained "gainful occupation" would be required, along with their employers, to participate in a program which required attendance of classes one-half day a week. In 1912 the first school was established in Milwaukee with R.L. Cooley (see # 504) as the first director of vocational education. Classes were first held in the Manufacturer's Home Building on Mason St. at the river, but were soon outgrown. In 1916 a lot was purchased at 7th and Highland and architects Eschweiler and Gerrit DeGelleke began the plans for the first unit of the present school. Two additional units, handled by DeGelleke, were put up in 1921 and 1927, completing the $3,000,000 complex. By 1936 it filled the square block and had become the largest vocational school in the nation.

200. Milwaukee County Court House
901 N. 9th St. 1929-31

The first two courthouses in Milwaukee were built on what is now Cathedral Square (see #62). When a new and enlarged facility was required, a nationwide competition was held for the design. From the 33 plans submitted, that of New York architect, Albert Randolph Ross, was selected. The ten-million dollar project, executed by 28 contractors, is faced with Bedford (Indiana) limestone. It is the last major building here that was influenced by the 1893 World's Fair in Chicago. The basic character of the building is established by the monumental Roman, fluted, Corinthian columns. The building's monumental proportions did not, however, impress Frank Lloyd Wright, who called it a "million dollar rock pile."

HABS

201. Trinity Lutheran Church
1046 N. 9th St. 1878
One of the state's finest examples of Victorian Gothic design, Trinity Church has been carefully maintained and is in an unspoiled and nearly original condition inside and out. An unusual feature here is the matched pair of cornerstones at the base of the buttresses flanking the main entrance. One is the traditional "Erected 1878," but its twin displays in bold letters ... "F. Velguth Architect." While an architect's name on a building is not unusual, it is rare to see such a proud and boastful signature. The CCB structure is trimmed with limestone and wood with a slate roof and sheet copper ornament. The mother church of the Missouri Synod in Wisconsin, this congregation was founded in 1847.

202. Pabst Brewing Company
917 W. Juneau Ave. 1880 and later
Milwaukee's oldest operating brewery, Pabst, was founded in 1844 by Jacob Best. Later his son Philip's daughter married a Great Lakes steamboat captain named Frederick Pabst (see #230). He was taken into the business and by 1889, when he had become its president, the company's name was changed to Pabst. At that time it was the largest brewery in the world. None of the original buildings remain, but most of the present complex is highly picturesque and dates from the last decades of the 19th century. Mostly CCB, they all resemble the pictured general office built in 1880. This is trimmed with sheet metal and buff sandstone and has battlemented parapets like most of the other buildings.

203. Forst Keller
1037 W. Juneau Ave. 1872 and 1898
This CCB Gothic building was built in 1872 as the First German Methodist Episcopal Church. After two decades of conducting services in the shadow of the Pabst Brewery, the congregation's patience with the noises and smells ran out. They built a new church on 21st and Highland in 1896, and sold this one to Pabst. Brewery architect Carl L. Linde converted the old church into a battlemented Gothic castle compatible with the other buildings. It was designed to become a Teutonic beer hall and was originally decorated with "armor and antlers and countless other evidences of the sturdy hunters." It was finally closed to the public in September of 1973.

204. Commerce Street 1884

What is now Commerce Street was once the Rock River Canal. It runs from a spot near the intersection of N. 3rd St. and W. McKinley Ave. northward parallel to the west bank of the Milwaukee River and ends just south of North Ave. Before railroads destroyed its practicality, many early settlers banked on a canal project to become the great commercial highway to the Mississippi River. Byron Kilbourn (see Kilbourntown), the driving force behind the canal, had been an engineer on a similar venture in Ohio. In 1836 planning began which would take the waterway northwest along the Menomonee River and end up at the Rock River near Fort Atkinson. Only the North Ave. dam was built (see #205) and this short section of canal. It was filled in and paved in 1884.

205. North Avenue Dam
Milwaukee River just south
of North Ave. 1891

This historic site was first developed with a dam in 1842 as a part of the ill-fated Rock River Canal project (see #204). The original dam, built by Capt. John Anderson, was 430 feet long and 18 feet high, and was composed of large green trees with all their branches on, stacked with their trunks pointing downstream. 100,000 yards of gravel and 4,000 cords of wood finished the structure, which supplied water power through a lock to the mile-long canal. Grist mills (see #206), tanneries, a woolen mill, and other factories paid $75 per year for the power (based on a flow of 100 cubic feet per minute). An 1866 spring flood destroyed ¾ths of the original dam and encouraged customers to switch to steam. The present dam replaced the old series of rebuilt structures in 1891.

206. The Eagle Mill
On Milwaukee River near
Vliet St. & N. 3rd St.   1866 and later

John B.A. Kern & Son (see son's house, #130) grew to become one of the largest flouring mills in the country. Located on the water power (the now filled-in canal: see #204) this huge structure began in 1866 as a 40 x 130-foot mill with seven run of stone. In subsequent additions, including the introduction of the new steam roller system in 1878, the building grew to 180 x 135 feet and six stories high with a daily capacity of 1,500 barrels of flour. In this building Kern proved that, as he had long suspected, there was a bonanza concealed in the flour business if properly handled. The business was originally founded by Col. John Anderson, who had built the canal, and Dr. Erastus B. Wolcott (see #133).

OLD CITY OF MILWAUKEE

A century ago the city of Milwaukee was bounded by what is now E. Burleigh Street on the north and Lincoln Avenue on the south. It extended from the lakefront to Washington Avenue (now N. 27th Street) on the west. Within this area were the three pioneer settlements (see *Juneautown, Kilbourntown* and *Walker's Point*) the lake front developments (see *Prospect Avenue Area* and *North Point*) the near east side and part of the *Grand Avenue Area.*

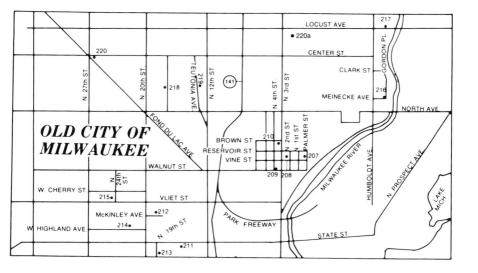

207. Casper Melchior Sanger Residence
1823 N. Palmer St.   **c. 1871**

Sanger, a native of Westphalia, Prussia, began business here, in 1862, as a tanner. He later founded a successful sash, door, and blind factory. When he built this house, its address was on Short Street, which became Island Ave. in 1876, and Palmer Street in 1931. The Italianate design is executed in CCB and trimmed with brick quoins and carved wooden brackets. The original front porch and cornice brackets have been removed. For years it was the home of Milwaukee's 16th mayor, Joseph Phillips.

208. Frederick W. von Cotzhausen Residence
1825 N. 2nd St.   **c.1855-58**

No builder or date of construction has been found for this structure, but all evidence points to its having been an early rental house. In 1863 it was purchased by von Cotzhausen, whose father, Ludwig, was president of the Electoral College under Napoleon I. Frederick, who had been presented to royalty and was educated in great European colleges, came here in 1856 as a lawyer with the title of baron. He built the Metropolitan Block on 3rd and State Streets (destroyed by fire in 1975). Famous Milwaukee painter, Robert Schade, lived here until his death in 1912. A finely proportioned CCB residence with basic Federal styling and later Italianate wooden cornice brackets and south bay, it has unusual wooden window and entrance lintels flush with the brickwork.

209. German Y.M.C.A.
1702 N. 4th St.   **c. 1856**

Originally said to have been a hotel, this building became the first home of Mount Sinai Hospital in 1903. It was rented at $50 per month, and after six years a $7,000 addition was made. The hospital finally outgrew its old quarters and in 1913 started construction of a new building on the site of the present 12th St. complex. The 4th Street building was once the north side branch of the YMCA as well as a boarding house, run in the 1880,s by a brewer, Emmanuel Burgy, and his wife, Elizabeth.

210. St. Francis of Assisi Roman Catholic Church
1927 N. 4th St.   **1876**

One of Milwaukee's oldest Romanesque churches, St. Francis of Assisi is part of a monastery which was begun here in 1869 by the Capuchin order. The present structure replaced a small frame church and was under the supervision of Rev. Lawrence Vorwerk. The CCB walls are set on a coursed rubble foundation and are trimmed with limestone. New York architect, William Schickel, drew the plans for this 60x140-foot sanctuary with its high nave and low, buttressed side aisles. The cut and carved limestone entrance porch was added in 1900.

211. St. George Syrian Catholic Church
1617 W. State St.   **1917**

The only surviving Byzantine-Melkite rite church in the state, this parish was organized by Archbishop Sebastian Messmer in response to requests from Milwaukee's Syrian-Lebanese community. As the Syrian immigrants began to arrive in 1895 and inhabit the neighborhood roughly bounded by Kilbourn, Highland, 6th and 20th Streets, they also sought a church and service with which they were familiar. Milwaukee architects Erhard Brielmaier & Sons designed this simple structure with its 3 bulbous "onion" omes of sheet metal. All of the stained glass, including the circular panel of their patron, St. George, over the main entrance, is original.

HABS

212. Robert Machek Residence
1305 N. 19th St.   **1893-94**

The only house of its kind ever built here, this Austrian half-timber cottage was the work of a wood carver from Vienna. No ordinary craftsman, Machek was awarded a silver medal by King Milan I of Serbia for his work on the royal palace at Belgrade. His house shows superb skill and quality carving, from the carved faces, dolphins, and ram's head on the exterior to the fine panelling, cabinets, and furniture inside. The applied, chamfered, boards only simulate true timberwork, but their layout shows an understanding of the principles and structural requirements of the real thing. The coach house, connected on the rear, was designed and built by the present owner to match the original structure and includes many authentic details salvaged from 19th century buildings.

HABS

213. Homrighausen Flats
950-960 N. 19th St.   **1894**

August G. Homrighausen, a mason-contractor who lived around the corner on State Street, erected this picturesque structure for 6 flats. Architects Marshall & Ryder drew the plans, and specified pressed tan-orange brick, with orange terra-cotta trim. Among the ornamental details are scallop shells, vines, buds, and two cartouches carrying the date of construction ...18, and 94. The twin chimneys are trimmed with a very unusual copper cornice molding.

214. Highland Avenue Methodist Church
2026 W. Highland Ave.   **1896**

Founded in 1846, the first German Methodist Congregation in Milwaukee built this church to escape the unfavorable location of their previous structure (see #203) which was nestled among brewery buildings. Their first church, a small Greek Revival design, stood on Fifth Street near Highland. This Victorian Gothic ediface is built of orange pressed brick and is trimmed with terra-cotta ornament of a matching color. Two entrance canopies and the western gable have pierced Gothic bargeboards made of wood. The unusual steeple makes the transition from square to octagonal by splitting into one large and four small spires.

215. St. Michael's Roman Catholic Church
1453 N. 24th St.   **1892**

This imposing limestone church was designed by Milwaukee architects, Schnetzky & Liebert. One of the favorites of the city's German aristocracy, Eugene R. Liebert received much of his education in Germany and subscribed to numerous architectural periodicals from the old country to keep in touch with achievements there. This Milwaukee County limestone church shows the influence of his national background in a Gothic style. Among the unusual and interesting details are the carved stone triple capitals atop the entrance columns which are embellished with faces, grapevines, and leaves.

216. Octagon House
2443 N. Gordon Place   c.1851-55

Milwaukee's only remaining octagon house was obviously influenced by Orson Fowler's book *A Home For All*. In fact, the floor plan is so close to one offered in the famous 1849 pattern book, that there is no doubt about its influence. Octagons, Fowler argued, were "far better, every way, and several hundred percent cheaper." While there were about two dozen built in Wisconsin, there were comparatively few in Milwaukee. It appears that only 3 were ever built here. Humble as it is, this is our last memento of a national novelty which spread like a prairie fire and died as suddenly as it appeared.

217. Charles Whitnall Residence
1208 E. Locust St.   1851

Originally this little brick house stood in the middle of a 20-acre tract which was occupied by many members of the Whitnall family. Charles, who built this house, was a painter; and his brother, Frank, was one of Milwaukee's pioneer florists and seedsmen. This location was so remote in the early days that its address was listed on Humboldt Ave., since Locust had not yet been cut through to the river. Whitnall sold a piece of his property to the city and in 1894 the bridge was completed, connecting Locust to the East side. Behind this house, at 2942 N. Dousman St., is the old 14-room home where Charles B. Whitnall, "father of Milwaukee parks" (see #351), was born. There were once extensive greenhouses on the property, which extended from Humboldt to the river.

218. Carl Sandburg Residence
2469 N. 18th St.

One of America's most prominent literary figures, Carl Sandburg, married a Menomonee Falls high school teacher, Lilian Steichen, in Milwaukee in 1908. At that time he was a district organizer for the Socialist Party in Wisconsin. He later became the personal secretary of Milwaukee Socialist Mayor Emil Seidel in 1910. In 1911 the Sandburgs lived in this house on N. 18th St.; and it was here that their first child, Margaret, was born. The next year he quit his job at the *Milwaukee Leader* newspaper office and moved to Chicago to work for the *Chicago Socialist*.

219. Beth-Israel Synagogue
2432 N. Teutonia Ave. 1925

The larger of two Byzantine-styled synagogues built here, this imposing structure was designed by Milwaukee architect, Herman H. Bruns. It was once the hub of the city's Orthodox community and the seat of Rabbi Solomon Scheinfeld. Built with an orange-brown scratch-face brick the building is trimmed with cut and carved limestone and wrought iron balconies. The 12-sided lanterns and their hemispherical domes are made of sheet copper. Although it was sold in 1960, to become the Greater Galilee Missionary Baptist Church, the old stained-glass Star of David is still in place over the entrance.

220. Van Ellis Building
2654 W. Fond du Lac Ave. 1903

An excellent example of an architectural style seldom seen in Milwaukee, this store and dwelling was erected by George Van Ellis, at a cost of $7,000. Its stepped gable is reminiscent of the picturesque buildings of Holland and Flanders built during the Renaissance. Although the ground floor has been completely altered, the upper stories have managed to remain in unspoiled condition. The building is basically red pressed brick trimmed in painted sheet metal. The architects were Leiser & Holst and the Hartkopf brothers did the mason work.

220a. Daniel H. Richards Residence
2863 N. 1st St. 1837

The oldest house in Milwaukee stands at the highest elevation in the city. From this promontory, 150 feet above Lake Michigan, the view of the Menomonee River Valley is spectacular. When the house was new there were only a few buildings in the village and this was the only dwelling on a 160 acre farm. Daniel Richards had come to this frontier settlement to found the first newspaper ever published here, "The Milwaukee Advertiser". His frame house was a symmetrical Greek revival design with wings on each side. Over the years the house has suffered two fires and has lost one of its wings. The rare foundation is composed of round field-stones which were no doubt picked up on Richards' own acreage.

GRAND AVENUE AREA

"West Wisconsin Avenue" is the least attractive of the three names that this street has been given since the pioneer days. It was originally a dirt road named Spring Street after the numerous natural springs which were once found along its length. Until the late 1840's, when a high bluff near 8th Street was graded down, the upper and lower street did not connect; and it was necessary to go blocks out of the way to avoid this interruption. In the 1850's James Higson Rogers purchased 160 acres on western Spring Street and subdivided the land for sale. To encourage what he guessed would become a choice residential area for the city's wealthy merchants, Rogers built a $60,000 mansion on 15th and Spring Street. He guessed correctly, and in the 1870's the street was lined with so many imposing mansions that it was considered necessary to give it a more appropriate name. Grand Avenue was chosen and remained the title until its present name was adopted. Like Prospect Avenue, Grand encouraged similar costly developments on the nearby parallel and intersecting streets.

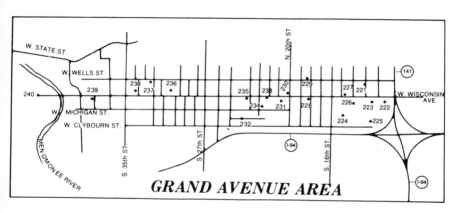

221. Abraham Lincoln Speech Site
W. Wells St., S.W. corner N. 13th St.
1859

This bronze tablet commemorates a speech given by Abraham Lincoln at the Wisconsin State Fair grounds, which included this property, on September 30, 1859. Described as "a real farmer's talk", it was directed to the subject of agriculture. No platform was provided, and at the last minute, a lumber wagon was drawn up to provide the necessary elevation for Lincoln. The tablet is no longer in its original, authentic, location. When it was erected, by the Old Settlers Club of Milwaukee in 1928, it stood about midway between Wells and Kilbourn on the west side of 13th Street. Then it was affixed to an immense boulder taken from the Milwaukee River.

222. Johnston Hall
1131 W. Wisconsin Ave.　　**1906-07**

The oldest Marquette University building, this hall was named after Robert A. Johnston, who gave the money for its construction. The founder of the Johnston Biscuit Co., he came forth with the donation when the old Marquette College, the Milwaukee Law School and the Milwaukee Medical School were working toward a university charter. He had been a contributor to the Gesu Church (see#223) and his son, Harry Johnston, had been a student at Marquette College. Designed by Milwaukee architect, Charles D. Crane, it is a picturesque, almost Venetian, Gothic building. Basically tan pressed brick on a Bedford stone foundation, the trim is executed in carved limestone; the cornice, with its crocketed pinnacles, is sheet metal.

223. Roman Catholic Church of the Gesu
1145 W. Wisconsin Ave.   1893 and 1902

Of all the Gothic churches to come out of Victorian Milwaukee, Gesu stands out as the most imposing and the one which follows most accurately the European historical precedent. Strongly French Gothic, this monumental structure is typically cruciform in shape, has two immense towers and a fleché (a small tower) over the crossing of nave and transept. A Gothic arcade with polished granite columns cuts across the gray limestone facade above the rose window. Architects H.C. Koch & Co. are responsible for the original church and Herman J. Esser designed the triple-arched entrance portico which was added in 1902 as a gift of the Lonstorff family. The pipe organ, was taken from the Studebaker Theater in Chicago, in 1911, and reinstalled here.

224. Chapel Dedicated to St. Joan of Arc
Marquette University Campus
15th Century

Obviously the oldest building in Milwaukee, this chapel was originally built in the early 15th century in the little French village of Chasse. In 1927 Gertrude Hill Gavin, daughter of American railroad magnate, James Hill, had the then-dilapidated building taken apart and shipped to her 50-acre estate at Jericho, Long Island. Mr. and Mrs. Marc. B. Rojtman, who later owned the estate, presented the chapel to Marquette in 1964. The chapel was again dismantled and shipped here for reassembly. Numerous furnishings from the same period were also a part of the gift. The original name of the Gothic structure was Chapelle de St. Martin de Sayssuel.

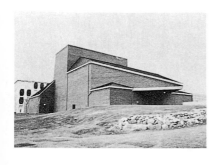

225. Evan P. & Marion Helfaer Theater
525 N. 13th St.   1975

Marquette University's theater was erected by the late philanthropist, Evan Helfaer, as a memorial to his wife, Marion. Milwaukee architects Brielmaier, Sherer & Sherer used a trapezoid as the plan shape and built the walls with a brown brick accented by concrete bands. The strongly faceted roof shapes are made of weathering steel with standing seams. This will rust to a dark brown and then seal itself against further corrosion. The building complex provides a 226-seat theater, scenery shop, instruction rooms and studios.

226. Biltmore Grand Apartment Hotel
1341 W. Wisconsin Ave. 1925

Originally planned to be an 8-story building, this quarter of a million dollar project ended up with only four floors. In 1953 Jacob Meister, the original developer, again considered the feasibility of adding the additional floors for which the foundation was prepared. Architects Rossman & Wierdsma designed two identical 4-story blocks which extend to the sidewalk and enclose a courtyard. Between them is a recessed one-story entrance faced entirely with ornamental terra-cotta. Five ogee Gothic arches, terminating in poppyhead finials, form an arcade which protects the entrance doors. Both wings are also faced with terra-cotta in two colors (light buff and white mottled) from the ground to their pierced Gothic balustrades at the roofline.

NR WRL

227. Elizabeth Plankinton Residence
1492 W. Wisconsin Ave. c.1890

Milwaukee's best remaining residential example of the Richardsonian Romanesque style was built as a wedding present for Elizabeth by her millionaire meat packer father, John Plankinton. According to tradition, her fiance ran away with another woman and Miss Plankinton rejected the house. After its completion, she walked in once, looked around the first floor, and left, never again to set foot in the house. The heavy rock-faced limestone construction is trimmed with richly carved buff sandstone, granite columns, terra-cotta tiles, ornamental sheet metal work, and a slate roof. The exterior is almost completely unspoiled and a great deal of the fine woodwork and fireplaces remain inside.

228. Sovereign Apartment
1810 W. Wisconsin Ave. 1929

This 142-family apartment building is one of the most important major projects to be built here in the art-deco style. The 8-story concrete structure is faced with light orange brick and trimmed with glazed and mottled terra-cotta trim. The entrance is faced with marble into which ornament is incised along with the name "Sovereign" in art-deco letters. Bronze is used for a pair of lanterns flanking the entrance and for the grilles in the side windows. Instead of a cornerstone the building is signed, on a bronze tablet to the right of the entrance, "Bruce Uthus/Architect A.D. 1929." Polychrome terra-cotta ornament at the roofline gives the apartment most of its style.

229. Milwaukee State Normal School
1820 W. Wells St.　　　　1885 and later

Between 1870 and 1876 the Normal, or teacher training, department of the Milwaukee Public School system was attached to the high schools. In 1881, the Board of Normal Regents finally agreed to establish State of Wisconsin Normal School #5 here in the city. In the beginning there were 60 pupils enrolled; facilities included a model class, elaborate laboratories, and manual training rooms. The original section of the building, with its three triangular gables, was roughly square and built with ornamental red and yellow brick, trimmed in sheet metal and terra-cotta. Additions have subsequently extended the structure east and west to fill the entire block.

230. Capt. Fredrick Pabst Residence
2000 W. Wisconsin Ave.　　　　1890

NR WRL

Milwaukee's most important residential landmark was built at the time when Pabst became president of the family brewery and its name was changed from Best to the Pabst Brewing Company. Architect George Bowman Ferry (of Ferry & Clas) drew the plans for this distinguished Flemish Renaissance mansion. Its handsomely proportioned facade, with corbie-stepped gables, is made of pressed tan brick on a Wauwatosa limestone foundation. The strapwork ornament is executed in matching terra-cotta and the red pantile roof is trimmed with copper rainwater heads and downspouts. The conservatory on the east end of the house was originally an exhibit pavilion for the display of Pabst Brewing Co. products (most likely at the World Columbian Exposition in Chicago, 1893). Made almost entirely of terra-cotta, the baroque design is ornamented with beer steins, barley, and hop vines and was designed by architect Otto Strack. Both inside and out, the house is in a remarkably unspoiled condition.

231. Sylvester Pettibone Residence
2051 W. Wisconsin Ave.
c.1854 and later

What may be Wisconsin Avenue's oldest house is buried under more than half a dozen remodellings. The original structure, for which no picture has been found, was built in or before 1854 by Sylvester Pettibone as a farmhouse. His property, which eventually grew to 250 acres, extended west of 20th Street and south of Wisconsin Avenue. Later owners enlarged and remodelled the original structure so many times that it is difficult to determine its shape. Pettibone was the first postmaster of Waukesha, a blacksmith, a farmer, and he was responsible for the first grading of a Milwaukee street (Water St. in 1836).

232. Pettibone Place
25th St. between Michigan
and Clybourn

This short dead-end street is named after one of Milwaukee's earliest settlers, Sylvester Pettibone. It runs east from 25th Street over what was once a part of his 250-acre farm. The old farmhouse, many times remodelled, is still standing on W. Wisconsin Ave. (see #231). Although very wealthy at one time, Pettibone was comparatively poor at his death. He had been overly generous and had often endorsed paper for his friends, only to be forced to pay up for their bad debts. This accounted for the shrinkage of his extensive acreage, which in the end amounted to only a few small lots.

233. Grand Avenue Congregational Church
2133 W. Wisconsin Ave.   1887

Unique among the city's churches, this Richardsonian Romanesque structure was a spectacular break in tradition for the time. A large semicircular arch and square turrets atop buttresses frame the main entrance. The parish, organized in 1847, moved here from their third church which then stood on the southwest corner of Sixth and Grand (now W. Wisconsin Ave.). When it was new, this $38,000 building was considered to have one of the largest audience rooms in the city. Its CCB walls rest on a rock-face limestone foundation; trim is stone and wood, with ornamental brickwork.

234. C.H. Rische Flats
626-630 N. 23rd St.   1898

Architects Rische & Kiesslich designed this highly picturesque pair of 3-story apartment buildings. Set on high English basements, these unusual eclectic facades are flanked by a pair of cylindrical brick towers with conical caps. The entrances are tucked under 3-story bartizans which are covered with imitation timberwork and shingles. The CCB structures have a limestone water table and are faced with stucco on the ground floor. Gothic and Romanesque forms are mixed with touches of the Flemish Renaissance and features that look like the battlemented parapet walls of a medieval castle.

235. Eagles Club
2401 W. Wisconsin Ave.   1925

This powerful and highly individual design was executed by architect Russell Bar Williamson. The steel fireproof construction is faced with stone and is trimmed with wrought iron, sheet copper, and pantiles. A very large bas relief frieze at the roofline depicts objects and purposes of the fraternity and humanitarian movements inaugurated by the order. At one time there were 4 twelve-foot statues flanking the giant arches of the Wisconsin Ave. entrance. They represented Liberty, Truth, Justice, and Equality. Inside is a "million dollar" ballroom which for years has attracted the nation's most important bands and orchestras for public dancing.

236. Tripoli Temple Shrine Mosque
3000 W. Wisconsin Ave.   1926-28

Built by the Ancient Arabic Order of Nobles of the Mystic Shrine, this Masonic fraternal clubhouse is a completely unique example of Islamic Indian architecture. The bulbous dome raised on a drum and the entrance pavilion with its huge arch were obviously inspired by the Taj Mahal at Agra, India. Clas, Shepherd and Clas were the architects and Bently Bros., Inc., the general contractors. The imposing mosque is faced with alternating bands of orange and brown brick, with colorful designs in glazed tile for trim. Corner minarets are capped with sheet copper, the unusual windows made ornamental with leaded glass. The dome is covered with 4 colors of glazed tile and topped with an 11½-foot-tall copper finial.

237. George J. Schuster Residence
3205 W. Wells St. 1891

A jobber in cigar leaf tobacco, Schuster employed architects Crane & Barkhausen to create his red castle. An eclectic design, it shows strong leanings toward the French Romanesque and the German Renaissance. Three red materials give this mansion an unusual character in a city which was predominantly yellow at that time. The foundation and first story facing are rock-faced sandstone with smooth elt courses. The upper walls are pressed red brick and trimmed with red terra-cotta ornament. A large "S" in a wreath can be seen at the top of the stepped gable and one of a pair of lions holding shields with the date of construction has survived.

238. Henry Harnischfeger Residence
3424 W. Wisconsin Ave. 1905

One of only a few mansions built in Milwaukee in this unusual German modern style. It shows influences of the previous New Rennaissance style which changed the face of Germany in the late 19th century, but there are very "modern" touches which tend away from ornament. Built for a co-founder of the present Harnischfeger Corporation, the house was designed by architect Eugene Liebert. The basic materials are dark brown pressed brick trimmed with cut limestone with a red pan-tile roof. A cylindrical molding which is a part of the brick adds a touch of refinement around openings. The corner bartizan is roofed with copper and sports an unusual finial. Two large knights in armor, carved in wood, support the southeast corner porch on the second floor.

239. Drott Tractor Co. Building
3841 W. Wisconsin Ave. 1928

A good, relatively unspoiled, example of early modern architecture with polychrome terra-cotta facing. Although the basic fireproof concrete construction and massing of elements is modern, the ornament is an unusual eclectic blend of historical forms. The basic masonry of the facade is terra-cotta made to look like large chiselled blocks of ashlar stone. Window trim is glazed brown and purple terra-cotta with ornament. The name, "Drott Tractor Co., Inc.," is handsomely applied in Roman serif stand-off letters of gold-leafed bronze.

240. Grand Avenue Viaduct
W. Wisconsin Ave. from
38th St. to 44th St. 1907-11

Edwin Thacher, a New York engineer, won a $1,500 prize for his design of this 2,088-foot link between Milwaukee and the town of Wauwatosa. It took half a million board feet of lumber to build the complex forms for the huge arches and 900 tons of steel to reinforce the mountain of concrete required. 300 workers took four years and $550,000 to complete the job of spanning the Menomonee River Valley above Pigsville (see #254).

SAUERKRAUT BOULEVARD

In 1870 Highland Avenue (then Prairie Street) extended west only as far as 12th Street. Six years later it was cut through to 27th Street and shortly after 1890 the area between 27th and 35th Streets was developed as a prestige residential area. At this time the street was continued west, but then as a wide boulevard named Highland. Among the many families to build mansions there were the Pabsts, Kieckhefers, Zinns, Manegolds, Millers, Pritzlaffs, Usingers and Krulls. Because the neighborhood was so heavily German, it acquired the nickname, "Sauerkraut Boulevard". At least one lady remembers receiving a letter from Germany addressed to a resident of the street with that name.

W. McKINLEY BLVD.			248 •	247 •							
N 35th ST	N 34th ST	N 33rd ST	N 32nd ST	N 31st ST	N 30th ST	N 29th ST	N 28th ST	N 27th ST	N 26th ST	N 25th ST	N 24th ST

W. JUNEAU AVE

HIGHLAND BLVD — 245 • — 244 •

• 246

W. STATE ST — 241 •

242 • — W RICHARDSON PL • 243 — 249 •

SAUERKRAUT BOULEVARD W. KILBOURN AVE

241. Colonel Theodore Yates Residence
2710 W. State St.   c. 1865

Yates, a Civil War hero and inventor, was commended for his gallantry in the Battle of Vicksburg, where he was severely wounded. After the war he was transferred to an administrative job in Milwaukee, where he met his wife and built this "country" home. Originally a 6.81-acre estate, the property was virtually in the country then, and the now small lot still contains the old vertical board and batten stable with a cupola. The house is a 2½-story CCB (painted) on a limestone foundation. The original full-width front porch and ornamental woodwork in the gable are now gone, but the Gothic label moldings over the windows are still intact.

242. Dr. Robert J. Faries Residence
3011 W. State St. c.1850

Built in sections and twice remodelled, this painted CCB house once fronted on the Watertown Plank Road (see #243), which originally cut through just north of State St. Dr. Faries was Wisconsin's first dentist and was considered without equal in the Midwest. He won a gold medal for a set of teeth at the 1867 Paris Exposition. He was also a gunstock engraver and produced woodcuts for early city directories. Also an amateur astronomer, Faries built the first telescope in the state and it is said that the flat roof on the house was added as an observation deck. Later owner, Philetus Yale, added the unusually tall 4½-story

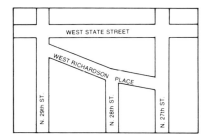

WEST STATE STREET

WEST RICHARDSON PLACE

N 29th ST.

N 28th ST.

N 27th ST.

243. W. Richardson Place
Just south of State St. between
27th St. and 29th St. 1848-53

This is the only remaining segment of the old Watertown Plank Road in the central city. Called the "Avenue to Wealth," this pioneer road was built before railroads were dreamed of and served as the gateway to the West for immigrants arriving in Milwaukee by boat. Originally the road began near 11th Street and wound for 58 miles through Wauwatosa and Oconomowoc to Watertown. As the city's street grid expanded, the old meandering roadbed was plowed under in favor of a more geometrically perfect layout. For some unknown reason this two-block-long diagonal segment, with a slight bend, was not destroyed. Beyond N. 35th Street, the road followed what is now State St. and in Wauwatosa the original name, "Watertown Plank Road," resumes and continues out through Elm Grove. Originally the road was paved with oak planks 3 inches wide and 8 feet long.

244. Second Church of
Christ Scientist
2722 W. Highland Blvd. 1913

Milwaukee architect, Carl Barkhausen, drew the plans for this distinctive classical church. Roughly patterned after the Pantheon in Rome, it has the same basic colonnaded portico in front of a large do ne-capped room. The square auditorium block, with its chamfered corners, supports a cylindrical drum which, in turn, supports the flat-crowned dome. The 174-foot-high structure is crowned with an octagonal copper lantern. The basic material, pressed buff brick, is trimmed with glazed terra-cotta ornament. An unusual combination of materials, the fluted limestone columns are topped with terra-cotta Corinthian capitals.

245. Frederick Pabst, Jr. Residence
3112 W. Highland Blvd. 1897

One of the first six mansions erected on Highland Blvd., this has outlived its contemporaries to become the most important survivor on a once elegant street. Its Classic Resurgence design is dominated by a handsome portico supported by four fluted Ionic columns. Each column is made from a single block of limestone and has the proper entasis (a slight swelling or curve in the middle). The finely pointed yellow pressed brick is trimmed with cut and carved limestone, wrought iron, copper, and a slate roof. Frederick Pabst, Jr., became president of the Pabst Brewery, which was founded by his father.

246. George J. Koch Residence
3209 W. Highland Blvd. 1897

Now a part of Concordia College, this formal, almost institutional structure was once a private residence. George Koch was cashier of the West Side Bank (see #192), where Adam Gettelman (see #253) was president. The CCB house is set on a limestone foundation and is trimmed with cut stone, cast iron and a sheet metal cornice with balustrade. Milwaukee architect, Edward V. Koch, drew the plans which include a skylight on the roof and a high English basement. Remodelings have concealed the original main room which once rose to the roof and had stencilled designs in its skylight well.

247. Theodore Sternemann Residence
3112 W. McKinley Blvd. 1903

Architect Herman W. Buemming designed this house which is almost the twin of his own residence on Pleasant St. (see #79). Its owner, Theodore Sternemann, was a partner in the leaf tobacco firm of Sternemann Brothers & Hayden. Although the size and basic proportions of the two Buemming designs are almost identical, there are variations in detailing which give them different characters. Both have fluted Ionic columns and the same lunette window in their triangular pediments, but the window and door treatments and the pronounced dentil moldings, give this house a Georgian look, while its counterpart is more Greek.

248. Three-Story Duplexes
3238 McKinley Blvd. to corner
of N. 32nd St.   1906

This row is one of the city's best remaining examples of three-story frame duplexes. Still present by the thousands, these practical and spacious two-family flats cover hundreds of square blocks in Milwaukee, especially in the central city. This stretch, on the north side of McKinley Blvd., is well preserved and very typical. The house on the left was built and owned by carpenter Frank Hunholz for $4,500. Although the basic dimensions (24' x 52') and layouts were the same, all street facades were purposely varied in detailing.

249. Joseph B. Kalvelage
Residence
2432 W. Kilbourn Ave.   1896

Designed by Otto Strack, this mansion was intended to be the first of many fine homes on what was then Cedar St. Kalvelage guessed that the area would become another Sauerkraut Boulevard, but it never developed. Then, as now, the house stands as a castle among cottages. The baroque design, inspired by late Renaissance forms in Germany and France, is executed in tan pressed brick with richly sculptured terra-cotta trim. The wrought iron railings and balcony, made by Cyril Colnik, are among the finest remaining examples of this craft in the city. In later years it was a hospital and then the Wisconsin headquarters for the Ku Klux Klan.

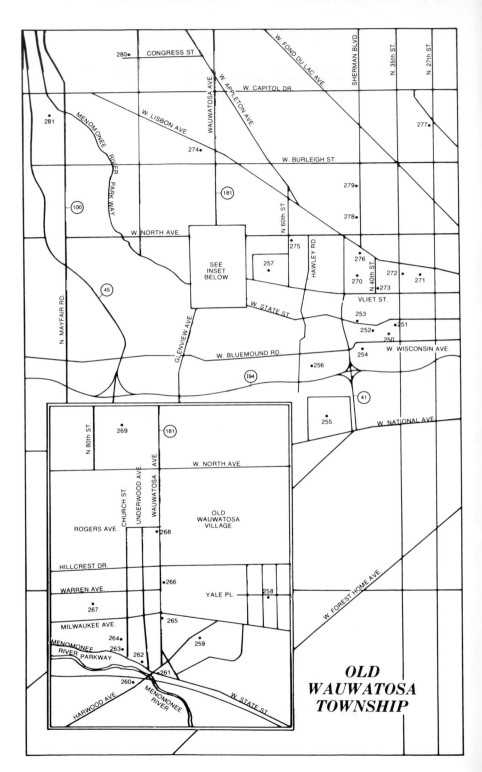

OLD WAUWATOSA TOWNSHIP

In 1842 this township, which was then attached to Milwaukee, presented a bill for incorporation to the territorial legislature. The proposed names were Bridgeport, Rushville (after Rushville, New York) and Wauwautosa. The latter was selected, but through a spelling error, it lost the "u" in the second syllable and has ever since been *Wauwatosa*. Most of the 36-square-mile town was farmland with an important cemetery(see #256), two breweries (see #252 and #253) the prestigious National Soldier's Home (see#255) and a number of extraordinary gentlemen-farmer houses (see #272 and #274) located on the major roads. The village of Wauwatosa was settled almost as early as Milwaukee and grew up around the Charles Hart Grist Mill on the Menomonee River. It was at this important intersection that there were eventually three streets, a railroad, a streetcar line, and the river coming together at one point.

250. Story School
3815 W. Kilbourn Ave. 1936

Organized in 1849, this school was first known as the 8th District School of the Town of Wauwatosa. It was renamed Story after a farmer and philanthropist, Alfred Story, who owned a sizeable parcel of land in this vicinity and who was known to have been a supporter of education. This handsome "moderne" structure was designed by architect G. E. Wiley and is made of orange brick trimmed with limestone and copper. Especially interesting are the decorative brick panels made with alternating brick and blue-glazed tiles in a herringbone pattern. The semicircular entrance pavilion has the name spelled in typical 1930's lettering and art-deco leaded glass transoms over the doors.

251. Frederick Miller Residence
3713 W. Miller Lane c. 1884

This is the only remaining house which was built and occupied by pioneer Milwaukee brewer, Frederick Miller. It also marks the location of the famous Miller Beer Garden, which sprawled over the bluff above the brewery. When it was new, the house was surrounded by large shade trees, a grape arbor, pansy beds, and it was painted pearl gray with white trim. With the original front porch gone and the clapboards covered with later siding, the only architectural interest is the 3-story octagonal tower with its weather vane.

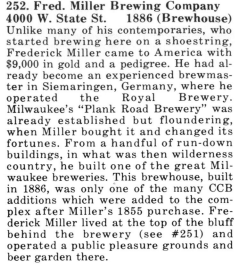

252. Fred. Miller Brewing Company
4000 W. State St.   1886 (Brewhouse)
Unlike many of his contemporaries, who started brewing here on a shoestring, Frederick Miller came to America with $9,000 in gold and a pedigree. He had already become an experienced brewmaster in Siemaringen, Germany, where he operated the Royal Brewery. Milwaukee's "Plank Road Brewery" was already established but floundering, when Miller bought it and changed its fortunes. From a handful of run-down buildings, in what was then wilderness country, he built one of the great Milwaukee breweries. This brewhouse, built in 1886, was only one of the many CCB additions which were added to the complex after Miller's 1855 purchase. Frederick Miller lived at the top of the bluff behind the brewery (see #251) and operated a public pleasure grounds and beer garden there.

253. Gettelman's Menomonee Brewery
4400 W. State St.   c. 1854
These two attached CCB buildings are all that remains of the historic Gettelman Brewery. The foundations for this business were laid in 1854 by Strohn & Reitzenstein, but an epidemic of cholera that year killed both partners. George Schweickhart bought the assets and built the "Menomonee Brewery" from the ground up. In 1870 he sold it to his son-in-law, Adam Gettelman, whose family continued the operation until the company was purchased by the Miller Brewing Company. The large structure to the rear was the malt house and had grain bins for barley storage. The little office in the front is said to have been the home of the Gettelman family.

254. Pigsville
Menomonee River Valley under and south of the Grand Ave. Viaduct
(see #240)
Long before this valley had substantial homes and streets, a man named Fries had a small farm on the fertile bottomland. According to local tradition, a group of squatters, who occupied a small piece of the land to the north, named the area after the numerous loud-squealing pigs raised by Fries. The nickname caught on and was used for so many years that, in the early 1900's, it began to appear in city map guidebooks. The valley eventually became a neighborhood of workers from local industry and the St. Paul Railroad shops to the south.

255. National Soldier's Home
Wood, Wisconsin   1866 and later
The National Home for Disabled Volunteer Soldiers was created by an act of Congress on March 21, 1866; and four homes were established nationwide. Augusta, Maine; Hampton, Virginia; Dayton, Ohio; and Milwaukee, Wisconsin, were selected as sites. The main administration building (pictured) was designed by Edward Townsend Mix in the Gothic Revival style and is CCB set on a limestone rubble foundation. The tremendous 6-story tower, with its variety of Gothic arched windows can be seen for miles from its prominent hilltop site. Here, too, is the city's best remaining example of 3-color ornamental slate work on the mansard roof.

256. Calvary Cemetery Chapel
5503 W. Bluemound Rd.   1899
This CCB Romanesque structure crowns a beautifully formed hill which has always been the focus of Milwaukee's principal Catholic cematary. Originally, a large wooden cross was, and now the chapel, is so well situated as to be seen for miles. Nicknamed "Jesuit Hill" because it has always been reserved as a burial place for clergy, it rises 100 feet above the drive. Architect Erhard Brielmaier created a distinguished cruciform plan which is basically a tall cube with projecting pavilions on all four sides. Three of these are terminated in semicircular half-domed bays, while the fourth is both nave and western porch. An octagonal lantern crowns the main block.

257. Washington Highlands
60th, 68th and Lloyd Sts. and Milwaukee Ave.   1919
This beautifully planned subdivision was once a hop farm owned and operated by the Pabst family. Its rolling hillside landscape, which once contained only a caretaker's house, is now a carefully laid out complex of winding streets, private parks, plazas, and substantial homes. The street plan, according to local tradition, was purposely made in the shape of a German helmet. All purchasers automatically become members of the Washington Homes Association, a corporation organized for the protection of all members. A comprehensive set of restrictions are outlined for members, including the amount of setback, cost and square footage of improvements, limits on usage and ownership, and a mandatory approval of plans by the association.

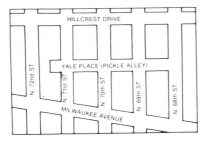

258. Pickle Alley (Yale Place)
N. 68th to 71st St. between
Milwaukee Ave. and Hillcrest

There was a time when Wauwatosa claimed to be the "pickle capitol of the world." A large pickle factory, owned by James Stickney and his son, Charles, once sprawled along the north side of Milwaukee Avenue between 72nd and 73rd Streets. They owned, among others, an 8-acre cucumber plot near 83rd and Aberdeen Court. During cuke season wagon loads from the fields would rumble down 73rd Street to the factory and that street even showed up on maps as "Pickle Lane." Yale Place began at 68th St. and ran into the Stickney property. It was first called Lake St., perhaps after the private pond behind the factory, but its popular nickname became "Pickle Alley."

259. Irvington Hotel
7335 Harwood Avenue   c. 1892

Once the "scene of social activity," this 3-story frame structure was sold in 1937 and converted into light housekeeping rooms. Tradition says that a Mrs. Luther B. Gregg came from Milwaukee to visit her sons at the Milwaukee Sanitarium and was disturbed at finding no hotels to relax in before a return trip. She had inherited this property from her father and took it into her hands to build this badly needed facility. Mr. and Mrs. Gregg operated the hotel for years, and it was here that the Wauwatosa Woman's Club held their evening meeting in 1895. Before the clapboards were covered with asbestos shingles, there was an interesting common lintel design connecting all 3 third-floor windows. There was also a second level to the two-sided porch which can still be imagined by the notch and columns on the west wall.

260. Old Wauwatosa Post Office
7720 W. Harwood Ave.   1854

Built originally as a dwelling place for Dr. Levi C. Halsted, this little frame structure became the social, political, and commercial center of Milwaukee's most important suburb. Being only a few feet from the railroad tracks, it was instantly pressed into use as a depot. When the Postal Service commandeered it as a station, it was on its way to becoming the catch-all building for most ctivities in this pioneer community. At one time it served as a general store, express office, circulation library, Republican Party headquarters, harness shop, grocery, and plumbing shop. Some years it functioned in six of these capacities simultaneously. Moved once, in 1950, it has miraculously staved off doom for more than an expected lifetime, to become one of Wauwatosa's most valuable historical landmarks.

261. Charles Jacobus Saloon
7616 W. State St. c.1902

This prominent landmark, on one of the principal corners in the old village of Wauwatosa, was built by the Pabst Brewing Company. Like most Pabst-owned saloons, this was probably designed by the company architect and it does have the same characteristics found on most of their buildings, including the brewery (see #202 & #203). Built by mason Fred Yahle, the CCB walls are set on a limestone foundation and display the Gothic arches and battlemented parapets so often associated with Pabst. At the top of the tower is a badly deteriorated Pabst emblem of the type seen on saloons built by the company throughout the Midwest.

262. Dittmar Building
1417 Underwood Ave. 1897

Dittmar was a blacksmith, whose shop was located just north of the present building. This important anchor, on one of the original corners of the old village, has always been a hardware store. In the beginning, when it was occupied by A.I. Smith, there were two apartments upstairs and the offices of a doctor and a dentist. The CCB building is triangular in shape, and its principal feature is a two-story octagonal bartizan with a lantern pierced by eight porthole windows. The unusual signage on the east wall, "Dittmar 1897 Bldg.", is cut into four stones laid flush with the brick. Inside, a rare hand-powered, mostly wooden, freight elevator is still in use.

263. First Congregational Church of Wauwatosa
1511 Church St. 1919-21 & 1959

The Congregational Church was the first to organize and is the oldest in Wauwatosa. The first meeting, in 1842, was in the small log house of Deacon Richard Gilbert Sr. on North Avenue just west of Highway 100. This site was purchased from Charles Hart for $50, and the original building was erected in 1853. A white frame structure with a central steeple, this small church was later remodelled by adding a large vestibule on the front and removing the spire from the belfry. The present structure, designed by architect E.D. Kuenzli, is made of red brick with limestone and wooden trim and has a very finely proportioned steeple. In 1959 a major office and Sunday school addition was built on the south.

264. Thomas B. Hart Residence
1609 Church St. c.1850

The oldest house, on what was probably Wauwatosa's first residential street, has the county's finest remaining example of bargeboards. These pierced, scroll-sawn wooden boards at the edges of the gables are delicately designed; one was worked with a carver's chisel after cutting. There are six patterns in all, including the ones on the vertical board-and-batten garage. The Gothic Revival-influenced design is also enhanced by a fine original porch and half octagon bays. The builder has not been determined, but the man who owned it longest was Thomas B. Hart, brother of the first permanent settler in Wauwatosa.

265. Wauwatosa Woman's Club
1626 Wauwatosa Ave. 1924-25

In 1894, a small group of ladies met at the home of Mrs. Alonzo Kellog, on Church St., and organized the Wauwatosa Woman's Club for "the social and intellectual development of women through a free interchange of thought by a course of careful study, essays and discussion." Early meetings were held in members' homes and the Irvington Hotel (see #259), but in 1914, Emerson D. Hoyt offered this lot for a clubhouse. The first mayor of Wauwatosa, Hoyt added a restriction, that the clubhouse include a museum to preserve the history and artifacts of early families here. The museum exists today and contains about 350 items. The red brick Georgian clubhouse was designed by Milwaukee architect, Roger Kirchhoff.

266. Rev. Luther Clapp Residence
1828 N. Wauwatosa Ave. 1856

When this historic house was built, its side porch was actually the front verandah and it faced Milwaukee Avenue. The well designed "front" door with sidelights was added later. Rev. Luther Clapp was the pastor of the First Congregational Church (see #263) from 1845 until 1872. A native of West Hampton, Massachusetts, he was graduated from William's College and studied for the ministry at Andover Theological Seminary. At the age of 25, he came here and assumed his position with the church. Luther and Harriet Clapp also held early school classes in the parlor of their home.

267. Dr. Fiske Holbrook Day Residence
8000 W. Milwaukee Ave. c.1870

This imposing three-story mansion, old Wauwatosa's largest, was built by the county physician who was attached to the nearby Milwaukee County Institutions. A pioneer doctor, who arrived here in 1853 from New York State, Day first lived on lower Church Street (which is now a part of Menomonee River Parkway) in a small frame house nicknamed "The Bird House". In 1854, he built a fine Gothic Revival cottage, of brick and wood, on the spot where the Congregational Church's parking lot is today (see #263). The 1870's house, set on its huge 250 x 320-foot lot on top of a hill, was occupied by Day until 1895. It was abandoned by a later owner in the depression and lay vacant for 10 years during which time its interior was severely vandalized.

HABS NR WRL

268. Lowell Damon House
2107 N. Wauwatosa Ave. 1844-46

"In 1844, Oliver Damon, wheelwright and cabinetmaker, migrated from New Hampshire to what is now Wauwatosa. He and his son-in-law, Jonathan Warren, built this house using oak and black walnut from land he purchased in 1841. In 1846 Damon's son, Lowell, came to Wisconsin and added the front portion of the house. The Rogers family gave the house to the Milwaukee County Historical Society in 1941 as a museum and period home."

269. First Baptist Church of Wauwatosa
Wauwatosa Cemetery/Wauwatosa Ave.
just north of North Ave.   **1852-53**

The oldest church building in Wauwatosa, this historic structure was also the first to be erected in that pioneer settlement. When the Baptist congregation was organized in 1845, it met in the old Gilbert schoolhouse which stood near North Ave. and Highway 100. In 1852, when the present building was begun, the congregation guessed that the center of the village would be at North and Wauwatosa Avenues, and the church was built near that intersection. Around 1900 it was acquired by Frederick D. Underwood, one-time president of the Erie Railroad, and remodeled as an armory for the Wauwatosa Light Guard, complete with cannons in the front yard. In about 1908 he moved it from its original location to the cemetery, where it was used for a chapel. Today it has a new front porch and is missing its original windows and square belfry, but the venerable Greek Revival church still has a limestone lintel over the front door with "1852" chiseled in handsome style.

270. Goethe & Schiller Monument
Washington Park above the
Blatz Temple of Music   **1908**

This is believed to be the only monument to Goethe and Schiller in the United States. The larger-than-life bronze statues are set on a granite base and are a replica of a monument in Weimar, Germany, by Ernest Rietschel. Both Johann Wolfgang von Goethe and Johann Christoph Friedrich von Schiller were 18th century poets, dramatists and philosophers. Among the greatest literary geniuses in German history, these men were attracted by each other's work and remained close friends for life. When the Northwest Expressway cut through the area in 1959, the statues were moved to a different location in the park and rededicated.

271. Frederick Koenig Residence
1731 N. 32nd St.   **1897 and earlier**

Before 1896, this house sat in the middle of what is now 32nd Street, and its front faced W. Lisbon Ave. It was part of a four-acre gentleman's farm and had a large frame barn on a stone foundation. When 32nd Street was cut through the property, by condemnation, the house had to be moved. Koenig, who had purchased the property from the Uhrigs (see #272), took that opportunity to subdivide his holdings and sell lots. He hired architect F. W. Andree to change the Victorian eclectic house into a "modern" mansion in the Classic Resurgence style. There is reason to believe that buried under the remodeling there are two earlier houses, one dating back to the 1850's.

272. Franz Joseph Uhrig Residence
1727 N. 34th St.   **1851**

Built on a 20-acre estate, this stately Italianate mansion was once the summer home of wealthy St. Louis brewer, Franz Joseph Uhrig. Originally it sat in splendor at the top of the hill, surrounded by shade trees, lilacs, gooseberry bushes, flowers, and an apple orchard. Of the many original outbuildings, including a windmill house, pheasant and chicken houses, and a barn, only the gardener's house survives at the corner of two alleys behind the mansion. Of CCB, it has a wooden porch, bracketed cornice, and cupola. Two wings were added by architect L.A. Schmidtner in 1871. The east wing was partially removed when 34th Street was cut through the property in 1903.

273. Ludwig von Baumbach Residence
1440 N. 40th St.   **c.1856 or older**

Originally a one-story house, this unusual structure was moved in the 1870's from its first location near 39th Street south of Vliet St. It was then jacked up and the first floor was built under it. Scars can still be seen where the 12" x 12" beams used in moving were placed. Ludwig von Baumbach came from the royal household in Kircheim, Prussia, and was for years the president of the Landtag of Hesse Cassel. After his move to Milwaukee he became the imperial consul to Germany. One of his six sons, Ernst, who lived in this house also, was recognized by President Grant as consul to the double monarchy of Austria-Hungary.

274. Samuel D. Luscombe Residence

7709 W. Lisbon Ave.   **c.1852**

Mr. Luscombe, who had come to Milwaukee with $50 in 1843, acquired what was then a small fortune of $60,000 in the wooden tub and pail business by 1851. He built this CCB Italian villa on the old Lisbon Plank Road as a "gentleman's farm". After many owners, including a retired sea-captain (Edward Stanford), the estate was sold to a genuine farmer. For 59 years the property saw the raising of dairy cattle, corn, wheat, oats and hay.

275. Herbert W. Tullgren Building

5919-27 W. North Ave.   **1924-25**

One of Milwaukee's best examples of polychrome terra-cotta facing, the Tullgren building numbers among only a few, such as the Bertelson building (see #99) and the Watts building (see #64). It was designed by architects Martin Tullgren & Sons, and has Mediterranean-inspired stylism. The glazed terra-cotta facing is highlighted by highly colorful ornament. The three principal elliptical arches on the North Ave. facade and the cartouches above, with their flower garlands, are perhaps the most richly colored terra-cotta in the city. Being hard-glazed, this material can be easily cleaned to almost new appearance.

276. Frederick William von Steuben Monument

Sherman Blvd. Entrance to Washington Park

Baron von Steuben, who had gained military honor in seven campaigns for the King of Prussia, came to America at his own expense to join the fight for independence. In 1777, he wrote a letter to . Congress stating his desire to be given an assignment. He became a major general and served with great honor. At the close of the war, George Washington wrote the last official letter before his resignation to von Steuben. The text of both letters is reproduced on bronze tablets on the sides of the granite base.

277. A.O. Smith Corporation
Research and Engineering Building
3533 N. 27th St. 1930

One of the most revolutionary and modern buildings in its day, this important landmark is a finely detailed and engineered structure even by today's standards. The original problems included the flexibility of constantly changing laboratory and product development areas and an easily maintained building with up-to-date design. Although parts of the building are easily recognized as 1930's speed-line and art-deco architecture, the basic concepts were so advanced for their time as to be modern 45 years later. Chicago architects, Holabird & Root, worked with the A.O. Smith engineering department to produce this U-shaped facility, which has extruded aluminum mullions and black benedict stone on the exterior and formica, black enameled steel, formica panels, and terrazzo on the interior. The floor of this main lobby has a geometric design which is illuminated with three-quarter-inch ground plate glass panels and underfloor lighting.

278. Washington High School
2525 N. Sherman Blvd. 1913-15

A fine example of English Tudor school design, this structure, like Riverside (see #157), was the work of Milwaukee architects, Van Ryn & DeGelleke. Basically light tan scratch-face brick, the building is set on a limestone ashlar foundation and is trimmed with cut and carved stone. The entrance pavilion, with its battlemented parapet and random quoins, is decorated with richly carved panels and corbels.

279. Third Church of Christ Scientist
2915 N. Sherman Blvd. 1922

Like the First Church on N. Prospect Ave. (see #90) and the Second Church on Highland Blvd (see #244), this building is still another variation of the denomination's favored classical stylism. Milwaukee architect, Frank Howend, drew the plans and the structure is built of light buff pressed brick trimmed with limestone ashlar. Smooth, Ionic-inspired, columns flank the large arched windows, and the shallow dome, with its sheet copper covering, rests on a cylindrical drum.

NR WRL

280. Annunciation Greek Orthodox Church
9400 W. Congress St. 1959

One of Frank Lloyd Wright's last commissions, this spectacular concrete church was completed after his death. According to Wright, this structure "is one of a series of five sectarian churches I have designed in the past few years, each inspired by what I could feel of the character and beauty of the particular services and faiths of each, and that I have tried to make worthy architecture." Wright emphasized that this was not a slavish copy of Byzantine forms, but a simple and fresh design preserving the beauty and tradition of the ancient period without copying a single feature. The dome is covered with a light blue mosaic, and the cream colored concrete is accented with the basic gold and blue color scheme.

WHM

281. Milwaukee County's First Airport
Currie Park — Hwy. 100 at
W. Capitol Dr. 1919

"One of the earliest publicly-owned airports in the United States was established here on July 3, 1919, by the Milwaukee County Park Commission. The nation's first commercial air transport, the Lawson Airliner (see #803), took off from this field on August 27, 1919, on a demonstration flight to New York City and Washington, D.C., and returned on November 14, 1919. This two-engined biplane, 95 feet in wingspan, carried 16 passengers and two pilots. Milwaukee's first airmail was flown from here on June 7, 1926, by the Charles Dickinson line, operating from Chicago to St. Paul via Milwaukee and LaCrosse. This airport was deactivated during November 1926, when the need for more space led the county to purchase Hamilton Airport, the site of present General Mitchell Field."

WALKER'S POINT and SOUTHWEST

One of Milwaukee's three original pioneer settlements (see *Juneautown* and *Kilbourntown*) this area south of the confluence of the Milwaukee and Menomonee Rivers was named after its founder, George H. Walker. Called by many, "Colonel Walker", he was a native of Lynchburg, Virginia, and first located at Skunk Grove (see #807), where he ran a trading post. In 1834 he built a log cabin here on a 12-foot-high point of land jutting into water and marsh land near what is now First and Seeboth Streets. He claimed 160 acres, laid out streets, and began to sell lots. A delay in clearing his title to the claim put him at a disadvantage in the speculation competition between the three original rivals. Walker later served two terms as mayor of Milwaukee.

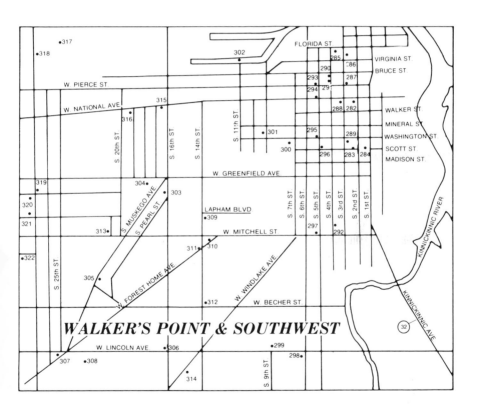

282. Frederick M. Bahr
Grocery Store
801-05 S. 2nd St. 1887

This is one of the most elaborate and picturesque commercial buildings of its size in the city. Built by a native of West Prussia, the structure is an excellent example of creative eclectic design. Segmental arches above the second floor windows serve only as hoods for the highly decorative lintels over the windows. Basically brick trimmed with stone, the building's real character comes from the cylindrical bartizan, with its oversized brackets, and the cupola over the entrance. Supported by two huge pilaster/brackets, this cupola sports the builder's name, the date of construction, triangular gables and an iron finial atop its ogee-mansard roof.

283. Scandanavian Evangelical
Lutheran Church
202 W. Scott St. 1882

In 1852 the city's Norwegians formed a congregation in a cobbler's shop. They later built a wooden church on this site and in 1882 replaced it with this large CCB structure. Architect Andrew Elleson set the cornerstone in an unusual location on the rock-faced limestone foundation. It faces southeast from the base of an angle buttress on the corner of the building. The brick walls are trimmed with buff sandstone and a deeply molded wooden cornice. The original chamfered frame doors are still intact, but the steeple was removed in 1923 when the building was converted into a candy factory. The "Chocolate House" was also responsible for the demise of the Gothic windows.

284. Allen-Bradley Company
1201 S. 2nd St. 1919 and later

In 1909 Milwaukee surgeon, Dr. Stanton Allen, provided the financial backing and encouragement to start the Bradley brothers (Harry and Lynde) in what would become one of the city's largest industries. The business began in a small office over a grocery store on Clinton St. and is now a million square-foot complex, one of the largest in Milwaukee. Major additions were made periodically until the famous clock tower was completed in 1963. It is the largest four-faced clock in the world, and the 15-foot 9-inch hands move over a 40-foot face. Each face, illuminated by fluorescent tubes, requires 34.6 kilowatts of power.

285. Double Townhouse
329-331 W. Florida St.   **c. 1869**

The original occupant and builder of this structure seems to have been Herman Benson, who was an insurance agent here. It is a very well proportioned example of the townhouse variation of the Victorian Italianate style. Basically a 3-bay composition, the center, or entrance, pavilion projects and becomes the focal point with its segmentally arched cornice and the double doors. Over the entrance is a porch canopy supported by three brackets. The original front doors, with their heavily molded panels, reflect the character of the similar roof cornice. Set eleven steps above an English basement, the two-story house looks like three.

286. Abel Decker Residences
408-410 S. 3rd St.   **c.1857**

Although grocer, Abel Decker was a resident on this street as early as 1851, he did not own this lot until 1855. Built with CCB, these two houses, now painted, have chimneys in the side walls which extend above the roofline. This feature, characteristic of the Federal style, is mixed with wide cornice boards and wooden brackets which lean to the Italianate. The dressed stone window lintels on the second floor front, have raised margins and are a better than average refinement. Both porches have been modified.

287. Jasper Humphrey and James Sheriffs Residences
634 and 640 S. 3rd St.   **c.1868**

Number 634 was the residence of Jasper Humphrey and his son-in-law, Henry W. Thompson. A New Yorker, Humphrey came here as a sailor and marine inspector and died in this residence, in 1892, as "one of the city's best-known lake men." A fine example of early Italianate design, this painted CCB house is set on a random rubble limestone foundation and has wooden trim. The handsomely proportioned facade is topped with a cupola. James Sheriffs, proprieter of the Vulcan Foundry, located in this area, built the house at 640 about the same time. It, too, has painted brick walls, the original wooden cornice, and a similar cupola on the roof.

HABS NR WRL

288. Durr, Schneider, Hilbert Residences
821, 813, 803 S. 3rd St.
1875, 1870, 1870

These houses, once in the center of southside society, afford a rare opportunity to compare three variations of the Victorian Italianate style side-by-side. Emil Durr's house (821) was built last and shows a tendency toward more ornament (much has been removed or covered by asphalt siding). It is a frame structure with a hip roof. Liquor wholesaler Emil Schneider's house (813) is built with CCB and has the original carved wooden brackets supporting the eaves, but lacks its front porch. Heliodore Hilbert's house (803), like Schneider's, is cream brick and has semicircular arched windows, but it has gable ends with broken pediments. Hilbert was a civil engineer, but served terms as president of the Common Council and city treasurer. Durr, who was also active in civic affairs, was a prominent lumber dealer.

289. Wisconsin Telephone Company Branch Exchange
239 W. Washington St.   1899

This handsome Classical building was the first branch exchange of the Wisconsin Telephone Co.. Designed by architect H. J. Esser, it is built of light tan pressed brick on a limestone foundation. The door canopy and cornice are made of sheet metal. In 1945 the Catholic Archdiocese of Milwaukee owned the building and commissioned architects Brust & Brust to convert it into a church for use as a Mexican mission.

290. Holy Trinity Roman Catholic Church
605 S. 4th St.   1849-50

Built for the German-speaking Catholics on the southside, this CCB church was designed by the same Milwaukee architect (Victor Schulte) who drew the plans for St. Mary's (see #73) and St. John's Cathedral (see #63). The octagonal steeple, which is set on two graduated octagonal drums, was added in 1862 by architect Leonard A. Schmidtner. One of the city's oldest churches, it is, like the other two by Schulte, an example of the Zopfstil style (the German equivalent of the American Federal style). The unusual character of the exterior comes from the use of raised brick framing or panelling of the surfaces in a manner similar to the structural exoskeletons in today's modern architecture. Within these panels and including the steeple, are repeated the dominant semicircular arches of which there are at least 7 sizes.

291. Holy Trinity School
621 S. 4th St. 1867

The oldest school building in Milwaukee, this structure is owned by the Holy Trinity parish (see #290) and was erected to replace a residence, which served as a school, on the same property. It is an excellent and unspoiled example of Victorian Italianate design and is built of CCB on a coursed limestone rubble foundation. The original porch, with its carved brackets, is still intact; and the cut limestone trim includes an unusually shaped stone between the second and third floors with raised borders and letters spelling, "Holy Trinity School." The corners of the two end pavilions begin with brick imitation quoins on the first level and turn to flat pilasters from there to the wooden cornice.

292. Public Natatorium
1646 S. 4th St. 1895

The original stated purpose of Milwaukee's natatoria was "to encourage healthful swimming and cleanliness facilities for those not fortunate to have their own baths." The first structure was built on Prairie St. near 7th and was such a success that bonds were issued in 1893 to build this one. Designed by Milwaukee architect, Eugene Liebert, the striking Classical Revival facade is built with pressed red brick on a limestone foundation and trimmed with red terra-cotta and sheet metal. The interior is designed with a balcony, supported by cast iron columns, which surrounds the central pool. A central skylight, now modified, once supplied illumination. Originally the pool was a steel tank, and it had to be drained once a week before the water was filtered. This is now the oldest survivor of Milwaukee's five natatoria.

293. Charles Harms Grocery Store
639 S. 5th St. 1887

When Mr. Harms came to Milwaukee, from Onondaga County, New York, in 1857, he worked as a cooper. By 1870 he had established the grocery and dry goods business here and later erected this 2-story CCB building which provided his business space as well as an upstairs apartment. Set on a limestone foundation, the brickwork is laid in a decorative manner, and the whole is trimmed with limestone and sheet metal. Three pairs of very tall sheet metal brackets and the owner's name and date appear at the ornamental roofline.

MILWAUKEE / WALKER'S POINT and SOUTHWEST

159

294. Tivoli Palm Garden
729 S. 5th St.   **1901**

Charles Kirchhoff, whose firm had designed the nationally famous Schlitz Palm Garden on Third Street, downtown, was also the architect of this large building. The two-story structure was originally three store fronts on National Avenue, with the Palm Garden at the rear or north end of the complex. Built with pressed tan brick and trimmed in carved Bedford limestone, the entrance is decorated with the traditional trademark of Schlitz saloons (the globe with belt buckle), executed in sheet metal. Originally the tile-roofed barroom was embellished with carving and stained glass. There was a cafe upstairs, and bowling alleys and a barbershop in the basement.

295. Commercial Building
1037 S. 5th St.   **1887**

This CCB corner building is, with the exception of the remodeled 5th St. front, a well-preserved and unusual example of the eclectic extremes to which late nineteenth century architects resorted. Six-foot-high paired brackets support the cornice, and a frame bay window projects from the south wall; but the most unique feature of the building is the raised corner which, like a bartizan, wraps around two sides. Made of sheet metal, it consists of even taller brackets, two triangular pediments, and a diagonal plaque where it is likely that the original name of the owner was spelled out.

HABS

296. St. Stephen's Evangelical Lutheran Church
1136 S. 5th St.   **1901**

Architects Uehling & Griswold were charged with the responsibility of completely rebuilding and making additions to an older church, built in 1854. According to the building permit, the old tower remained and was covered with face brick. The cornerstone, at the base of the southwest corner buttress, carries both dates — 1854 and 1901. Basically red pressed brick, laid with colored mortar, the structure is trimmed with cut limestone and sheet metal. An unusual feature of this heavy Gothic design is the huge poppyhead finial over the south transept window. A fleché, sheathed in sheet metal, rises over the crossing of nave and transept.

297. St. Stanislaus Roman Catholic Church
1681 S. 5th St. 1872-73

St. Stanislaus is the third Polish parish in the United States and it also founded the nation's first Polish elementary school. This distinguished building, designed by Leonard Schmidtner, resembles the German Renaissance style and is basically CCB trimmed with limestone. The mother church of the Polish community, it was extensively remodelled in 1962. The original sheet copper domes were replaced with welded aluminum over a steel frame which was then covered with 23-karat gold leaf. Slab glass replaces the original stained glass. The old entrances were rebuilt with cut and carved limestone.

HABS NR WRL

298. St. Josaphat Basilica
601 W. Lincoln Ave. 1897-1901

Milwaukee's most impressive and richly decorated church, this neo-Renaissance structure is also said to have the sixth largest dome in the world. Father Wilhelm Grutza, St. Josaphat's pastor, engaged architect Erhard Brielmaier to prepare drawings. As these plans were being made, Father Grutza became aware of and ultimately purchased the salvage material from the old Chicago Post Office which was then being razed. For $20,000 he bought a 500-car trainload of limestone blocks, marble, granite columns and woodwork. Brielmaier made new drawings, rearranging these materials into a new cruciform design. In 1929 it was designated a basilica by Pope Pius XI, the third church to be so honored in the United States.

299. General Thaddeus Kosciuszko Monument
W. Lincoln Ave. near S. 9th St. 1904

This bronze equestrian statue was erected to honor the Polish general of the American Revolution. Created by Florentine sculptor, Gaetano Tertanove, it was dedicated, according to the inscription on the stone monolith, "To the hero of both hemispheres by the Poles of Milwaukee." Once located at the Becher Street entrance of Kosciuszko Park, it was later moved to its present location. The monument was once flanked by two large cannons.

HABS NR WRL

300. St. Patrick's Roman Catholic Church
1105 S. 7th St.   **1893-94**

Organized in 1876, as an outgrowth of St. Gall's parish, this church was intended to serve the first English-speaking congregation on the south side. It was designed, in Gothic style, by Chicago architect, James J. Egan. Made of CCB and set on a rock-faced limestone foundation, this creative variation on the style has a square tower that turns into an open belfry with tracery and then into a chamfered square which becomes a pyramidal spire. A row of glazed dormers on the roof takes the place of the traditional clerestory. The stained glass windows come from the Tyrolean Art Glass Company in Germany. An earlier (1870's) CCB Italianate school is adjacent to the church on the south.

301. Walker Square
W. Washington, S. 9th.,
W. Mineral, and S. 10th Sts.   **1837**

Prior to 1889, Milwaukee had no park board; and its green public spaces consisted of numerous small patches, squares and triangles around the city, most of which had been donated by community-spirited citizens. One of the earliest of these parks, which together totalled only 59 acres, was Walker Square. A gift from Colonel George H. Walker, founder of Walker's Point, this little parcel contains two and one-tenth acres.

302. S. Eleventh St. Swing Bridge
S. 11th St. and Burnham Canal   **1886**

Of the 223 bridges maintained by the city of Milwaukee, only one is a swing bridge. They were at one time very popular here but in 1896 the whaleback steamer, *Christopher Columbus*, collided with the Buffalo St. swing bridge and caused a reaction which led to the planned obsolescence of all those remaining. When the Pleasant Street Bridge was destroyed in 1972, this became not only the last of its type, but the oldest of the city's bridges. By an interesting coincidence this aged structure carries one of the heaviest loads in the city. It is continuously pounded by 25-30-ton truckloads of concrete and scrap metal traveling to and from the "mainland" and the island between the Burnham slip and the south Menomonee Canal.

303. Richard D. Whitehead
Horse Watering Trough
S. 16th, S. Pearl, W. Bow Sts. 1910

This is one of the last remaining horse troughs in the state. They were once plentiful and ranged in size from a quarter-sphere of cast iron attached to a building to huge fountain pools such as the Henry Bergh Monument, which at one time stood in City Hall Square (see #1). According to the inscription on the back this was "erected by R. D. Whitehead, Supt. of the Badger State Humane Society in remembrance of my faithful friends. Horse: George — Dogs: Dandy, Pet, Punch, Judy & Shorty — Cats: Frank & Henry — Birds: Browney & Dick." Above the granite trough is a bronze bas relief of George and Dandy.

304. Bow Street Swamp
Vicinity of Bow St. and
S. Muskego Ave.

South Muskego Ave. once crossed a swamp near Bow Street. It was first paved in 1876, but the roadway continued to settle for years, and the 11th ward had to spend hundreds of dollars to keep it above water. The large amount of landfill continued until the whole marshy area was dry, and it was then developed. But, since most of the houses in the area were built before the ground was firm, they began to sink. Today dozens of structures in the Muskego, Pearl Union and Bow St. vicinity are leaning to an astonishing degree. The three pictured here are 1424 to 1430 Union St., N.E. corner Bow St.

305. Lorenz Paetzold Residence
1942 S. Muskego Ave. 1878

One of the city's rarest one-of-a-kind oddities, the frame house is completely encapsulated in slate shingles. Considered unusual even in Victorian times, today it may be the only one like it in the Midwest. Lorenz Paetzold was a carpenter and slater who had done work on such prominent homes as the Alexander Mitchell residence (see #178). No one knows why he built his own house with this unusual material, but it might have been to display his specialized skill. There are five different patterns of slate used for siding, window and corner trim. Even the chimneys were once covered with slate.

306. Carl Kunckell Residence
2221 S. 16th St.   c. 1857

Built by a pioneer soda-water manufacturer, Carl Kunckell, this fine Italianate residence is an uncommon Milwaukee example with a free-standing tower. While most Italianates are low or rambling, this variation, with its CCB tower standing a full story above the roof line, is rare. Kunckell's estate (6 acres) has now been whittled down to a small city lot, supported on all sides by a retaining wall necessitated by the later grading of the original hill on which the mansion was built. The present owner, only the second in the building's history, has inherited a rare, unspoiled piece of history with the original hardware and lighting fixtures.

307. Layton House Hotel
2504 W. Forest Home Ave.   1849

Built in the year of the California gold rush, this three-story CCB building is Milwaukee's oldest remaining hotel. It was designed by architect John Rugee and cost $4,000. John Layton, an important early meat packer and one-time partner of John Plankinton, wisely predicted the need for this establishment. Its location on the Janesville Plank Road (now Forest Home Ave.) insured that hundreds of farmers carrying potatoes and grain to the Milwaukee market would welcome the opportunity to make this a halfway house or stopover. Before the western wing was taken off and the addition was made on the front, it had a long wooden verandah.

HABS

308. Forest Home Cemetery Chapel
2405 W. Forest Home Ave.   1890-92

Forest Home, founded in 1849, is one of Milwaukee's most beautiful and historic cemeteries. Among the many improvements built there over the years, the chapel/crematorium stands out as a gem. It was designed by architects Ferry & Clas and is roughly Gothic in style. Red sandstone, laid random ashlar, is the principal material, and the porte cochere at the entrance is framed with wooden Gothic construction. Laid out like a cruciform church, the floor plan includes the traditional longitudinal nave intersected by a transept. What distinguishes this variation is that the transept on both sides is constructed of a light metal framework filled with leaded glass. Like a greenhouse, it is filled with living plants and provides a beautiful backdrop for the two arcades of the nave.

309. South Division High School
1321 W. Lapham Blvd.   1898-99

The city's oldest public high school building, South Division was designed by Milwaukee architect, Didrik C. Ottesen. The huge block-long structure has been expanded three times, in 1911, 1916 and 1951. The ground and first floors are decorated with banded rustication and limestone string courses. The school's focal point is a four-story square tower with a sheet copper dome supported on a polygonal drum.

HABS

310. St. Jacobi Evangelical Lutheran Church
1321 W. Mitchell St.   1905-06

St. Jacobi Church has dominated the west end of the Mitchell Street shopping district since 1905. At the important three-street intersection (S. 13th St., W. Mitchell St., and Forest Home Ave.) this imposing edifice has been the western anchor of a district which begins with St. Stanislaus (see #297) on the east. Organized in 1873 by former parishoners from St. Peter's (then located on 3rd Ave. and Scott St.), the parish engaged Milwaukee architect Otto C. Uehling to draw plans for this structure. The red brick Gothic building has been for sale since 1969. Both an apartment building and a national hamburger chain have threatened this landmark's existence, but it is still temporarily serving the original parish.

311. Milwaukee Public Library, Forest Home Branch
1432 W. Forest Home Ave.   1966

Milwaukee architects Von Grossman, Burroughs, and Van Lanen drew the plans for this distinguished and well proportioned modern structure. Large concrete panels and I-beams of weathering steel are composed in what has been called "an alive and creative solution to small scale public architecture." This project was the recipient of an honor award from the Wisconsin Chapter of the American Institute of Architects in 1967.

312. St. Hyacinth Roman Catholic Church
W. Becher St., corner S. 14th St.
1882-83

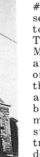

By 1882, the St. Stanilaus parish (see #297) had become so large that a group separated and St. Hyacinth was created to serve the families west of 11th St. This handsome church was designed by Milwaukee architect Henry Messmer and is built with walls of solid CCB set on a limestone foundation. By dividing the walls into bays with brick pilasters and framing windows with stone and brick pedimented casings, a very richly modelled effect was achieved. Buff sandstone was used for carved details and trim on this Italian Renaissance-inspired design.

313. St. Vincent de Paul Catholic Church
W. Mitchell St., N.W. corner of S. 21st St.
1900

By 1888 St. Hyacinth's parish (see #312) had outgrown its church, and a group left to form St. Vincent's. The first building on this corner was a large brick combination school and church. In 1900 they engaged Bernard Kolpacki, the Polish architect who seems to have been the favorite on the south side. This 182-foot-tall structure is among his most spectacular designs and is reminiscent of the German Renaissance. Pressed light tan brick is set on a rock-faced limestone foundation, and trim is executed in sheet metal and cut limestone. The roof, gutters and downspouts, and the two domes are made of sheet copper. A fleché is set over the crossing of the nave and transept.

314. St. Cyril & Methodius Catholic Church
Intersection W. Hayes Ave., W. Windlake Ave.& S. 15th St.
1893

This Victorian Gothic church was designed by the south side's favorite architect, Bernard Kolpacki. The Polish congregation was organized in 1893 by Fr. J.F. Szukalski, who had just come here from St. Michael's parish in Beaver Dam. The parishioners were drawn mostly from St. Hyacinth (see #312) and St. Josaphat (see #298). The cornerstone is actually a part of the northwestern corner buttress, and the three principal arches have greatly exaggerated keystones. The cream-colored brick is trimmed with orange terra-cotta and sheet copper detailings.

315. Badger Mutual Fire Insurance Company
1635 W. National Ave.   1937

One of Milwaukee's finest, unspoiled examples of the "moderne" style of the 1930's, this smooth-finish limestone building is still occupied by the original owners. Designed by Milwaukee architect Herbert W. Tullgren, the entrance mantel is of special interest. Over the doors are three cast metal grilles which match the design of the geometric leaded glass windows in steel casements. A stone shield, with a badger and the date of the organization (1887), is flanked by carved leaf ornament at the top of the grilles. The company's name appears in low-relief stone letters in a style which was popular at that time.

316. Pythian Castle Lodge Building
1925 W. National Ave.   1927

The fraternal organization, the Knights of Pythias, commissioned Milwaukee architect Richard E. Oberst to design this commodious facility. Founded in 1864 in Washington, D.C., the Knights organized a lodge here in 1870. This building was erected with light tan brick and cut and carved limestone trim. It is a well detailed structure, with a fine complement of materials. The 3-story entrance pavilion is embellished with two tiers of spiral-twist columns and carved stone ornament. A wrought iron balcony, the tile roof and two sheet copper oriel windows with leaded glass complete the list of quality materials.

317. Jacque Vieau Cabin Site
Mitchell Park, 550 S. Layton Blvd.
1795

The first house in Milwaukee was built on this site by Jacque Vieau. He established a fur trading center here for the Northwest Fur Co. and selected this spot because it was at the intersection of the Green Bay-Chicago Trail and another trail which led to Mukwonago. In 1925 this bronze tablet was affixed to a boulder and dedicated by descendants of Vieau and Solomon Juneau under the auspices of the Old Settlers Club of Milwaukee County. For years a replica of Vieau's cabin stood nearby, but it has since deteriorated and been removed. The marker is located in the northeastern quarter of the park.

318. Mitchell Park Horticultural Conservatory
550 S. Layton Blvd. 1959-67

Mitchell Park, one of the earliest established by the park commission, has had a plant conservatory since 1898. Six years later the old building, which resembled a giant greenhouse, was complemented with a sunken garden to the south. In 1955 the first structure was razed to make way for the three geodesic domes designed by Milwaukee architect, Donald L. Grieb. The basic construction consists of a precast concrete shell with an outer skin of aluminum and glass. The outside surface is held away from the substructure on metal supports. Each dome, measuring 87 feet high and 140 feet in diameter, houses a naturalistic display of plants, flowers and trees in different climatic conditions.

319. St. Lawrence Catholic Church
1434 S. Layton Blvd. 1905

This imposing Romanesque church was designed by Milwaukee architects, E. Brielmaier & Sons, and built by mason Sylvester Wabiszewski. The parish was organized in 1889. The structure is made of orange brick on a rock-faced limestone foundation and is trimmed with cut stone and sheet metal. A typically Romanesque semicircular apse finished the eastern end and a larger-than-life-sized statue stands on the roof in place of the fleché which, in Gothic churches, decorated the crossing of the nave and transept.

320. St. Joseph's Convent Chapel
1501 S. Layton Blvd. 1914-17

Built for the School Sisters of St. Francis, this is the finest of Milwaukee's Romanesque Revival churches. Architect Richard Philipp, of Brust & Philipp, toured Italy to gain a first hand knowledge of the historical forms before beginning this commission. Textured brown brick, laid in Flemish bond, is the principal material, with the first floor being dressed limestone. An octagonal dome over the crossing of the nave and transept and a pair of square towers with octagonal lanterns create a fine medieval Italian skyline. Brick corbels, inlaid colored tiles, and cut stone are used for ornamental trim. Inside, a rich use of various marbles with inlaid gold and colored mosaics completes this distinguished composition. The 127-foot by 210-foot structure was built by Paul Reisen's Sons, masons.

HABS

321. Sacred Heart Sanitarium
1545 S. Layton Blvd.   1893 and later
The School Sisters of St. Francis began this large three-story complex in 1893 and made the first major addition in 1911; the south wing was completed in 1929. An unusual, but picturesque, design, it has characteristics of Romanesque, French Renaissance, and Gothic styling. The five-story brick tower is decorated with a pyramidal roof, four pointed dormers, and a turret on each corner. Originally developed for hydrotherapy and possessing a spa-like atmosphere, the institution later became the first hospital in Wisconsin to be accredited for its program of physical rehabilitation. It is now called the Sacred Heart Rehabilitation Hospital.

322. Arthur L. Richards Residences
2714-34 W. Burnham St.   1915-16
This row of "cottages" was designed by Frank Lloyd Wright for the Milwaukee developer, Arthur L. Richards. In 1912 Wright worked with the same man on the Hotel Geneva at Lake Geneva, Wisconsin. The exterior construction on both projects was stucco, with trim executed in stained cypress boards. Built on a small (55' x 52') lot, the total area of one floor in each house is only 847 square feet, including the porches. Since the project was not personally supervised by Wright, the quality of workmanship and attention to detail, which is normally associated with his work, is missing.

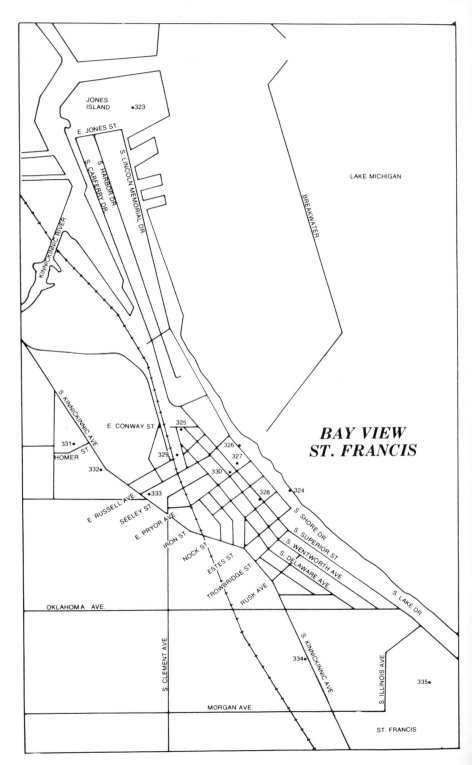

JONES ISLAND •323

E. JONES ST.

S. HARBOR DR.

S. CARFERRY DR.

S. LINCOLN MEMORIAL DR.

KINNICKINNIC RIVER

LAKE MICHIGAN

BREAKWATER

BAY VIEW ST. FRANCIS

S. KINNICKINNIC AVE.

E. CONWAY ST.

•325

331•

HOMER ST.

329

•326

•327

332•

•330

•328

•324

•333

E. RUSSELL AVE.

SEELEY ST.

E. PRYOR AVE.

IRON ST.

NOCK ST.

ESTES ST.

TROWBRIDGE ST.

RUSK AVE.

S. SHORE DR.

S. SUPERIOR ST.

S. WENTWORTH AVE.

S. DELAWARE AVE.

S. LAKE DR.

OKLAHOMA AVE.

S. CLEMENT AVE.

334•

S. KINNICKINNIC AVE.

S. ILLINOIS AVE.

335•

MORGAN AVE.

ST. FRANCIS

170

BAY VIEW/ST. FRANCIS

The old village of Bay View was made a part of the 17th ward of the city of Milwaukee in 1887. Before that it was an important industrial village in the township of Lake. Having been the location of the pioneer Milwaukee Iron Company, Bay View could claim the honor of being the foundation of Milwaukee industry. In addition to the mill were numerous humble workers' cottages, saloons, churches and a yacht club. St. Francis, to the south and on the lakefront, developed around the St. Francis of Sales Catholic Seminary (see #335).

323. Jones Island
The Milwaukee and Kinnickinnic Rivers at Lake Michigan

This modern international shipping port, with its boat slips, warehouses, railroad yard and petroleum tank farm was once a quiet fishing village. Named after James M. Jones, who established a shipyard there in 1854, the original property was a real island. In 1857 the first harbor entrance was abandoned, and a new "straight cut" was made nearly a mile to the north (the present harbor entrance). The old channel was eventually filled in, creating the peninsula shape which it is today. At one time the village consisted of a main street, "Mahnawauk," which ran north and south with numerous cross streets. There were 350 houses, taverns, a bakery, a general store, a post office and a population of 750. The last resident moved away in 1943.

324. South Shore Yacht Club
E. Nock St. at Lake Michigan   1913

Organized in the lakefront home of William Barr in 1913, the South Shore Yacht Club had as its first permanent home, an old three-masted schooner. Named the *"Lily E."*, it was one of the last working sailing vessels on Lake Michigan. It was built in 1869, and after retiring from the lumber and cordwood trade, was purchased by the club and sailed here, in 1915, from Sheboygan. After the boat was wrecked in a 1922 storm, the club set up quarters on a barge which, in turn, was broken up on the beach in a 1929 storm. Seven years later the present clubhouse was built. Early in its history the club merged with the Steel Mill Yacht Club, which had been organized in 1915 by the Illinois Steel Company for its employees.

171

325. Globe Tavern
2414 S. St. Clair St. c. 1895

Located across the street from the Bay View Rolling Mills, this tavern no doubt conducted a booming business with the hot and thirsty steel workers. It was built by the Schlitz Brewing Co. which, like all of the big Milwaukee breweries, owned and operated hundreds of saloons in the Midwest. Sheet metal globes, with the belt and buckle and the name "Schlitz", can still be found in Milwaukee (see #294) and Chicago. This specimen, however, perched on its octagonal bartizan, is an unusually large one, and while most are slightly domed on a wall, this is a full sphere.

326. Joseph A. Starkey Residence
2582 South Shore Dr. c.1878

While Bay View was essentially a working man's community, with many humble cottages built by the steel mill, there were a few finer houses occupied by the management. Joseph Starkey, superintendent of the North Chicago Rolling Mills' two blast furnaces, lived in this handsomely proportioned structure. A native of Yorkshire, England, Starkey came to Racine County, but then moved back East, where he worked at steel mills in Youngstown, Ohio, and Wheatland, Pennsylvania. He finally came to Chicago in 1872, where he took charge of two furnaces owned by the same company which ran the Bay View operation, and was subsequently transferred to this mill.

327. Warren Brinton Residence
2590 S. Superior St. 1871

Built for the superintendent of the Bay View Rolling Mills, this little frame house is said to have been designed by Warren Brinton and constructed by mechanics from the mill. It has no basement, and the front porch is a later addition. Mrs. Beulah Brinton raised funds for, and established, the first lending library in Bay View, a collection which later started the Llewellyn Branch of the Milwaukee Public Library. Mrs. Brinton taught English and homemaking skills to the wives of immigrant mill workers in much the manner of later social centers.

328. Welsh Congregational Church
2739 S. Superior St.   1873

Originally a branch of the Milwaukee Welsh Church, this congregation was founded in 1868. In the beginning there were only six families or about thirty members of the adult congregation. Services were held in their native tongue. They met in the village schoolhouse until 1873 when this humble church was built. Although the original entrance porch is still intact, a new all-aluminum extension was added on the east and a stained glass transom window over the old front doors was removed. The clapboard building is now occupied by the Christian Science Society.

329. Puddler's Hall
2463 S. St. Clair St.   1873

One of the many local taverns built to accommodate the thirsty steel workers at the old Milwaukee Iron Co. Just to the north of this building was one of the gates to the giant plant which once occupied 128 acres along the lakefront. This tavern also served as a union hall for the Sons of Vulcan, later the Amalgamated Association of Iron and Steel Workers. A frame building with mansard roof and dormers, it has been re-sided and remodelled extensively. The old factory later was called North Chicago Rolling Mills, and finally, in 1889, the Illinois Steel Company. The behemoth, with its blast furnaces and a forest of smokestacks, was finally acquired by the city in 1938 and torn down.

330. Artesian Well
1700 block E. Pryor Ave.

Of the many mineral springs and artesian wells which once served Milwaukee, only one is now listed and approved by the health department. The expanding urban population has increased pollution to the point where all others had to be capped and discontinued. This well is said to be so deep that it draws pure water from a great distance beyond the city. The health department checks the water every two months, and it is heavy in iron content. Decades ago it was just a pipe sticking out of the ground, but now a concrete structure provides an animal watering trough, a bubbler, and spigots for filling jugs. It flows under its own pressure 24 hours a day.

331. Joseph Williams Residence
606 E. Homer St. 1865

This may be the only house, still standing in Milwaukee, which was built and occupied by a man who originally claimed his land from the Indians. In the beginning Joseph Williams lived in a log cabin near the corner of Linus Street and Woodward Avenue. In 1865 he erected this 2-story CCB Italianate house at the highest spot on his 160-acre farm. The rear (west) wing may be much earlier, and in fact could be the oldest in the city. In 1926 the hill in front of the house was cut away, and construction was begun on the Avalon Theater and apartment building. The original front door now faces a brick wall.

332. St. Lucas Evangelical Lutheran Church
2605 S. Kinnickinnic Ave. 1888

This handsome Victorian Gothic church, the second built by the congregation, is made of CCB set on a rock-faced limestone foundation. The architect listed was H. Schnetzky and the trim is carried out in ornamental brickwork, wood and sheet metal. The buttressed tower is the most interesting feature in the design, and it stands 145 feet to the top of the steeple. An unusual architectural stained glass window surmounts the main entrance. As the tower rises above the roof, its corners are chamfered. Above the 4-faced clock are 4 gables which blend into the octagonal steeple. Three bells were installed in the tower in 1901.

333. Church of the Immaculate Conception
1023 E. Russell Ave. 1907-08

This neo-Classical church was founded by Irish employees of the Milwaukee Iron Company, which donated the land on which it stands. Architects Buemming & Dick designed the light tan pressed brick structure which was enlarged in 1959 by Brust & Brust. The building rests on a limestone foundation and is embellished with brick quoins, a sheet metal cornice, and an octagonal tower with a dome of sheet metal. The 1,000-seat addition moved the main entrance from the original Russell Ave. side to South Kinnickinnic Ave.

334. Russell Bennett Residence
3317 S. Kinnickinnic Ave.   1855

The last Gothic Revival residence in the city once commanded a beautiful view of a 160-acre farm. When Russell Bennett built this house, he was allowed to purchase the brick from a new brickyard which had been set up nearby for the construction of buildings on the St. Francis Seminary grounds. Much of the ornamental detail, so characteristic of the Gothic style, was taken off years ago (bargeboards, carved wooden finials, and Gothic fretwork porches). Bennett was one of the county's earliest pioneers.

NR WRL

335. Henni Hall-St. Francis
Catholic Seminary
3257 S. Lake Drive   1855-56

Victor Schulte, the architect of St. Mary's (see #73), St. John's Cathedral (see #63), and Holy Trinity (see #290), had so impressed Rev. John Martin Henni (bishop of Milwaukee) with these works that he was given the commission for the Seminary of St. Francis of Sales. It changed his life, and he moved to a farm in this area during the construction of the seminary. Bricks for the project were made on the spot by the brothers of St. Francis while the sisters cooked for all the workmen. A large five-story CCB Italianate structure, Henni Hall has wrought iron and sheet metal balconies, oak doors with carved lion heads, and a well proportioned octagonal dome with a sheet metal lantern. The beautiful grounds and incomparable view of Lake Michigan have been matched by the fine reputation and successful training of young men for the priesthood.

OAK CREEK/FRANKLIN/GREENFIELD

All three original townships were laid out in the usual square configuration, being six miles on a side and containing 36 six-mile-square sections. Both Franklin and Oak Creek have remained principally agricultural as they were in the beginning, and they contain the cities of South Milwaukee, Franklin and Oak Creek. Greenfield, however, has all but disappeared and is now subdivided into Hales Corners, Greendale (see #348), and West Allis; and part has gone to the city of Milwaukee.

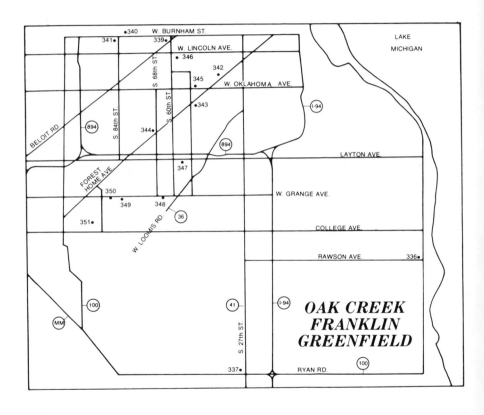

336. Edward Rawson Residence
1020 Rawson Ave.   1893

Built by one of the family after which Rawson Avenue was named, this eclectic Victorian house was designed by Racine architects, Davis & Wilson. Edward's family once owned 320 acres in this area, and his father first lived in a log house to the south of the present structure. Shortly after 1891, the Bucyrus Erie Company (then of Ohio) purchased a large segment of the original farm and began the construction of the huge plant which still stands across the street. Originally the 12-room house was painted a light red color, and a spacious verandah wrapped around the tower.

337. Painesville Cemetery and Chapel
2740 Ryan Road   1852

This historic chapel was built as a meeting place for a group of German Protestant "free thinkers" who came here to escape the suppression of freedom of thought and religion. Built by New York state carpenter, Henry Roethe, this frame Greek Revival structure originally stood on fieldstone pillars instead of a full foundation. The cemetery has been called the only exclusive burial place for free-thinkers in the world. In 1937 the historic chapel was about to be destroyed, when the Painesville Memorial Association was organized to save it and the building was restored.

338. Peter Juneau Residence
6014 W. Lincoln Ave.   c. 1845

Solomon and Peter Juneau were among the first permanent white settlers at the Indian crossroads which became Milwaukee. Solomon is recognized as the city's founder and its first mayor. Peter, his brother, once owned the 156 acres which was downtown's old third ward (see Old Third Ward chapter). He later moved to Greenfield Township, acquired a 200-acre farm and built this house. Twice moved, many times remodelled, and covered with new siding, the old farmhouse is difficult to imagine, but Juneau descendants assure us that it was once a pretty sight, surrounded by a garden and trees. In the basement hand-adzed oak joists and sills hint that this is the oldest building in West Allis.

339. Joseph Juneau Farmhouse
6014 W. Beloit Rd.   c. 1875

The third white child born in Milwaukee, Joseph Juneau was the son of Peter Juneau. He lived on his father's large farm for 70 years, first in the Lincoln Ave. house (see #338), then in a second house which was razed in the 1920's. He built this frame farmhouse about 1875 which was occupied by his descendants as late as the 1950's. His well kept farm has been whittled down to a small lot, while the house has lost its commodious verandah and its ornamental window casings and has been covered with new siding.

340. Honey Creek Settlement
N.E. corner S. 84th Street and
National Avenue

A steam sawmill built on this site in 1855 by Bigelow Case and Edwin Youmans was the first substantial industry on Honey Creek, which later became a part of West Allis. Lumber from the mill was used for the Mukwonago Plank Road and many other pioneer needs. The mill was discontinued in 1885 due to the lack of suitable timber. Three times each week a stage served the Honey Creek community, consisting of a blacksmith shop, schoolhouse, homesteads, sawmill and post office. Among the early settlers were Cornwall, Douville, Smith, Strong, Sheldon, Marsh, and Marlott.

341. 5th District Schoolhouse
8405 W. National Ave.   1887

This is the third school to stand on the same property, designated for educational purposes in 1840. The first building was of log construction. In 1849 an adjacent acre was added to become the cemetery, which is immediately behind the present structure. The materials in this Romanesque design are CCB on a rock-faced limestone foundation with buff sandstone belt courses and capitals. The bell cupola, added in a recent restoration, replaced the original which was missing for many years. Today the old school is the museum and office of the West Allis Historical Society.

342. Commerce and Arts Statue
W. Forest Home Avenue in
Jackson Park   1879

Originally this larger-than-life-size white pewter statue stood over the entrance to the old Chamber of Commerce building at 225 E. Michigan St. (see #23). It was taken down in 1909 and moved to Jackson (then Reynolds) Park, where it was placed on a red granite base by the South Division Civic Association. The statue, later called "Lady of the Woods", is surrounded by a wrought and cast iron fence. There was a similar statue called "Progress" on the Mitchell Building next door to the Chamber of Commerce. It was taken down in 1935 and was supposed to have been given to the park commission, but it disappeared and has not been seen since.

343. Deutsche Evangelische
Zions Kirche
W. Forest Home Ave. & S. 52nd St.
1858

Built by the first Evangelical congregation in Wisconsin, this humble CCB church replaced the original log structure which was erected in 1844. Called Zion Church, it became "The Centennial Historical Museum" of the Wisconsin Conference of the Evangelical United Brethren Church when the nearby Memorial Church was built in 1929. The simple 28 x 36-foot building is trimmed with flush wooden lintels and a wooden cornice. Next to the old church is the first Evangelical cemetery in Wisconsin.

344. St. John's Evangelical
Lutheran Church
6802 W. Forest Home Ave.   1896

The German parish, founded in 1846, erected this handsome CCB Gothic edifice in 1896. It rests on a rock-faced limestone foundation and is trimmed with buff sandstone, sheet metal, and wooden cornices. The tower is of special interest with its set-back buttresses and an octagonal belfry with a clock. Four triangular gablets enclose the spire. The front is flanked by two corner towers with pyramidal spires and, which like other areas in the design, have sunken panels trimmed at the top with a diagonal zig-zag brick cornice. The chancel is a half-octagon, and a small flèche decorates the roof ridge.

345. St. Sava Serbian Orthodox Cathedral
3201 S. 51st St.   **1956-58**

The only Serbian Byzantine church in this area, St. Sava's follows the traditional cruciform layout with a central dome and four subsidiary domes at the corners. Peter Camburas, of the Chicago architectural firm, Camburas & Theodore, drew the plans for this very handsome Fond du Lac limestone structure. The sheet metal domes rest on octagonal stone drums with semicircular arches and are surmounted by gold-leafed crosses. The wood joist/steel truss roof is cylindrical and sheathed in copper. Cut limestone trim, some of which is richly carved, accents the random ashlar walls.

WHM

346. John Lendrum Mitchell Residence
5301 W. Lincoln Ave.   **1884**

The son of banker and railroad magnate Alexander Mitchell (see #178), John L. Mitchell became a U.S. senator from Wisconsin. He was the father of General William (Billy) Mitchell, one of the great prophets of the air age. Originally the Mitchell estate consisted of 480 acres, a pond, and a private racetrack where the senator practiced his trotters. The 4-story brick mansion, designed by Edward Townsend Mix, was one of the largest Queen Anne buildings in the state with 14 bedrooms. It is highly picturesque with its ornamental wood and terra-cotta trim, shingle siding and dozens of stained glass windows. Part of the estate, once called "Meadowmere," is now the St. Joseph's Home for the Aged, and large additions have accordingly been made to the house.

347. John Finen/Bodamer Log Cabin
W. Layton Ave. near S. 56th St.
       c. 1834

Originally this log structure stood on the land which was homesteaded by John Finen in the vicinty of S. 76th St. and W. Coldspring Rd. As the years passed and it became the home of the Fred Bodamer family, various remodellings and additions concealed the first one-room house. Later an abandoned schoolhouse was attached to the rear, one and a half stories were added on top, porches were built on three sides, and the whole assemblage was covered with siding. In 1965, the real estate firm which owned the house was about to have it burned by the local fire department for a training exercise. The newly chartered Greenfield Historical Society moved quickly and, with volunteer labor and donations, disassembled the house and saved the original logs. It was restored and dedicated as a museum in 1969.

348. Village of Greendale
Loomis Rd. & W. Grange Ave. 1936-38
"A town designed for healthy living and industry; of a size that makes possible a full measure of social life, but not larger; surrounded by a rural belt; the whole of the land being in public ownership or held in trust for the community." This was written by Ebenezer Howard (1850-1928), the English inventor of the "Garden City" concept. In 1936, the Resettlement Administration conceived this $7,000,000 project as a model for future private development. As with similar areas in Cincinnati and Washington, this provided "work for idle hands" and a needed housing development for middle-income families. Seven-hundred-fifty living units were created, mostly of painted concrete block, along with schools, industry, and shopping facilities. The pictured village hall, a brick building, faces into central Broad Street from Northway.

349. Jeremiah Curtin Residence
8685 W. Grange Ave.   c. 1840
Curtin came to Milwaukee with his parents in 1837 and settled on a farm. This house, probably the only example of an Irish immigrant cottage in the state, is built with fieldstone walls 18 inches thick. Jeremiah was graduated from Harvard College in 1863 and became an expert linguist, translator, ethnologist and diplomat. The master of approximately 70 languages, he traveled the world speaking in native tongues and was appointed to the American legation in St. Petersburg, Russia, by Abraham Lincoln in 1864. He translated Henry Sienkiewicz's novel "Quo Vadis" from Polish into English and worked for the Bureau of Ethnology of the Smithsonian Institute.

HABS NR WRL WHM

350. Werner Trimborn farm and Lime Kilns
8881W. Grange Ave.   c.1842-1870

Once the city's dominant supplier of lime, the Trimborn facility once covered 530 acres and employed up to 40 men to haul limestone to the 6 kilns and take away the finished product. There were bunkhouses for the workers, horse barns, a granary, stables for cattle, pigs and fowl, and a fruit house. Remains of the historic kilns can be seen on both sides of Grange Ave. The CCB dwelling occupied by Trimborn is pictured. Among the other remaining buildings is a very important stone barn which has a roof constructed with hand hewn oak timbers. Remains of two limestone quarries are on the north side of the road.

351. Whitnall Park
Root River between W. Grange Ave. and W. Rawson Ave.

The largest park in Milwaukee County was named after Charles B. Whitnall who is commonly called the "father of the Milwaukee county parkway system." Whitnall, a soft-spoken visionary who was once secretary of the City Land Commission and a 40-year member of the County Park Board, envisioned this park as one piece of a vast network of public wilderness. Largely through his efforts miles of potentially threatened farmland were acquired for the city and converted into Milwaukee's highly renowned park system. Whitnall Park is a 618-acre tract of native woods, rolling countryside and streams which has been preserved with much•of its originality. In addition to a bog, a lake, a prairie, and numerous wooded areas, there is a formal botanical garden named after Alfred L. Boerner, the landscape architect responsible for the layout of many county parks. When Whitnall died in 1949, his ashes were scattered in a favorite area in the woods here.

Opposite: Thomas Irwin farmhouse Page 188 No. 363

OZAUKEE
COUNTY

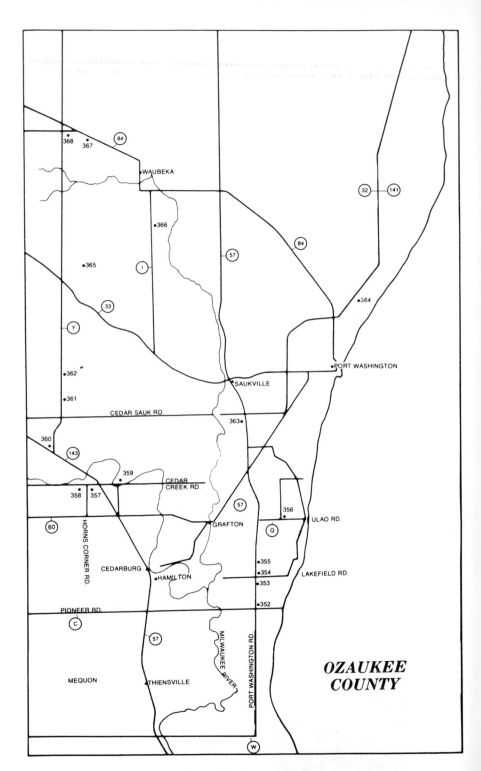

368 367

84

WAUBEKA

32 141

366

57

84

365

I

364

33

Y

PORT WASHINGTON

362

361

SAUKVILLE

CEDAR SAUK RD.

363

360

143

359

CEDAR
CREEK RD.

358 357

57

356

60

HORNS CORNER RD.

GRAFTON

ULAO RD.

Q

355

CEDARBURG

HAMILTON

354

LAKEFIELD RD.

353

PIONEER RD.

352

C

57

MEQUON

THIENSVILLE

MILWAUKEE RIVER

PORT WASHINGTON RD.

**OZAUKEE
COUNTY**

W

OZAUKEE COUNTY

Mostly agricultural contryside, Ozaukee County has prominent banks of clay along the Lake Michigan shoreline which are often 75-80 feet high. It was once a part of Washington County, and the county seat was located in Hamburg (later named Grafton). In 1853 the old county split and Ozaukee was formed, with Port Washington becoming the new county seat. By 1870 the population was seven-eighths German by birth or descent. The Milwaukee River and Cedar Creek provided excellent water power, and at least six substantial industrial settlements grew up on their banks. The first town to be founded was "Wisconsin City", which later became known as Port Washington.

352. Louis Hovener Farmhouse
308 N. Port Washington Rd.   1890

This substantial stone house was built two decades later than its style and construction would indicate. Louis Hovener had a quarter section farm in 1873, but 20 years later his property had grown to 233 acres. The 2½-story house once had a flat roof, but a hip roof was built over it in 1939. The neatly coursed limestone masonry is finished with quoins and lintels that are bush-hammered with chiseled margins.

353. Johann Friedrich Hennings Farmhouse
1143 Lakefield Rd.   1872

This farm has been occupied by the same family since 1842. It was in that year that 4-year-old J.F. Hennings came here with his parents from Germany. The attractive 2-story fieldstone structure was built by a Mr. Burhob and it has dressed quoins. Among its numerous fine details are the segmental-arched window lintels, the ornamental wooden cornice, and one of the most beautiful porches to be found on a farmhouse anywhere. Scroll-cut ornament of this type is usually seen only on fancy city houses.

354. St. John's Evangelical Lutheran Church
1142 Lakefield Rd.   1902

This congregation, founded in 1866, first met in a tavern and dance hall which once stood on the site of the house next door east. The pastor lived on the first floor and the upstairs became the church. This humble, frame, Gothic building with a broach spire was built, in 1902, for $3,000. It was abandoned about 10 years ago and now serves as a toy factory.

355. E. Schnabel Farmhouse
628 N. Port Washington Rd.   1875

This is one of the most finely finished and detailed of all the stone houses in Ozaukee County. Under the front gable peak is an exceptional date stone with a five-piece frame which matches the roof angle. The inscription, "E. Schnabel 1875," is recessed in a panel which is surrounded by a dentilled molding and has a flower ornament. The fieldstone walls are embellished with bush-hammered quoins that have chiselled margins and chamfered edges.

356. Luther Guiteau Residence
782 Ulao Rd. (Hwy. Q)   c.1850

The man who assassinated President J.A. Garfield spent his boyhood in this house. His father, Luther Guiteau, was one of the earliest settlers in this area which became known as Port Ulao. The son, Charles, described as "nervous and high-strung," later became a lawyer in Chicago. On July 2, 1881, he shot the President in a Wahington, D.C., railway station. After a sensational trial he was hanged in June of 1882.

357. W.H. Seegers Farmhouse
1588 Horns Corners Road   c.1868

Once the focal point of an 80-acre farm, this fine stone residence has a number of notable details. Its fieldstone walls are trimmed with dressed quoins and five-piece stone segmental arches over the windows. Although the fieldstones appear to have been selected at random, with no uniformity of size or color, a unifying effect was created by inscribing horizontal course joints in the mortar which conform to the spacing of the quoins.

358. Christian Poggenburg Farmhouse
1685 Horns Corners Road   c.1855

This beautifully preserved Greek Revival farmhouse was owned by the original family for over a century. The land, which eventually grew into 101 acres, was purchased in 1848, and a 2-story log house was built. The present structure was begun in the 1850's by Christian Poggenburg, and the north kitchen wing was added later by his son, Fred. The Greek Revival dwelling is made of fieldstone with dressed uoins and has a Victorian porch.

359. Red Bridge
Covered Bridge Road
1½ mi. N. of Hwys. 60/143   **1876**

This is the last surviving covered bridge in Wisconsin. At one time there were more than 40 throughout the state, but when the Boscobel bridge was razed in 1937, only this one remained. It is a lattice truss construction made of pine logs cut and milled at Baraboo. The 3x10-inch planks are overlaid and secured with two-inch hardwood pins, and the roadbed is floored with 3-inch planks. The center support pier was added in 1927. The bridge was retired in 1962.

HABS NR-WHM

360. Deckers Corners Tavern
2090 Highway 143   **c.1873**

The triangle bounded by Pleasant Valley Road, Granville Road (Highway Y), and Highway 143 was a logical location for this building which, since it was erected, has always been a tavern. The two-story structure is made of fieldstone with inscribed joints and tooled quoins. The stucco was added in later years. There is a one-story fieldstone wing on the rear and a 2-story frame addition made about 1910.

361. Martin Wollner Farmhouse
2690 Highway Y   **1862**

This was the homestead of one of four Wollner brothers who settled around this intersection. The well-constructed house is built with roughly squared fieldstones laid with inscribed mortar joints and dressed quoins. The sills are neatly finished with chiselled margins. A two-story frame wing was added by the original family around 1900. On the barn is a well-crafted cornerstone reading, "M. Wollner, 1871."

362. Frank Bach Residence
and Cheese Factory
3018 Highway Y   **c.1865**

Part of this house, which was built in two sections, was used as a cheese factory. No one remembers which was built first, but the 2-story front block is constructed of fieldstone with roughly squared fieldstone quoins. The rear block, which is set at 90 degrees, is of similar masonry but has 2½-stories and the additional refinement of a four course cornice of orange brick laid in a decorative manner.

363. Thomas Irwin Farmhouse
1235 Sauk Road c.1870

This is a superb, unspoiled example of an eclectic Victorian farmhouse. Once set on a 148-acre farm, the frame, clapboard structure has finer-than-average detailing and is still in almost original condition. The broad front porch, with its beautifully proportioned scroll-cut ornament, is the highlight of the house. Dentil moldings decorate the main gable and the little circular attic windows.

364. Dundlinger Farmhouse
Highway LL, 1½ mi. N. of 84 c.1868

This is one of the rare few fieldstone farmhouses to have windows with semicircular arches. Although the stones selected are of random size and color, they are laid with more than usual attention to horizontal courses. The window openings are finished with CCB frames and sills. A long porch once extended across the full length of the south wing. There is a vaulted fruit cellar under the kitchen.

365. Riveredge Nature Center
Highway Y between
Hawthorne Dr. and Highway 33

This plant and wildlife sanctuary, along the Milwaukee River, is owned and operated by the privately funded Riveredge Nature Center, Inc. There are 250 acres of fields, streams, wetlands, deciduous forest and river frontage accessible by self-guiding nature trails. These are designed especially for the handicapped and are paved with hard surface or wood chips.

366. Pioneer Village
Highway I just N. of 33

Located in Hawthorne Hills County Park, overlooking the Milwaukee River Valley, this hilltop site contains over a dozen historic buildings moved to this location and restored. The Village is operated by the Ozaukee County Historical Society and includes houses, farm buildings, and shops dating from the pre-Civil War period. Most of the structures are made of logs or timbermasonry construction (fachwerk).

367. Louis Glunz Dance Hall
W4777 Highway 84   **1918**

This barracks-like structure was once used to house German prisoners during World War II, but it was originally built as a dance hall by a Chicago entrepreneur. This building, and the one next door, were at one time a restaurant, bar, hotel, and grocery complex, but after nine years they were abandoned and lay vacant until war prisoners were housed here. By day the Germans were bussed to a canning factory in Fredonia to work. Now the complex is the New Tribes Institute Missionary Training Center.

368. Herman F. Beger Farmhouse
W5011 Highway 84   **1871**

In 1846 five-year-old Herman Beger came from Saxony, Germany, with his parents, and settled in the township of Fredonia. Their original 140-acre homestead is still owned by the family. This handsome and stately fieldstone house has inscribed mortar joints and is trimmed with point-dressed and chiselled quoins. Door and window lintels are finely dressed with raised margins. The hog and chicken barn is equally well constructed.

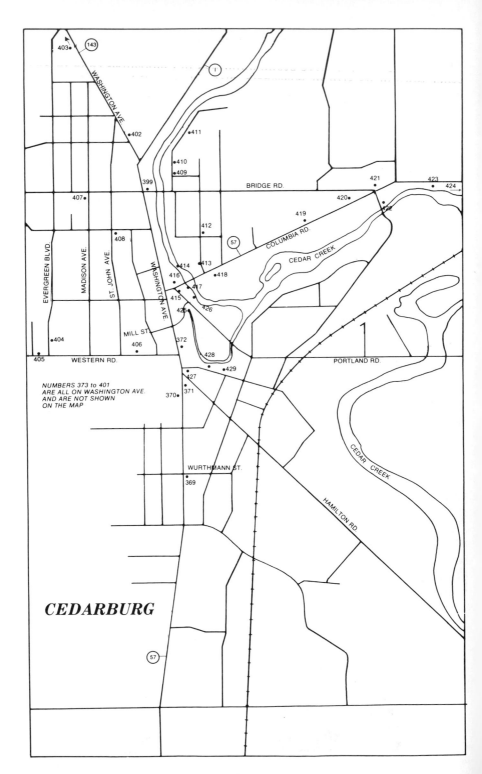

CEDARBURG

NUMBERS 373 to 401
ARE ALL ON WASHINGTON AVE.
AND ARE NOT SHOWN
ON THE MAP

CEDARBURG

There are, perhaps, more stone buildings in Cedarburg than in any other town of its size in Wisconsin. Not only was this area fortunate to have a virtually unlimited supply of limestone in its local quarries, but it also had the skilled German masons to take advantage of the material. Another natural resource, Cedar Creek, was actually responsible for the location of a settlement here. It provided a beautiful natural setting and generated so much water power that, by the turn of the century, five dams had been built in the vicinity, and each supplied a mill or factory with its energy. The predominantly German community sported a brewery, a number of mineral spring resorts and offered good fishing and boating. An unusually large percentage of the early nineteenth century residences, commerical buildings, factories and churches still survive here in good condition.

369. Erhardt G. Wurthmann Residence
W61 N358 Washington Ave. 1866
One of Cedarburg's most beautiful Victorian houses, this was the home of a German-born painter and decorator. He came to America as a young boy and was apprenticed under his uncle, who was a master painter in this vicinity. Erhardt eventually had a store downtown (see # 386) and 14.33 acres on which this house stands. A painting of three cherubs on canvas, thought to be his work, decorates the front porch ceiling.

370. John Schuette Sr. Residence
W61 N439 Washington Ave. c.1855
One of the most unusual houses in Cedarburg, this humble structure is set on what was once a 22-acre tract at an odd angle to the street. The saltbox appearance of the end walls came later when a lean-to addition was made on the rear. The greatest mystery about this house is why a limestone rubble building has a brick front wall. It may have been added when the Victorian porch was erected.

371. St. Francis Borgia Roman Catholic Church
Hamilton Rd. & Washington Ave. 1870
Like St. Mary's in Port Washington (see #465), this handsome limestone church dominates the town. It is set on an important intersection, at a high elevation, and it faces the main business thoroughfare. A marble datestone on the tower credits Rev. Hugh McMahon for erecting the church. Although the door and windows are Romanesque, the buttresses, pinnacles, and spire are Gothic in design.

372. Immanuel Evangelical Lutheran Church
W61 N498 Washington Ave.   1882

Built under Rev. E.G. Strassburger, this stone Gothic church was erected by a congregation of German Lutherans to replace a smaller, earlier building. The original members had split into two congregations in 1862, (see #408) one of which stayed at this location. The present building has rough quarry stone sides and a more formal rock-faced limestone facade with a buttressed tower. A 3,000-pound bell hangs in the tower.

373. Wirth Building
W61 N513 Washington Ave.   1871

J.P. Wirth, a shoemaker, who settled here in 1846, founded what became one of the largest businesses in the city. According to a marble date stone at the second floor level, he erected this substantial stone, Italianate store in 1871, dealing in shoes in one half and groceries, dry goods, clothing, etc., in the other. There was once a bay window with an iron balcony on the south wall.

374. Central House Hotel
W61 N518-20 Washington Ave.   1853

One of the many early hotels on Cedarburg's main street, this small establishment was operated by Henry C. Nero. The central house boasted, "First class accommodations, choice wines, liquors and cigars. Good stabling and large stock yard." The triangular dormer on the roof and the large first floor windows were added later.

375. J. Lauterbach Building
W62 N553 Washington Ave.   c.1865

This is one of the few commercial buildings here which is still owned and used in its original capacity. Originally Lauterbach tailored custom-made suits and sold ready-made clothing, hats, caps, and "gents' furnishing goods of all kinds." The original building entrance was a doorway with two flanking windows framed in wood. The first floor has been altered, but the paired brackets and wooden cornice survive.

376. Union House Hotel
W62 N557 Washington Ave. 1883

Built by J.C. Kuhefuss, this CCB hotel once had a fine ornamental balcony over the main entrance. Below the marble date stone, which reads, "J.C.K. 1883," one can still see the blocked-up door which led to that cast iron balcony. Kuhefuss also operated a livery and boarding stable in conjunction with the hotel and was a dealer in buggies and sleighs.

377. John Grundke Residence
W62 N562 Washington Ave. 1853

Mr. Grundke married the daughter of William Schroeder (see #384) and was, perhaps through this relationship, connected to the operation of the Cedarburg grist mill. This residence is said to have begun its life as a small frame house which was later enlarged and cased with brick. The present roof was built over an older one which still survives within the structure. The 2-story brick residence is trimmed with stone lintels.

378. Cedarburg State Bank
W62 N570 Washington Ave. 1908

This sturdy Romanesque facade is made of heavy, rock-faced limestone blocks. The trim and cornice molding are of carved and smooth-finished cut stone, and the margins of the vertical pilasters' blocks are chiseled to a line. The building was later occupied as a post office. At one time the Wisconsin Telephone Company operated a switchboard on the second floor.

379. Washington House Hotel
W62 N573 Washington Ave. 1886

The first Washington House was built in 1846 by Conrad Horneffer. Thirty years later it was acquired by Fred Jaucke (see #839), who built the northern (3-story) half of the present structure in 1886. At one time, below the words, "Washington House," at the cornice level, there was a similar stone with raised letters which read, "18- F. Jaucke -86." The unanswered question is... did Jaucke buy the original frame structure and replace it with this 2-piece hotel, or had Horneffer already built the south half? The buildings are fine examples of decorative bricklaying.

380. Italianate Commercial Buildings
W62 N577 Washington Ave.   c.1865
Here are three similar business buildings at the most important intersection
in Cedarburg. The two southernmost
were built of stone, while the other is
made of CCB, but they all have similar
twin-bracketed wooden cornices. L.E.
Jochem's general merchandise store
(left) also was once a post office. Next
door (middle) was Jacob Becker's Saloon.
The brick building was the store of
"general merchant", Juergen Schroeder
(see #383).

381. Louis M. Hoehn Residence
W62 N582 Washington Ave.   c.1870
Hoehn was both an undertaker and a
furniture dealer, a combination which
was common in the nineteenth century
(see #704). Next door to this residence,
on the north, was his two-story frame
furniture store with a false front. The
CCB Italianate house has a double-
bracketed wooden cornice and limestone
trim. Later, when the structure became
the Farmers and Merchants Bank, one
of the rusticated brick pilasters and two
round arched windows were removed to
make one large elliptical arched window.

382. C.W. Lehmann Hardware Store
W62 N588 Washington Ave.   1874
Called the "finest business block in the
city", in 1893, this imposing Italianate
structure replaced the Lehmanns' first
frame store built in 1867. It once had a
large anvil, with a letter "L" on it, in the
triangular pediment at the roof line. The
first floor and basement were occupied
by the hardware business, the second
was residential, and the third was used
as a lodge hall. The rock-faced limestone
is from the Anschuetz quarry.

383. Juergen Schroeder Residence
W62 N589 Washington Ave.   c.1870
Before this house was built,the
Schroeder's lived above their general
store (see #380) down the street.
Juergen's descendants still occupy the
house, but at one time the family owned
all of the Washington Ave. frontage between the store and William Schroeder's
house (see #384). This otherwise simple
CCB structure is made beautiful by the
splendid original porch with its cast iron
cresting and delicate scroll-cut gingerbread.

384. William H. Schroeder Residence
N62 W591 Washington Ave. c.1885
A beautifully preserved example of the Queen Anne style, this 2½-story frame residence was built for $4,000. William, who worked as a bookkeeper for a Milwaukee company and commuted every day, first lived over the family store to the south (see #380). The clapboards, shingle siding, projecting bays, stained glass, scroll-cut ornament, and the spindle and lattice work give the house a picturesqueness typical of that style.

385. German Free School
W62 N593-5 Washington Ave. c.1855
This building is said to have been a dance hall before Trinity Church (see #418) acquired it, in 1864, and made it into a school. For years it was the only school in Cedarburg, and it eventually closed in 1932. A very unusual and interesting detail can be seen on the limestone building's corners. The dressed quoins, which are properly functional, have been cut in such a way as to create the effect of a raised corner pilaster. The first floor windows have been altered.

386. E.G. Wurthmann Store
W62 N594 Washington Ave. 1888
An unusual example of a Queen Anne false front commercial building, this was the downtown store of painter and decorator, Erhardt G. Wurthmann (see #369). After practicing his trade for three years in Chicago, he came to Cedarburg, in 1866, and began what was to become a substantial business here. In this building he displayed an extensive assortment of paints and wallpapers and employed up to ten people in his "busy season".

387. John Armbruster Jewelry Store
W62 N620 Washington Ave. 1913
This is one of the few buildings in Cedarburg that is still owned and occupied by the original business. Armbruster came to Cedarburg from Germany in 1882 and established his business here two years later. This building, faced with white glazed terra-cotta, once had an ornamental pediment with a letter "A" in a cartouche. The now-rare cast iron sidewalk clock was made by the Brown Street Clock Co. of Monessen, Pa. The interior is mostly original.

388. George Fischer Residence
W63 N627 Washington Ave. 1849

When Fischer packed and left for the California gold rush, he sold this house to Edward Blank. Since that sale, in 1854, this dwelling has been continuously occupied by five generations of the Blank family. The original structure is the two-story frame Greek Revival north block which projects toward the street. In 1864 Mr. Blank, who was Cedarburg's second postmaster and who once ran Hilgen Spring Park, built the stone south wing.

389. Henry Roth Residence
W62 N628 Washington Ave. c.1870

This fine Greek Revival-influenced house has a southern wing built of CCB (now painted). The main, original block is made of limestone with inscribed mortar joints. The carefully dressed quoins are embellished with chiselled margins. The rear addition of fieldstone was made in recent years. Henry Roth ran the old saloon (see #397) across from the Wittenberg Mill.

390. Cedarburg Grade School
W63 N643 Washington Ave. 1894

Built by stonemason John Vollmar, this substantial building originally contained both the graded school classes and the high school, which was on the south half of the second floor. It was constructed with rock-faced limestone blocks from Cedarburg's Anschuetz quarry. The basic massive shapes and semicircular arches are Romanesque, but the wooden brackets and gable ornaments are Victorian.

391. Cedarburg High School
W63 N645 Washington Ave. 1908

This massive stone structure was built by the same mason (John Vollmar) and with the same Anschuetz quarry stone as the "old" school (see #390). For years it was known as the "Washington Building" to distinguish it from the grade school, which was called the "Lincoln Building". Here the style leans more to an Italian palazzo with its flat roof and modillioned cornice.

392. John Roth Residence
W63 N664-6 Washington Ave. c.1870

John, and his brothers Henry and Phillip, married three sisters who were the daughters of a local German baker, George Stiehle. Henry built the rooming house nearby on the corner of Bridge Street (see #397), and John operated a billiard hall and saloon. This Greco-Italianate house is built of CCB and has many characteristics of the Greek Revival, but the arched window and door openings belong to this later period.

393. Charles Gottlieb Friedrich Residence
W63 N672 Washington Ave. c.1873

This pleasantly proportioned CCB building served Friedrich as a cobbler shop as well as a residence. The 2½-story CCB dwelling has a simple pitched roof and elliptical brick arches over window and door openings. The window sash are finished with sharp-cornered segmental arches, but the brick arches have rounded corners which were made with tapered bricks.

394. Leopold Jochem Residence
W63 N673 Washington Ave. c.1898

The largest late Victorian mansion in Cedarburg, this was once the home of the proprietor of a grocery and general merchandise store (see #380). The eclectic design has elements of the Romanesque, Queen Anne, and Classical Revival styles. It is built with red pressed brick on a stone foundation and lavishly ornamented with leaded potmetal and prism glass windows, shingle siding, wooden moldings and sculptured terracotta.

395. August Weber Residence
W63 N676-78 Washington Ave. c.1870

This was one of many Cedarburg houses owned by John Weber, the proprieter of the Brewery (see #410). August, his son, also worked at the Brewery and lived in this house. The two-story CCB Italianate dwelling is ell-shaped, has a bracketed cornice and a flat roof. There is a subtle dignity about the facade which comes from its fine proportions and panelled effect created by brick corner pilasters and horizontal bands.

396. Groth Family Store
W63 N692-96 Washington Ave. c.1876
This substantial two-story limestone commercial building was erected by William Groth for Henry G. Groth and his brother-in-law, John F. Bruss. The north half was occupied by Bruss as a general merchandise store; and the south half became the Groth Brothers Hardware Company, a business which survived until 1963. The hip-roofed structure has an Italianate character and has a twin-bracketed wooden cornice.

397. Henry Roth Rooming House
W63 N697 Washington Ave. 1888
Before this building was erected, there was a small two-story frame structure on the lot with a sign that read, "Beer Saloon, H. Roth". Once the first assistant chief of the Cedarburg Fire Co., Mr. Roth then built this impressive eclectic Victorian block out of CCB. The ornamental brickwork in spandrels, false arches, and stringcourses gives the building a rich and decorative character.

398. Cedarburg Woolen Mill Office
W63 N702-6 Washington Ave. 1864-65
Founded by Frederick Hilgen (see #427), Diedrich Wittenberg (see #400) and Joseph Trottman, this pioneer Cedarburg industry was situated on Cedar Creek and powered by water. The corner building, a three-story stone Greek Revival structure, was built in 1864-65 as the office, and the north wing was added later for storage. The factory at the rear (see #399) turned out woolen and worsted yarns, flannels, frocking, skirting, blankets and mackinaws.

399. Cedarburg Woolen Mill
N70 W6334 Bridge Rd. 1864-65
This building has been twice enlarged. The original mill, built during the Civil War, is the northern half of the present structure. An almost identical addition was made to the south (along Bridge Rd.) about 30 years later. Both had a low-pitched Greek Revival roof, and the earlier section sported a decorative cupola. In 1907 both roofs were removed and a third story was added with the present almost-flat roof.

400. Diedrich Wittenberg Residence
W64 N707 Washington Ave. 1864
Built by one of the founders of the Cedarburg Woolen Mill, this CCB mansion is an excellent example of Victorian Italianate design. Its basically square plan is relieved by a projecting entrance pavilion with a broken pediment. The original cornice brackets remain, but the old front porch was replaced. Wittenberg's Mill was conveniently located across the street (see #398).

401. Adolph Martin Boehme Residence
W64 N717-19 Washington Ave. c.1860
When this stone house was built it stood on a two-acre lot. It is one of Cedarburg's finest examples of quality stone masonry. The severe design is made elegant by carefully proportioned openings and the degree of finish in the construction. The walls are made of local limestone laid with heavy mortar joints. The neatly dressed quoins are raised slightly above the wall surface, and horizontal course lines are inscribed in the mortar, using the quoins for spacing.

402. Dr. Fred A. Luening Residence
W64 N758 Washington Ave. c.1862
This Gothic Revival-influenced house was once the home of the builder of Columbia Mill (see #422). By 1865 it had become the residence of Dr. T. Hartwig and, in a photograph taken that year, the doctor and his family are shown on the lawn in front of the house. The attractive scroll-cut wooden porch with its cast iron cresting had not yet been added, and a wing to the rear with three Gothic windows and a Gothic door shows clearly.

403. Michael Sullivan Farmhouse
1167 Washington Ave. 1854
Once the manor house of an 80-acre farm, this well built stone structure is a fine example of fieldstone construction. Heavily mortared joints, with inscribed lines, give smoothness and uniformity to the irregular stones; and the corners are finished with dressed limestone quoins. There is a smaller frame wing on the rear.

404. Founders Monument
Evergreen Rd. between
Western Ave. and Center St.   1887
Located deep in a wilderness area, this limestone monument contains a German inscription and the names of 26 of Cedarburg's earliest settlers. It was erected by Trinity Lutheran Church (see #418) in what was known as "Groth Cemetery" after Ludwig Groth, one of the settlers buried here. This is the oldest cemetery in Cedarburg and one of the oldest in the state.

405. Carl Dobberpuhl Residence
N50 W6890 Western Rd.   c.1865
Ludwig Groth, who once owned 120 acres in this area, built a house here about 1844. Almost immediately thereafter he sold 80 acres and the dwelling to his brother-in-law, Carl Dobberpuhl. Trinity Cemetery (now Founders Park, see #404), was on this original tract and a gift from Groth and Dobberpuhl. This house, probably built later, is a well-preserved limestone structure that has mortar joints with inscribed horizontal course lines.

406. Milwaukee Northern Substation
N57 W6406 Center St.   1907
Now a photographer's studio, this building once served as an interurban station on the Milwaukee Northern Line (see #414). It was used as a passenger waiting room, a freight storage facility, and a generating station to assist in supplying electricity to the system. The side pictured shows the overhanging canopy of the trackside platform. After the building was abandoned in the late 1940's, it was occupied first as a sign shop.

407. F. Moegenburg Residence
W66 N695 Madison Ave.   c.1863
The Moegenburgs were a family of many carpenters and masons. Which one built this house has not been determined. In fact, there were three F. Moegenburgs listed in the 1900 Ozaukee County Directory and two of them on this street (which was then called Velvet). The well built two-story stone section was built first and the south, or kitchen, wing came later. The porch is a relatively recent addition.

408. First Immanuel Lutheran Church
N60 W650 Cleveland St. 1891

This CCB Gothic church was built by the congregation which broke away from Immanuel Evangelical Lutheran Church in 1862 (see #372). Since both buildings contain the identical German inscription (Ev. Luth. Immanuels Kirche), this congregation adopted its present name to avoid confusion. Built on land donated by Gottfried Bruss, the church is made of Port Washington brick and is set on a limestone foundation.

409. John Weber Residence
N.E. corner Riveredge Dr.
and Adler St. c.1860

This two-story CCB, Greek Revival house was the home of the owner and operator of the brewery next door. It was probably built by one of the original founders of that business. Weber came here from Germany in 1854, and under his management the brewery employed six men. He was also president of the Cedarburg Wire and Nail Company (see #423).

410. Engels & Schaefer Brewery
W62 N718 Riveredge Dr. 1848

One of the oldest breweries in southeastern Wisconsin, this complex of stone buildings, with its dressed quoins, ceased operation in 1920, a victim of Prohibition. It reached its peak under the ownership of John Weber when it was called the "Cedarburg Brewery". The average annual production was only 2,200 barrels, but the product was then "noted for its delicious taste, its purity and its refreshing qualities".

411. Ernst F. Kafehl Residence
W61 N764 Riveredge Dr. c.1860

Kafehl was an early employee of the Weber Brewery (see #410), and he no doubt purchased this house because of its proximity to his place of work. The original owner has not been determined, but the diminutive Greek Revival structure is a beautifully built example of stone masonry with dressed quoins. The front porch, with its fluted Doric columns, was added in the twentieth century.

412. E. Mielke Residence
N65 W6128 Tyler St.   **c.1867**

This handsome stone house was built for one of three Mielke brothers. During its construction a young boy, John Vollmar, who was 14 years old at the time, helped the stonemasons. He was later to become one of Cedarburg's prominent stonemasons and was resonsible for many important buildings here, including the grade school (see #390), and the high school (see #391). He also built the Ozaukee County Courthouse at Port Washington (see #475).

413. City Hall, Firehouse and Jail
W61 N619-23 N. Mequon St.   **1908**

A disastrous fire destroyed the old firehouse/school building and the adjoining "Cedarburg House" in 1907. This two-story CCB structure was immediately begun to replace the old facility and provide additional space for city offices and a jail. The fire station doors have been modernized to accommodate new equipment, but the old 5-story brick tower, with its mansard roof, has survived intact.

414. Milwaukee Northern Bridge
Cedar Creek behind Fire Station 1907

Now abandoned, this riveted iron bridge once served the Milwaukee Northern Interurban "Rapid Transit" Line. The company, which began about 1906, ran from Milwaukee to Sheboygan, with Cedarburg the first stop, and Port Washington the second. Car barns, which were erected here, still stand behind the police station on Hanover Ave. and are now used as the Kiekhefer Plant #2.

415. Wadhams Pagoda
Filling Station
N58 W6189 Columbia Rd.   **1926**

More than one hundred filling stations, designed like Japanese tea houses, were built by Wadhams Oil and Grease Company of Milwaukee. The prototype, built in 1917 at Fifth and West Wisconsin Ave. in Milwaukee, was designed by architect Alexander C. Eschweiler. The basic style was eventually adopted by Texaco, Inc., for their national chain. Of the few now remaining, this is a good example of the larger variety which had "pagoda" cupolas on the roof with hanging lanterns.

416. Hilgen-Schroeder Mill Store
N58 W6194 Columbia Rd.   c.1856

Built as living quarters and a store, this three-story CCB structure was once under the proprietorship of J. Trottman. It was erected by Frederick Hilgen as a retail outlet for flour and feed from the Cedarburg Mill across the street (see #417). Since 1941 it has been used for bar and restaurant purposes and the first floor has been altered and enlarged.

417. Cedarburg Mill
N58 W6181 Columbia Rd.   1855

For over 120 years this huge 5-story stone grist mill has dominated the Cedarburg landscape. It was built by Frederick Hilgen (see #427) and William Schroeder to replace an earlier log structure. The handsome Greek Revival design is executed in limestone, quarried on the site, and has broad wooden cornices. Many of the original 12-over-12-light sash still remain. One of the finest mills in the Midwest, its lower walls are 32 inches thick.

418. Trinity Evangelical Lutheran Church
N60 W6047 Columbia St.   1891

Designed by architect William H. Hilgen, this handsome rock-faced limestone church was built by masons John Weber and John Vollmar, with tin work by C.W. Lehmann (see #382). This congregation, founded in 1843, built its first log church adjacent to the graveyard which still survives as Founders Park (see #404). This structure's limestone walls are trimmed with buff sandstone and an unusual pair of cornerstones. The left corner reads "A. 18" and the right reads, "D. 91".

419. Adam Gleitzmann Residence
N67 W5540 Columbia Road   c.1855

Built by an early Cedarburg cooper, this finely proportioned limestone house is a two-story Greek Revival design with a one-story ell-wing. Mr. Gleitzmann's cooperage shop still stands to the west of the house and close to the road. In this building he made barrels for Milwaukee packing houses. Adam had come to America from Bavaria, at the age of 19, and first settled in Grafton.

420. E. Hilgen Residence
N69 W5316 Columbia St. 1869

This finely finished limestone house is one of the most attractive examples of its style in Cedarburg. Over the front door is a wide keystone with "E. Hilgen, 1869", clearly chiseled on its face. The rough quarry stone is finished on the corners with dressed quoins, and the nicely molded wooden cornice is double-bracketed. Another refinement is found in the little scroll-cut details on the wooden window casings right under their arches.

421. Eilert Stallman Residence
N70 W5266 Columbia Rd. 1865

This is one of the finest of all the stone houses in Cedarburg. It was built by a carpenter, Eilert Stallman, who had a one-third interest in the Columbia Mill (see #422) along with E. Hilgen and C. Barthel. Stallman's dwelling, located conveniently across the street from the mill, is a two-story limestone structure with finely dressed quoins and a carved front door casing that contains a keystone with the inscription, "E. St 1865."

422. Columbia Mill Remains
Cedar Creek at Highland Drive 1846

One of many water-powered industries on Cedar Creek, the grist mill which once stood on these massive stone foundation walls was known as Columbia. The street, which served as a short-cut to the mill, was named after that enterprise. It was built by the community's first physician, Dr. Frederick A. Luening (see #402). The last of many names attached to the building was the Weber Milling Co. when it was razed in 1975.

423. Excelsior Mill and Residence
4807 Columbia Road c.1866 and later

Henry Wehausen purchased this property in 1866 and probably built this Gothic Revival cottage as his dwelling. In 1871 he erected the Excelsior Flour and Sawmill, which is still standing behind the house. That imposing stone structure was gutted by a fire in the 1880's and stood empty until John Weber bought it, in 1890, and turned it into the Cedarburg Wire and Wire Nail Co. The last roll of wire was produced there in 1969. The house, built on a slope, is decorated with scroll-cut gable and window ornaments.

424. Peter Anschuetz Residence
4309 Columbia Rd. 1869

Heinrich Anschuetz came to this vicinity, in 1836, and opened the great limestone quarry out of which came the material to erect most of the buildings in Cedarburg. Part of the original 640-acre land purchase was given to his sons, and he built this stone house for one of them. Peter did not become active in the quarry, but farmed his land instead. A keystone over the entrance is inscribed, "P.A. 1869".

425. Methodist Episcopal Church
N56 W6093 E. Portland Rd. 1905

Founded in 1900, the Cedarburg Methodist congregation first met in an old saloon. They commissioned architect William H. Hilgen to draw plans for this structure. It is a frame, clapboard-sided, Gothic design with a square tower and open belfry. The pleasantly proportioned Gothic windows have intersected tracery and hood moldings. Other Gothic details include the bargeboards at gable ends and the poppyhead finial atop the tower. Since 1965 the building has served the Ozaukee Baptist Church.

426. Cedar Creek Marker
Portland Rd. at Mill St. 1969

"The Indians called the stream "Mequonissippi". By the 1830's, when Wisconsin Territory ws surveyed, settlers had named it Cedar Creek. The waters were harnessed to turn sixteen mills which sawed timber, milled grain and produced goods. They provided food, transportation and recreation. They also carried away waste residues of urban and rural development. Cedar Creek winds through hills and marshes on its 32-mile journey from the Cedar Lakes to the Milwaukee River...falling 350 feet on the way."

427. Frederick Hilgen Residence
N47-W6033 Spring St. c.1853

The founder of Cedarburg built this house. Known as "Father Hilgen," he was involved in almost every enterprise responsible for the growth of the village. He was a co-founder of the grist mill (see #417), the woolen mill (see #398), the Bank of Cedarburg, and the Hilgen Manufacturing Co. He also operated Hilgen Spring Park, a 74-acre summer resort with two hotels. The frame Greek Revival house originally was approached from Hamilton Rd. The brick rear section (now the front) and the roof were added later.

428. Richard Hilgen Residence
N47 W5862 Spring St. c.1865

This was one of the many Hilgen-built houses on the street that led to the Hilgen Spring Park Resort. "Father" Frederick Hilgen lived a short distance west (see #427), and to the rear of this house (north) was the Hilgen Manufacturing Company. The 2½-story CCB house has a one-story wing and two different window arch shapes.

429. Hilgen Residence
N47 W5840 Spring St. c.1880

There is no direct relationship between good taste and money spent. This humble frame house, another of the many Hilgen-built dwellings, is a good example of how a pleasant design can be achieved with what was obviously a limited budget. The 2-story clapboard structure is well proportioned and is trimmed with just enough ornament to keep it from being dull. The front window frames, in two different shapes, give just enough character.

GRAFTON

The village of Grafton was originally known as "Hamburg." This early designation is thought to have come from one of the area's earliest settlers, Jacob Eichler, a native of Hamburg, Germany. At that time, in the 1840's, Washington County was much larger and included what is now Ozaukee County. In 1844-45, on the southeast corner of what is now 12th Avenue and Bridge Street, a two-story "stone block' was built to serve as a courthouse and jail. The village was then the county seat of Washington County, and it was renamed Grafton. The old stone courthouse still stands, but it has been so abused as to be almost unrecognizable. In 1853 the county was split, and one part became Ozaukee County. Four years later the village of Grafton was renamed "Manchester", but the new name was abandoned in 1862 and the present name was restored.

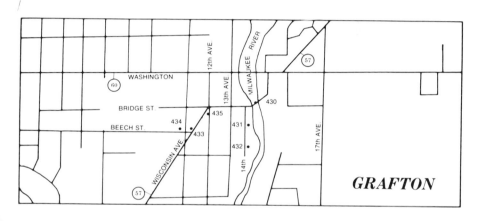

430. Old Iron Bridge
Bridge Street at the river   1888

At one time this single lane, riveted iron bridge was the only way across the Milwaukee River in the village of Grafton. It is proudly signed and dated on a decorative cast metal plate above the entrance arch which reads, '1888, builders, Wisconsin Bridge & Iron Co., Wauwatosa, WI.". Just below the bridge is the dam which supplied water power for both the grist mill (see #431) and the woolen mill (see #432).

431. Grafton Flouring Mill
1300 14th Ave. **c.1884**
The first dam was built here in the early 1840's and a grist mill was erected then by I. Edwards, William Bonniwell and P.M. Johnson. The present structure, which may contain a large section of the original mill, was built in the 1880's. Once the operation was run by H. Schmith & Co., and it had five runs of stones with a capacity of 100 barrels of flour a day. The brand name, "White Lily", is said to have been a popular flour among bakers in Milwaukee.

432. Grafton Woolen Mill
1350 14th Ave. **1880**
A branch operation of the Cedarburg Woolen Mill (see #398), this complex was once described as "the only worsted mill in the West". The 3-story, all-stone, structure contained "two sets of woolen machinery and one of worsted". The latter machines were imported and described as the "most modern kind". For a while the buildings were used as a tannery, and they were then refitted as the Badger Worsted Mills by William J. Roebken in 1902.

433. Kohlwey Blacksmith Shop
1327 Wisconsin Ave. **1868**
This was the building occupied by two generations of blacksmiths in early Grafton. The original craftsman, Frederick Kohlwey, lived one block west in a house which is still standing (see #434). His son, Henry, is probably the one whose initials appear on the handcrafted keystone over the front door which reads, "1868 - H.K.". The roughly dressed stone building is finished with chamfered quoins and a twin-bracketed wooden cornice.

434. Frederick Kohlwey Residence
1327 11th Ave. **c.1860**
Hidden under what looks like a late Victorian facade is one of Grafton's earliest dwellings. It was built by the family of blacksmiths who also erected the stone shop on Wisconsin Ave. (see #433). When this foundation was excavated, bedrock was found to be right under the surface. In the 1920's the basement was cut deeper with air hammers. A hand-hewn beam and a hand-forged door latch (probably made by Mr. Kohlwey) can still be seen in the basement. The scool-cut gable ornaments are exceptional.

435. Grafton Hotel
1312 Wisconsin Ave.   1892

An earlier hotel on this site, the Wisconsin Haus, served as a tavern, a steamship ticket office and a hotel. The present 3-story structure was built by Edward Mueller and in its day was a spectacular centerpiece for this little village. At one time the CCB walls were more picturesque with a spire on the corner bartizan and a raised ornamental gable over the western bay window. The building is still being used for a hotel and tavern.

HAMILTON

This picturesque little village, at the crossing of Cedar Creek and the old Green Bay Road, is older than Cedarburg. It was originally named "New Dublin" by a group of Irish immigrants who settled here. According to local tradition, William Stephen Hamilton, son of Alexander, passed through the settlement after a cattle drive to Green Bay in 1847. He is said to have spent a night in a local tavern-hotel and enjoyed a "boisterous" evening buying drinks for the townspeople. The new Dublinites renamed their community in his honor. Edward H. Janssen, who later became Wisconsin state treasurer, built the Concordia Mill (see #442), the Turner Hall (see #437) and his own house (see #436), all of which still remain.

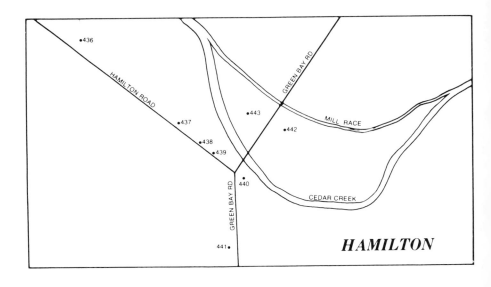

HAMILTON

436. Edward H. Janssen Residence
264 Hamilton Rd.   1854

This fine stone house was erected by the man who built the nearby Concordia Mill (see #442). The Janssen house was once set in a beautifully laid out eight-acre tract with formal gardens and an orchard. The 2½-story masonry structure is trimmed with dressed quoins and lintels. Although influenced by the Greek Revival style, this dwelling has, with its original recessed porch, the feeling of a Dutch Colonial farmhouse. The two dormers, on the front, were added later.

437. Turner Hall
240 Hamilton Rd. 1867

The German-speaking Turnverein was organized in Cedarburg, in 1853, and called the Cedar and Hamilton Society. In 1867 the Hamilton members broke away and built their own meeting hall here. The two-story fieldstone structure is trimmed with local limestone quoins, lintels, and sills; but its date stone, inscribed, "Turn Halle 1867", is a fine buff limestone from Waukesha or Wauwatosa. The upper dance floor cuts across the tall front windows and has a skylight cupola. For years the building was used as a shoe and slipper factory.

438. Valentine Hand Residence
232 Hamilton Rd. c.1848

One of Hamilton's earliest settlers, Hand purchased 80 acres, in 1845, and built a hotel across the street from this house. His fieldstone dwelling has heavily mortared joints with inscribed horizontal course lines. The quoins are hand-dressed and trimmed with chiselled margins. Window lintels are made of wood and are detailed with raised moldings.

439. Henry Hentschel General Store
228 Hamilton Rd. c.1860

Hidden under the awnings and glass block are two fluted columns with capitals which once decorated the entrance to this building. A molded stone lintel, which still exists above the remodelled entryway, indicates the size of the once-spacious show windows and front door complex. The 2½-story fieldstone structure is trimmed with dressed quoins and lintels and has a lunette window under the gable peak.

440. Daniel E. Callahan Residence
210 Green Bay Rd. c.1847

This interesting structure is said to have first been an inn and horse relay station on the old Green Bay Road. The rear wing, made of fieldstone with dressed quoins, was probably built first. The front section is made of brick and was later covered with wooden siding. The property was owned by Callahan until 1861. In 1889 it was purchased by Wilhelm Barthel in whose family it remained until 1930.

441. Eggert Lau Residence
189 Green Bay Rd.   c.1864

This beautifully crafted and well proportioned stone dwelling was the home of a wagon builder. Mr. Lau and Carl Binge built buggies and sleighs and sold harnesses in a nearby shop. Across the street his partner had a blacksmith shop where fittings for their wagons were made. This handsome limestone house is trimmed with dressed quoins, a double-bracketed wooden cornice, and lintels that have sunken bush-hammered panels. The porch is a later addition.

HABS NR WRL

442. Concordia Mill
252 Green Bay Rd.   1853

Edward H. Janssen (see #436), his brother Theodore, and William Gaitzsch built this stately grist mill in 1853. Its name and date are incised in the lintel over the main entrance. The gambrel-roofed limestone rubble structure was influenced by the Greek Revival style. After the death of his partners, Janssen sold the mill to Andreas Bodendoerfer, who built a large "barracks" for workers across the street (now gone). During World War II the mill was used as a distillery.

443. Bodendoerfer Barn
251 Green Bay Rd.   c.1860

This substantial fieldstone structure was originally the stable barn which served the boarding house that Andreas Bodendoerfer built closer to the road. That large, 24-room facility provided lodging for employees of the Concordia Mill across the street (see #442) and the local shoe factory (see #437). Its interior was gutted by a fire in 1924, and the remaining walls had to be razed.

MEQUON

The city of Mequon is actually a civil township which is two miles wider than the usual six-mile-square town. With the exception of Thiensville, which is a separate village near its geographic center, Mequon has no "downtown" or town center. Among the earliest settlers were the Bonniwells, a family of six brothers, one sister and their mother, who came here in 1839. It was on their land that the first schoolhouse was built; and, when Ozaukee was still a part of Washington County, the home of William T. Bonniwell became the meeting place and thus the county seat. In 1843 that honor was shifted to Grafton. The Bonniwells are remembered in the name of one of Mequon's principal east-west roads.

444. Log Slaughterhouse
behind 7625 Mequon Rd. c.1848
For years Christoph Herbst owned 18.5 acres on the southwest corner of this intersection and operated a butcher shop here. This log building is believed to have been built originally as a slaughterhouse, and possibly for the nearby meat market. The two-story structure has neatly joined corners and some of the original chinking between the logs. It has been altered and is now in relatively poor condition.

445. Jacob Zaun Farmhouse
8516 W. Mequon Rd.   c.1855 and later

The first segment of this large residence was built of fieldstone in the 1850's and has 21-inch thick walls. That two-room structure is now the rear, or north, wing of the present house. The second segment, the long block parallel to the road, was built later and once had a long porch which extended along the front. The scroll-cut window casings have an unusual shape. The last addition was the 2½-story front section with the bay window.

446. John O'Brien Farmhouse
12510 Wauwatosa Rd.   c.1848

A fine example of fieldstone masonry, this house has inscribed horizontal courses in its heavy mortar joints and neatly dressed quoins. O'Brien acquired the property from the Bonniwell family in 1846 and sold it to John Peuschel in 1855. The eastern addition, or kitchen wing, carries the date, 1870, in a stone above the back door. The stone barn is dated 1874. The house remained in the Peuschel family until 1964.

447. John Reichert Farmhouse
14053 Wauwatosa Rd.   c.1885

This Victorian eclectic residence is unusually fancy for a farmhouse, and it has survived with most of its original ornament intact. The two-story frame structure still has its scroll-cut gable ornaments and front porch. Of special interest are the two shallow, shingle-covered, false roofs above the windows on the street facade. These, with slightly projecting framing, create a bay window effect.

448. Jonathan Morrell
Clark Residence
13615 Highway 57   1848

This fine stone Greek Revival house has an unusual application of two types of masonry in one building. The side walls are of regularly coursed fieldstone with heavy mortar joints; while the gable end, or formal front, is made of "fancier" material, including roughly squared limestone blocks. Quoins, lintels, and sills are made of tooled limestone.

449. Trinity Evangelical Lutheran Church
Granville Rd.
S.W. corner Freistadt Rd.   1884

The oldest Lutheran church in Wisconsin was founded here, in 1839, by German immigrants fleeing religious persecution in the fatherland. Twenty families gathered in this vicinity to create the Colony of Freistadt and built the state's first Lutheran church, a log structure. The present building was designed by the same architect, Frederick Velguth, who drew plans for Milwaukee's Trinity Lutheran Church (see #201), which was an offshoot of this congregation. This Gothic edifice is beautifully constructed of Cedarburg limestone.

WHM

450. Wisconsin Lutheran Seminary
11831 N. Seminary Dr. 65 W. Mequon
1929

This complex of buildings was designed to resemble the "architectural patterns of the Wartburg, where Luther translated the New Testament into German". Milwaukee architects, Clas, Shepherd and Clas, drew the plans for the original structures. Today there are a few additions, but they are all compatibly arranged around what looks like a medieval quadrangle. On 80 acres are offices, classrooms, 17 separate houses, dormitories and a Romanesque gateway tower. Pictured is the slate-roofed chapel and gymnasium wing.

451. Thoreau School
6006 W. Mequon Rd.   1892

Built between a feed mill and a cemetery, this was the District Number 2 Public School in Mequon. The original front door was located where the middle window is today and was protected by a canopy. The otherwise plain clapboard design is enhanced with diamond-shingled panels and a bell cupola. The last classes were held here in 1952, and the building is now used as the American Legion's Howard J. Schroeder Post #457.

452. Octagonal Barn
13669 N. Port Washington Rd. c.1895

At one time there were fourteen octagon barns scattered along a stretch of N. Port Washington Road. Most of them were built in the decade from 1890 to 1900 by Ernst Clausing, whose father, Frederick, settled in Wisconsin in 1848. The unusual shape was practical in that a greater floor area could be enclosed with fewer running feet of walls. The octagonal shape also withstood wind better than a square barn. One of Clausing's barns has been moved to Old World Wisconsin (see #632).

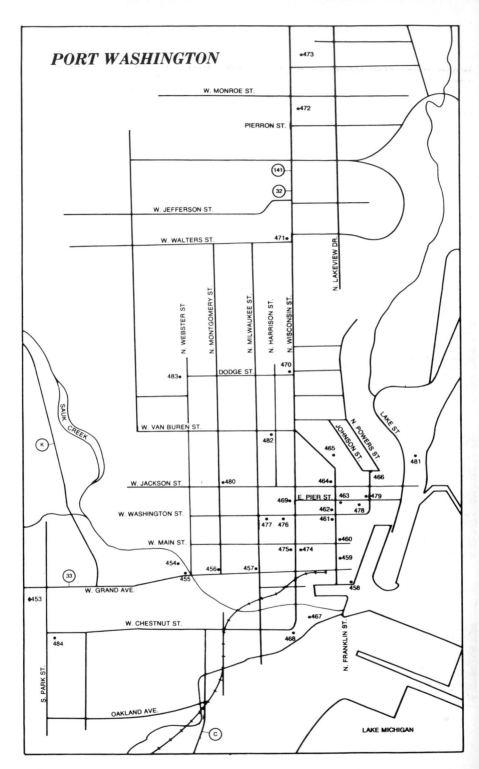

PORT WASHINGTON

PORT WASHINGTON

When Worcester Harrison first saw "the little city of seven hills" in 1833, the landscape was just as the Indians had left it. He recognized here, on the banks of Sauk Creek, a logical and beautiful site for a city. His plat was entered and recorded at the Green Bay land office in 1835, and the new settlement was named "Wisconsin City". Two years later, in the Panic of 1837, the land speculation came to a halt, and almost overnight most of the buildings were abandoned and the area became a ghost town. Harrison returned, in 1843, with another group of settlers and the town was renamed "Washington". When this was discovered to be a common name, it was changed to "Sauk Washington" and later "Port Washington". When Ozaukee County was separated from Washington, the county seat was established here and a courthouse was erected.

453. Teed-Bohan Residence
829 W. Grand Ave.　　　c.1850
Believed to have been built by mason-contractor, Louis Teed, this house was later the home of John R. Bohan, first clerk of Ozaukee County. Bohan was also the publisher of the *Ozaukee County Advertiser*. This is a well proportioned, clapboarded, frame Greek Revival house with a hipped roof. The front facade is set back with four square columns supporting the overhanging roof.

454. John R. Bohan Residence
Behind 440 E. Grand Ave.　　1855
A rare surviving example of the Gothic Revival style, this house was built by publisher and politician, John Bohan. Its grounds were once quite large, and the original entrance faced Sauk Creek. The steeply pitched roof and the scroll-cut "gingerbread" bargeboards at the gable ends are characteristics of the style. Note the creative use of cut shingles for ornamental panels and siding.

455. Residence
426-28 E. Grand Ave.　　c.1865
This simple pitched-roof dwelling has been enlarged and remodelled, but the original front possessed a special beauty and dignity. There the windows, with segmental arches, are set in recessed brick panels with matching arches. This detail and the overall proportions gave the house elegance. The south half of the house and the porch made of cast concrete parts are later additions.

456. Byron Teed Residence
316 W. Grand Ave.   1872
Now called the "Eghart House", this unspoiled Victorian cottage was purchased from Teed in 1881 by Judge Leopold Eghart. Only these two families have occupied the house in its more than a century of existence. The judge's daughter, Elsa, lived here until her death in 1969. Then a group of local citizens saved the house from an impending parking lot and restored it as a public museum.

457. Hoffmann House Hotel
200 W. Grand Ave.   1895
Called a "first class" hotel in every respect, this three-story building was erected by F. Louis Hoffmann. Its simple, but nicely detailed, CCB walls are trimmed with stringcourses which conform to the two different window arches. The corner two-story bartizan has panelling, ornamental swags, brackets and moldings, all made of sheet metal. A fine, decorative brick cornice edges the roofline.

458. Port Washington Harbor
E. Grand Ave. at Lake Michigan   1867
Said to be the first artificial harbor in the United States, the dredging here was begun in 1867 with county and matching federal funds. The present harbor was completed in 1935. A large wooden stock anchor, similar to the one in Union Cemetery (see #484), is displayed at the intersection of the two harbor channels. In 1889 a wooden pier light with a gas lantern was built at the end of the north pier.

459. First National Bank
118 N. Franklin St.   1927
This imposing Classical Revival building, which is unusually formal for Port Washington, is actually an older structure with a new facade. It was erected shortly after the First National Bank was incorporated in 1909. The present face, added in 1927, is made almost entirely of white glazed terra-cotta. The bold, but simple, composition is composed of a deep entablature supported by two fluted Corinthian columns and two corner pilasters.

460. The Wilson Hotel
200 N. Franklin St.   1892

Advertised in the nineteenth century as "Port Washington's popular hotel," this three-story structure replaces the earlier "Union House Hotel," which once stood on the same lot. Unlike the city's other early hotels (see #457, #463), this one is still operating as a hotel and retains the name that Frank Wilson gave it before the turn of the century. The corner bartizan is covered with wood, ornamental sheet metal and shingles.

461. Mike Bink's Block
231 N. Franklin St.   1891

Originally built as a saloon, this two-story Victorian eclectic building has a cylindrical corner bartizan which rises a full story above the roof. Unlike many of the simpler saloons built here, this deluxe building was made with an unusually rich complement of materials. Basically brick set on a stone foundation, it is decorated with wood, carved limestone, ornamental cut shingles, and has a sheet copper dome.

462. Schumacher Monument Co.
302 N. Franklin St.   c.1931

Designed by Port Washington architect Edgar Berners, this smooth-faced stone building was originally a showroom for grave markers and monuments. Set on a granite foundation, the limestone ashlar walls are ornamented with low-relief carving and a receding, or reverse, cornice. This facade, with its many subtle details, is the city's best example of the art-deco style.

463. Wisconsin House Hotel
312 N. Franklin St.   1855

The first building on this lot, in 1845, was the "United States Hotel". When Wisconsin achieved statehood in 1848, its name was changed to the "Wisconsin House", but four years later it burned down. The present structure was built on the old foundation but was enlarged by about 20 feet in both directions. The 3-story CCB Italianate building is distinguished by its chaste brick cornice and the two-story sunken panels into which the windows are set.

464. James W. Vail Residence
403-05 N. Franklin St. c.1870's

This eclectic Victorian frame house was built by a local banker but has been longer associated with the name of Mrs. Frances Kuhl, whose family lived here around 50 years. The original front porch has survived with its unusual scroll-cut brackets, each of which has a five-pointed star. Another uncommon detail is the pair of main entrance doors side-by-side under a double lintel.

465. St. Mary's Catholic Church
430 Johnson St. 1882

Set on an angle on top of a high bluff and centered on the city's main thoroughfare, St. Mary's dominates Port Washington in the same way that medieval cathedrals dominated the humble dwellings clustered around their foundations.The first church built for the parish was a frame structure on this lot. The present Gothic edifice is made of rock-faced limestone from the local Druecker quarry and was dedicated by Archbishop Heiss in 1884.

466. U.S. Coast Guard Lighthouse
311 Johnson St. 1860

Situated on a bluff, 106 feet above the lake, this painted brick building replaced an earlier lighthouse built in 1848. The present structure, set on a stone foundation, has an unusual decorative brick cornice and an equally uncommon brick recessed date tablet. There was once a square tower on the roof with a standard iron lantern house (see#132) which contained an oil burning lamp. This station, called a "4th order fixed white light," could be seen for 20 miles.

467. Port Washington Power Plant
146 S. Wisconsin St. 1930

This facility was built as a generating station for the transmission line loop around the Milwaukee metropolitan district. The original "unit" was erected by the Milwaukee Electric Railway and Light Company at a cost of approximately $7,500,000 and had a capacity of 80,000 kilowatts. This site was selected because it was right on the harbor and had access to coal ships, there was cold water for condensing, and it was close to Milwaukee.

468. Edward Dodge Residence
146 S. Wisconsin St. 1848

Wisconsin's finest remaining example of beach pebble architecture, this was once the home of a pioneer Port Washington blacksmith. Both Dodge and his wife gathered the beautiful smooth pebbles for this house along the nearby beaches and sorted them for color and size. The 20-inch-thick walls are basically limestone rubble with a thin facing of carefully selected, water-washed cobbles and pebbles. Laid in horizontal lines of different colors, a banded effect was achieved with 5 rows per quoin. The Greek Revival design is trimmed with rough-dressed limestone quoins and a wooden cornice. Originally the house stood about 125 feet to the north of its present location on the south bank of Sauk Creek. When the plant (see#467) was built here, the Dodge house was moved and restored to become the gate house for the complex. Inside are displayed relics from the steamer *Toledo* (see#484), which turned up during dredging of the channel near the power plant in 1931.

469. Port Washington High School
315 N. Wisconsin St. 1892

This imposing structure was the fourth school to be erected on this site, the first building having been constructed of logs in 1845. The CCB walls are set on a limestone foundation and trimmed with beltcourses of red sandstone. There was once an ornamental spire atop the tower, which has the bold Romanesque entrance arch at its base. The building now serves the Milwaukee Area Technical College.

470. Columbia Park
601 N. Wisconsin St. c.1865

Built by Matt Adam, this building was later part of a beer garden which included a dance hall (still standing to the rear) and grounds covering about one square block. Drinks, cigars, food and band concerts made this a popular summer garden around the turn of the century. The building is a modified Greek Revival design; the corner pilasters and ornamental cornice are made of brick. The original entrance was centered on the Wisconsin Street side.

471. Herbert Labahn Residence
Wisconsin St. N.W. corner
Walters St. 1920-21

Herbert and Charles Labahn, two members of an old brewing family, ran the "Old Port Brewing Corp." Herbert's father, Ludwig, was president of the brewery which preceded "Old Port". This house was built by contractor Joseph Ubbink in the Classical Revival style and is still set on its imposing, well-landscaped corner lot. A piece of the family brewery still survives behind a new front as the American Legion Clubhouse at 435 Lake St.

472. Peter N. Pierron Farmhouse
1112-1114 N. Wisconsin St. c.1870

Like many houses around old Port Washington, this farmhouse was originally surrounded by open space, but today it is set in a more densely populated area. Once a center of activity on the 110-acre "Pleasant View Farm," the 2½-story CCB residence still has more spacious grounds than many of its neighbors. There have been many remodellings and alterations, but the formal two-wing composition is still impressive.

473. Fischbach Farmhouse
1314 Husting St. 1878

Although built by Fischbach, this structure has long been known as the Michael Schmit farmhouse since that family occupied it from 1887 until the 1920's. Although still handsomely proportioned, the house lacks much of its original charm. The once tall and stately front windows have been shortened, and the cornice has been altered. Fortunately much of the original porch is still intact.

474. Thill's Hotel
103 W. Main St. 1902

This dignified three-story structure replaced an earlier hotel, the "American House," which was built on this lot in 1853. It was operated by four brothers and three sisters, all children of Peter Thill. Rates around the turn of the century were $1.50 per day, and the hotel offered omnibus service to the train station. The walls are CCB, and most of the ornamental trim is made of painted sheet metal.

475. Ozaukee County Courthouse
109 W. Main St.   **1901**

The first county courthouse was erected here in 1854 and was a three-story brick building. This massive rock-faced structure replaced the original and is built with limestone from the Cedarburg quarry. Its Richardsonian Romanesque design was drawn by Milwaukee architect Fred Graf, and the contractors were Wurthmann & Vollmer. Ornamental trim was carried out in Bedford limestone, and a gold-leafed eagle surmounts the tower.

476. John Brabender Residence
109-11 W. Washington St.   **c.1850**

Like its neighbor to the west (see #477), this house once stood at the same vertical elevation as Washington Street. It was the home of an early cooper in Port Washington, John Brabender. A large and imposing house for its day, this Greek Revival structure has now been sided with asbestos shingles. While lunette (half-circle) windows are not common in houses of this style, two lunettes might be considered truly rare.

477. M. Mamer Residence
119 W. Washington St.   **c.1870**

This nicely detailed frame Victorian house once stood level with the street but it became the victim of an ambitious grading project. Washington Street, once a well-known bobsled hill, descended to a level area and then dropped a second time to Wisconsin St. The Mamer house was situated on that horizontal segment until the top of the bluff was cut down and the low section was filled with the graded soil.

478. Rooming House
211-213 E. Pier St.   **c.1855**

Before the harbor was dredged out, Port Washington had three privately built and operated piers. The second built, known as "Blake's Pier", once extended eastward from the foot of Pier Street. This three-story CCB structure is said to have been a rooming house or hotel which catered to the understandably heavy sailor traffic on this street. Its walls are distinguished by the ornamental brick cornice and the panelled fenestration of the first floor (similar to that on #455).

479. Heinrich Mueller Residence
230 E. Pier St.   **1856-57**
Built right up to the sidewalk, this simple early dwelling was influenced by the Federal style. It is a townhouse type of structure which was more often found side-by-side for many running blocks in larger and more densely populated cities. The painted brick building is trimmed with limestone and has projecting lintels.

480. Jacob Schumacher Residence
232 W. Jackson St.   **1891**
Few private dwellings have cornerstones, but, since this was the home of the owner of Schumacher's Statues and Monuments Company (see # 462), it is easy to imagine who supplied the idea and, no doubt, the engraved stone for this house. The inscription reads "Jac. Schumacher - 1891." Although the architectural design is unimportant, this house is distinguished by the quality and variety of its trim. Stone beltcourses, carved wood, and three styles of slate shingles complement the CCB walls.

481. Band Concert Shell
N. Lake St. north of Jackson St.   **1934**
This substantial band shell was given to the city in memory of Edwin and Mary Jaehnig, who operated a general store in Fillmore, Wisconsin, and lived in Port Washington after retiring from business. The reflecting half-dome is fully enclosed in a structure made of "antique" cream brick. Its low-pitched roof and symmetrical side wings resemble the Greek Revival style.

482. Evangelical Friedens Kirche
455 N. Harrison St.   **1889**
Organized in 1854, this German-speaking congregation first held services in a public schoolhouse. Their fine CCB Gothic church was erected in 1889 and now is the Friedens United Church of Christ. The brick walls are set on a rock-faced limestone foundation, and the buttresses are trimmed with sheet metal. The walls are framed with brick pilasters and corbelling. An unusual round window in the tower has a four-pointed star surrounded with circles.

483. St. Mary's Cemetery
N. Webster St. at Dodge St.   1854

One of the prettiest little cemeteries in southeastern Wisconsin, this was begun by Fr. Francis X. Sailer, who was the first resident priest at St. Mary's (see#465). A fine set of four cast iron posts support wrought iron gates at the entrance, and there are numerous mausoleums and iron grave crosses here. The remains of Fr. Sailer are buried under the floor of a small CCB Gothic chapel which has a stencil-decorated, vaulted ceiling.

484. Anchor From Steamer *Toledo*
Union Cementery S.E. Corner
Park and Chestnut St.   1856

In one of Port Washington's early marine disasters, the propeller steamer *Toledo* sank in a storm near the present harbor (see #458) in October of 1856. In 1900 the boat's anchor was recovered and displayed in a small vacant lot adjacent the Wilson Hotel (see #460). It was later moved to its present site in Union Cemetery where it marks the common grave of the 46 victims of the sinking.

SAUKVILLE

The unusual village "square" in Saukville is actually a triangle which was determined by a very important intersection of roads. On the north is E. Dekora Street which was the old Dekorra Military Road. Opened by General Dodge in the early 1830's, this road ran from Dekorra (which is now a ghost town near Portage on the Wisconsin River) to Port Washington. Today it is Highway 33 and as it passes through Saukville, it becomes East and West Dekora Street (spelled incorrectly). On the south of the triangle is the important Green Bay Military Road which was surveyed in the 1830's from Chicago to Green Bay. Today it enters town as Main Street (or Highway O) and becomes E. Green Bay Avenue along the " square". At one time there were more hotels in Saukville (five in 1899) than other town its size in the county.

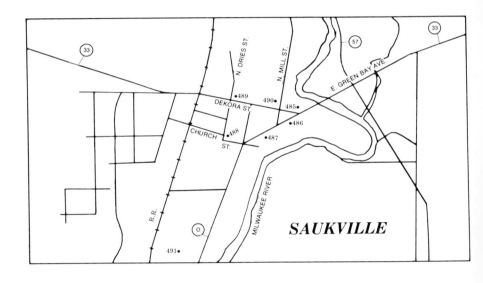

485. Pulaski Hotel
310 E. Green Bay Ave.   1848
William Payne erected this three-story, frame, Greek Revival hotel and, in spite of its officially christened name, it was always known as Payne's Hotel. The first manager was William Richards; and at that time, the building had a large front verandah and 18 rooms. Dances held in the third floor hall drew crowds from a thirty-mile radius. The building was later a grocery, a tavern, and after 1917 it became residential.

486. Eagle Hotel
241-245 E. Green Bay Ave.   c.1885

This frame hotel was one of three in early Saukville, and the upper half of its bracketed, Italianate facade is completely original. The lintels over the second floor windows and the front door are decorated with an unusual geometric ornament. In 1892, when the proprietor was Joseph Niesen, the Eagle boasted, "first class accommodation for travelers — board by the day , week, or month — neat clean and conveniently located. Good stabling and livery attached."

487. Residence
173 E. Green Bay Ave.   1874

This highly unusual dwelling looks more like a commercial building with its brick false front concealing a pitched roof. The CCB structure is accented with red bricks; and the date, 1874, which appears at the sides of the attic window, is ingeniously constructed with cut bricks. The whole house, with its mismatched second floor arches and overdone brick cornice, appears to have been designed by its creative, but non-professional owner.

488. Immaculate Conception Catholic Church
140 W. Church St.   1875

This impressive Romanesque church easily dominates the little village of Saukville. It is one of the finest examples of stone masonry in the county. The side walls are rough stone, heavily mortared, but the principal facade is finished with fine straight courses of dressed limestone and is trimmed with point-dressed, chamfered quoins. The original windows are true, heavily stained glass.

489. St. Peter's Evangelical Church
166 W. Dekora St.   1876

One of only two major churches in early Saukville, the German Evangelical Lutheran congregation was organized on June 16, 1876. It was set up as a mission and was served by a Rev. Frank of Port Washington. The CCB Gothic design features an unusually large date stone with boldly incised letters. The front is framed by brick pilasters and ornamental brick corbels.

490. Commercial Buildings
133 N. Mill St.   c.1865
This is an exceptional pair of painted brick, false-front, commercial "blocks". Both are relatively unspoiled on the exterior, and they have numerous unusual details. The building on the left, which was for years the Peter Feltes Tavern, still has its original 16-light, first-floor windows. These have a rare refinement in their little corner ornaments. Each building has an unusual, and different, decorative brick cornice.

491. St. Mary's Cemetery Chapel
South of town on Main St.   1889
This picturesque hillside cemetery has many interesting and unusual details. At a high elevation is an 18-foot cast iron "cemetery cross" made by M.H. Wiltzus & Co. of Milwaukee. The representation of Christ and the three statues around its base are cast white metal or zinc. The CCB Gothic chapel is dated by inscriptions in window keystones on opposite sides of the building, "A.D." on one side and "1889" on the other. There are numerous cast iron crosses on graves here.

THIENSVILLE

A village within a city, Theinsville is located in the geographic center of the city of Mequon. When the post office was established here, in 1840, the community was named Maquon River, Wisconsin. Later a German immigrant, Joachim Heinrich Thien, settled here, laid out the village and built a mill. The name, Maquon River, survived until 1883, when it was changed to Thiensville in his honor. Until it was incorporated, in 1912, Thiensville was considered a part of Mequon.

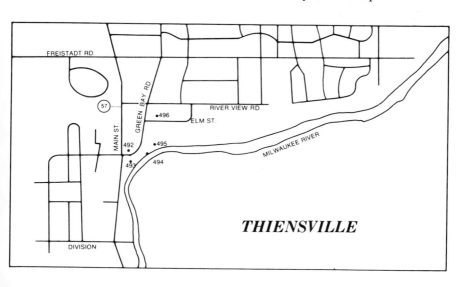

492. Thiensville Village Hall and Fire Department
101 Green Bay Rd.   **1914**

The-hose drying tower on this dual-purpose building is more than twice the height of the main block. This, and its position on an important intersection, make the building a well-known, and striking, landmark. The 2-story CCB structure was used for municipal offices upstairs and engine house below. Organized in 1859, the all-volunteer department first rented area garages and then used this facility from 1914 to 1960. The original bell will be mounted in front of the new station.

493. Thiensville State Bank
118 Green Bay Rd.   **1930**

This "Moderne" art deco building was designed by Minneapolis architect A. Moorman, a specialist who characterized himself as the "bank builder". This bank, which was founded in 1910, had to move an old house, once owned by P. J. Kroehnke, about 75 feet west to make way for the new structure. It is made of scratch-face orange-brown brick and is trimmed with sandstone. Ornament is carved in low relief in stone and appears on the copper burglar alarm grille.

494. Thienville Mills
Green Bay Rd. at river   **1876-1968**

This decorative wall, built with used CCB, contains the old stone letters from the five-story grist mill which once stood nearby. The mill and the village were named after Joachim Heinrich Thien who came here from Germany in 1842. When the stone mill was torn down, in 1956, these letters somehow ended up in the river. Twelve years later they were dredged out of the mud and set in this wall. The original spelling was "Thienville Mills", and the "s" from "mills" was used to make the present spelling.

495. Thienville Mill Stable
Green Bay Road at river   **1867**

J. H. Thien's first mill was followed by a two-story stone structure built by his son. That burned down and was replaced by the five-story stone mill from which the letters have been saved (see #494). This fieldstone building, with its roughly squared quoins, predates the last of the three mills and is now the only surviving piece of architecture from this pioneer complex. Once used as a stable, it is dated in a stone over the entrance.

496. Van Buren School
228 Elm St.   1866

Wedged between two additions, and disguised under a uniform coat of paint, the old Thiensville Van Buren School is still recognizable to the inquisitive eye. When it was built, in 1866, it stood alone in an open field and had a hipped roof with a ventilated wooden cupola at its peak. The building was erected to replace the area's first school, which had served since 1846. The fieldstone walls have heavily mortared joints with inscribed course lines, and the corners are finished with dressed quoins. The windows are surrounded with brick and have keystoned elliptical arches. Among those to attend this school was the late H.V. Kaltenborn, the nationally famous "dean of newscasters". Around 1900 the old building was expanded with the addition of two rooms on the east, and the last classes were held here in 1923. Three years later A.L. Gilbert founded a children's shoe company and purchased the school for use as a factory. It has since been remodelled and enlarged many times.

WAUBEKA

This town was named after the Indian chief, Waubeka, who had a village here on what is now the Milwaukee River. In the 1870's a pioneer railroad told the farmers and townspeople that it would be more costly to bring their tracks to Waubeka than to continue them straight north. When they asked for investors, the local residents turned them down and the railroad went to Fredonia instead. In those days being bypassed by a transportation artery often meant doom for a small town; but as the locals predicted, their waterpower would insure continued prosperity. By the 1880's there were seven industries in this thriving little settlement.

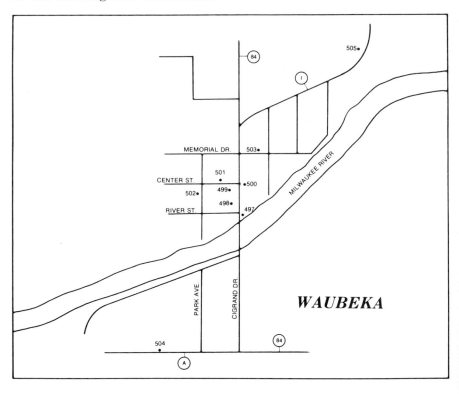

497. Bidinger Residence
N5406 Cigrand Dr.　　　　　c.1850
Among the oldest remaining houses in Waubeka, this stuccoed brick building was the residence of one of the towns four blacksmiths. His shop, now abandoned, still stands next door. It is a fine fieldstone structure which was also stuccoed at an early date. The cornice returns, a common characteristic of the Greek Revival style, are missing on the house, but nailing grounds in the masonry prove their one-time existence.

498. Heinrich Klessig Store
N. 5411 Cigrand Dr. c.1860

Built as a combined general store and residence, this frame, Greek Revival structure has had numerous additions and remodelings. Originally a one-story wing, the dwelling was later raised to become two stories. In 1903 William Arndt opened a hardware store and tinsmith shop here, and the building has served in that capacity ever since. The north addition came in 1922.

499. Eagle Hotel and Dance Hall
N5419-23 Cigrand Dr. c.1880

The first Eagle Hotel was built in 1859 across the street on the northwest corner of Cigrand Drive (formerly Waubeka St.) and Center St. After it burned down, the present structure was erected by a Luxembourger, Mike "Pop" Mueller. The dance hall, attached on the south, may have been built at the same time. Although there are a couple of rooms on the second floor front, the rest of the building is one huge dance hall with a bar and a balcony.

500. Wadewitz Butcher Shop
N5426 Cigrand Dr. c.1884

This pleasantly detailed building looks as though it might always have been a residence, but it once had a square false front which extended above the present roofline. What is now the living room was a butcher shop, and there was a sausage kitchen in the basement. Eventually the raised front was trimmed down to the pitched roofline, and a new cornice was added to finish its appearance.

501. Waubeka Firehouse
410 Center St. 1904

This tiny, but functional, building is typical of the minimum firehouse facilities to be found in small towns. Since the fire fighters were volunteers and summoned by bells to the fire station, there was no need for living quarters or office space. Here was just enough room for equipment storage and a prominent tower to elevate the all-important bell for maximum efficiency. Compare this with the Newburg fire station. (see#565).

502. T. Borchardt Residence & Shop
N5415 Park St. c.1875

This T-shaped building was the residence and workshop of Waubeka's tailor. He had four sons who became tailors, and a few of them moved to Milwaukee. A common practice in small towns was to combine one's dwelling with a business as in this structure. The shop segment has a pitched roof, but the two corners are raised to a horizontal cornice, creating a partial false front.

503. St. John's Catholic Church
W4088 Memorial Drive c.1855

When this fieldstone Gothic church was erected, it had an octagonal belfry with louvered openings and a spire. A priest from Little Kohler made regular round trips to serve the parish. About 1910 the Catholics moved away, and the building was later used as a storage facility for a local automobile dealer. The spire was subsequently removed, and finally the present owners, St. Paul's Community Church (UC of C), acquired the building.

504. Warren Cooley Residence
W4156 Highway A 1851

This Federal style house was built by Mr. Cooley and his young son Charles, who, three years later, became the man of the house when his father, a sister and a brother-in-law died at the same time of cholera. Charles later married; and his son, Robert Lawrence Cooley, was born here in 1869. Robert founded the Milwaukee Vocational School (see #199), the first of its kind in the country. The two-story CCB house has a one-story wing and a captain's walk.

505. Birthplace of Flag Day
N5595 Highway I 1885

Bernard J. Cigrand, a navy lieutenant, professor of dentistry and historical author first celebrated the birthday of the U.S. flag here at Stony Hill School. In this humble fieldstone building he held the first recognized observance of the congressional adoption of the Stars and Stripes (June 14, 1877) on June 14, 1885. After crusading for thirty-one years, Dr. Cigrand finally achieved his goal when president Woodrow Wilson instituted national Flag Day in 1916.

Opposite: Walter Demmon farmhouse Page 238 No. 511

WASHINGTON
COUNTY

WASHINGTON COUNTY

In the beginning, Washington County bordered on Lake Michigan and averaged 27 miles in width. Between the eastern edge of Dodge County to the lake, it included 648 square miles. It was set off from the original Milwaukee County in 1836, but after lengthy hot debates it was finally split to create Ozaukee County in 1853. The rolling landscape still shows the residual effects of the last ice age. Gravel beds, kames, kettles, eskers and small lakes abound, especially in the north central area. Germantown was the first permanent community in the smaller Washington County. It was settled in 1839, and all the land had been claimed by 1845.

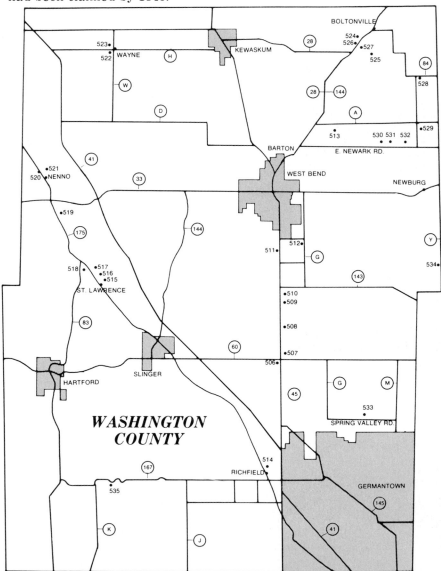

506. Frankin Grist Mill Office
3623 Highway 45 c.1855

The original mill on this property, built by a Mr. Nauth, burned down in 1862. It was rebuilt in brick by Ehlers & Eggert, in 1866, and operated by them for eight years. The mill is now gone, but remains of its foundation and the dam survive on the property. Until 1975 the mill office was covered with 12-inch cedar vertical board-and-batten siding. When the siding was taken off the log structure a layer of wheat chaff, possibly added for insulation, was revealed.

507. Francis Everly Log House
N.E. corner Hwys. 45 & 60 1844

The Francis Everly family settled here in 1843, and the next year the father and his three sons (Francis Jr., Frederick, and Jacob) erected this two-story dwelling. This is believed to be the first log house in the area. Later in the nineteenth century, before it was considered desirable to preserve log structures, this one was covered with clapboard siding. It remained disguised until about 10 years ago.

508. Peter Hoffmann Farmhouse
4136 Highway 45 1851

This unusual dwelling is constructed of fieldstone of random sizes and colors with roughly dressed quoins. The segmental arches over the first floor windows are made with cream brick, but those over the second floor are orange. It is possible that this house was allowed to deteriorate for a time and that the gable had to be rebuilt with brick. If this was the case, it would explain the window arches near that repair.

509. J. Spaeth Farmhouse
4720 Highway 45 1866-73

The Spaeth family owned the 50-acre farm, on which this house was built, from before the Civil War until the 1970's. The residence was built in two stages with the brick section first, in 1866, and the fieldstone wing added later, in 1873. The CCB block is set on a fieldstone foundation and has a full triangular pediment with a denticulated brick cornice. Its date is scratched into the brick work.

510. Henry Rogge Farmhouse
4802 Highway 45   1885 and earlier
Until the present owners acquired this house in 1960, the farm had been owned by the Rogge family since the Civil War. The substantial fieldstone house is carefully constructed with heavy mortar joints and inscribed course lines. The front two-story block is dated on a stone which reads "H. Rogge — 1885", but the other section may be as much as 20 years older. Just north of the house is a finely-crafted fieldstone pig barn with the date, 1882, inscribed in the mortar.

511. Walter Demmon Farmhouse
5545 Highway 45   c.1860
This beautifully detailed structure is one of the West Bend area's finest brick dwellings. Its CCB walls are trimmed with applied, scroll-cut, wooden ornaments over the lintels and a decorative brick cornice. Demmon, a native of New York state, settled in this area in 1846 and built what was described as a "superior" log cabin. The same word was used to describe the farm which he spent 35 years developing on this land.

WRL

512. F.W. Schroeder Farmhouse
5657 Highway G   c.1860
Mr. Schroeder was a farmer, dairyman, stock raiser and manager of the West Bend Cheese Factory. His son, Carl (1856-1944), developed one of the first registered Holstein-Friesian herds in Wisconsin and from it were bred many registered herds throughout the world. From this "cedar lawn" herd came two world champion cows. This fine painted-brick house, of a modified Greek Revival design, has segmental-arched lintels with an ornamental brick molding.

NR WRL

513. Lizard Mound State Park
Highway A between Indian Lore Rd. and Highways 28-144
In this area are thirty-one well-preserved burial mounds built by prehistoric Indians. Almost unique to the state of Wisconsin, these oddly formed earthworks, called "effigy mounds", were made in the shapes of birds or animals. They usually contained the remains of one or two Indians, along with tools, weapons, and pottery. Pictured here is the lizard effigy after which the park was named.

514. Adam Maurer Hotel
1891 Railroad St. 1873-1903

By 1873 Maurer's name began to be associated with this building, but a part of it was already standing as an earlier tavern. Just who built the first section, and what it looked like, has not been determined, but the two subsequent additions were dated. A marble tablet with the inscription, "A. Maurer-1885", marks the first hotel and dance hall addition. In 1903 the north wing was added. The CCB, Italianate structure has fine wooden brackets and faces the railroad tracks.

515. St. Lawrence Catholic Church
4890 Highway 175 1880

This very imposing Gothic structure was built under the aegis of Rev. Martin Weiss and has a fine, typically cruciform ground plan. Very little has changed since it was erected in 1880, and the original colored, grisaille-type windows are in a fine state of preservation. Even the front doors, which are often among the first items to be modernized, can still be seen. The parish was organized in 1846.

516. Ziegelbauer Residence and Blacksmith Shop
4928 Main St. 1867

A beautiful and colorful effect was achieved in this dwelling/shop by the use of split fieldstones laid with heavy mortar joints and window arches which are made of yellow brick. The low section, originally used as a wagon-maker's and blacksmith's shop, was later occupied by a carpenter and cabinetmaker. The quoins are also made of unusually large split fieldstones.

517. John Sell Farmhouse
5134 Highway 175 1866

This imposing two-story fieldstone residence once surveyed a 146-acre stock and grain farm. The land was settled before the Civil War by John Sell, who first purchased 120 acres. A date stone above the southern gable peak contains the inscription, "1866". Here is a good example of roughly split and squared fieldstone quoins. The window frames and front doorway date from relatively recent times.

518. Jacob Weninger Farmhouse
5191 Highway 175 **1883**
This remarkably unspoiled dwelling has a number of unusual refinements and still has its original porch and chimney (two of the most frequent victims of decay and replacement). The date stone above the second floor is marble instead of the usual limestone. In addition to the inscription, "J. Weninger-1883", there are two carved ornaments on the tablet. There is an unusual carved wooden detail above the attic lunette window.

519. John Schumacher Farmhouse
4929 Highway 175 **c.1855**
This well constructed log house, with its one-and-a-half story frame wing, is located just south of the intersection of two historic roads. Now called Addison Center, this is where the old Winnebago Indian trail (Highway 175) and the Dekorra Road (Highway 33) crossed. The latter thoroughfare was blazed, in 1832, by General Dodge to connect Port Washington to Dekorra (an Indian village on the Wisconsin River).

520. S.S. Peter and Paul's Catholic Church, Rectory and School
7001 Highway 175   **1867-1904**

Here are three exceptionally interesting and well preserved buildings side-by-side in the middle of farmland. They have not only architectural interest but many important historical associations. Rev. Michael Heiss, who later became archbishop of Milwaukee, once served here as a missionary. His nephew, Rev. John Michael Heiss, later became the first resident pastor of this parish. Another important man to labor here in the 1850's and 60's was Fr. Caspar Rehrl, who founded the Sisters of St. Agnes Convent in Barton (see #600). The first Catholic settlers came to this vicinity in 1844 and were mostly of German and Irish origin. Four years later Fr. Charles Schraudenbach, who had previously served many of these parishioners at St. Lawrence (see #515), built the first church. This small log structure was enlarged in 1852 and served the parish until the present building was erected.

Church

The first part of the present church was erected in 1867 with CCB on a fieldstone foundation. Its Gothic windows are topped with brick hood moldings and are recessed in stepped brick jambs. The glass has fine grisaille-type painting. Each window is framed in panels which are created by brick pilasters. The handsome buttressed tower was built in 1904 and has an octagonal lantern with eight gables supporting the spire. When this was added, the 1867 roof was removed and its pitch was made steeper. The interior is unusually fine for a country church and contains three carved and gilded altars.

Rectory

Built in the same year as the church (1867), this attractive residence was constructed with brick made on local farms. Its unusual design resembles the Gothic Revival with lacy scroll-cut bargeboards. The windows are topped with interesting sinuous hood moldings. The gable angles and front porch are more typically Victorian. The interior was completely rebuilt about the turn of the century.

School

Originally a convent and school combined, this CCB structure was built during the pastorate of Fr. John Wernich (1874-1878). It replaced a log schoolhouse which had served since 1845. Its highly unusual false front may have been added as an afterthought to more closely match the church. Its Gothic windows are set in three bays divided by brick pilasters. The cornice is decorated with squares which are recessed in the brickwork.

521. Mike Gehl General Store
7010 Highway 175   **c.1880**

This rare survivor of the nineteenth century is still being operated as a general store and tavern. Inside are the original shelves, counters and display cases, along with the doors, moldings, and wooden ceiling, which were there when the building was new. The second floor was once a hotel and has 7 bedrooms and a large hall. The 2-story CCB eclectic Victorian structure still has its full-width porch canopy with scroll-cut ornament.

522. Wendel Petri Barn
Highways W & H, S.W. corner   **c.1860**

Once the Petris owned three of the four corners at this intersection known as Wayne Post Office. On the northeast corner they operated a cheese factory, and around this crossroads they had a general store and a warehouse. This building was a barn, and for years calves were butchered inside. The two-story fieldstone structure is Greek Revival in style and has wooden cornices.

523. German Evangelical and
Reformed Salem's Church
Highway W just North of H   **1879**

The datestone over the entrance to this church may be the only one like it in Wisconsin. It is rare in that not only are the church and date shown, but a commercial message, "West Bend Marble Works" is chiseled into the tablet. This congregation organized in 1857 and built a church the same year. Their original name was Evangelical Lutheran St. Jacob's Congregation. In 1878 they reorganized under the new name and shortly thereafter built this pretty little Gothic church. The spire rises from a well-proportioned octagonal bell cupola with eight gablets. The beautiful, well-kept grounds include straight rows of mature trees, three buildings, and a graveyard. The school, church, parish house, and outhouse are all built with CCB.

524. Odd Fellows Hall
Scenic Dr. and Bolton Dr.   **1888**

This handsome CCB Italianate building was erected by the "Kickapoo Lodge" of the International Order of Odd Fellows. Founded in 1870, the fraternal lodge disbanded after 30 years and sold its clubhouse to the "Modern Woodmen of America", who added the frame dance hall in 1906. The well preserved structure still has its original ornamental wooden cornice, and the carved date stone with the I.O.O.F. symbol. Its beautifully proportioned entrance facade is framed with brick corner pilasters.

525. St. John of God Catholic Church
1488 Highland Dr. 1891
Founded in 1859 by Rev. Patrick Bradley, this parish was predominantly Irish. The first church, built in 1860, was a 31x49-foot brick structure. The present Gothic building was made of CCB set on a fieldstone foundation. The church is now a mission of St. Michael's. West of the graveyard and church are the ruins of two large fieldstone buildings with dressed quoins.

526. Fred C. Schuler Residence
9286 Bolton Dr. c.1868
This handsomely proportioned CCB dwelling was erected by the partner of Harlow Bolton, after whom the town was named. Schuler and Bolton ran the Reliance Roller Mills and built the local cheese factory. The mill was continued, after 1894, by Fred's son, who later became a banker in West Bend. This structure has an unusual wooden cornice which curves down at the corners and an original frame porch. The bricks were made at the Diesterhaupt yard.

527. William Riley Farmhouse
9060 Hwy. 28-144 c.1865
This well-constructed fieldstone farmhouse has been owned by the same pioneer Boltonville family for over a century and a quarter. The Riley family first settled in this vicinity in 1847 and later built this sturdy dwelling with local stones and neatly dressed quoins. A one-story frame wing is attached to the masonry dwelling.

528. The Saxonia House
421 Highway 84   **1855**

This rare example of German fachwerk-bau architecture is one of the largest buildings of its kind in Wisconsin. In November of 1855, a celebration was held to christen the new structure as a brewery, a residence for the brewer's family, a social hall, and an inn to serve new settlers in the township. It is set on the outskirts of the village of Fillmore and once was the focal point of an 89-acre tract called "Spring Brook Farm". The building was erected by Ernst Klessig, a brewer, and used partially for the manufacture of beer. Further south on the property the aging "cellars" can still be seen as a large "cave" dug into a small hill with a huge stone entrance arch. The Farmington Township turnverein was organized here and held its meetings in the building until 1867, when members were able to construct their own facility. Although the exterior has been covered with stucco, careful inspection will reveal the outlines of the timber construction. The spaces between the hand-hewn, pegged timbers are nogged with soft orange-colored bricks. Much of the interior has been changed, but a few old doors remain. The Victorian porch was added later.

529. Braatz/Foley Barn
7540 Highway M   **c.1850**

This rare fachwerk and log barn was probably built in two stages. The northern section is made entirely of logs with a central pass-through. The southern segment, which is covered with vertical board siding, is actually a fachwerk structure of hewn timbers nogged with CCB. The builder of this barn has not been determined, but the Foley family owned the land for nearly a century. Henry Braatz, the previous owner, probably built at least a part of the building.

530. Peter Schwin Farmhouse
1060 E. Newark Drive   **c.1860**

Green Lake was once named Schwin Lake for Peter Schwin who came to this territory in 1848 and bought 400 acres. He gave away most of the land to his children, and, by the time that Michael Schwin came to own the parcel, it had dwindled to 109.48 acres and the lake had been renamed. In 1892 Michael's tract was called "Green Lake Farm". This well built fieldstone house has inscribed mortar joints and CCB lintels.

531. St. Peter's Church
1010 E. Newark Drive 1861
This fine fieldstone church, of the rural German type, has dressed quoins and an interesting cross near the front gable peak executed in reddish stones. An elongated half-octagon apse is on the rear; and the church still retains its old linens, reed organ, and candles of unbleached wax. It is now used as a cemetery chapel, and mass is said twice a year for historical and sentimental reasons.

532. Peter Kessel Farmhouse
720 E. Newark Drive c.1857
This exceptionally well built fieldstone dwelling once dominated a 140-acre farm. Its handsome walls are laid with heavy mortar joints and prominently inscribed horizontal course lines. The quoins are neatly dressed, and the sills are embellished with chiselled margins. A scar on the southern (front) wall indicates that at one time a long porch stretched across the full width of the house. Of the two barns on the property, one is made of fieldstone.

533. David's Star Church
Spring Valley Rd., 2/10 mile west
of Church Rd. 1856
This fine limestone country church was the second house of worship built by a German Lutheran congregation which was founded here in 1843. Although it is partially obscured by a recent vestibule, the unusual date stone can still be seen over the original entrance. Inscribed thereon is the name of the congregation in German (David's Stern), the date (1856), and a six-pointed star. A clapboarded octagonal belfry supports the squat spire.

534. St. Augustine
Roman Catholic Church
5479 Highway Y 1857
This was built to serve a mission which was established by Father Caspar Rehrl (see #600). It is a fine early example of heavily mortared fieldstone work with dressed quoins. In early years a school was conducted in the basement by the Sisters of St. Agnes from Barton. There are two unusual features about the church, the octagonal roof on a square belfry and the fact that its back faces the road.

535. Holy Hill
Highway 167 between K and CC

One of the highest and most beautiful wooded hills in southeastern Wisconsin, this 289-foot peak was called Butte des Bois by French traders in the days before statehood. For years it was known as Lapham's Peak, but that name was later transferred to another eminence (see #615). As years passed, it was also called Government Hill, Big Hill, and finally a 15-foot-high wooden cross was erected on the summit, in 1858, and it was renamed St. Mary's Hill. In 1863 a log church was erected here, and nearly twenty years later it was replaced by a substantial brick, Gothic structure. About this time it became known as Holy Hill. The shrine became the responsibility of the Discalced Carmelite Fathers in 1906, and a monastery was erected near the church. The present imposing Romanesque church, with its pair of 192-foot spires, was completed in 1931. Designed by Chicago architect Herman Gaul, this brick and stone edifice still shelters the original white oak cross which was erected over a century ago by Father Haselbauer.

GERMANTOWN

The village of Germantown is actually a 36-square-mile civil township similar to the city of Mequon in Ozaukee County. Almost all of the early settlers were German; and this, no-doubt, led to this area's name. One of the first non-German land owners was Alexander Mitchell (see #178) who settled in Milwaukee to become one of the richest men in the state of Wisconsin. Germantown was incorporated in 1846.

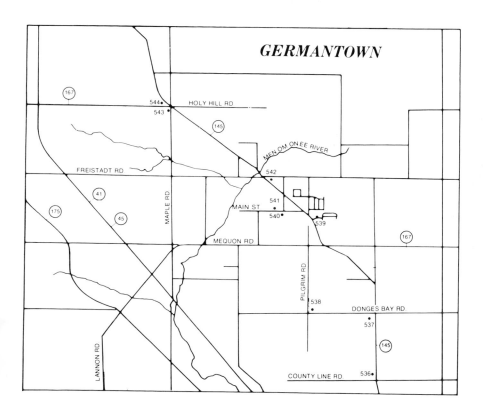

536. Henry Leonhardt Farmhouse
N96 W14424 County Line Rd.   c.1860
Once called "County Line Farm," this original 80-acre tract has been in the Leonhardt family since before the Civil War. The Greek Revival-influenced house is an unusually large structure and is beautifully built of coursed limestone rubble. The entrance is a later addition. All lintels are smooth and flush with the walls. The gable ends have two quarter-circle windows at the attic level.

537. St. John's Evangelical Church
N104 W14181 Donges Bay Rd. 1869
This handsomely detailed church was built by a German congregation which was established in 1843. A fine example of stone masonry, it was built with limestone rubble quarried on the land owned by three members. Peter Brown, also a member, was the mason. The beautiful Greek Revival influenced design, with its constrasting quoins, is said to have cost the congregation a $30 architect's fee.

538. Jacob Schunk Farmhouse
N104 W15446 Donges Bay Rd. c.1858
Schunk was one of Germantown's earliest settlers, having arrived here in 1841. His limestone, Greek Revival dwelling has a two-story frame wing. Of special interest are the two quarter-circle windows at the attic level. No doubt a variation on the lunette window (see #439), this detail is less common; and this example is more prominent than usual.

539. Frederick Witzlib Farmhouse
W154 N11474 Hwy. 145 1842
This well-preserved log house has been altered in many ways, but much of the heavily chinked original wall surface can still be seen. The porch and the dormer are additions; and the gable ends, cornice, and dormer have been covered with aluminum. Once set on a 76-acre farm, the house and its owner have appeared on early maps with various spellings; i.e., Witzlieb, Witzleb.

540. Germantown Mutual Insurance Company Marker
N116 W16150 Main St.
"Chartered by a special act of the State Legislature April 1, 1854, Wisconsin's first mutual insurance company was organized by a group of farmers for protection against fire losses. Its first office was in Stage Coach Tavern. From 1870-1911 the home office building was located in Dheinsville on the old Milwaukee-Fond du Lac Trail and moved to this site in 1911." (Also see #543.)

541. Diefenthaler & Co. Store & Saloon
N116 W16322-34 Main St.
1885 and later

This large building complex began, in 1885, with what is now the center section on the Main Street front. It was used as a general store and saloon. About 1892 the eastern section was built and for years was occupied by the Germantown State Bank. The western addition came in 1924. The CCB structure had elliptical-arched windows which have been squared off; there is an unusual tower at the rear with an ogee mansard roof.

542. Staats Brewery House
N120 W16701 Freistadt Rd.   1871

This is believed to be the residence of the man who operated the old brewery which still stands a short distance to the southeast. The brewery was founded by a Mr. Staats and was later owned by A. Hilgendorf and then Albert Reingruber. The 2½-story stone house has numerous scroll-cut brackets with drop finials arranged in pairs to support the eaves. Nailing grounds, imbedded in the south wall, indicate that the pediment was once a full triangle.

543. Germantown Mutual Insurance Company
N128 W18875 Highway 167   1870

The design of this handsome office building is an unusual variation of the Victorian Italianate style. Over the semicircular-arched transom of the front door is a rare round date stone which gives the name of the company (see #540) and the date of construction. There was once a wooden-cornered captain's walk on the roof with an iron railing. When the building was converted to a residence, the round arches of the windows were eliminated, but their keystones can still be seen.

544. Christ Evangelicial Church
N12808 Fond du Lac Ave.   1862

Founded in 1842, by German immigrants, the Evangelische Christus Kirche first worshipped in a school and then built a log church in 1850. This limestone Gothic structure was erected 12 years later on land donated by Philip Dhein. In the adjacent cemetery is a rare cast iron grave marker designed in an architectural Gothic manner. It is covered with a marbleized glaze, and the name of the deceased appears on a two-color enamelled plate as an insert.

HARTFORD

Hartford, the fourth name for this town, was designated by the territorial legislature in honor of the earliest settlers who had come here from Connecticut (perhaps from the town of Hartford in that state). The first name was Wayne, then Benton and then Wright. In 1842, three Rossman brothers in Prairieville (now Waukesha) sent John Thiel and Nicholas Simon to the north on an expedition to locate a power site for a grist mill. They came to the south shore of Pike Lake and followed the Rubicon River to the site of the present dam in Hartford. A saw and grist mill was erected and the town began to grow, with mostly "Yankees" from the northeastern states. The Rossmans, considered the founders of Hartford, are honored in a present street name, a school and a subdivision.

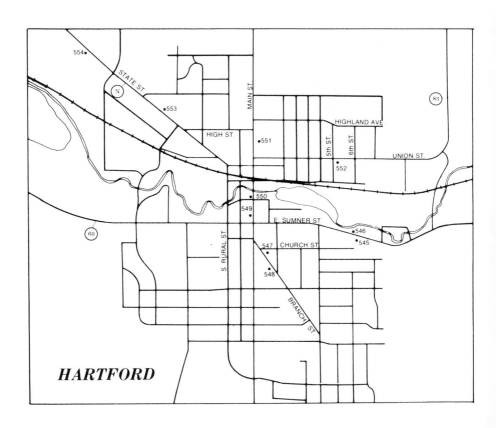

545. Dr. Frederick W. Sachse Residence
305 E. Sumner St. c.1870

The original owner of this house has not been determined, but after 1910 it was the home of the respected Hartford physician, Frederick Weston Sachse, M.D. The dwelling is an unusual variation of the Italianate style. Instead of the more common L-shape or the large front-smaller rear block, this plan is T-shaped with two wings symmetrically placed on both sides of the main structure. The eaves are supported by scroll-cut brackets.

546. Kissel Motor Car Co. Marker
E. Sumner St. between Michigan and Grand Aves.

Across the river from this marker was the plant where Kissel manufactured passenger cars, trucks, ambulances, funeral cars, taxicabs, and firetrucks. Founded by George and William Kissel, in 1906, the company grew into a 3-million-dollar operation which turned out up to 4,000 units a year. The "Gold Bug" and "White Eagle Speedster" models attracted many celebrity purchasers to Hartford and they are now prized as collectors' items. The company ceased production in 1931.

547. First Congregational Church
108 Branch St. 1853-1898

Organized in 1847, this congregation built its first church in 1853. Twenty-one years later it encased that humble 32x50-foot frame structure with cream colored brick and entirely changed the interior. In 1898 a large addition was completed which gave the church its present appearance. By then the entrance vestibule and two towers had been added. One, on the northeast corner, has since been cut down to the roofline.

548. Fred Bloor Residence
155 Branch St. 1898

This is certainly one of the most spectacular displays of late Victorian eclecticism in southeastern Wisconsin. The basic massing of elements follows the Queen Anne style which was beginning to lose popularity by that time, but the house derives its character from its two amazing porches. The L-shaped ground floor porch is a picturesque ensemble of turned posts, spindles and balusters blended with scroll-cut trim.

WASHINGTON / HARTFORD

251

549. P. Kreutz Block
41 N. Main St.   1893

Built as a hotel and tavern by Peter C. Kreutz, this two-story CCB commercial building is still being used for its original purpose under the name "Central Hotel". Although it has been rebuilt for other uses, the old stable, which served Kreutz's guests, is still located behind the hotel. While it was not uncommon for buildings of this vintage to be signed and dated in the masonry, the example near the roofline here is unusually large.

550. Hartford City Hall
109 N. Main St.   1930

This handsome Georgian-inspired structure was partially built on an old foundation. Before 1930, this lot was occupied by two buildings, an older city hall, which was built in 1892, and the historic Wheelock & Co. flouring mill. Milwaukee architects Robert A. Messmer & Bro. drew the plans. The red brick walls are trimmed with cut Bedford limestone, and an octagonal sheet copper cupola with a flagpole marks the entrance bay.

551. Residence
444 N. Main St.   c.1870

This unusually long dwelling is set with the narrow end to the street. A scar on the south central projection suggests that the original entrance was located there and that the house might once have faced Union Street to the south. What was already a long and narrow building became even more extended with later additions to the east and west. There are a few original, nicely molded, four-panel doors still in use here.

552. Smith M. Seeley Residence
304 5th St.   c.1860

This frame residence, set on a fieldstone foundation, has Gothic Revival characteristics. While the main gable angles are ordinary, the one over the front door is tall and acute. This and the scalloped trim over the windows hints that there may have been major Gothic bargeboards on the gables. A wide front porch has been removed. Seeley came here in 1857 and built a foundry. Later he joined Lewis Rowell in the Hartford Plow Works, which was only a block from this house.

553. Gottfried Falkenstein Residence
410 W. State St.   1900

This frame dwelling has two very well preserved original porches with scroll-cut ornaments and spindlework. In the gables are adjustable ornaments which were purchased out of a catalog. They came in three pieces and could be made to fit any angle, with the center segment being trimmed to length. Next door east is an excellent opportunity to compare an almost identical house which has had its ornament removed.

554. Albert Schroeder Farmhouse
759 W. State St.   c.1870

For generations this CCB farmhouse was the home of the Schroeder family, and their land extended into what is now central Hartford. The Greco-Italianate design has characteristics of the Greek Revival style on the gable ends, but otherwise it follows the Victorian Italianate mode which became popular later in the century. Of special interest are the segmental window arches of the second floor, with their brick dentils, which interrupt the horizontal cornice molding.

KEWASKUM

The township of Kewaskum once belonged to West Bend and was called "North Bend." Later the town and village were named after Chief Kewaskum of the Potawatomies. His name is said to mean "the turner", or a man who is able to "turn' fate to his advantage. While Milwaukee, Waukesha, and especially Ozaukee County are filled with Indian names, Kewaskum is the only town with such a name in Washington County. The first settlers were Mr. and Mrs. William P. Barnes in 1844.

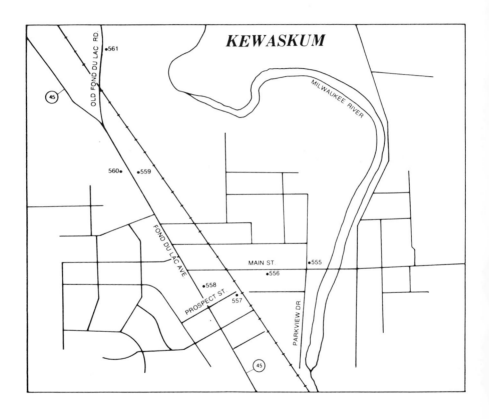

555. Herman Krohn Shop
402 Main St.   c.1900
This humble commercial building, which is attached to a house, affords an excellent opportunity to study a typical sheet metal cornice at close range. While these galvanized sheet iron and hammered zinc constructions are usually two to six stories above the sidewalk, this one is close enough to appreciate and it is in excellent condition. Two brothers, Charles and Herman Krohn, used this building as a tailor and barber shop.

556. Holy Trinity Catholic Church
249 Main St. 1905

This impressive, twin-towered Gothic church was consecrated in 1906, by Archbishop Sebastian G. Messmer from Milwaukee. Its massive facade is given verticality by the use of buttresses, two towers and the intersected tracery in the three windows above the main entrance. The CCB structure is set on a granite foundation and is trimmed in cut limestone.

557. J.M. Mueller Residence
131 Prospect St. c.1885

This eclectic Victorian dwelling is essentially an ordinary frame, clapboard structure. What gives it character are the two original porches with their decorative columns and false arches. The arches are an unusual application of scroll-cut wooden "gingerbread" which is pierced with a series of holes. The side of the house which faces the railroad tracks is shown here with its second floor porch and shingle siding.

558. Templar Hall
1230 Fond du Lac Rd. 1877

This simply designed brick structure was erected by the International Order of Good Templars for use as a meeting hall. Through the years it has served other societies, as well as the Kewaskum German Methodist Church. The unusual front window, with its brick hood mold, was once the top of an arched main entrance doorway. The building has a recessed date stone over that door which reads..."Kewaskum Lodge I.O. of G.T. No. 181, 1877".

559. Dr. Hausmann Residence
1554 Fond du Lac Rd. 1894

This elaborate frame house was designed and built by a local carpenter/contractor, Louis Brandt. One year after its construction, Brandt is said to have sold the same plan, with modifications, to Otto Backhaus and talked him into building with solid brick (see #561). Dr. Hausmann's dwelling is now sided with aluminum, but all of the original porches can still be seen with their elaborate turned spindle work. Two engraved sandblast glass panels survive in the front doors.

255

560. Charles Miller Residence
1603 Fond du Lac Rd. c.1865

This Greek Revival-influenced house is made of CCB with a pinkish cast and is set on a fieldstone foundation. It is trimmed with an ornamental brick cornice and has unusual lintels made by setting the brick vertically and at alternating depths. Miller owned a local brickyard and manufactured the bricks for the Washington County Jail in West Bend (see #590). The large front porch is a later addition.

561. Otto Backhaus Farmhouse
9376 Old Fond du Lac Rd. 1895

One of the most elaborate farmhouses in the county, this was designed and built by Louis Brandt, a local carpenter-contractor. The original landowner, Gottlieb Backhaus, came here from Germany and bought 135 acres in 1851. His son, Otto, built this solid CCB structure, which is still occupied by a descendant of the original family. It is similar, in floor plan, to the Hausmann residence (see #559). The eclectic Victorian house still has all of its original porches and trim.

NEWBURG

Barton, which is now a part of West Bend, was founded by Barton Salisbury, who built a sawmill there in 1845 (see #598). In 1848 he came to this area and founded Newburg. Salisbury built a dam and erected a sawmill and gristmill here. He also began to construct the Webster House Hotel, but died in an accident on the site (see #563). This important Wisconsin pioneer is buried in Newburg's Union Cemetery. His first name is honored as Barton Avenue in West Bend (Barton) and his last in Newburg as Salisbury Street.

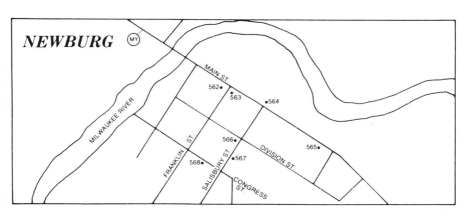

562. Fischer's General Store
527 Franklin St.   c.1870

This two-story commercial building, with its attached residence, is a fine example of ornamental brick masonry. The decorative horizontal banding is accomplished by laying bricks vertically and on a diagonal. By using one of these bands and two additional brick patterns, above and below, a very picturesque cornice was created. On the store's second floor windows, limestone corbels are chamfered down to an inset brick window frame.

563. Webster House Hotel
526 Franklin St.   1849

The founder of Barton, Wisconsin, died in an accident while this hotel was being built. Barton Salisbury was working on the roof when a rafter broke and he fell to the ground. He and his two nephews were erecting what was to be the first hotel in Newburg. It is a three-story frame Greek Revival building, and in later years it was known locally as the "White House". Mr. Salisbury was laid to rest in Newburg's Union Cemetery.

564. Max Weinand Saloon
518 Main St.　　　　　　　　c.1875

This 2½-story false front tavern is one of the best, unspoiled examples of its type still standing. Since it was built, the frame structure has always served in its original capacity as a tavern. The clapboard facade is cheerfully decorated with ornamental shingle work, a modillioned cornice, diagonal siding and colored-surround windows. There are many other original details including hardware, interior ceiling, and large pane front windows.

565. Newburg Fire Station
423 Main St.　　　　　　　　c.1887

This humble frame building once had a tall false front which rose above the peak of the present roof to a horizontal cornice. With that facade the structure appeared to be more substantial, and the east door then had an arch like the original west door. The bell tower, with its unusual diamond windows, is original. Newberg's first fire "engine" was purchased in 1886 and was a hand drawn pump cart with wooden water tanks.

566. Nicholas Maas Cobbler Shop
423 Salisbury St.　　　　　　　1859

Mr. Maas sold his boots and shoes in the 2½-story corner block and lived in the low south wing. This unassuming Greek Revival-influenced CCB building has many unusual details. All of the original display shelves and bins survive in what was once the salesroom. Handmade iron espagnolette bolts can be seen on the windows, and V-shaped drain grooves are cut in the wooden sills. A very rare signature was made on a grained door jamb by its craftsman, Robert Klein.

567. Newburg Grade School
412 Salisbury St.　　　　　　1902

This otherwise ordinary schoolhouse has a number of unusual details. Its CCB walls are set on a fieldstone foundation, and above the windows are straight horizontal drip courses of brick. A bay window above the entrance is half-octagon in plan and matches the louvered octagonal cupola at the intersection of roof ridges. The date and inscription, "Public School", appear in raised letter on a sheet metal sign.

568. Holy Trinity Catholic Church
517 Congress St.   1899

A very impressive Victorian Gothic structure, this was built to succeed what was described as a "sober looking" earlier brick church erected in 1859. The cornerstone from that old church was laid along with the 1899 stone in the present foundation. The CCB walls are trimmed with cut limestone and sheet metal. Before a bell was purchased for the old church, in 1862, the parishioners were summoned by striking a steel hoop.

SLINGER

Baruch Schleisinger Weil, a German-Alsatian, had 527 acres of Polk Township platted for a village in the 1840's. It was called Schleisingerville, after him, until 1921 when ten letters were dropped from the name and the town was re-incorporated as "Slinger". Weil also erected a distillery and was responsible for the coming of the railroad to this town. It was not long before hotels, blacksmiths, shoemakers, wagon builders and merchants began to crowd the area. Weil eventually moved to West Bend, in 1853, where he built a house at the top of the 8th Avenue hill (see #595).

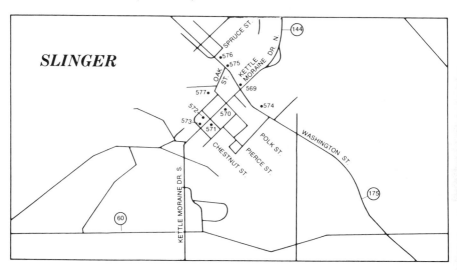

569. Roth's Hotel Barn
N. Kettle Moraine Drive
just east of Washington St.   **1862**
The first hotel on this corner was erected in 1861 by Fred Roth. A year later he built a large dance hall and this substantial barn. The old frame hotel was replaced by another in 1910; but the dance hall, which attracted people from a wide area for seasonal affairs, still stands next door to the north. For those events, and for church services, this barn provided space for up to 80 horses. The fieldstone walls have dressed quoins and brick arches.

570. St. Paul's Lutheran Church
200 S. Kettle Moraine Dr.   1886

Until this church was erected, the congregation, which was organized in 1875, held all of its services in private houses and in a public hall. Its first pastor was Rev. Albert Opitz, and the name was the "German Evangelical Lutheran Congregation of Schleisingerville". The CCB Gothic structure is set on a fieldstone foundation and is trimmed with cut sandstone.

571. Dr. J.E. Reichert Residence
308 S. Kettle Moraine Dr.   c.1885

This 2½-story CCB residence was the home of Dr. Reichert, who married one of the Rosenheimers and who, therefore, is buried in the family cemetery (see #576). The brick house has a steeply pitched roof and stick gable bracework. Heavily striated buff sandstone is used for lintels, and a 45-degree chamfer is cut into the bottom edge of each one. Original scroll-cut ornament survives on the bay window and the front porch.

572. Odd Fellows Hall
309 S. Kettle Moraine Dr.   c.1870

This unusual CCB Italianate structure was originally used as a meeting hall for the Odd Fellows Fraternal Organization. A date stone, under the gable peak, contains the inscription, "I.O.O.F." (International Order of Odd Fellows) and their symbol, a three-link chain. A projecting pavilion, in the middle-front, causes the wooden cornice to make unusual bends. The original entrance was probably in this section. All cornice brackets are 3-piece, scroll-cut laminations.

573. E. Penoske Residence
315 S. Kettle Moraine Dr.   c.1865

The original builder of this house has not been determined, but it is the least spoiled of three similar houses in this block. One is next door west, and the other is across the street. Each dwelling has an excellent, decorative, wooden porch and all three designs are different. The Penoske house is made of CCB and has segmental window arches with integral drip courses. The basic stylistic influence is Greek Revival.

574. St. Peter's Roman Catholic Church
208 E. Washington St.   **1892**

This parish first worshipped in a log church erected in 1856 and was served by missionary priests from St. Lawrence and Barton. This handsome Romanesque structure was built under the aegis of Rev. Charles Grobschmit. The CCB walls are set on an unusual foundation which is all fieldstone except for those areas under the buttresses, which are rock-faced limestone. The 138-foot high steeple contains three bells.

575. Lehman Rosenheimer General Store
200 W. Washington St.   **1860**

A native of Dormetz, Bavaria, Lehman Rosenheimer came to America in 1840 and to Milwaukee two years later. In 1855 he bought an 80-acre tract here which comprises most of present-day Slinger. This large frame Greek Revival store has been enlarged and remodelled many times, and it is now hidden under aluminum siding. In its heyday there was a tavern at ground level and staircases leading up to the store from both corners. Mr. Rosenheimer established the family cemetery nearby (see #576).

576. Rosenheimer Family Cemetery
W. Washington St. at Spruce Ave.
     c.1868

This beautiful two-acre cemetery is one of only a few privately owned cemeteries in the state. Established by Lehman Rosenheimer, around 1868, this has been the burial ground for 56 people from four generations of his family. Eight of Lehman's 11 children are buried here around a large central monument which contains the names of the original family. The bordering Spruce Ave. was named for the 100-year-old row of Norway spruce trees which Lehman planted on the grounds.

577. 6th District Grade School
201 Oak St.   **1885**

Built originally to serve as a school and city hall, this CCB structure now houses the Slinger Fire Department and the village clerk. Before the eastern wing windows were filled with brick and doors were cut through the wall, the building was symmetrical and had a taller bell tower with a pyramidal roof. The walls are decorated with ornamental brickwork.

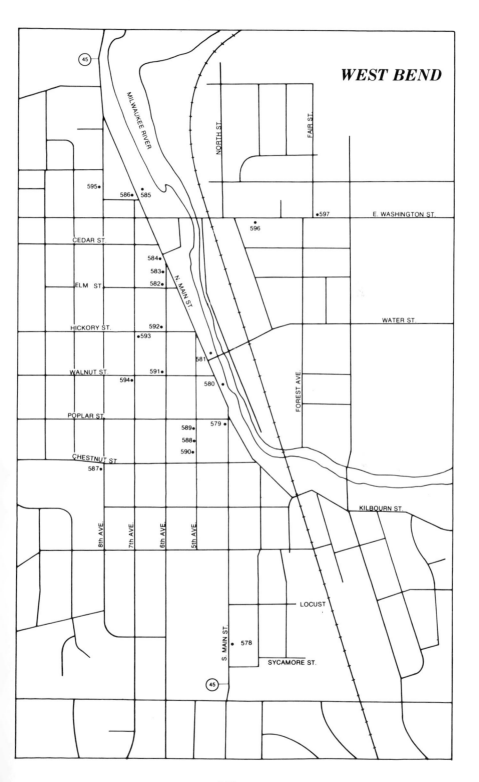

WEST BEND

WEST BEND

When the territorial legislature authorized the building of a road from Milwaukee to Fondulac, Bryon Kilbourn (see *Kilbourntown*) Erastus B. Wolcott (see #133) and James Kneeland recognized an opportunity here. In 1845 these men found only a squatter living in a shack on the river here. That man, E.N. Higgins, joined the three Milwaukeeans in purchasing the village site of 720 acres. Kilbourn was the one who created the name, West Bend, for the new venture. In 1853, when old Washington County was divided to form Ozaukee County, West Bend became the new Washington County seat. The town grew to become an important industrial and commercial center, while the residential areas were located on the surrounding hilltops.

578. Amity Leather Products Co.
735 S. Main St.   **1924 and later**
A fine example of "moderne" factory architecture, this tan pressed brick structure has been Amity's main plant since the low north wing was completed in 1924. Founded in 1915, by Robert H. Rolfs, the company has grown into the largest manufacturer of billfolds and personal leather accessories in the world. When the addition was built in 1930, Rolfs commissioned Chicago architect Fred Dolke to disguise the necessary sprinkler system water tank in a modern tower which has become a company symbol.

579. Leander Frisby Residence
304 S. Main St.   **c.1853-61**
This fine Italianate house is built of CCB and has a large cupola on its hipped roof. The wooden cornice, with its brackets, extends around the half-octagon bay on the Poplar St. side. Frisby was a prominent early judge and politician who became attorney general of Wisconsin in 1881. The brick walls of his house are said to be concealing an earlier frame structure. The original porches were removed and replaced years ago.

580. Gottlieb Schlegel Bakery
229 S. Main St.   **1907 and earlier**
This old bakery was originally a two-story pitched-roof building without any ornamental detail. In 1907 Mr. Schlegel decided to update and improve the street facade by extending the front wall above the roof line, creating what is commonly known as a "false front". The painted brick addition is decorated with sheet metal cornices, ornamental panels, the owner's name and the date.

581. Treverani's Hotel and Saloon
149 S. Main St. 1886

John Treverani built this commercial structure and established a saloon in the south half of the first floor. In the north half was a kitchen and dining hall while the transient rooms and family living quarters were located upstairs. Treverani closed the hotel after nine years and continued the saloon. Since then the building has been used as a meat market and a building and loan office. The bracketed wooden cornice is especially noteworthy.

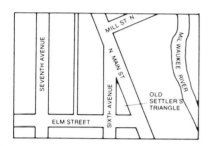

582. Old Settlers Triangle Marker
Main St., 6th Ave., Elm St.

"In West Bend's early days, this plot was a community gathering place. For over 90 years, the Triangle and the building which stood there were at the center of business, social and political life, and served as a meeting place for the old settlers. Through a gift from Community Trust, the Triangle is dedicated to the early settlers and leaders of the community."

583. Masonic Temple
220 6th Ave. 1922

A group of Free and Accepted Masons assembled on the Fourth of July, 1862, and began the organization of West Bend Lodge No. 138 F. & A.M. Their first home was in the Lemke building and, after two subsequent moves, built this structure as a permanent home in 1922. The Classical design, which resembles a Greek temple, consists of six pilasters supporting a triangular pediment. The pressed brick building is trimmed with cut limestone.

584. Washington House Hotel
228 6th Ave. 1864

For years this imposing three-story CCB hotel was the largest and finest building on the main street of West Bend. It was built in less than a year to replace an earlier frame hotel of the same name that burned to the ground on New Year's Day, 1864. Fresh vegetables for the dining room were grown in a backyard garden, and a spring well in the basement supplied drinking water. The first floor and roofline have been altered.

585. Eagle Brewery
445-59 Main St.   **1856 and later**

The first brewery building on this property was erected by Christopher Eckstein in 1856. Later in the century, when it was owned by Adam Kuehlthau, this company merged with the West Bend Brewing Company and continued until lack of local support caused the plant to close in 1972. The office building (left in the photograph) has an especially interesting cornice made with decorative brickwork over which are mounted nine elaborate scroll-cut wooden brackets to support the eaves.

586. Carl Mayer Residence
710 Beech St.   **1859 and later**

The large central section of this house was built by a German immigrant, Carl Mayer, who became a local brewer. In 1865 the north wing was added, and about five years later it was balanced by the addition of the south wing. The painted CCB Greek Revival house has fine ornamental brick cornices and a full triangular pediment. In 1875 it became the home of Andrew Pick, who married Mayer's daughter and was co-operator of West Bend Brewing Co.

587. McLane School
833 Chestnut St.   **1939**

Once called "the finest educational facility of its day", this building was originally named West Bend Grade School. In 1942 it was redesignated McLane Grade School in honor of a former superintendent of schools, D.E. McLane. St. Louis architects, O'Meara and Hills, drew a plan which blended modern conveniences with traditional forms. The building's focal point is the recessed corner entrance with two-stepped, octagonal drums surmounted by a sheet copper cupola. The red-brown brick is trimmed with carved stone and three bas-relief panels entitled, "character", "body", and "mind".

588. Courthouse Square
5th, 6th, Poplar &
Chestnut Streets 1853

This square block of land was deeded to Washington County, in 1853, by William Wightman, Byron Kilbourn, James Kneeland, E.B. Wolcott, and their wives. It was set aside as a permanent site for county buildings. Today it is occupied by the courthouse annex (see #589), the old jail (see #590), and there is a bronze statue of a doughboy, marking a monument to the county residents who lost their lives in the Civil, the First and Second World Wars, and Korea.

589. Washington County Courthouse
320 S. 5th Ave. 1889

The first courthouse, a two-story frame structure, was built in 1854-55 and moved to Main Street when this imposing building was erected. The Romanesque design is centered around an eight-story tower with a pyramidal roof which is flanked by eight similar caps on corner turrets and dormers. The massive entrance arch is repeated over many windows, and the CCB walls are accented with buff terra-cotta ornament and stained glass. Note the huge terra-cotta panel on the north wall.

590. Washington County Jail
340 S. 5th Ave. 1886

This well-preserved CCB jail was designed by architect E.V. Koch and replaced an earlier structure built in 1854. It is in remarkably unspoiled condition inside and out and still retains its original ornamental wood porch. The sheriff lived in the finished quarters at the front of the building and could look through a slit-window into the cell-block at the rear. All of the original iron floors, walls, grilles, and doors remain. The building now serves as the Washington County Historical Society.

591. St. Johannes Evangelical
Lutheran Church
146 S. 6th Ave. 1864

Organized as the German Evangelical Lutheran St. Johannes Society of the Unaltered Augsburg Confession in 1858, the congregation had no place of worship until this church was built. The original structure faces 6th Ave., and the large rear section was added in 1897. When the building was new, an octagonal belfry with a spire rose from the roof ridge and there was no front porch. The brick cornice molding is exceptionally wide and complex.

592. West Bend City Hall
100 S. 6th Ave. 1900

The design of this picturesque eclectic building was once described as "modern colonial style". It once housed both the city offices and the fire department. The stables and horse-drawn fire engines are long gone, but the department's hose-drying tower, with its bell cupola, is still there. The CCB building, is trimmed with sheet metal and has an octagonal cupola with an ogee dome.

593. Holy Angels Catholic School
105 S. 7th Ave. 1880

The original Holy Angels Church was built on this site in 1853. It was moved away, in 1879, and became a storehouse and granary when this CCB structure was erected. The Gothic design is distinguished by brick pilasters and corbels and the unusually simple brackets supporting the eaves. A very attractive and most uncommon detail can be seen above the windows where the "dripstones" are made of bricks set diagonally. The building was a school until 1926.

594. Baptist Church
S. 7th Ave. S.W. corner Walnut St.
1872

This very useful church has served many religious groups since it was built. The brick Gothic structure was erected by the Baptists of West Bend and once had a tall spire. It is set on a fieldstone foundation and has nicely proportioned lancet windows with brick hood moldings. The bulding has served the German Methodist Episcopal Church, the Assembly of God, and now is the Bible Baptist Temple.

595. B. Schleisinger Weil Residence
440 N. 8th Ave. 1853

The city of Slinger, Wisconsin, originally called Schleisingerville, was named after Baruch Schleisinger Weil, who founded that community in the 1840's. He moved to West Bend in 1853 and erected this house at the top of the 8th Ave. hill. It was designed and built by an early cabinetmaker, Peter deTuncq. The unusual brick cornice stops short of the corners, and the windows are asymmetrically spaced. Two fine scroll-cut porches were added by a later owner.

596. Charles M. Mayer Residence
131 E. Washington St.   1875-76

Once one of West Bend's finest mansions, this CCB Italianate structure originally was the home of Mrs. Maria Mayer and her son, Charles. They owned a large parcel of land east of the river which included the popular resort, "Schlitz Grove", and which later was subdivided into almost 100 lots. The original front porch, a delicate turned-post affair with a spindle frieze, was eventually replaced by the present Classical verandah.

597. Fred Karsten Residence
224 E. Washington St.   1879

Karsten settled here, in 1856, and had to clear timber from his land. This house, built 23 years later, remained in the family until 1937. Above the date stone, which reads "F. Karsten - 1879", is a very unusual denticulated drip molding made with brick. The two-story house and its one-story wing are made of CCB with decorative brick window and cornice treatment.

WEST BEND (BARTON)

Now a part of West Bend, this was once a distinctly separate community to the north. It began, in 1845, when Barton Salisbury built a sawmill here (see #598). At first the village was called "Salisbury's Mills" like so many pioneer settlements which used the name of the central and supporting business establishment. But this man and his operation were so successful and influential that both the township and the village were given the name of Barton. In 1848, Salisbury moved seven miles east and founded Newburg. He died there, in a construction accident, while building a hotel (see #563).

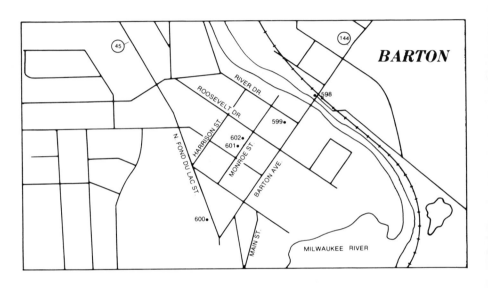

598. Barton Roller Mill
1784 Barton Ave.   1865

The original sawmill on this property was built by Barton Salisbury (see #563) in 1845 and converted into a flour mill two years later. This structure burned down in the early 1860's and was rebuilt by Robert R. Price in 1865. Fire again struck in 1914, and caused serious interior damage. It was again rebuilt with more modern equipment. The three-story CCB structure has a gambrel roof and has had numerous sections added through the years. It is located near the Milwaukee River Dam from which it drew power.

599. Residence
415 River Drive c.1855

This humble CCB dwelling is a beautifully proportioned example of a common early style in this area. Among the first houses in Barton, it has survived with less exterior alteration than its contemporaries. The Greek Revival design has the common offset entrance and only a single window at the second floor level. Its simplicity is relieved by wooden lintels with scroll-cut ogee arches and a decorative brick cornice.

600. St. Agnes Convent
1386 N. Fond du Lac St. 1858 and later

Father Caspar Rehrl founded the Congregation of the Sisters of Saint Agnes on this Barton hillside in 1858. The newly-formed order of sisters were trained here to become teachers in the many parishes that he established in southeastern Wisconsin. Three of the original buildings survive. Closest to the road is what remains of a twice-enlarged chapel with Gothic windows. Behind that is Father Rehrl's own fieldstone house (pictured) and an 1878 fieldstone barn.

601. St. Mary's Immaculate
Conception Catholic Church
Monroe St. between Roosevelt
and Jefferson 1900

Founded by Father Caspar Rehrl (see #600), the parish's first church was built of brick in 1857. The present structure, consecrated by Archbishop Katzer from Milwaukee, contains the old cornerstone and the tower clocks from the original church. The CCB Gothic design has unusual rock-faced limestone quoins on the tower and is trimmed with sheet metal.

602. St. Mary's School
Monroe St. S.W. corner Roosevelt Dr.
1876

This handsome Italianate school was erected nearly 20 years after the first St. Mary's Church (see #601), but before the rectory, which was built in 1882. Although the entrance has been altered, the building still retains most of its original details and proportions. The principal facade is divided into three bays by brick pilasters. These, the corbelled cornice, and the water table are CCB and form large panels.

Opposite: Jonathan Parsons residence Page 284 No. 631

WAUKESHA
COUNTY

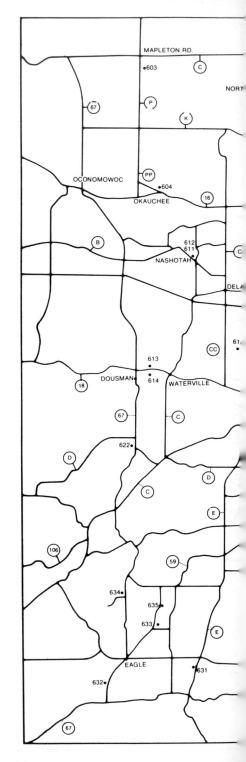

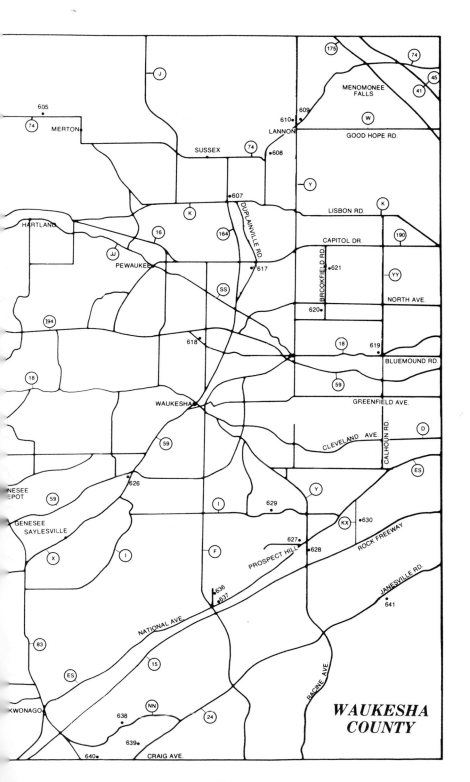

WAUKESHA
COUNTY

WAUKESHA COUNTY

The topography of Waukesha county is its principal asset. Having been sculptured by the glaciers, the area is replete with lakes, kettle holes, and hogs' backs. There are over 14,000 acres of lakes, 35 streams, 8 rivers and over 11,000 acres of public forests, parks and wildlife areas. The highest point in the county is Lapham Peak (see #615), and the largest lake is Pewaukee (4½ miles long and with an area of 2,310 acres). In the northern half of the county, called "Lake Country", is a group of a dozen major lakes around which many resorts grew up in the 19th century. Oconomowoc was the largest lake resort and Waukesha the principal mineral water resort. All of Waukesha county's resorts, however, gladly welcomed social, recreational and health seekers.

603. St. Catherine's Catholic Church
Hwy. P just south of Mapleton   1886
Originally this CCB Gothic church had a louvered belfry and a tall octagonal spire with four gablets. Its unusual cornerstone has the date "1886" and some shamrocks sculptured in high relief on a sunken panel. The fine, old, colored grisaille-style windows are still intact, and the foundation is made of fieldstone. A half-octagon apse is attached to the rear and has the same lancet windows as the nave. The parish was organized in 1847.

604. Okauchee House
34880 Lake Dr. 1841

This fine Greek Revival stagecoach inn was built by Israel McConnell at the main intersection of roads in Okauchee. McConnell originally owned 210 acres of the village center and there was once a small lake near the inn. Erected on a 30-inch thick fieldstone foundation, the walls are made of solid oak. In this rare construction technique, called *laminated wall*, 2x8 boards are stacked horizontally and dowelled to hold them together. The resulting wall, 8 inches of solid wood, was then covered with clapboards. The three-story main block has a two-story ell to the rear. Once a long porch extended across the front of the building and a second floor entrance was located directly over the present front door. The 32-room inn has a large third floor ballroom with a vaulted ceiling which is flanked by eight servants rooms on two sides. The basement contains a large fieldstone cistern and a brick oven with a built-in iron cauldron next to it. Between the two eastern-most ground floor windows on the first floor was a door to what used to be the tavern room.

605. John M. Hall Farmhouse
W29724 Highway 74 1868

A farmer and stock raiser from Cayuga County, New York, Mr. Hall settled at Merton Township in 1842. His first residence was a 12-foot square shanty without doors or windows and with a blanket hanging over the entrance. He built two others before erecting this final CCB Italianate structure. The main block has a two-story east wing and a one-story wing on the rear. Note how the bracketed, wooden cornice curves to accommodate window arches.

606. Trevor R.R. Depot
North Lake
Hgwy 83 & 74 1886

This frame depot building, with its deep bracketed overhangs, once served the Soo Line at Trevor, Wisconsin, just north of Antioch, Illinois. When the Milwaukee Road pulled out of North Lake, leaving nothing but tracks, the "Kettle Moraine Railway" was established and is operated by railroad buffs to preserve a part of the steam era. Two locomotives, a 2-6-2 Prairie from California and a 2-8-2 Mikado from Washington State, pull the rolling stock.

Admission Charge for rides.

607. William Greaves Farmhouse
N52 W23248 Hwy. K 1871

A smooth stone tablet between two second floor windows reveals the builder's name, the civil town in which he located, the number of the section where he bought land and the date of construction. This unusual gravestone-shaped piece reads, "W. Greaves, Lisbon Sec. 35, Waukesha Co., Wis., 1871". The very well built limestone structure has lintels, sills and a water table which are finished with the bush hammer and have chiselled margins.

608. St. James Catholic Church
W220 N6588 Hwy. 74 1848 & 1886

This parish, organized in the pioneer Irish settlement between old Lannon Springs and Templeton, held its first service in a log cabin owned by James Brogan in 1841. The main block of the church, built in 1848, was dedicated by Fr. James Colton, its first pastor. While this section has Gothic styling, the buttressed tower, completed in 1886, has all Romanesque arches. Both are built with rock-faced Lannon limestone.

609. Saloon
7300 Lannon Rd. c.1895

Ordinarily, a corner tavern in a small crossroads community would have been of wood frame construction, but here, where the owners of a local quarry built a dozen workers' homes of stone, the neighborhood of his saloon is built of limestone. The building's otherwise plain design is enhanced by a square corner bartizan supported over the entrance by two scroll-cut brackets. It is partially sided with cut shingles and has a straight-sided mansard roof.

610. Joe Cordie Store & Residence
7297 Lannon Rd. c.1890

While many merchants lived on the floor above their establishments, this configuration is a less common side-by-side relationship. The ell-shaped building has a pitched roof, but the business facade has the often used "false front" which rises above the actual roof and has a bracketed horizontal cornice. For more than 60 years the Walter family operated a butcher shop on the premises.

611. Nashotah House
Episcopal Seminary
3442 N. Mission Rd.   1842 and later

The oldest chartered academic institution in Wisconsin, this historic theological seminary was originally founded to be a mission to the Indians. The first building (right) was erected in 1842 at a cost of $400. The gift of a can of blue paint to Dr. Breck, one of the founders, was used to coat the new structure. Until this day it has been known as "Blue House". The second building, "Red Chapel," was built in 1843 and later moved to this site.

NR WRL WHM

612. Chapel of St. Mary the Virgin
Nashotah House (see #611)   **1859-66**

Originally dedicated to St. Sylvanus, this distinguished perpendicular Gothic church was designed by the renowned New York architect, Richard Upjohn. Almost twenty years earlier Upjohn had drawn the plans for New York City's famous Trinity Church at Broadway and Wall Street. This Waukesha County limestone structure was patterned after a buttressed English parish church and has seen major interior alterations in 1897 and 1907.

613. Elisha Edgerton Farm
Hwy. 18 just east of Dousman
1856 & 1874

This complex of buildings is all that survives of a great "Wisconsin premium" farm which was built by Edgerton on land that he settled in 1836. The small Gothic Revival carriage house, built in 1856, is made of limestone and trimmed with carved wooden window casings and bargeboards. Episcopal services were once held in a chapel upstairs. In 1865 the farm was purchased by George Washington van Brunt, whose initials, "G.W.V.B." and the date, "1874",can be seen on the westernmost building in marble.

WHM

614. Wisconsin Masonic Home
36225 Sunset Dr. (Hwy. 18)
1923 and later

In 1905 Willard van Brunt, nephew of the wealthy inventor-manufacturer, George Washington van Brunt, gave the old Edgerton farm (see #613) to the Masonic Grand Lodge as a home for old members. Previously, after G.W. van Brunt's death, his children had turned the property, over 300 acres, into the "Springdale Resort" which failed. When the Masons acquired the complex, they commissioned Milwaukee architect, Armand D. Koch, to design the main building in 1923. Subsequent additions were made in 1924, 1957, and 1964.

615. Lapham Peak
Kettle Moraine Drive
2 miles south of I-94   1916

The highest point in Waukesha County, this was called Government Hill until it was renamed in 1916. At an elevation of 1,233 feet, it is the third highest peak in Wisconsin, with only Blue Mounds and Rib Mountain being higher. The area was renamed by the U.S. Geographic Board in honor of the distinguished scholar and scientist, Increase A. Lapham, who conducted weather studies here and earned the title, "Father of the U.S. Weather Bureau".

616. Albert Campbell Farmhouse
3115 Highway 83   1848

One of the earliest settlers in Delafield Township, Campbell arrived here from Oneida County, New York, in 1837. By 1880 he was called a "leading farmer," and his 320-acre claim on the Bark River was considered to be a "fancy" farm. In his dairy barn, which still survives, the stalls were varnished, v-groove wainscoting (which has since been whitewashed). The CCB house is a 2-story, Greek Revival design with a hip roof. It is trimmed with brick corner pilasters and a deep wooden cornice.

617. Amos W. Griswold Farmhouse
W223 N3481 Duplainville Rd.   1856

A native of New York State, Griswold came here in 1844 and settled on 188 acres of land. He first lived in a log cabin and then, in 1856, built this two-story Greek Revival house with limestone from the newly-opened Sussex quarry. The well preserved Victorian porch was added later, and the original stone masonry has been covered with stucco. Mr. Griswold once was a supervisor of the Town of Pewaukee and its justice of the peace.

618. John Hodgson Residence
24198 W. Bluemound Rd.　　c.1843

A native of Yorkshire, England, Hodgson came here in 1828 and, at the age of 21, became a deputy government surveyor working in Michigan, Indiana and Wisconsin territories. His 2-story house has 23-inch-thick walls of limestone and flush dressed lintels. The unusual eaves brackets are supported by a stringcourse, and they alternate with modillions. Inside is a walnut staircase and 17 rooms.

619. Michael Dousman Residence
15670 Bluemound Rd.　　c.1843

Originally the home of a Mackinac, Michigan, fur trader, Michael Dousman, this historic mansion was later operated by Charles Dunkel as a wayside inn. Dousman, whose son, Hercules, built Villa Louis at Prairie du Chein, was said to have brought the men who built his mansion from Mackinac. The 2½-story frame Greek Revival structure, with its one-story ell, is original, but the double verandah is a later addition. After 1884 a third floor ballroom was the scene of many social events.

620. Robert J. Kiekhefer Residence
2275 N. Brookfield Rd.　　1929

An excellent example of French Provincial architecture, this imposing mansion was built by the founder and president of the American Lace Paper Co. Set on a 230-acre hillside estate, with an unsurpassed view of the hills 23 miles away, this Waukesha limestone house has a tile roof, copper gutters and downspouts, and some authentic half-timber work. Its highly picturesque silhouette, designed by Milwaukee architect Richard Philipp, includes two towers with conical roofs and weathervanes.

621. Oak Hill Cemetery
3462 N. Brookfield Rd.

Part of the land grant of pioneer, Joseph Ewbank, this historic cemetery is the burial ground for Yankee, English and German settlers, and one Revolutionary War soldier. The latter's headstone, broken in two and later strengthened with a concrete support, reads, "Nathan Hatch - Died Nov. 10, 1847 - Aged 90 Years - A Soldier of the Revolution". Hatch, who came here in the 1840's, was buried elsewhere and was later moved to this cemetery.

622. Ottowa Town Hall
W360 S3337 Highway 67　　**1874**

When the Ottowa Civil Township held its annual meeting in 1868 and the subject of building a new town hall was brought up, the resolution was defeated. It was not until 1874 that a "yes" vote insured the construction of a 20 by 40-foot brick or stone building "not to exceed $800 all completed". The well constructed limestone coursed rubble building is dated and identified on a stone above the entrance.

623. Stone Farmhouse
S50 W30732 Old Village Rd.　　**c.1865**

Little is known about this well-built limestone residence, but its fine masonry construction is noteworthy. The two-story pitched roof structure is finished with cutstone details and prominent quoins. For years the Greene family lived here and had a millinery shop in the parlour. It is said to have once been a trading post.

624. Union House Hotel
Hwy. 83, N.W. corner R.R. tracks　1861

Erected by P. Lynch, this old frame hotel was made the center of activity in Genesee Depot by Fred Schwinn. During the years of his ownership, Schwinn set up the first telephone switchboard for the community in this building, and it was operated by his sister and local girls. He helped to bring electricity to the community; he brought the first movies to the local hall and owned the first automobile in the area.

625. St. Paul Catholic Church
W314 S4200 Hwy. 83　　**c.1870**

Before 1870 the Roman Catholics in the area around Genesee Depot were served by a visiting priest from Waukesha. In 1863 they purchased this land and around seven years later built the frame Gothic church. At that time they became an out-mission of St. Theresa's parish in Eagle (see #654) and were served by their priest. In 1963 the United Pentacostal Church took over the building as the "Genesee Tabernacle".

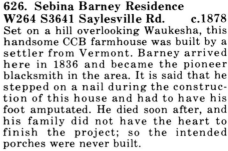

626. Sebina Barney Residence
W264 S3641 Saylesville Rd. c.1878
Set on a hill overlooking Waukesha, this handsome CCB farmhouse was built by a settler from Vermont. Barney arrived here in 1836 and became the pioneer blacksmith in the area. It is said that he stepped on a nail during the construction of this house and had to have his foot amputated. He died soon after, and his family did not have the heart to finish the project; so the intended porches were never built.

627. Freewill Baptist Church
19750 W. National Ave. 1858-59
The first Freewill Baptist Church in Wisconsin, this historic frame structure is now the home of the Prospect Aid Society, one of the oldest women's organizations in Waukesha County. The church was organized in 1840 in Rev. Rufus Cheney's house (see #628). The Ladies' Aid Society, originally of this church, took over the building when the congregation disbanded in 1925 and dropped "Ladies" from their title. The beautiful fan ornament in the triangular pediment, was once called a "sunrise."

628. Rev. Rufus Cheney Residence
S. Racine Ave. just south
of National Ave. c.1840
Called the "father of Prospect Hill", Rev. Cheney organized the first Freewill Baptist Church in Wisconsin (see #627) in this house on July 11, 1840. A native of Antrim, New Hampshire, he settled here, in what was then "Wisconsin Territory", in 1837 and built this house out of walnut trees sawn in a nearby field. He directed the founding of the first school in the area, which also met here in the early years.

629. John Konrad Meidenbauer
Log House
21800 Lawnsdale Rd. Early 1840's
When Bavarian-immigrant Meidenbauer purchased the farm, in 1848, this hand-hewn log house was already standing. Its notched corner joints are flush, non-locking dovetails. Another log building, four pigs, a sheep, 12 chickens, two acres of potatoes, seven acres of wheat, a one-acre garden and 50 head of cabbage were also included in the original $800 purchase. The present owner is one of 12 children of John Meidenbauer (a nephew of Konrad), born in the house.

630. Henry Schreiber Barn
4908 S. Calhoun Rd. 1898

One of the rare few round barns in the Midwest, this structure stands nearly 60 feet high to the top of its cupola. Unlike most cupolas, which illuminate and ventilate the barn, this one is actually the top of a silo which rises from the ground and supports the roof. Set on a fieldstone foundation, the basic construction consists of elm timbers cut on the farm. Most of the shiplap wooden siding is now covered with roll roofing, but the cupola is still original. Schreiber bought the 160-acre farm from the Gilbert family in 1892.

631. Jonathan Parsons Residence
W341 S9585 Highway E 1859

One of Wisconsin's finest Italianate farmhouses, this CCB structure was erected by a farmer who served in the Territorial Assembly of 1842. With the exception of two additions to the south and west, this excellent specimen is almost completely unspoiled. The beautifully proportioned composition is still complemented by all of its original porch trim, eaves brackets, window sills and lintels, and the fine cupola on its roof.

632. Old World Wisconsin
Highway 67, ¾ mile south of Eagle

"A 550-acre multicultural outdoor museum that conserves Wisconsin's 19th century heritage and makes history come alive through the preservation of the homesteads and artifacts of those pioneers of many nationalities who built our great state. Distinctive architectural styles may be seen as well as the furnishings and costumes of various ethnic groups." Pictured here are three buildings in a Finnish farmstead and the Friedrich Koepsel house from the farm representing the Pomeranian Germans. Other groups of carefully restored buildings, taken from all over Wisconsin, will include east and central European, Welsh, Cornish, English, Belgian, Dutch, Danish, Swedish, and Norwegian.

Admission charge

NR WRL

633. Ahira Rockwell Hinkley Residence
W354 S7910 Hwy. 59   1848

Hinkley, who came here in 1836, was the first settler in Eagle Township. His farmhouse, one of Wisconsin's finest examples of cobblestone construction, is a two-story Greek Revival design. The foundation is made of large fieldstones, but the section showing below the water table is faced with baseball-sized stones of uniform diameter. The rest of the walls are made of smaller smooth stones which were probably dropped through a hole in a board to insure uniform size.

634. P. Hinkley Farmhouse
W364 S7310 Hwy. 67   c.1865

Numerous Hinkleys came to Eagle Township from New England. A.R. Hinkley (see #633), located nearby, was from New Hampshire. When Oramel and Phoebe Hinkley arrived here from Vermont, they first stayed with A.R. and then acquired part of this 320-acre family tract. Their son, Edward, purchased 80 of the acres in 1872 after his service in the Civil War. This limestone rubble house, shown on the 1873 atlas for "P. Hinkley", may refer to Phoebe, who had been a widow since 1855.

635. Palestine School
W351 S7510 Hwy. 59   1928

"Although education in one room schoolhouses was a part of pioneer living, it continued in rural areas even to modern times. Palestine School, the last one-room school district (grades 1-8) in Wisconsin, operated until June, 1970." This land was originally the gift of A.R. Hinkley (see #633), and the first building was a log structure erected in 1846. That was replaced by a frame building in 1854 and this brick ediface in 1928. Today it is a kindergarten room for Eagle Elementary School.

636. Reformed Presbyterian Church of Vernon
W234 S7710 Big Bend Dr. 1854

The only church of its denomination in Wisconsin, this congregation was organized in 1848 by a group of Scotch settlers in the northeastern corner of Vernon Township. They were called "Covenanters" because they had supposedly "made a covenant with God". Each family was assigned a pew, and no musical instruments were allowed in the service. The beautifully proportioned frame Greek Revival building has unusual triple-hung sash (12-over 12-over 12.

637. Vernon United Presbyterian Church
S71 W23280 National Ave. 1857-59

Organized in 1847 by Scotch immigrants, this congregation first met in homes, a barn, and a schoolhouse. The fine, original, Greek Revival block, with its corner pilasters and full triangular pediment containing a "sunrise" ornament, resembles the Freewill Baptist Church on Prospect Hill (see #627). The frame porch was added in 1938, and a new educational wing, kitchen, and tower were built in 1950. The original frame structure is set on a fieldstone foundation.

638. Randall V. Craig Farmhouse
S104 W26630 Hwy. NN 1876

This well proportioned Victorian farmhouse has been preserved in almost mint condition. It is believed to have been built by the Porter family, one of whose pioneer gravestones was found in a nearby field. The date, 1876, is written in mortar inside the fieldstone foundation. There is also a date painted inside a cabinet in fancy script with the name "John Miller". While he might have been the original owner, that could also have been the builder's signature.

639. Jesse Smith Inn
S107 W25620 Hwy. 24 c.1848

One of southeastern Wisconsin's most famous plank-road inns, this three-story fieldstone structure once lodged as many as 100 guests overnight. Teamsters (going to and from the lead mines) and farmers traveling the Janesville Plank Road first were hosted by Mr. Smith in 1842 in a frame house. When this burned in 1847, the present Greek Revival-influenced stucture was erected. Jesse, a native of Andover, Vermont, owned 350 ncres here.

640. Perry Craig Farmhouse
S110 W26660 Craig Ave. 1848

A native of Hamburg, New York, Perry Craig came to Wisconsin in 1841 and spent his first five years in Mukwonago as a carpenter. He worked on such jobs as Judge Field's house (see #675) and the mill at Saylesville (see #723). In 1846 he began to acquire this 240-acre farm, most of which is still owned by his descendants. After two years in a wooden "shanty," he built this substantial fieldstone house with dressed quoins. The front of the 2-story main block has been altered.

641. St. Paul's Evangelical Lutheran Church
S66 W14325 Janesville Rd. 1905

Founded in 1857 as a mission station serving 12 families, the German congregation laid the cornerstone for this CCB Gothic church in 1905. Architect C.L. Lesser signed the structure in a stone to the left of the tower. The true cornerstone, on the other side of the entrance, is a very unusual three-foot-square limestone block with bevelled edges. It rises from the water table and has the date, "1905", in a large circle with an "A" above and a "D" below.

DELAFIELD

This village was once called "Hayopolis" supposedly because of the abundance of hay to be found here. It was later named "Nehmabin", which was probably an Indian name first given to the two nearby lakes. The lakes still carry the name but it is now spelled "Nemahbin". Then, in 1843, the town was renamed after Charles Delafield, who had come here from New York to start a mulberry grove. Once described as the "chief point on the road between Watertown and Prairieville", Delafield boasted three hotels.

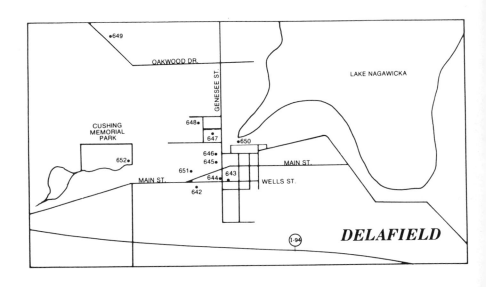

642. Hawks Inn
420 W. Wells St.　　　　　　　1847
Once a popular stagecoach stop on the Milwaukee-Madison line, this beautifully proportioned three-story Greek Revival inn was once located on Genesee St. Built by Nelson Paige Hawks (1799-1863), a cultured Yankee, this historic establishment was noted for its excellent food and drinks. In 1960, when its lot was sold for a gas station, the building was moved to this site and restored and furnished by local citizens. The structure is made of hand-hewn timbers and handmade nails.

NR WRL

643. Delafield Presbyterian Church
606 Genesee St. 1869

When the congregation was organized, in 1866, it held its first meeting in a log schoolhouse. This frame church was built three years later and was in continuous use until a new building replaced it in 1967. A Sunday school was added in 1924, and the entire structure was moved 25 feet north to a new concrete foundation in 1953. For a while the former sanctuary was used as a theater, but has now been adapted to a commercial building.

644. Pearmain Residence
617 Genesee St. c.1865

This unusual story-and-a-half CCB house is said to have been built by one of Delafield's early settlers, and it once had a fountain in the front yard which was fed by water piped from a spring far to the south. The simple, but handsome front porch is embellished with scroll-cut wooden ornament. The house was later sold to Nelson C. Hawks (son of N.P. Hawks see #642), who was the founder of the town's first newspaper, *The Young American.*

645. Hawks Inn Dance Hall
715 Genesee St. c.1850

This narrow building was once connected to Hawks Inn (see #642) by a short hallway and was originally used as a dance hall. After Hawks died in 1863, William Jacques moved the building a short distance to the present site. Built as a frame structure, it was then remodelled with a brick face and turned into a shoe shop and post office. From 1875 to 1969 it served as the Delafield town hall and had, for many years, a large front porch.

646. Andrew Proudfit Residence
727 Genesee St. c.1850

A native of New England, Proudfit moved here in the earliest days of Delafield's settlement and engaged in numerous businesses. As a builder he was responsible for a number of the town's structures, including his own house. In 1846 he purchased the local mill (see #650) and made many changes in its operation. Eventually his businesses failed, and he moved to Madison to become a successful banker. The Greek Revival house has a later porch and north addition.

NR WRL

647. St. John Chrysostom Church
Genesee St. at Church St.   1851-53
This humble frame church is a very fine example of Gothic Revival design executed in the vertical board-and-batten technique. From the pointed lancet windows to the scroll-cut bargeboards at the gable ends, this design follows the characteristics of a well known plan published by the architect of New York's Trinity Church, Richard Upjohn. The church's name honors a 4th century bishop whose eloquent sermons earned him the name Chrysostom (Greek for "golden tongue").

648. St. John's Military Academy
Genesee St. at St. John's Rd.   1884
Sidney T. Smythe, who was completing studies for the Episcopal ministry at Nashotah House (see #611), founded this academy in 1884. It grew from a two-room frame building to a 180-acre campus with 20 buildings. Most of today's structures, designed by Milwaukee architect Thomas Van Alyea, have English Gothic and medieval castle styling. Within the ivy-covered, battlemented stone walls a maximum of 400 cadets in grades 7-12 are schooled.

649. Bishop Jackson Kemper Residence
W153 Oakwood Dr.   c.1846 and later
Kemper was elected the first missionary bishop of the Episcopal Church in America in 1835. In 1842 he inspired the founding of Nashotah House (see #611) and for 16 years, as Bishop of Wisconsin, he traveled throughout the state creating missions and churches. This house, which he occupied from 1846 to 1870, is said to have been built in three stages...the first section in 1846, the two-story clapboarded section in 1852, and the limestone block in 1861. Note the row of ancient maples in the front yard.

650. John Heath Grist Mill
627 Mill St.   1840
Delafield's first grist mill, this 3½-story limestone rubble building was erected by John Heath, who also built the first frame house in the village. The otherwise coarse masonry is neatly finished with dressed quoins and chiselled sills. In 1846 the mill was purchased by Andrew Proudfit, who refitted it with a steam engine and a new race, and raised the dam.

651. Wisconsin State Fish Hatchery
417 Main St. 1907

This handsome English Tudor building was constructed with granite fieldstone and trimmed with cut limestone. Originally set on a 40-acre tract along the Bark River, the complex of six large outdoor ponds and two indoor processing ponds was a bass hatchery, the third to be established by the State Conservation Commission. Once it supplied a large quantity of bass fingerlings for stocking lakes in Wisconsin, but now is used as a research and experimental station.

652. Cushing Memorial Park
and Monument
Cushing Park Rd. at Main St. 1914

"Perhaps the most conspicuously daring trio of sons of one mother of any whose exploits have been noted in the pages of history." That comment, by biographer T.W. Haight, is part of a bronze tablet depicting the three Cushing boys on their granite obelisk monument. After spending their boyhood in Delafield, they all became military heroes. Alonzo died at Gettysburg, William sank the Confederate ironclad, Albermarle, and Howard was killed by Apaches in Arizona.

EAGLE

In 1836, a group of prospectors saw a bald eagle rising over the prairie they were crossing and named the area "Eagle Prairie". When the village was begun, it was called "Eagleville." Then a Mr. Pittman platted the new settlement, and it was temporarily named after him. After the railroad, which was mainly responsible for the growth of the town, arrived in 1851, the official name became "Eagle Center". Everything was calm, until 1876, when a 16-karat diamond was discovered in a nearby well. The craze that resulted turned Eagle into a boom town overnight. Speculators and prospectors crowded into the town and left no stones unturned trying to find what they were sure was a diamond lode and a quick fortune. The hill where the first stone was found was named "Diamond Hill," and the local inn became the "Diamond Hotel". Many mines were dug, but not another gem was found. The original stone was displayed at Tiffany's in New York and was later moved to the American Museum of Natural History there.

653. Kline's Hotel
Highway 59 at railroad tracks   1863
Originally called Kline's Hotel for one of the three pioneers who platted the village in 1851, the name was changed to the Diamond Hotel after the big discovery of 1876 (see Eagle story). At one time this three-story frame building contained offices, a barber shop, and special rooms where salesmen, who stopped over periodically from the depot, (which once stood across the street) were said to have laid out their merchandise for local business.

654. St. Theresa Catholic Church
132 Waukesha Rd.   1895-96
Before 1852, visiting priests attended to the religious needs of Eagle's Catholics. Then a small frame church was built on this site, which served the area until, under the direction of Rev. Anthony J. Nickel, the present structure was built. The cornerstone for the Victorian Gothic church was laid in 1895 on a rock-faced limestone foundation, and the CCB walls are trimmed with sheet metal and stone.

HARTLAND

Herseyville was the first name of this little village in Merton Township. It was named after the man who operated the first saw mill on the Bark River, Christian Hersey. The mill was erected in 1841 and it was not until thirteen years later that the railroad reached this area. A grist mill was built on the river in 1860. The area, originally Potawatomi Indian land, was first settled by white men in 1838.

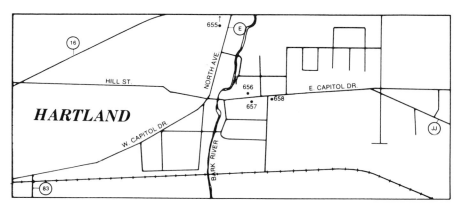

655. George McCurlie Residence
W300 N5573 County Hwy. E   c.1850

"Swallow's Corners," the popular name of this intersection for many decades, was so called because of the 133-acre farm belonging to Henry Swallow on the southwest corner. Swallow bought the McCurlie house in 1864 with gold he obtained in the California goldrush. He called the farm "Swallow's Nest," and his sons were named Martin and Robin. The carpenter-Gothic clapboard structure, with its scroll-cut brackets and bargeboards, is still owned by a descendant of the Swallow family.

656. Congregational Church Annex
230 E. Capitol Dr.   c.1871

Now owned by the First Congregational Church of Hartland, this CCB structure was once a fine private residence. Although its original owner has not yet been determined, the name of its builder is known. He was John Spillman, a carpenter from Denmark. The lower cream-brick section of the house has an Italianate character, with its semicircular arched windows, but the steeply pitched roof and the pierced bargeboards at the gable ends are related to the Gothic Revival.

657. Stephen Warren Residence
235 E. Capitol Dr. c.1855

When Mr. Warren arrived here in 1838, there was wilderness in all directions. He was the original owner of the Village of Hartland, having acquired, by 1880, 270 acres of land including both sides of Main Street (now E. Capitol Dr.). Listed as a farmer and stock dealer, he was a member of the Wisconsin Assembly in 1855. His two-story CCB house is framed with brick pilasters and is trimmed with a wooden cornice and limestone sills, lintels, and water table.

658. Burr Oak House Hotel
315-17 E. Capitol Dr. 1848

This imposing three-story Greek Revival hotel was one of the first buildings erected in Hartland. Built by Patrick Kelley, the Burr Oak House was a stage coach stop, tavern and hotel. In the 1890's it was half-a-mile from the railroad depot and it had 6 rooms, accommodating 10 guests at $2 a day or $10 a week. The roof extension to the rear, which gives the frame building a "saltbox" look, was an addition. At the turn of the century Dr. H.V.B. Nixon used it as "Hartland Emergency Hospital".

MENOMONEE FALLS

Frederick Nehs bought 720 acres here, in 1844, and built a lime kiln and a stone house. It was suggested that the settlement, which was developing, be called "Nehsville" in his honor. He objected and instead requested that the name should reflect the waterfall and its potential power. The name "Menomonee" came from the Indian tribe which lived in this area. This was the only location in Waukesha County where Menomonees could be found. Their name, "Min-no-minee", means "wild rice". Both water power and the generous supply of limestone attracted settlers. The first town meeting was held in 1842, and by 1880 there were many businesses and factories, including two mills. It was then stated that "considerable business is done at this place, for its size and population."

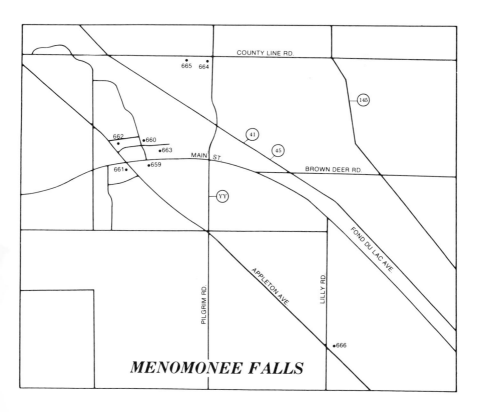

MENOMONEE FALLS

659. Enterprise Roller Mill
N88 W16447 Main St. 1891

Simon Peter Schlafer built this grist mill across the river from an earlier mill with which he was first associated. That stone structure, the Nehs & Lepper Mill, was razed in 1964 for the present bank. Schlafer made two trips weekly to Milwaukee, taking orders for flour from the bakeries there. The substantial four-story limestone building was once called the "Enterprise Roller Mill of Schlafer, Huebner & Co.".

660. Albert R. Baer Residence
W166 N8990 N. Grand Ave. c.1885

This fine, small example of the Queen Anne style was built for a local tax assessor, grocer, and insurance salesman. It is said to have been built for Baer by his father. Generally an undistinguished frame structure, the house derives all of its character from the one projecting bay/pavilion. This finely detailed element includes clapboards, cut shingles, fan ornaments, panelling and rich moldings.

661. Frank Koehler Residence
N88 W16621 W. Appleton Ave. 1893

The unusual commercial appearance of this residence can be attributed to the fact that it first served its builder as an office as well as a home. Koehler is said to have run a tin shop and a wagon repair business. The CCB facade is trimmed with rock-faced limestone and fine bush-hammered stone window sills with chiseled margins. The building's date appears above the entrance in sheet metal.

662. St. Paul's United Evangelical Congregation Church
N89 W16856 Appleton Ave. 1880

Organized in 1868, this German congregation did not hold regular services in English until 1934. Members first purchased and occupied a vacant Methodist Episcopal church on these grounds and, in 1880, laid the cornerstone for the present Lannon stone structure. Much of the original design has been destroyed or hidden by a series of remodellings begun in 1955. The well proportioned belfry, once painted in contrasting colors, and the now-painted shingles of the spire displayed colorful geometric designs.

663. St. Mary Church
N89 W16297 Cleveland Ave.   **1905**
Archbishop Sebastian Messmer granted permission to organize this parish in 1904, and a year later the cornerstone was laid for this edifice. The famous "Lannon" limestone deposit comes near the surface here, and three feet of it had to be removed before construction could begin. Milwaukee architects, E. Brielmaier & Son, drew the plans for this handsome Romanesque church, built of CCB with cut stone and sheet metal trim.

664. Old Falls Village
County Line Rd., S.W. corner
Pilgrim Rd.   **1845 and later**
The fine Greek Revival house pictured was built of coursed limestone rubble, in 1858, by German immigrant, John Fehr. Part of his original 36-acre estate has been developed by the Menomonee Falls Historical Society, and additional buildings of local importance have been moved to the property. Among these are the old railroad depot and a log cabin built by Gregory Umhoefer in 1845.

665. Log House
N96 W16247 County Line Road   **c.1861**
Very little is known about this restored log house. The date, which is cast in a concrete tablet above the door, was added by the present owner. Once set on a 40-acre farm, the house is built on a fieldstone foundation and now has a 2-story frame wing on the rear.

666. St. Anthony Catholic Church
N74 W1604 Appleton Ave.   **1867**
One of the most spectacular rural stone churches in southeastern Wisconsin, this edifice was erected on a hill which had once been an Indian gathering place. The unusual side walls are divided by buttresses into five bays, each of which has a gable. The fine limestone masonry includes the uncommonly large octagonal belfry which gives the structure much of its character. The parish was organized in 1844 and held its first services in a log building on the corner of Lilly Rd. and Appleton.

MERTON

The first settler here, William O'Dell, built his house in 1840. Six years later Henry Shears and George Trowbridge bought a piece of land on the Bark River and soon built a grist mill. It was Shears' wife who suggested that the name of the settlement be "Moreton", after the town in England of the same name. The spelling was later changed to "Merton". Before this time the village and the township were known as "Warren" after an early pioneer, Sylvanus Warren. Basically a one-street town, Merton is rich in well-constructed buildings in a variety of design styles.

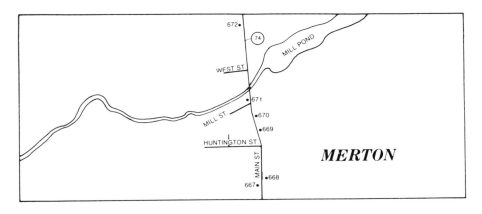

667. Octagon House
6985 Main St. c.1860

The original owner and the age of this humble octagon house seem to be lost in history. The one-story frame dwelling, with its hip-roofed wing, is now covered with aluminum siding, but nothing can disguise its unique shape. Like the houses in Pewaukee (see #721) and Milwaukee (see #216) its builder was doubtless inspired by Orson Fowler's influential book, *A Home For All, or The Gravel Wall and Octagon Mode of Building*, first published in 1848.

668. First Baptist Church
6996 Main St. 1855

Founded by natives of New England, this congregation began in August of 1843 with nine members. Their church, built in 1855, is basically a Greek Revival design, but its octagonal belfry and spire reflect the regional tastes of the founders. Before the new entrance vestibule was added, the front doors were flanked by a pair of triple-hung, 6-sash/36light windows. The building is sheathed in clapboard and flush siding.

669. John Mitchell Residence
7084 Main St.   1888

Built by an early Scotch immigrant, this house once stood on the Main Street edge of a 53-acre farm. Mitchell's fine Victorian frame residence is still owned by his descendants. He was the community banker, justice of the peace, and a member of the school board. A date stone, imbedded in the foundation under the projecting central pavilion, reads, "Mitchell 1888". Window lintels, stick-style gable ornaments and the pair of scroll-cut porches are original.

670. Bark River Hotel
7134 Main St.   1889

For many years the most well known symbol of the village of Merton was this three-story frame hotel. It is actually the third building to be erected on this lot. The first, built by W.W. Caswell, burned in 1884 and was rebuilt. The second structure burned in October of 1888, and the townspeople formed a bucket brigade from the river to the hotel to fight the fire. Only by spreading wet rugs on the roofs and dousing the walls with water, was it possible to save the adjacent buildings.

671. Phillip Schneider Residence
7167 Main St.   1875

The builder's initials, and date when this house was erected, appear in a most unusual fashion at the peak of the main gable. A large square stone, which is pierced by a circular attic window, has the letter and number inscriptions in each of the four corners. Beginning with John Schneider in the 1850's, the Merton Grist Mill was owned by that family until 1924. This was the miller's house and it was built by John Schlicher, a German mason.

672. Jacob Schneider Residence
7371 Main St.   c.1867

This handsome stone dwelling was built for the brother of John Schneider, the miller (see #671). It was the work of the same German stonemason, John Schlicher, who built Phillip Schneider's house. The walls are 22 inches thick, and the basement ceiling is vaulted. The stone fence was added later by Dr. Samuel A. Barrett, an anthropologist for the Milwaukee Public museum. The property was once part of the John Schneider farm.

MUKWONAGO

The first village plat to be recorded in Waukesha county was that of Mukwonago in 1836. It had been surveyed that year by Ira Blood and Martin Field. Before that this land was a major Indian village, said to have been the "capital" of the Potawatomie tribe. The Indian word, originally spelled "Mequanego", means "the place of bears". This is believed to mean the location of the bear clan of the tribe and not that there were real bears here. The first brick house in Waukesha County was built in this village in 1842 by Sewell Andrews (see #674). An 1880 description called the surrounding countryside "beautiful and rich; the place has good water power, and the inhabitants are well-informed and generally well-to-do."

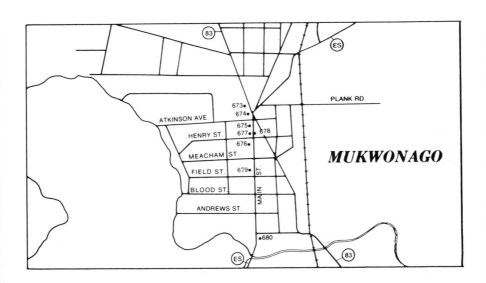

673. Mukwonago House Hotel
111 Rochester St. c.1845
This historic three-story Greek Revival hotel was built by Ed McGee. In its early days the street front had a large three-story porch supported by square columns with chamfered corners. Simple sawn wood ornamental arches stretched between the columns, and a balcony was supported between two of them at the second floor level. The off-center patch over the entrance marks the doorway which opened to that balcony. The two-story north wing was added later.

674. Sewall Andrews Residence
101 Main St. 1842
The first brick house in Waukesha County, this handsome Greek Revival structure was built b a pioneer from Andover, Vermont. Andrews, one of the three earliest settlers in Mukwonago, built this community's first store, in 1837, and was its first justice of the peace. The orange brick of the house is trimmed with finely chiselled limestone and wood cornice moldings. The entrance, unusually fine for its day, is framed with carved rope moldings and leaves and has two sidelights and three transoms.

675. Judge Martin Field Residence
201 Main St. 1843 and later
Built for the first probate judge in Waukesha county, this 2-story frame house was erected in three stages. The first section, which looks like a wing on the south, was built in 1843. The large block was added in the 1860's and once had a long Victorian porch, which has since been removed. Finally, a second floor was stacked on the original section. Field was one of the early pioneers here and a co-surveyor of the village.

676. Laurel Andrews Residence
307 Main St. 1880
Built by a nephew of Sewell Andrews (see #674), this frame Victorian eclectric house retains much of its original details and trim. Laurel Andrews was an active local merchant who served on the school board and as a postmaster. Scroll-cut window lintels and an unusual picket-fence-like fascia are complemented by black cast iron cresting on porches and bays. The house was once equipped with inside shutters on all windows.

677. Baptist Church
Main St., N.W. corner Henry St. 1880
Mukwonago's first regular church services were initiated by the Baptists in 1837. Their first church, built in 1840, burned down and was later replaced by this frame structure set on a fieldstone foundation. In later years it became Woodman Hall and was used as a theater, dance hall, and meeting place. Mount Olive Evangelical Lutheran Church, organized in 1921, purchased the old hall and made it into a church again.

678. Unitarian & Universalist Church
Main St., N.E. corner Henry St. 1879
Sewell Andrews (see #674) was among the organizers of the unusual merger which resulted in the erection of this church. A very large building for a community of this size, the frame Gothic structure was completed in August of 1879 at a cost of $3,000. Among the notable pastors through the years, was Rev. Olympia Brown Willis, a pioneer women's rights advocate, who came from Racine to conduct services here.

679. Wallman & Lotz Furniture Store
411 Main St. c.1878
In the partnership which operated stores in two cities, Wallman ran the business in Waterford, and Lotz took care of this store. The two-story frame structure, with its practical pitched roof, was designed to conceal that fact with a typical false front. A horizontal wooden cornice, supported by brackets, tops the facade and supposedly gives the building a look of greater solidity. An unusual tall cupola, with four windows, is set on the roof.

680. Stockman House Tavern
802 Main St. 1852
Ulysses S. Grant is said to have spent a night in this old inn when he passed through Mukwonago after the Civil War. The three-story Greek Revival building was erected with black walnut beams by Charles and John Stockman, whose family owned a nearby farm. Once a spacious verandah stretched along the Main St. facade, which was then the main entrance. Today most of the building is hidden by asphalt and aluminum siding.

OCONOMOWOC

Called "the Newport of the West", Oconomowoc was once the crown jewel of Wisconsin's resort country. Around 1870 the natural beauty of this area, between Lac LaBelle and Fowler Lake, was "discovered". First as summer guests and later to build houses, the people started pouring in from all over the Midwest. As Oconomowoc's popularity grew, the size and quality of its summer homes increased until they began to resemble palaces and castles. Millionaires from Chicago, St. Louis and Milwaukee moved into their summer "cottages" each season and dazzled the town with gala social events, luxurious attire and lavishly appointed horses and carriages. But before this excitement began, it was a just a beautiful hunting and fishing ground for the Indians who created its name. There has been much disagreement over the true meaning of the word, but most concede that it was originally spelled, Con-no-mo-wauk. The translations vary from "river of lakes" and "waterfall" to "place of the beaver" and "home of the winds." In 1837 the first white settler, Charles B. Sheldon, built a log house here. The credit for founding and building early Oconomowoc is given to Sheldon and the man who built the flour mill, the dam, and the lumber mill — John S. Rockwell.

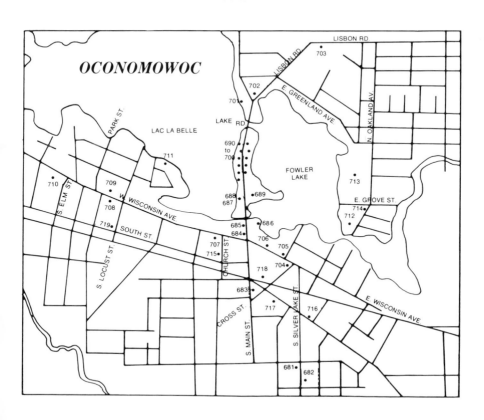

681. David Edwards Residence
414 Silver Lake St. c.1875

A native of Connecticut, Mr. Edwards came to Oconomowoc in 1865 and built this unusual CCB house. The pierced, scroll-cut bargeboards are pure Gothic Revival, but the window openings relate more to the later Italianate period. The large front porch was added much later. A very similar house across the street demonstrates, by contrast, the importance of bargeboards in this design. These bargeboards, unlike most, are first scroll-cut and then carved in the round.

682. George F. Westover Residence
505 Silver Lake St. c. 1874

One of Oconomowoc's most distinguished Italianate houses, this was built for Westover's second bride, the sister of Dr. McL. Miller (see #690). The house once had a fine square cupola atop its hipped roof, but it was removed after being damaged in a fire. The 2-story frame structure has an unusual cantilevered balcony on the north side and an equally uncommon hexagonal attic window over the entrance. Paired scroll-cut brackets support the eaves.

683. St. Jerome Catholic Church
211 S. Main St. 1889

Oconomowoc's Catholics were originally served by Father Hobbs of St. Catherine's church in Mapleton (see #603), who visited here as a missionary. The first church on this property was a red-painted frame building erected in 1860 and sold for $60 just before the cornerstone was laid for the present structure. This CCB Gothic edifice is set on a limestone foundation and still has its original windows and ornamental cedar shingle designs on the spire.

684. Mann Block
106-110 N. Main St. 1871

Once called "Mann's splendid brick block," this three-story commercial building was erected by Curtis Mann, who was once the county's wealthiest resident. The well designed Italianate structure was built with Watertown brick (CCB) and, according to an 1880 description, contained "an elegant hall used for Masonic purposes, with a separate one used for theatrical performances ... both located on the third floor." The building still has its double-bracketed wood cornice and a statuary niche on the eastern facade.

685. Kellogg Drug Store
114 N. Main St. 1891

This lot was originally given by J.S. Rockwell to the Methodist Church for a building site. The structure was dedicated in 1850 and used for seven years. Later this rock-faced limestone building was erected and for many years was occupied by Harry Kellogg as a drugstore. A carved, irregular, pentagonal stone, near the roof peak, contains the date and a symbol of the Masons, who used the second floor for meetings.

686. Peter Klos Saloon
125 N. Main St. 1879

A fine example of late Victorian masonry construction, this humble saloon building was built by Peter Klos, whose name and the date appear in raised letters on a semicircular stone near the roofline. Later the E.N. Tuckerman saloon (1916), this building still serves as a bar. The CCB walls are decorated with an ornamental brick cornice and stone lintels with delicate incised scrollwork.

687. Oconomowoc Public Library
212 Lake Road 1849-59

Three of the oldest buildings in the city have been joined to create the present library complex. The southernmost structure, built in 1849, and identified in the old photograph as "Bruce's Cheap Store", was built by Oconomowoc pioneer John S. Rockwell. The center building, originally two stories high, was also built by Rockwell (about 1855) and later increased by one story. Both Rockwell buildings were stores, one a hardware operated by Warren Daily and the other a general store run by Joseph Rector (see #719). The northern third of the trio was built by D.W. Small (see #711) in 1859 and became the Summit Bank, the first bank in town. When it was abandoned by the financial institution in 1870, this building served as city hall, fire department, a bakery and finally as the Telephone Company. The Oconomowoc Public Library was founded in 1893 and acquired the central building in 1901, the southern section in 1907, and the old Telephone Co. building in 1954-56.

688. Griffins
212 Lake Road

These griffins originally came from Chicago to the Charles Kohl summerhouse on Lac La Belle. In 1922, when Mrs Kohl bought Draper Hall, one of the city's resort hotels, they were moved to a spot near that building's entrance. When it was razed, they were moved to this location in front of the library (see #687). The mythical, half-lion, half-eagle creatures have twins in front of Milwaukee's Mitchell Building (see #22). Another pair was exhibited at the Philadelphia Centennial Exhibition in 1876.

689. Zion Episcopal Church
135 Rockwell Place   1889

This fine limestone Romanesque church is set on a beautiful wooded peninsula jutting into Fowler Lake. It replaces an earlier brick church that had a structural defect which forced its demolition after only 36 years of service. The congregation, founded in 1846, first met in a little log schoolhouse and was served by Rev. Lemuel Hull, who came once every four weeks from St. Paul's Church in Milwaukee (see #56).

690. Dr. McL. Miller Residence
234 Lake Road   1859

Once this Gothic Revival mansion stood across the street, to the east, on the Zion Episcopal Church property (see #689). In 1945 it was raised off its foundation and trundled directly across Lake Road to the present site. The original front facade, as a result, now faces the lake; and the rear has been so greatly remodelled that it bears no resemblance to the old front. The most beautiful remaining detail is a 5-sided Gothic bay window which once faced Lake Road.

691. David Gould Residence
238 Lake Road.   1860 and later

A St. Louis millionaire, Gould came to Oconomowoc and rebuilt this old frame house around 1899. Originally built by a local butcher, Mr. Kohlman, the house was then enlarged and re-faced. Its "foundation" was made of granite fieldstone, and the first floor was covered with red sandstone; the upper floors were sided with shingles. Inside the 16-room mansion was fitted with 11 fireplaces. The once broad lot was laid out with sunken gardens and tennis courts.

692. Captain Scudder Residence
307 Lake Road   **c.1895**

This monumental frame mansion was once fitted with a huge verandah which wrapped around the building and made it appear half again as large. Locally known as Scudder's "cottage," it was one of the area's most impressive Classical Revival buildings. The St. Louis family occupied the house until the 1920's. The fine narrow clapboard effect has been covered by aluminum siding, but the exceptional oval window in the triangular gable survives.

693. H.J. Brookins Residence
317 Lake Road   **1889**

A St. Louis lumberman, Brookins summered here sporadically, with the house sometimes unused, except by servants, for years. The coach house in the rear was unusual in that the living quarters were on the ground floor and carriages were kept below ground. The mansion was used as a summer home until the 1920's. Its eclectic design combines the Queen Anne and Classical Revival styles. The massive 3-story octagonal tower has an unusual porch opening on 3 sides at the top floor level.

694. Harold Peck Residence
318 Lake Road   **1882**

This 2½-story Queen Anne mansion was built by one of the four sons of Madame Peck (see #699). Mr. Peck died during the construction, and the house was completed by his widow. Over the entrance is an unusual gable set on a short pitched roof section. The entire street facade is faced with ornamental shingle-work. The building later became the "Wilhelm" hotel, which lasted until the 1950's.

695. James C. Hitchcock Residence
404 Lake Road   **1875**

A native of Augusta, New York, Hitchcock first moved to St. Louis, where he sold house-furnishing hardware. In 1861 he came to Oconomowoc, opened a hardware store and became the proprietor of the La Belle Spring. He built this house on a lot which was shared with his friend and neighbor (see #696). A rare example of the "Swiss-cottage" style, it has a deep overhang and numerous scalloped and scroll-cut details.

696. Medbury Residence
412 Lake Road   **1875**

Both this house and its next door neighbor (404 Lake Road, see #695) were designed by Milwaukee architect James Douglas. Medbury and Hitchcock were friends; and while their houses are different in certain details, the basic massing of elements and the floor plans are the same. Both were built in the same year, but this house, with its roof and stick-style gable, is more typical of Douglas' work.

697. Mrs. H.G. Fuller Residence
423 Lake Road   **1884**

In most respects this large house is an undistinguished frame example of the Queen Anne style, but its one spectacular asset is the northern side wall. The second and third floors are framed by a huge triangle which comprises most of the wall. An unusual window layout, a scroll-cut, decorative panel at the third floor level, and the ornamental shingle siding give the house its character.

698. Dr. Hosea Townsend Residence
430-434 Lake Road   **1845 and later**

Built for the first physician to establish his practice in Oconomowoc, the south house was the original structure. After a few years an old office building was moved here and attached to the house. Later, the imposing northern wing was added; and, in 1887, when it was purchased by Clarence Peck, the stately Ionic collonnade was erected. In 1922 the two segments were divided and occupied as separate houses.

699. Albert Rockwell Residence
503 Lake Road   **c.1870**

Built by the son of John Rockwell (see #687), this two-story frame Italianate house was erected on the lot next door to his stepmother's house (see #700). In 1884 Clarence Peck, (see #698), bought the house for his mother, Madame Peck. There was once a sprawling verandah which wrapped around two sides of the house. In 1927 it was remodelled into apartments and named the "Lakeview."

700. Foster/Rockwell Residence
517 Lake Road   c.1840 and later

The back part of this house is one of the oldest buildings in the area and was occupied by two famous names in Oconomowoc's early history. The first house in the village (a log cabin) was erected on this lot, in 1837, by Philo Brewer. G.A. Foster built part of the present structure a few years later and eventually sold to John S. Rockwell (see #687). The Rockwells allowed the old cabin to stand for many years before finally tearing it down. Albert Rockwell and his mother erected the stone wall around the property in 1868.

701. Marjorie Ward Residence
800 Lake Road   1926

Once called the "finest example of French Provincial manor-type architecture in the Middle West", this imposing mansion was built by the daughter of A. Montgomery Ward of Chicago. The pink common brick structure was designed by a Chicago architect named Clark. It is trimmed with red brick and wrought iron, and has a carved Bedford limestone entrance and a slate roof. The huge 140-foot-long structure was enlarged in 1934 and is now used as a retirement home.

702. Clark Residence
128 Lisbon Road   c.1873

Now nearly hidden by large additions and remodellings, this once imposing mansion is said to have been the home of the Clark sewing thread millionaire from Chicago. It is supposed to have been built on Lac LaBelle and later moved to the present site on the north side of Fowler Lake. The most significant remaining detail on the building is an unusual third floor balcony and lancet window, framed by the gable-end ornaments.

703. Henry Schuttler Residence
371 E. Lisbon Road.   1879-80

Built by a Chicago wagon manufacturer, this $50,000 mansion was set on the old 158-acre Starkweather farm. The spectacular house, called "Mon Bijou" by Mrs. Schuttler, was designed by Milwaukee architect, G.A. Gombert. Although vestiges of the octagonal towers and turrets survive, most of their spires have been removed, along with the original porches and solarium. However, much of the richly designed CCB masonry and buff sandstone trim can still be seen. The building is now a summer resort.

704. Notbohm Block
203 E. Wisconsin Ave. 1896

Still occupied by the original business, this handsome three-story late Italianate commercial building was erected by C.W. Notbohm & Son for their "furniture and undertaking" firm. In 1915 the furniture business occupied the first and third floors and a printer the second. Built with orange pressed brick, this structure is trimmed in cut limestone and has ornamental brick panels and arches and a well preserved sheet metal cornice with the date.

705. City Hall
174 E. Wisconsin Ave. 1886

This large civic building still serves as the mayor's office and police and fire departments. Before it was painted, the CCB walls were more decorative with cut stone trim and orange brick beltcourses and accent lines. The original stained glass transoms still top most of the second floor windows, but the belfry is now gone. Once a series of vertical timbers supported a pyramidal spire above the clock faces.

706. Oconomowoc National Bank
138 E. Wisconsin Ave.
1920's and earlier

This handsome Bedford stone Classical facade was added to an old stable building in the 1920's. It was orginally the livery stable for the "Jones House Hotel" which, by the time it was razed in 1975, was known as the "Oconomowoc Inn". After the stable days, this building became a rocking horse factory (the Oconomowoc Wooden Toy Horse Company) and was eventually faced with a polished granite "foundation" and cut limestone.

707. Theodore Worthington Residence
231 W. Wisconsin Ave. 1860

One of the first settlers in early Oconomowoc, Worthington claimed 160 acres of land, most of which is now the center of town. He originally occupied the second house built in the village and in 1860 erected this large CCB Italianate structure with a steep, hipped roof. Both the first and second floor porches and the enlarged first floor front windows are later additions. Under the bracketed cornice is an unusual frieze decorated with elongated octagons.

708. Dr. Edward Harvey Hewitt Residence
513 W. Wisconsin Ave. 1887

Dr. Hewitt's father, George C., was one of Delafield's earliest settlers in 1847. The doctor was born here, in 1857, and received his education at the University of Wisconsin in Madison and the Pennsylvania College of Dental Surgery. He came to Oconomowoc and began to practice dentistry here in 1884. His house, a 2½-story frame Queen Anne design, is set on a limestone foundation and still has its original porch with cast iron cresting.

709. Dr. Louis A. Meyer Residence
514 W. Wisconsin Ave. 1894

A native of Oconomowoc, Dr. Meyer was the son of a boot and shoe maker from Saxony, Germany. His house, designed and built by Fred Urbutt, is one of the best preserved residences of its age in the city. An eclectic Victorian design, it shows a tendency toward the Queen Anne style. The narrow, closely-spaced clapboards and the commodious verandah give it an air of refinement.

710. O.L. Rosenkranz Residence
805 W. Wisconsin Ave. c.1860

This very dignified brick Italianate house was the home of an early Oconomowoc jeweler. The unusually refined appearance of this house can be attributed to the cornice and the window shapes and spacing. The uncommonly deep eaves are embellished with fine moldings and both a dentil course and modillions. The paired, and narrow, windows on the Elm St. side and over the bay window are tastefully positioned on large blank walls.

Old Hotel

Present Residence

711. Woodlands Hotel
335 Woodland Lane   1860

This oddly-shaped residence is actually a small segment of a once famous summer resort hotel. Named after the beautiful grove of trees, on the south bank of Lac LaBelle, where it was built, the Woodlands was also the home of its developer, D.W. Small (see #687). The 1860 structure soon proved too small for the increasing patronage; and a large addition was made in 1873, bringing the capacity up to nearly 100 guests. At this time it was also remodelled, and it was perhaps then that the mansard roof was added which gave the building a third floor and the distinctive look with its many dormers. In 1915 Frank Boyle and William Lachenmeir turned the building and property into the "Woodland Health Farm." Exercise facilities were built, and guests were taken on eight-mile walks around Lac LaBelle before breakfast each morning. The short-lived venture failed after one season, and the building was eventually torn down except for this section. The verandah and mansard roof were removed, and the brick was covered with stucco. Today's residence is the left end of the old Woodlands as it was seen from the lake.

712. Site of Townsend House
West of Oakwood Ave. just north
of Norway Bridge   1870 & 1874

Copeland Townsend has been called, "the originator of the summer resort business of the West." The great hotel he built on this site was the first in the state erected exclusively for tourists. Oconomowoc's greatest showplace, it was so successful that it became necessary to double its size in 1874. The three-story structure, with its two mansard-roofed towers, offered, "hot and cold baths, water in rooms, gas, telegraph, bowling, billiards, electric bells, and a bar."

713. Dr. James A. Henshall
Coach House
Oakwood Ave./Fowler Park   c.1860

This humble coach house is all that remains of a once spectacular Fowler Lake estate. Dr. Henshall's mansion was a Gothic-windowed, many-gabled extravaganza with numerous picturesque shapes, like the "Flemish" gable on the coach house. On this property Henshall experimented with America's first private fish hatchery and wrote an important book on black bass. He later moved to Washington and became U.S. Commissioner of Fisheries.

714. Our Saviour's Evangelical Lutheran Church
354 N. Oakwood Ave. 1872-?

This congregation of Norwegians first met at the house of Ole Halverson, who later donated the corner lot for the present structure. It was not until 1872 that the decision was made to build; within a year the basement was completed and ready for use, but the construction was still not finished in 1880. The painted stained glass windows are original and of the colored grisaille type. Note the interesting octagonal steeple with 8 gablets.

715. First Congregational Church
50 S. Church St. 1854

Organized in 1841, the Congregationalists erected this frame Greek Revival church which bears a resemblance to New England colonial architecture. In 1941 Milwaukee architects Eschweiler and Eschweiler added the entrance vestibule with such care and good taste that it looks as though it could have been part of the original design. Fourteen years later, a religious instruction wing was built, using lumber from Fond du Lac to continue a tradition started when oxen hauled timbers from that town for the original building.

716. Pliny Putman Residence
318 E. Summit Ave. 1859 and later

Built by a local cabinet maker, this greatly altered house began as a simple 1½-story Greek Revival design made of red brick. When the rotting roof was replaced in a recent remodelling, framing details indicated that it may have had a large cupola on top of the hipped roof similar to that on the Diedrichs house in Milwaukee (see #84). Once owned by Oconomowoc mayor, W.W. Collins, the house was later given a Classical Revival porch and, in 1915, the frame wing.

717. Gottlieb Maas Residence
217 Summit Ave. c.1870

Maas was the master brewer responsible for the beer which was awarded the highest premium at the Philadelphia Centennial Exhibition in 1876. He worked for the Blatz Brewery in Milwaukee and is said to have built this house close to the railroad depot to make his commuting more convenient. The CCB house has interesting brick window arches, a wooden molded cornice and the original porch which was later enclosed.

718. Milwaukee Road Depot
115 Collins St.   1896

Called "the only fieldstone depot left in the United States", this substantial edifice is said to have been erected due to the urging of Albert Earling, who would soon become president of the railroad, and wealthy Chicago meat packer, Philip D. Armour. The old facility, which overlooked the stockyards, was considered unsuitable for the reception of their distinguished guests. The granite depot is trimmed with red sandstone and heavy timber construction.

719. Joseph H. Rector Residence
504 South St.   c.1885

Oconomowoc's eleventh mayor, Joseph Rector, purchased this double lot in 1884 and probably built this house within one year. Called a "self-made man", he once ran a general store in one of the library complex buildings (see #687), and was the editor of the *Oconomowoc Democrat*, a short-lived weekly. The Victorian eclectic house still has its original porches with unusual columns, each of which has two side brackets resembling miniature hammer beams.

PEWAUKEE

Pe-wauk-ee-wee-ning was the original spelling of this town's name. Originally the site of a Potawatomie Indian village, this lakeshore settlement adopted the name it was given by that tribe. It means "snail lake", and the name describes a civil township, the village and the largest lake in Waukesha county. The first white settler was Asa Clark, who came here from Vermont in 1836 and built a dwelling and a mill. Many of the early settlers were "Yankees". Between 1878 and 1920 this huge lake became a valuable source of ice for the packing companies and breweries. During the winter, workers cut ice and stored it in insulated buildings, and the rest of the year this supply was shipped out of town. One icehouse is said to have shipped eight carloads a day to breweries in Milwaukee.

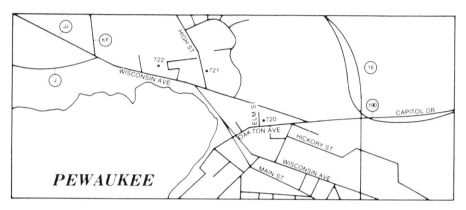

NR WRL

720. Odd Fellows Hall
227 Oakton Ave.   1876

This fraternal lodge hall, called the "largest and best in the Midwest when built", was the meeting place of the International Order of Odd Fellows (I.O.O.F.). Their three-link-chain symbol and the building's date appear in the circular panel near the roof peak. Also used as an early community center, this building once hosted touring minstrel shows.

721. Deacon West Residence
370 High St.   1856

One of the few octagon houses surviving in Wisconsin, this two-story specimen was built by the area's pioneer blacksmith; it replaces a log house on the same hillside site. In 1873 almost everything but the 18-inch thick walls was destroyed in a fire. The exterior is rough plaster over what might be a "gravel wall" (cement), the type which Orson Fowler recommended in his influential book on octagonal architecture. (See #667)

722. St. Mary's Catholic Church
449 W. Wisconsin Ave. 1868 and later
Organized in 1858, the parish first built a frame church here. In 1868 the parishioners (predominantly German and Irish) built their second edifice with rock-faced Waukesha limestone. This was later partially razed, and the side walls of the old church were incorporated into the present design with its newer buttressed Gothic tower.

SAYLESVILLE

Once called "South Genesee," this little settlement was later named for Stephen Sayles who, with his four sons, settled here in 1839. One of the sons, Whitman Sayles, became a partner with two other men (Orendorf & LeSuer) and built the first mill in 1842. They also erected the first store that year. In addition to water power, Saylesville offered a fine quarry which was opened, in 1844, by a Scotch immigrant, William Johnston. Stone from this excavation was used in building the state capitol at Madison, the first Carroll College hall in Waukesha and the first Milwaukee Sentinel Building.

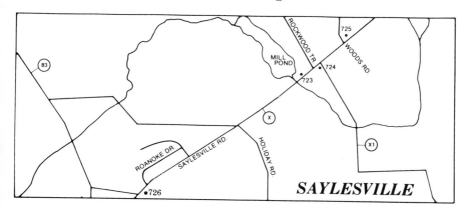

723. Grist Mill
Highway X at Mill Stream　　1876

The first mill in this location was built in 1841 by Whitman Sayles and others. George Vincent remodelled it, in 1866, with two runs of stone driven by Tyler turbines. Ten years later it burned, and the present structure was built in its place. The mill and its pond were the center of activity in all seasons. Summer was time to fish on the pond, and winter saw skating and ice-cutting for the local creamery.

724. Saylesville Community Hall
S52-W28731 County X　　1890

Originally built for use as a Sunday school, this clapboard frame structure was turned into a community hall in 1915. It was used for meetings, plays, a singing school, socials, suppers, weddings and funerals. Dances and card parties were forbidden in a clause which said that, if violated, the property would revert back to Whitman Sayles, the donor. (See #723)

725. Saylesville School
Highway X at Woods Rd.   1896

The original school here was a small one-room building with foot-and-a-half-thick grout walls plastered on the inside. A huge stone slab in the center supported the heating stove, and four children each sat at the pine desks attached to the walls. In 1896 this "modern" frame schoolhouse with a shingled bell cupola was built. The original foundation is fieldstone, and two subsequent additions have been made.

726. Alexander Rankin Residence
S57-W29687 Saylesville Rd.   1850

This Federal style residence was built by the first settler in Saylesville, Alexander Rankin, who came here in 1837. The limestone for its walls was taken from the pioneer quarry established by William Johnston in 1844. The house was heated by two fireplaces. Their chimneys, as is characteristic of this style, are a part of the end wall which rises above the roof.

NR WRL

SUSSEX

In 1880 Sussex was described as a "lovely little burg, the only one in the town of Lisbon". Even today it is the only village in the 36-square-mile township, and it still has much of the same charm described in that early account... "The place has a quiet, yet exceedingly attractive appearance, the streets and cemetery being very handsomely shaded and well kept." It was named for Sussex County in England, from which some of the early settlers had come. In 1854 some farmers opened a "Union Store" here, the first cooperative in Wisconsin. For half a century this district was the principal hop-growing area for the state. In 1925 Sussex and nearby Templeton merged to become a village.

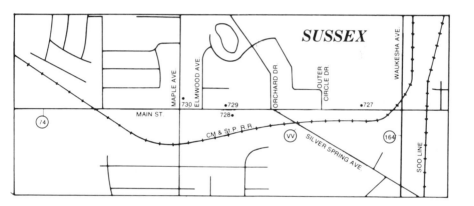

727. Andrew L. Davidson Residence
N64 W23420 Main St.   c.1874
This is a very well built example of limestone rubble construction with quoins. Mr. Davidson, who was a farmer and a skilled stonemason, built the house himself with material quarried on his own 54-acre tract. A native of Scotland, he settled here with his new bride, in 1850 and is said to have constructed many of the houses in this area.

728. Dr. Charles E. Wintermute Residence
N63 W23781 N. Main St.   **c.1878**

This well preserved Victorian eclectic house has been the home of five early Sussex physicians. It was built by Dr. Wintermute, but later was occupied by Doctors Chapman, Jones, Greulich, and Lawler in succession. Around 1911 the house was purchased by William H.S. Edwards, a Republican leader and one-time assemblyman. While the main block of the house is a relatively style-less clapboard block, it derives great character from the well maintained ornamental porch.

729. James Weaver Residence
N64 W23850 Main St.   **c.1866**

This two-story painted CCB house was the home of retired farmer, James Weaver. He was one of a large and important family of farmers who acquired great wealth in raising hops. The most notable feature of this otherwise humble house is the beautifully scroll-cut ornamental work on the front porch.

730. St. Alban's Episcopal Church
W239 N6440 Maple Ave.   **1866**

Named for the first Christian martyr in Great Britain, this parish was organized in 1842. Two years later the members built their first church, and in 1866 the present structure was dedicated by Bishop Jackson Kemper (see #649). The design is patterned after the Peasmarsh Village Church of Sussex County, England, which was the home church of some of the founders. The three-tiered square tower and its bell were added in 1875.

WATERVILLE

This picturesque little crossroads settlement is set in beautifully rolling and wooded country at the intersection of two roads and the Scuppernong River. More like a creek, the Scuppernong's clear and beautiful stream is fed by many springs. At one time there were nearly twenty homes clustered within a half-mile radius around the "village center". On the four corners were two stores, a blacksmith shop, and a tavern with a dance hall upstairs. Most of the early settlers here came from the northeastern states and New England. Two tornados, in 1880 and 1882, caused considerable damage to buildings and trees in the vicinity. When the railroad bypassed the town to the south, there was no incentive for continued development, and this pleasant settlement has remained the same until the present day.

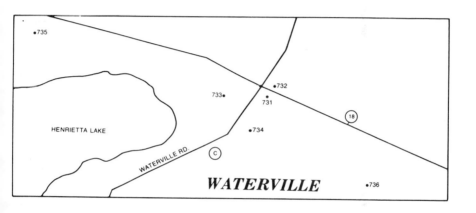

731. John Mills General Store
Highway 18 S.E. corner
Waterville Rd. 1876

The original builder and use of this structure has not been determined, but before it became a general store, it was operated as a tavern by a Mr. Deck. John Mills, who travelled this area of the country selling his goods from a wagon, was the last to occupy the building for store purposes around 1897. He lived upstairs, and evidences in the masonry indicate the possiblity that there were once lean-to additions on both sides of the building.

732. Charles Morgan Neff Residence
34742 Highway 18   **c.1844**

A native of Connecticut, Mr. Neff opened a blacksmith shop on this corner at the age of 21. In newly-settled farm country, his business boomed, and the little shop grew to require three forges and additional help to meet the demand. The original shop burned to the ground, and he replaced it with a larger one which lasted until 1928. Only his residence, with its one-story east wing, survives.

733. E.W. Barnard Residence
1201-13 S. Waterville Rd.
    c.1845 & 1904

Barnard came to Waterville from Hartford, Connecticut, and opened a general store on the corner of his property (Waterville Rd. and Highway 18) which also served as a post office. His Greek Revival house and its wing are the southern half of the present structure. In 1904 the present owner doubled the size of the building by adding the two-story set-back section with the porch. Henrietta Lake, behind the house, was named for Barnard's daughter.

734. Reed Residence
1226 S. Waterville Rd.   **c.1850**

The southern half of this house was built by Orson or Harrison Reed as a 1½-story Greek Revival frame dwelling. It was later jacked up and patched to become a full two stories tall. Both this section and the original one-story wing have log floor joists. The wing's framing is nogged with brick. In the 1920's Miss Gertrude Sherman, who owns the Barnard house (see #733), built the matching northern half.

735. J.M. Crummey Residence
35057 Highway 18   **c.1865**

This well preserved clapboard house was the residence of a prosperous local farmer who owned a 311-acre tract which ranged north and west from Lake Henrietta (see #733). The original front porch was once U-shaped, and it wrapped around three sides of the house. There are three additional porches around the sides and back. The house derives its pleasant character from the segmental-arched windows and its good proportions.

736. Capt. Stephen A. Hubbell Residence

Hwy. 18, east of Waterville Rd. c.1840

One of Milwaukee's most important Greek Revival temple-style houses, this historic structure was moved to Waterville in September of 1968. Its original location was on the east side of Commerce St. (see #204) between Walnut and Galena. Captain Hubbell came to Wisconsin from New York State, in 1836, and ran the *Badger*, the first steamboat ever built in Milwaukee, for Byron Kilbourn. In 1844 an English cabinetmaker, Thomas Youles, moved Hubbell's riverside residence up to N. 8th St. between old Winnebago St. and Juneau Ave. Thirteen years later Sebastian Brand purchased the house and from it was able to look down the hill and see the nationally known Brand Stove Company, which he owned. His factory, located on the site of the Vocational School (see #199), manufactured all types of cast iron stoves. When Brand moved away, in 1880, he began to rent the house; and for the next 88 years it deteriorated until, in 1968, its present owner saved it from the wreckers and moved it in two pieces. The one-story ell, added after the first move to 8th St., has tamarack rafters and is thought to have been a one-room claim shack built in the mid-1830's. Both sections are of braced frame construction and are made with pegged hewn-oak timbers.

Milwaukee

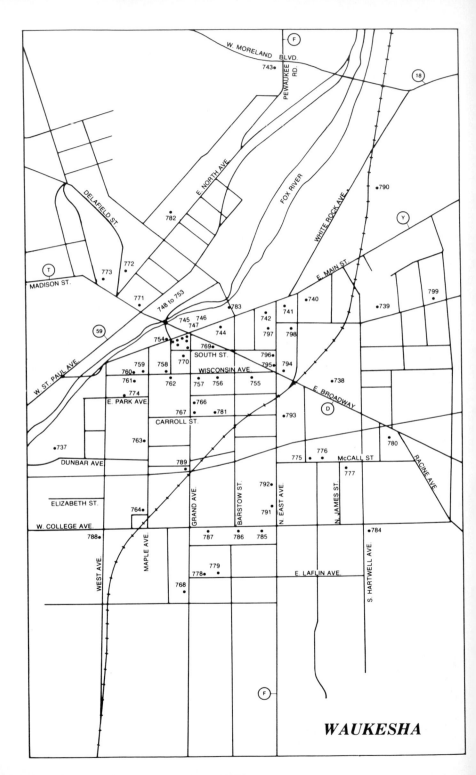

WAUKESHA

WAUKESHA

In 1868, Colonel Richard Dunbar took a drink of spring water that was to change the future fortunes of Waukesha. He was an ailing man and this mineral spring water, he was convinced, was responsible for his miraculous cure. About six months later a local newspaper made this statement about the "great discovery" ... "Thus, unbeknown to our people, there has gurgled forth a fount of God's elixer of life and the afflicted of every country shall look here for a revival of lost hopes. What Saratoga is to the East, Waukesha is ultimately destined to be to the rest of the world, a health-restoring resort for suffering humanity." The word was out, and almost overnight Waukesha was crowded with people clamoring for the water. Dunbar named his discovery "Bethesda" after a pool in Biblical Jerusalem. He then began shipping the water all over the country. As the crowds grew so did the number of springs and hotels to accommodate them. In the following decade Waukesha's boom created nearly 20 springs with names like Bethesda, Lithia, Silurian, Eureka, Clysmic, Arcadian, White Rock, Hygeia, etc. There was so much demand that other jealous producers were bottling water with labels that read...*Imitation* (small letters) *Waukesha Water* (large letters). Resort hotels began to appear in rapid succession, each one more elaborate than the last. The Fountain Spring House (see#768), was the largest hotel in Wisconsin, and it had space for 800 guests. Waukesha became "Spring City" and "The Saratoga of the West" and before long the social activity was enough to lure non-water-drinkers. Families arrived in fancy carriages and brought their servants and wardrobes to spend the summer. Up to 25 trainloads would pull into the depot daily, bringing the wealthy, the famous, and the curiousity seekers. Even Mrs. Abraham Lincoln paid a visit in 1872. Those who could not come, such as King Edward VII of England, had the water imported. But before all of this developed, Waukesha was the land of prehistoric Indians who built effigy mounds (see #742). Later white settlers came, in 1834, and the settlement was known as "Prairie Village" and "Prairieville". Much of the early architecture was made from local limestone.

737. Dunbar Oak Marker
Opposite 561 N. Dunbar
"Beneath this oak on or about August 27, 1868, Col. Richard Dunbar reclined after drinking freely from a nearby spring. Continued use of its waters healed him of a mortal ailment. He called the spring 'Bethesda' which signifies mercy. He sold the waters across the nation and beyond the sea. The names 'Bethesda', 'Waukesha', 'Dunbar', became household words. Thus began the glamorous and exciting summer resort era of Waukesha as the 'Saratoga of the West', 1868-1905."

738. Silurian Mineral Spring
Post Office Circle   **1840**

Called the "parent spring of Waukesha", this once famous watering place was originally used by the Indians and discovered by David Jackson in 1840. After years of piping the water to his nearby home through hollow logs, Jackson took advantage of the growing mineral water boom and began to bottle and sell the product. By the 1870's David Smeaton had developed the property, built a splendid Victorian pagoda "Fountain House" (now gone) and turned this into a major attraction.

739. Resthaven Sanitarium
915 N. Hartwell Ave.   **1900-08**

This large building on Arcadian Heights was originally planned as a hotel sanitarium for "rest and treatment." Three wings radiate from a central rotunda so that there are no inside rooms. The spectacular hilltop location, called "healthful and sightly," and the huge structure were billed as a "palatial hotel and famous resort" in 1912. It was converted into a hospital, in 1944, and made an annex of the Milwaukee Veteran's Hospital. Now it is occupied by the New Tribes Bible Institute.

740. Dr. Volney L. Moore Residence
307 E. Main St.   **c.1866**

This substantial CCB Italianate mansion was the home of a physician who arrived in Waukesha on June 16, 1865. Its massive 3-story tower is framed with brick corner pilasters and an ornamental brick cornice. High relief carved corbels and keystones decorate the window lintels. An unusual, and rare, carriage step can still be seen in the front yard. Inscribed, "Dr. Volney L. Moore M.D.", it is two steps carved in stone with corner ornaments.

741. St. Matthias Episcopal Church
111 E. Main St.   **1851-53**

Waukesha's oldest functioning church building, this historic Gothic Revival structure was built on the site of a prehistoric Indian mound (see #742). The congregation was organized in 1844, held their first services in a barn, and received their first regular priest two years later. The buttressed stone chapel, a gift in memory of one of the original vestrymen, Samuel H. Barstow, was added in 1887.

742. Old Waukesha County Courthouse
101 W. Main St. 1893

Milwaukee architects, Rau & Kirsch, drew the plans for this imposing Richardsonian Romanesque building. It replaces an earlier courthouse, built in 1846, which in turn was erected on a prehistoric Indian effigy mound. The turtle-shaped mound with its 36-foot body and 250-foot tail extended over the St. Matthias Church grounds (see #741). The picturesque building is trimmed with carved sandstone, buff terra-cotta ornament, stained glass, sheet copper, polished granite and it has a slate roof.

743. "Justice" Statue
515 W. Moreland Blvd. c.1893

For over half a century this hollow pewter representation of justice stood atop the old courthouse on Main St. (see #742). The nine-foot, 100-pound figure holding a copper scale is said to have come from France. It was taken down for painting in 1950. In 1965 and 1970 the scales blew off during storms. The statue was finally removed in 1972, restored by the lawyers' wives, and placed in the new courthouse.

744. National Hotel
235 W. Main St. 1871

Built by an immigrant from Bavaria, John Sperber, this was one of the important hotels during the "Spring City's" resort years. It once had a verandah which extended along the Main St. side and a two-story tower with a dormered mansard roof over the corner entrance. While most of the competition was open only during "the season," the National stayed open year round and became the leading commercial hotel. The finely crafted Waukesha limestone facade still has its original wooden cornice.

745. Putney Block #2
301 W. Main St. 1882

Frank Howell Putney, Foskett's son (see #746), razed the old Exchange Hotel and erected this handsome Waukesha limestone building as section two of a structure which would eventually fill the entire block. The original, bracketed cornice survives with its straight mansard roof section of sheet metal. A richly crafted sheet metal pediment on the Grand Ave. side displays the Odd Fellows' symbol, and the Main St. side has the emblem of the Masons (see #770) who once met upstairs.

746. Orient Block
816 N. Grand Ave. 1870

This was the first of three sections of the huge Putney block (see #745 and #747). At a time when the demand for resort hotels was pressing, Capt. Foskett M. Putney owned and operated the old wood-frame Exchange Hotel on the southwest corner of Main and Grand and he built this as an addition. The handsome rough-dressed limestone facade is accented with rock-faced panels above the windows and an arcade of cut stone. Putney operated this as the "New Exchange Hotel" until 1879, when he retired.

747. Putney Block
802 N. Grand Ave. 1891

Frank Putney erected this two-story stone building as the final addition to the block-long complex begun by his father (see #746) and continued by himself nine years earlier (see #745). He connected all three structures with a long hallway at the second floor level. Less attractive than the earlier sections, this one is distinguished by a cylindrical corner bartizan made of sheet metal with a conical slate roof.

748. Jackson Block
321 W. Main St. c.1854

Waukesha's oldest store building, this handsome three-story structure was built with dolomite (limestone) from a local quarry. In 1854 Calvin Jackson opened a drugstore and grocery here which flourished until he retired thirty years later. The unusual asymmetrical window openings are enhanced with richly ornamented lintels and bush-hammered sills. A fine corbelled sheet metal cornice caps the facade.

749. John J. Clark Dry Goods Store
325 W. Main St. 1888

John was the nephew of Betsy Clark who was said to have acquired more wealth by her own devices than any woman in Waukesha. The rock-faced limestone building originally served as a dry goods store and later was occupied by the Waukesha State Bank between 1944 and 1956. The structure's date, 1888, which appears in a rectangular panel, and the cornice below are made of sheet metal.

750. Barnes Block
329-33 W. Main St. c.1858

This distinguished Italianate business block and its almost identical twin next door west were erected by C.C. Barnes. A carved stone Masonic emblem, over the third floor windows, marks this as an early meeting place for the Waukesha lodge (see #770). Four different window lintels and a richly bracketed sheet metal cornice give the building its character.

751. Jameson & James Block
335 W. Main St. 1868

Orginally a clothing store, this two-story limestone building was erected by Reuben M. Jameson and Samuel D. James, who had been previously located in the Robinson block (see #754). The business continued in the James family, at this location, until 1904. The three semicircular windows of the second floor are framed by stone pilasters at the sides with a corbelled arcade and a bracketed wooden cornice at the top.

752. Angrave-Waite Block
337 W. Main St. 1868

Mrs. Jane Angrave and her son-in-law, John A. Waite, first shared a frame building on this corner lot. Waite was a butcher, and when Mrs. Angrave built the present structure, she lived on the second floor while he continued to sell meat on the first. His business remained in this location until 1902. This, like the other Waukesha buildings of its vintage, has the pleasant character of roughly dressed limestone laid in courses of varying thickness.

753. Nickell Block
340 W. Main St. 1901

Waukesha's Wheelman's Club once held regular meetings on the second floor of this commercial building, and there was once a post office on the ground floor. Possibly built by Addison C. Nickell, the rock-faced limestone structure is trimmed with three bay windows and a cylindrical bartizan made of sheet metal. The roof parapet wall, the odd domical structure and the inscriptions, "Nickell" and "1901" are also sheet metal.

754. Robinson Block
342 W. Main St.   **1856**

Charles L. Robinson built this three-story limestone structure as his place of business. With Martin Brown he made and sold harnesses and saddles on the first floor and rented the upstairs hall. The Federal style building is distinguished by its rounded corner, the fine stone masonry, and a large sheet metal cornice. Originally the second and third floors were a large hall which served as a social, cultural, political and entertainment center for the village.

755. First Methodist Church
121 Wisconsin Ave.   **1895-98**

Since their organization in 1839, as the Prairieville (See Waukesha introduction) Methodist Church, this congregation has built four houses of worship. The first three (one frame and two stone) were destroyed by fire in a 30-year period. This monumental building, designed by Milwaukee architect H.C. Haeuser, was damaged by a fourth fire 21 years after its completion. The imposing Romanesque structure features a huge 5,000-seat auditorium crowned by an octagonal lantern/skylight with lavender leaded glass.

756. Isaac Lain Residence
229 Wisconsin Ave.   **1848**

Waukesha county's finest example of the Greek Revival temple-style, this handsome house was built by a carpenter-contractor who later served as village president. Its fine proportions can still be appreciated from a distance, but, with the exception of the four Doric columns and the entrance casing, the entire building with all of its molding detail has been covered with aluminum siding. The building has been the home of the American Legion since 1944.

NR WRL

757. First Baptist Church
247 Wisconsin Ave.   **1872**

This handsome stone Gothic church replaced a beautiful Greek Revival structure built in 1844. The congregation, the second in the city to organize (1839), engaged Milwaukee architect Edward Townsend Mix to draw plans for the present building. Before the church was completed, a severe windstorm blew the spire down. The pastor, who thought it was "useless and costly", considered leaving it off, but was outnumbered, and the spire was fortunately rebuilt.

758. Richard Street Residence
348 Wisconsin Ave.   1871

This handsome Victorian eclectic house was built for an industrialist connected with the Waukesha County Manufacturing Company. Said to have been designed by an English architect, the CCB structure is set on a limestone foundation and is trimmed with carved stone arch corbels and keystones. The scroll-cut stick gables and a fine pair of original front doors with etched and engraved glass panels survives, but the large porch was built later.

759. Samuel Hadfield Guest House
402 Wisconsin Ave.   c.1879

One of the few surviving reminders of Waukesha's resort days, this small facility once boasted a 60-guest capacity, public parlours and a dining room. Hadfield, who had come here from England in 1852, had to move the old Putney house (see #760) four feet to the west to make room for this structure. The mansard roof lacks its ornamental iron railing, but the spacious verandah is still intact.

760. Aaron Putney Residence
406 Wisconsin Ave.   c.1870

Samuel Hadfield married the Putney's daughter, Eunice, in 1860; and when he erected his guest house next door east (see #759), he moved his father-in-law's residence four feet west to the present location. This relatively plain frame house is distinguished by its deep over hanging roof and the unusually prominent supporting brackets with drop finials. The oversized main drop finials, under the side roof peaks, are a true oddity.

761. First German Reformed Church
413 Wisconsin Ave.   1891

Led by German immigrant Rev. H. Kurtz, nine families organized in 1866 and purchased the old Prairieville Academy building. Said to have been the first entirely stone building in the state, it served the congregation for 25 years until this church was erected. The CCB walls, set on a limestone foundation, support a wooden tower with an octagonal spire. A nicely designed marble tablet, set in brick over the entrance, reads, "Erste Deutsche Reformirte Kirche 1866-1891."

762. Cutler Park
Wisconsin Ave. at Grand Ave.

Orginally the homestead of Morris Cutler (see #764), this centrally located park is filled with historical monuments. A tablet marks the spot where Cutler's house once stood, and there are three cannons and a gray granite Civil War monument. Near the west end of the park are three prehistoric Indian mounds which are survivors of the 55 once found in the city. The largest mound (pictured) was excavated in 1850, revealing human bones and fragments of pipes, shells and pottery.

763. William G. Mann Residence
346 Maple Ave.   1897

In 1896 a two-story frame hotel, called the "Morse House", burned to the ground on this corner. William Mann, a commercial photographer, married the hotel owner's daughter, Carrie Morse; and they built this house on the family property. The corner pavilion has an unusual ogee mansard roof with a cupola and two circular dormers. At one time the boldly detailed porch extended across the front to an engaged octagonal "gazebo" similar to that on the Chandler house (see #786).

764. Morris Derrick Cutler
Residence
401 Central Ave.   1845

Built by Waukesha's first white settler, this frame Greek Revival house once stood in what is now Cutler Park (see #762). It originally was located near the Civil War monument and faced north. Cutler, who came here in 1834, lived in this structure until his death in 1896. Five years later it was moved to the present location, a one-story ell wing was removed, the porch added, and asbestos siding was applied.

765. Waukesha Mineral Water Co.
550 Elizabeth St.   c.1928

This early stucco factory building is a good example of industrial architecture showing the influence of speed-line streamlining and the decorative tradition of the 1920's and 30's. It was the home of Waukesha Mineral Water Co., bottlers of "Silver King" and "Silurian Ginger Ale." In 1947 it housed the Federal Refrigerator Manufacturing Co.; it is now an industrial park for a number of smaller operations. The building is trimmed with a pantile cornice and decorative inset tiles.

766. Henry Totten Residence
515 N. Grand Ave.   c.1850

Built for a Waukesha druggist, this house originally stood on the northwest corner of Wisconsin Ave. and Grand. In 1873 an auction was held, and the home was sold and moved to the present site. The two-story Greek Revival design has a full triangular pediment, but the indented first floor porch is uncommon. Two fluted Doric and two square columns support the facade. Most of the original work is covered with aluminum siding.

767. Andrew J. Frame Residence
507 N. Grand Ave.   1880

One of the most distinguished Italianate houses in the county, this CCB structure was designed by Milwaukee architect Edward Townsend Mix. A handsome tower over the entrance was removed in the 1940's. Frame was president and board chairman of the First National Bank of Waukesha. He was once known as "America's greatest country banker." Under the original porch canopy two fine art-glass windows and the engraved "Frame" nameplate survive.

768. Site of Fountain Spring House
West side of S. Grand Ave.
North from W. Newhall Ave.
1874 & 1878

Called "the queen of the Northwest" and "the largest hotel west of the Allegheny Mountains," the fabulous Fountain Spring House was the foundation of Waukesha's resort days. It was built by Matthew Laflin, a Chicago millionaire who claimed to have been cured of "a painful and dangerous malady" by drinking mineral water here. The hotel opened in 1874 and became nationally famous for its first class accommodations. Four years later the southern half was destroyed by fire. Laflin retained the original 6-story octagonal tower and rebuilt the hotel to more than double its original size. At that time it was 450 feet long and accommodated 600 guests. People from all over the country flocked here each summer with their servants, nurses, horses, and carriages to enjoy the healthful water and the sociability. Surrounded by more than 100 acres of beautiful grounds, guests could enjoy the spring pavilion, a trout pond, boardwalks, parades, a bathhouse, and a spectacular dining room seating 500. The hotel finally closed in 1905 and became the headquarters of the Metropolitan Church Association. In 1957 Milwaukee real estate developers purchased the property, razed the buildings and erected the "Fountain Spring Apartments."

769. United States Post Office
235 W. Broadway   1913-14

Waukesha architect Oscar Wenderoth designed this impressive neoclassical structure on an historic triangle occupied previously by the First Methodist Church (see #755). The semicircular portico, supported by six fluted Doric columns, embraces half of the cylindrical lobby which features a Corinthian colonnade and a coffered dome with a stained glass skylight. The Bedford stone exterior is complemented with iron lanterns and railings, granite steps, bronze handrails and a copper dome on the roof.

770. Masonic Temple
317 South St.   1904-05

Waukesha Lodge #37 was organized in 1851 and held its first meeting in the Odd Fellows Hall. For years members met in rented quarters on the third floors of the Barnes Block (see #750) and the Putney Block (see #745). In 1904 they finally laid the cornerstone for this Classical rock-faced limestone building. Of special interest is their illuminated cross-shaped sign made of sheet copper and containing 10 stained glass panels with Masonic symbolism.

771. Louis Yanke Saloon
200 Madison St.   1892

This substantial late Victorian building was erected by Louis Yanke who operated a saloon on the street floor and lived with his family and other relations on the second floor. While the St. Paul Ave. side is all limestone, the unusual Madison St. side is made of rock-faced granite trimmed with rock-faced limestone. The bartizan, over the corner entrance, is made of wood and sheet metal.

772. Waukesha Water Utility
115 Delafield St.   1907

Devised as a public relations display in the 1930's, this greenhouse-like structure encloses an important functional operation. Deep-well water is pumped up at the rate of 577 gallons per minute and allowed to fall on an umbrella-shaped baffle and splash down to an underground reservoir which holds 290,000 gallons. In the process the water is aerated and loses its "ground odor." The utility, which succeeds an earlier (1887) franchise, was organized in 1907 and created this illuminated display to show off the water for which Waukesha is famous.

773. William Blair Residence
434 Madison St.   1876

This was the home of a director and president of the Waukesha County Manufacturing Co. (woolen mill), once the county's largest enterprise. Blair came here from Ayrshire, Scotland, in 1845, and established first a threshing machine plant and later an ironworks. His CCB residence still has its original iron roof cresting and stick-style gables. The most interesting design element is the windows with their corbelled sills and triple-keystoned arches. Each "keystone" has an incised fleur-de-lis.

774. Residence
603 N. West Ave.   1883

This is one of the few houses that boldly displays the date of its construction as a part of the design. In the triangular porch pediment, which faces West Ave., the number 1883 is displayed in raised, scroll-cut, wooden numberals. The eclectic frame design features an octagonal tower and three original porches. Note the way in which the two dissimilar porches flanking the tower make the same angular attachments to it.

775. Fabacher Residence
200 McCall St.   c.1895

This large Queen Anne style residence has a clapboarded first floor set on a rock-faced limestone foundation. The second and third floors are sided with cedar shingles. The unusual front porch, which was added later, extends beyond the house to become a porte cochere. Fabacher owned a restaurant in New Orleans' French Quarter, and he built this house as a summer home. Later owned by Judge David Agnew, it is now a fraternity house.

776. Henry Carl George Residence
210 McCall St.   c.1863

Mr. George, who was a stonecutter and mason, purchased this property in 1861 and may have built the house himself. It remained in the family until 1950, when it was sold at auction. Miss Susie George, the last of Henry's descendants to occupy the house, was a strong-willed seamstress who worked in the neighborhood and reportedly accepted no advice from her customers. The house was not equipped with indoor plumbing until after her death.

777. Greek Revival Residence
403 McCall St.   **c.1860**

Very little is known about this handsome 2½-story house on the corner of N. James St. Its coursed limestone rubble walls and wooden cornices are well proportioned and obviously well maintained. The stone-framed lunette at the attic level is decorated with a wooden fan ornament. The porch is a later addition, and there is a smaller wing on the rear.

778. Moses Weeks Residence
214 W. Laflin Ave.   **1908 and earlier**

Mr. Weeks came from Maine to Milwaukee and engaged in business there in the early 20th century. It is said that his mother-in-law was advised to come here for her health and the Bethesda water; so the whole family moved to Waukesha around 1908. He purchased this house and remodelled it, adding the well-proportioned Greek-temple portico with its five Doric columns.

779. Residence
210 W. Laflin Ave.   **c.1895**

A well preserved example of turn-of-the-century styling, this frame clapboard house shows both the influence of the Classical Revival and the picturesque eclectic Victorian periods. An unusual semicircular arch, which is subordinate to the angular porch gable, is reflected in a transom window over the front door. A quasi-Palladian treatment ties three rectilinear windows together above the porch.

780. John P. Buchner Residence
609 E. Broadway   **1879**

Buchner came from Bavaria, in 1840, and lived on a farm in New Berlin. In 1877 he moved to Waukesha and subsequently built this CCB house. In 1915 he gave the city a nearby 5-acre tract to make the park which is now named after him. The house is set on an unusual rock-faced granite foundation, above which is an equally rare, point-dressed limestone water table.

781. Daniel J. Hemlock Residence
234 Carroll St.   **c.1876**

This unusual CCB Victorian eclectic house was the home of a Waukesha lawyer, Daniel Hemlock. Its design in many ways resembles the "new American style" developed by Milwaukee architect James Douglas. Nicknamed the "termes mordax," or ant-hill style, it is distinguished by a complicated roof construction with dormers and "hills" (see #88). The front porch was added later.

782. Alexander Cook Residence
600 E. North St.   **1865**

Waukesha County's first district attorney, Alexander Cook, was elected in 1846 and served eight terms, the longest period in the history of that office. He had come to Prairieville (Waukesha), in 1845, from Syracuse, New York, and practiced here 52 years, establishing one of the longest legal careers in county history. His limestone house is dated on a stone near the gable peak. Its steeply pitched roof and unusual pointed window lintels give the house a Gothic Revival feeling. It is likely that ornamental bargeboards once decorated the gable end.

783. William P. Sloan Residence
912 S. Barstow St.   **1841**

The oldest stone house in Waukesha, this small structure is also said to be the very first one to be erected of that material here. It originally faced Main Street and was later moved to this location. The limestone for its construction came from Lyman Goodnow's quarry, which opened the year before and was the first in the county. Sloan was a lawyer and a board member of Prairieville Academy and Carroll College.

784. Caspar Melchior Sanger Residence
507 E. College Ave.   **1886**

This imposing mansion, one of Waukesha's largest, was once the focal point of the "Hickory Park Stock Farm." Sanger, a wealthy tanner from Westphalia, Prussia, lived in Milwaukee and bought the 80-acre Moss property here in 1885. When he built this "country gentleman's" residence, it had a large tower, of which only a 3-story stump survives. A fine painted window, the original porch, and unusual window lintels can still be seen.

785. William Powrie Residence
115 W. College Ave.   c.1897

This picturesque 2½-story frame house was occupied until the 1920's by William Powrie, and is believed to have been built by him. Obviously influenced by the Classical Revival, the design also includes a cylindrical three-story tower with a conical roof and a stepped main gable which is reminiscent of the Flemish Renaissance. In 1968 it was purchased by Carroll College and is now used as a faculty residence.

786. Walter Seymour Chandler Residence
151 W. College Ave.   1870

One of the finest and best preserved Victorian Gothic frame houses in southeastern Wisconsin, this was the home of a Milwaukee lumber dealer. It is rare to find so many original features on a frame residence of this age and complexity (such as the iron cresting on the roof, the porte cochere, tower balconies, the tower finial, and the porch with its integral corner pavilion which has a colored glass cupola). Even the grounds are unspoiled.

787. Methodist District Parsonage
239 W. College Ave.   c.1855

One of Waukesha's mystery houses, about which little is known, this handsome Greek Revival residence probably began its life as a parsonage for Methodist clergymen. Built of coursed limestone rubble, with scratched mortar joints, the well proportioned facade has a wooden cornice with the typical broken triangular pediment. The one-story ell wing has a canopy supported by 3 square columns and 2 pilasters.

788. Robert Jones Residence
501 W. College Ave   c.1896

Built by a railroad mail carrier, this well-preserved Victorian eclectic house has had only two owners in its lifetime. In 1911 it was purchased by Thomas Shephard, who owned a 200-acre farm, "Lily Grove," in Yorkville. Both the porch pediment and the front gable have fan ornaments, but the structure's principal feature is the fine two-sided verandah with its engaged gazebo.

789. Milwaukee & Madison Railroad Depot
319 Williams St. 1881

When it was new, this passenger and freight facility was described as "the finest in the northwest ... no depot in Milwaukee is as attractive in appearance." In 1882 it was taken over by Chicago & Northwestern, which used it for passenger service until 1957 and freight until 1966. President Harry S. Truman stopped here, in 1948, for a whistle-stop campaign speech. The CCB structure is trimmed with decorative shingle-work, pierced bargeboards and ornamental brackets.

790. Wisconsin Central Car Shops East of White Rock Ave.
near Frame Park 1886

The last of three railroads to enter Waukesha, the Wisconsin Central was the only one which brought its main line through the city. It was with great civic pride that early newspaper accounts described the "great Waukesha shops" where locomotives and other rolling stock were repaired. Now black with grime, the CCB building still has its large limestone inscription, "Wisconsin Central 1886." In 1908 the Minneapolis & Sault Ste. Marie Railroad (commonly called the Soo Line) bought the Wisconsin Central.

791. Carroll College
100 N. East Ave. 1846

Wisconsin's oldest college, Carroll was chartered in 1846 and named for Charles Carroll, one of the signers of the Declaration of Independence. It continued the work of Prairieville Academy (1841) (see #761) and erected its first "Old Main" in 1853. After that was destroyed by fire, the present structure was built in 1887 and enlarged in 1900. The limestone Victorian Gothic building is decorated with red sandstone, stained glass and unusual square-block belt courses on the tower.

WHM

792. Abram H. Hadfield Residence
232 N. East Ave. c.1878

This handsome Victorian eclectic house was built with stone from one of Hadfield's quarries. In partnership with his father and brother, Abram had an interest in the Pewaukee and Waukesha quarries, the latter being the largest shippers of stone in Waukesha County (up to 3,500 carloads a day in 1880). In 1915 the house was given to Carroll College by Mr. and Mrs. Samuel Quaw of Wausau. Now the "music annex", it is named "Shephard Hall" for a former Carroll School of Music director, Clarence C. Shephard.

793. Frank E. Allen Residence
425 N. East Ave. c.1888

Known for years as "Swan Cottage", this unusual house was built by a man from "tornado country" who took no chances with its construction. Major beams run both ways in the structure (for better bracing strength), and its flat-top hipped roof constitutes one half the height of the design. An interesting variation on the Queen Anne style, the two front pavilions protect the recessed entrance, which is hooded by the roof. The south bay window is fitted with a splendid example of etched, ruby-flashed glass.

794. First Congregational Church
701 N. East Ave. 1867 and later

The Congregationalists were the first church to organize in Waukesha (1838), and the present structure was erected in 1867. Wings were added to the north, south and east; and new stained glass windows were installed in 1899. These beautifully preserved windows are both painted and stained. It was not until 1922 that the large frame building, with its original steeple and many additions, was faced with brick.

795. Joseph Jackson Hadfield Residence
710 N. East Ave. 1885

Hadfield, whose father came to Prairieville from England in 1842, was a wool buyer and real estate dealer. Shortly after erecting this house, he became village president. Built with limestone from his father's quarry, this structure is an exceptionally fine example of masonry construction. Fortunately all of the stick-style gables and the original porches are still intact and in good condition.

796. Samuel D. James Residence
726 N. East Ave. 1871

Mrs. Elizabeth James was a sister of Addison C. Nickell (see #753), who lived in the house next door south; and it is believed that Mr. Nickell built both structures. Mr. James, a local banker and dry goods merchant, lived there until the early 20th century. The house later was occupied by a Carroll College fraternity and a funeral home. With few exceptions, this fine eclectic Victorian design has survived in unspoiled condition.

797. St. Joseph's Catholic Church
818 N. East Ave. 1888-90

This parish was organized in 1842, and the first mass was said by Fr. Martin Kundig, a missionary from Switzerland. Part of the stone walls of the first church, built in 1849, still survive in the present school. Chicago architect, A. Druiding, drew the plans for the present Gothic structure, and the cornerstone was laid in 1888. Unlike the angle buttresses used elsewhere on the building, there are cylindrical, turret-like buttresses on the upper tower.

798. Presbyterian Parsonage
121 Arcadian Ave. c.1885

Between the years 1901 and 1941 this frame house served as a residence for Presbyterian ministers, beginning with Rev. Chester H. Williamson and including, in order, Rev. Charles Bovard, Rev. Palmer and Dr. Ernest Wright. The building was purchased from its original owner (unidentified). A humble, but exceptionally well preserved example of the Queen Anne style, the house still has its original porch and decorative shingle, clapboard, and spindle ornament.

799. Jackson Residence
814 Arcadian Ave. c.1890

Otherwise an ordinary frame dwelling, this unique house derives its character from the 2½-story porch centered on its street facade. While stacked porches are not rare, it is unusual to find an enclosed extension of the attic supported above the upper deck. This house was built by a local piano tuner whose wife was organist at St. Matthias (see #741) and used to teach piano here.

Henry C. Miller residence Page 375 No. 883

RACINE
COUNTY

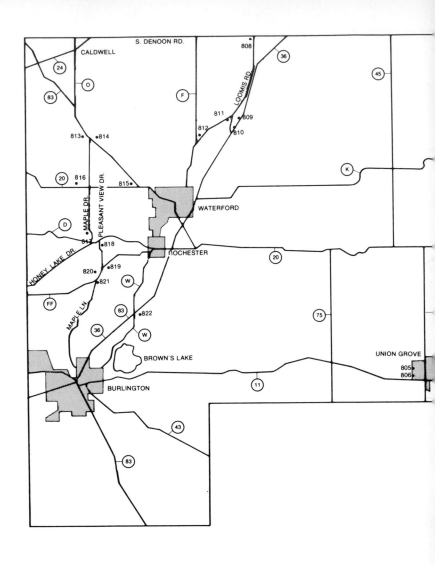

RACINE COUNTY

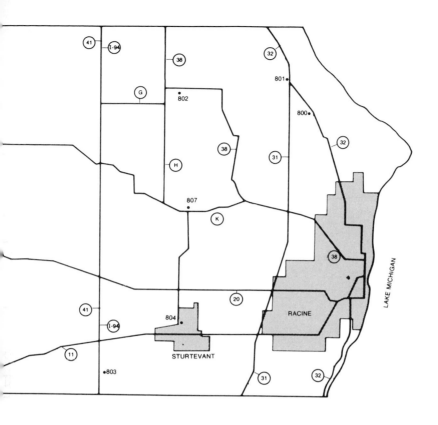

RACINE COUNTY

Originally a part of old Milwaukee County, Racine was separated in 1836. It first extended south to the Illinois state line and stretched for 26½ miles along Lake Michigan. In 1850 it was split laterally to create Kenosha County on the south. Before Wisconsin became a state (1848), Racine County was described as "generally even, or slightly rolling, and is destitute of timber. Burr oaks, hickory, etc., are found in occasional groves, and the remainder is a prairie." Architecturally the county is very rich, but these examples are clustered on the eastern and western extremes, leaving a 17-mile-wide band of relatively uninteresting farmland and prairie in between. Racine, on the east, is the county seat and it has one of the richest concentrations of landmark quality buildings in the Midwest. At the western end of the county, along the Fox River, are Waterford, Rochester and Burlington, each with numerous important buildings.

800. Green Bay Road Marker
Hwy. 32 at Intersection
of Five Mile Road

This often-overlooked concrete obelisk was placed on the west side of Highway 32 by The Wisconsin Society of Chicago. Its bronze tablet commemorates the pioneer road between Chicago and Green Bay which was surveyed in circa 1833. Roughly following an Indian trail, this "military road" was blazed and staked out by Army engineers Lt. A.J. Center and James Duane Doty (who later became a governor of Wisconsin). It passed through Milwaukee, Thiensville, Hamilton, Grafton, Saukville and Belgium on its way to Fort Howard in Green Bay.

801. 32nd Division
Memorial Highway Marker
Hwy. 32 just north of Hwy. 31   1960

This marker was erected to commemorate the world famous "Red Arrow" division which was organized under War Department orders on July 18, 1917. It was formed from National Guard troops in Wisconsin (15,000 men) and Michigan (8,000 men). In World War I they fought on five fronts and suffered 14,000 casualties. They were the first American troops on German soil at Alsace in May of 1918. The red arrow shooting through a line signifies their ability to penetrate enemy defenses. The French called them "Les Terribles", "the terrible ones."

802. St. Louis Catholic Church
Hwy. G just east of I-94   1901

A fine example of Romanesque design, this church follows the style more faithfully than most churches of the era which blend Gothic with Romanesque. Built of CCB, it is set on a granite foundation and is trimmed with limestone and sheet metal. The parish was begun in 1845, when Rev. Kundig celebrated mass in local homes in what was then called Lower Caledonia or Thompsonville. In 1857, parishioners built a frame church which served as a school on weekdays.

803. University of Lawsonomy
I-94 between Hwy. 11 & County Line
Rd. 1943

A 136-foot, illuminated, sheet metal sign announces a university that was never built. The 40-acre tract, with a few small buildings, is still maintained, but there were never more than four or five students at a time here. Established by industrialist-philosopher, Alfred W. Lawson, the "university" was intended to produce "master intellects of all times". His followers believe in vegetarianism, and they are opposed to vices. Before his educational aspirations developed, Lawson established a pioneer airline and began to manufacture airplanes in Milwaukee. Both ventures failed.

804. Corliss Hotel
2810 Wisconsin St. c.1901

Before it was called Sturtevant, this important railroad intersection had the name "Western Union Junction". In 1901 it was surveyed for the Brown Corliss Engine Company, and the village was called Corliss. A depot occupied the southwest corner of the intersection of two railroad tracks. It was only logical that a hotel be erected on the northeast corner of this important transportation hub. Ernest Klinkert, who had built a brewery in Racine, put up this hotel, which was first called the Corliss. Its unusual design includes three corner bartizans, with lookouts, supported on limestone corbels. Klinkert's name appears on a limestone block near the cornice, facing the tracks.

805. Union Grove
Congregational Church
11th Ave., N.W. corner Vine St. 1892

When this congregation was organized, in 1844, its title was The Congregational Church of Paris (for the only post office in that area). A second church, which stood on this site, burned down in March of 1892. This CCB Gothic edifice was erected on the old foundation the same year. Its yellow brick is trimmed with orange brick and cut limestone which, over the Gothic arches, is set flush with the wall surface. Its unusual silhouette has a frame bell cupola, a gable with sheet metal shingles and a mansard roof with cast iron cresting.

806. Union Grove School
11th Ave., S.E. corner Vine St. 1882

"Union School", the first built here (1846), is thought to have been partly responsible for naming the town. It was replaced, in 1859, by a two-room frame school on this site. In 1882, when this substantial CCB structure was built, the old school was moved away and converted into a residence. The present building has little window space, but an interesting pilaster and panel composition. The two-room wing was added later and, in 1914 and 1925, new schools caused it to be abandoned; it was sold to the Mason's Lodge No. 288.

807. Skunk Grove Marker
Hwy. K, intersection Hwy. H. 1973

"Skunk Grove was a stopping place for travelers in an uncharted wilderness on the mail route between Green Bay and Chicago. It was located about 200 yards southeast of this marker, where the trail crossed the stream now known as Hood's Creek. By 1832, in what was still Pottawatomi Indian Territory, two French brothers, Jacques and Louis Vieau, had the first known trading post in this area, "Jambeau's Trading Post."

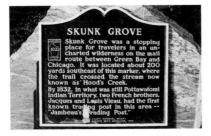

808. Hans Ellertson Farmhouse
Near S110 W20516 S. Denoon Rd. 1884

One of Racine County's most exceptional farmhouses, this was built by its owner, Hans Ellertson. The bricks were made at a tile and brick factory in Windlake, in which he was a partner. Hans was also a trained carpenter and he gave to the house many fine features which are uncommon in rural areas. Both the wooden cornice and the soffits are embellished with moldings and panels. The foundation is made of roughly squared granite blocks, one of which has the date, 1884, neatly chiselled in serif numerals. Inside, the moldings are rich and deep, and many first floor doors are wood-grained in up to five different patterns. Mr. Ellertson's pride and joy, however, were the doors of the parlour. Each has four panels with hawthorn branches painted in oils. Under the parlour windows are mountain landscapes realistically painted in sunken panels. At the side of the house is a large, roughly pyramidal, granite boulder with an iron ring attached. Used as a hitching post, it bears an inscribed date...May 1, 1895. Out back is a timber-framed granary with the date 1868 on one of its hewn beams. The large barn has an 1871 sandstone cornerstone.

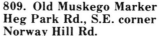

809. Old Muskego Marker
Heg Park Rd., S.E. corner
Norway Hill Rd.   1963

"Under the leadership of John Luraas, forty pioneers came to Muskego Lake from Norway in 1839, to found one of the most important settlements in Norwegian-American history. After temporary set-backs, the settlement flourished here through the leadership of Even Heg, Johannes Johanssen, Soren Bache, Elling Eilsen, James Reymert and Claus Clausen, who sent glowing reports to Norway and encouraged a large movement to this country. This settlement gave rise to the first Norwegian Lutheran congregation organized in America (1843) and published the first Norwegian-American newspaper. Old Muskego became well known as a mother colony to other settlements, schools and churches springing up on the new frontier. Countless wagonloads of newcomers stopped here before continuing west."

810. Norway Lutheran Church
Heg Park Rd., S.E. corner
Norway Hill Rd.   1869

The first Norwegian Lutheran Church in America worshiped here in a log building erected in 1845. After the present church was built, the old red oak log structure was moved to the Lutheran Seminary campus in St. Paul, Minnesota. This CCB, Romanesque building is set on a granite foundation and has a clapboarded frame belfry supporting an octagonal spire. Among the many Norwegians buried in the hilltop cemetery surrounding the church is Civil War hero Colonel Hans C. Heg (see #811).

811. Col. Heg Memorial Park
Loomis Rd. at Heg Park Rd.

Racine County's first public memorial park, this triangle of land is situated in the historic Norway Hill area and is named after Colonel Hans C. Heg. An outstanding Civil War hero, Heg was killed in action while commanding a Scandinavian regiment called the "15th Wisconsin" at the Battle of Chickamauga. A large bronze statue of Heg stands in front of the park, and an 1837 Norwegian log house was moved there in 1928 and restored. There is also an 1847 two-story frame farmhouse on the property.

812. Charles Buchholtz Farmhouse
5420 Loomis Rd. 1870

The stone for this house was quarried on the west side of the Fox River and hauled across the ice during the winter. Charles Buchholtz had owned the 160-acre farm since 1861. His house is set on a fieldstone foundation and is very neatly built of coursed, roughly-squared limestone with dressed quoins. The two-story main block faces south across a triangular intersection of roads and has a one-story north wing.

813. Mygatt Farmhouse
5924 Hwy. 83 c.1850

This was probably the home of Philip R. and Sarah Mygatt, whose daughter, Elizabeth, married Martin Beardsley. Martin's father, Elam, owned the farm across the road (see #814). In 1904, Elam Buttles, whose family farm bordered this one on the north, purchased the Mygatt property, and it is still occupied by his son. The house is a well-proportioned Greek Revival design with wide, molded cornice boards. The cobblestone walls are trimmed with limestone lintels and sills, and the quoins are made of CCB.

814. Elam Beardsley Farmhouse
5601 Hwy. 83 c.1855

Elam first settled in Racine County, in 1834, in the town of Caledonia. He later moved here and traded his old farm for this one which, in 1879, was called "The old Homestead". The two-story house has been altered, but retains its fine stone walls made of large, graded cobblestones. Corners are trimmed with dressed quoins. The fine scroll-cut wooden porch was a later addition. Later the farm was purchased by the Kelley family, which owned it for nearly a century.

815. Ira A. Rice Residence
31509 Hwy. 83 c.1865

Born in Oswego County, New York, Ira Rice came to Racine County, in 1836, and built a log house here. His son, John T. Rice, was the first child born in Rochester. Ira was a farmer and an attorney and was admitted to the bar in 1870. On this 230-acre tract he raised vegetables and wheat. His handsome Italian villa has survived with few exterior alterations and is one of the finest examples of that style as executed in wood. Especially notable are the scroll-cut porch brackets and the cupola atop the hipped roof.

816. Lewis Merrill Residence
3603 Hwy. 20 c.1850

This fine Greek Revival dwelling was probably built by Lewis Merrill who homesteaded this land around 1840. By 1858 the house was standing, and the 150-acre farm was then owned by Willard Lapham. The stuccoed main block of the house has a pitched roof, while that over the one-story eastern wing is hipped. That roof extends beyond the wall and is supported by fluted Doric columns to create an ell-shaped porch. The present owners are building an identical wing to the west.

817. Matthew Blackburn Farmhouse
Maple Drive, 6/10 Mile north
of Hwy. D 1847-48

An English immigrant, Blackburn once owned a 200-acre farm here. His residence, one of southeastern Wisconsin's finest examples of cobblestone construction, was trimmed with limestone hauled from the Genesee quarry. The finely proportioned Greek Revival design has a full triangular pediment with a triangular attic window. The wooden siding and front bay window were added over what was once a recessed porch with two full columns. As usual, the finely sorted small cobblestones were used on the front; the sides were done less carefully with larger stones.

818. District No. 3 Schoolhouse
Hwy. D, S.E. corner Pleasant View Dr.
1866

Once this sturdy schoolhouse had a wooden bell cupola with ornamental scroll-cut brackets. The cupola was removed and the building has been converted into a residence, but the bell was saved and remounted near the front gable peak. The well-built Greek Revival structure is made of limestone with raised mortar joints and has dressed quoins, lintels, sills and water table. Just below the wooden cornice is a datestone which reads "1866 Dist. No. 3". The last classes were held here in 1963.

351

819. Hoyt Residence
Hwy. FF, southeast corner
Pleasant View Dr.   c.1890

Like the nearby William Rowe house (see #821), this structure, and all of its trim, look to be at least twenty-years older than the evidence indicates. According to tradition, this house was built by one of the Hoyts (see #820) for a son who died of blood poisoning from a nail cut before the building was completed. The original homesteader here was William S. Hoyt, who claimed 400 acres in 1837. His son, Franklin, bred award-winning Ayrshire cattle and assumed numerous public posts, including state assemblyman.

820. Franklin E. Hoyt Residence
Hwy. FF just south of
Pleasant View Dr.   c.1885

One of the most unusual eclectic designs to be found in Racine County, this house is said to have been erected before the Civil War by Franklin E. Hoyt (see #819). Now a rambling, 14-room mansion, it is difficult to find any clues that indicate an earlier structure might be its core. What can be seen is a highly creative and picturesque blending of materials and design styles unlike anything else in the territory. The basic material is CCB set on a granite foundation with raised mortar joints. The second floor of the main block is sided with ornamental, stamped, sheet metal shingles and the window frames have a decorative panelled design. The first floor lintels are limestone, laid flush, and cut to form flat arches. With the ornamental hardware, stacked wooden porches, dormers and scroll-cut wooden trim, the dwelling's design resembles the Queen Anne and Eastlake styles. On the same property across the street is an old cider mill which has for years been called "The Jail". It acquired that title when a prisoner, being transported to Racine, was held there overnight. Just below its 1858 datestone are three unusual decorative panels of cobblestone masonry. Elsewhere on the property are three other barns, one of which has a cobblestone foundation.

821. William Rowe Farmhouse
Hwy. FF, just north of Maple Lane 1889
Although this house resembles a style which was popular twenty years earlier, closer inspection reveals details which are more characteristic for this date. In the 1860's and early 70's the Italian Villa style flourished and produced many dwellings with square towers like this one (compare #306). This is a rare survival of a then-unpopular style. The date "1889" is cut into bricks on the exterior and in the basement. Inside, the moldings and corner blocks have different designs in each room.

822. St. Francis Friary
Hwy. W just south of Hwy. 83-36
1930-31 and 1954
The Franciscans, the second largest religious order in the world, settled in Wisconsin over 85 years ago. They established the "Assumption Province" to minister to the needs of Polish-speaking people and set up headquarters in Pulaski, Wisconsin. In 1930 they purchased 300 acres here and broke ground for a friary and liberal arts college to train candidates for the priesthood. The plans were drawn by Chicago architects, Slupkowski and Piontek, and the Spanish baroque style of the buff brick and limestone complex reflects the Franciscan missions in California. A western wing was added in 1954. The college was discontinued in 1969.

BURLINGTON

Originally called "Lower Forks", this village site on the Fox River was later dubbed, "Foxville" when the mail service between Racine and Mineral Point started in the late 1830's. Its final name is said to have been taken from Burlington, Vermont. Like most early settlements, which grew up around water power, this one first spawned a dam and a grist mill. The earliest residents were from New York state and New England, but in the 1840's German immigrants began to arrive. By the turn of the century a sizeable proportion of the population was German. Burlington was incorporated as a village in 1886, and became a city in 1900.

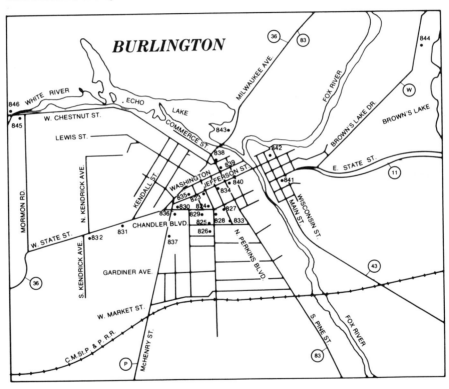

823. Charles A. Jones Residence
225 N. Kane St.   1896

One of the largest mansions ever built in Burlington, this imposing frame structure was the home of a real estate and insurance agent. His name, "C.A. Jones", is clearly carved on the street side of a two-level carriage step which has been moved close to the house. The date, 1896, is carved on a granite block inside the porch wall. The three-story Queen Anne / eclectic frame structure has cylindrical glass windows in the tower.

824. Italianate Residence
125 N. Kane St.   c.1875

This two-story CCB dwelling, which is otherwise an average structure for its date, is distinguished by a number of well designed details. The denticulated wooden cornice has larger than average dentils for the scale of the building and instead of being square, the dentils have a gentle ogee curve which gives them the appearance of small brackets. The canopy over the front door repeats the dentils and is supported by an unusually interesting pair of laminated scroll-cut brackets made of wood.

825. Oliver W. Chandler Residence
149 S. Kane St.   c.1855

This large Gothic Revival frame house was built for a well-known music dealer and piano agent. When it was new, a picket fence surrounded the grounds, and there were two porches flanking the entrance pavilion. The house has been considerably altered with an addition on the rear, two dormers cut through the roof in front, and aluminum siding. The original scroll-cut bargeboards remain, and there is a cast iron Gothic grille on a basement window. The unusual fence is a chain strung between cast iron posts, made to look like pruned logs.

826. Anthony Meinhardt Residence
201 S. Kane St. 1882

The showplace of Burlington, this fine mansion once was surrounded by 15 acres of beautifully landscaped grounds, including flower and vegetable gardens, an orchard, a pasture, a dense pine grove, fountains and tennis courts. Built by the founder of the Meinhardt Bank, the house was designed by Milwaukee's most influential architect, Edward Townsend Mix. The eclectic Victorian design is executed in limestone trimmed with buff sandstone. On the exterior corners are unusual, smooth-dressed, vertical stones which are not true quoins, but which frame each wall surface as neat panels. The original front porch was moved around to the side, and the large combination porch and porte-cochere was added in 1914 by Racine architects, Guilbert and Funston. Inside are two vestibule doors with beautiful decorative panels made of etched ruby flashed glass. Mr. Meinhardt set his children to work on the house. Francis designed and carved a walnut mantel, and the others were assigned the task of polishing the black walnut staircase with oil and pumice. It is said that this labor was never forgotten, and the children would not consider sliding down the banister. The carpenter, Fred Itzin, was such a perfectionist that one out of three loads of lumber was sent back because of imperfections. Anthony died, in 1891, assuming that his name would last forever in Burlington. But his widow, it is said, did not permit the three sons to marry, and the bank was eventually sold and renamed so that today the Meinhardts are almost forgotten.

827. Origen Perkins Residence
117 E. State St. 1846

This dignified, stuccoed residence shows the influence of both Greek Revival and Federal styling. Two fluted Doric columns support the front porch, and there is a shape on the hipped roof which hints that there may once have been a cupola there. A native of Connecticut, Perkins came here, with his wife, in 1837 as one of Burlington's earliest settlers. He first built a log house, then a frame dwelling and finally this residence. In 1850 he went to California for gold and was murdered for his money on the return trip.

828. Burlington Settlers Monument
E. State St. between
Kane St. and N. Perkins 1925

The bronze sailing vessel, set on a stone monolith, was erected in 1925 to the memory of the pioneers who first settled Burlington. It was a gift from Charles Dyer Norton, whose father, Edward Galusha Dyer, was the city's first physician. It was on this site, in 1840, that the Dyers built the first frame house in Burlington. Listed on th tablet are the names of 21 settlers who came here in a six-year period, beginning with Lemuel R. Smith in 1835.

829. Deacon T.W. Durgin Residence
117 W. State St. c.1848

As late as 1876, Durgin was listed as a farmer at this address, which was then 641 Liberty St. His handsome Greek Revival house was built in sections through the years. The front, or main block, is a well proportioned fieldstone structure with a wide and richly molded wooden cornice. The large front porch was added later. On the rear is a square block with a hipped roof. Inside, the original pine Greek Revival casings are still intact.

830. Jacob Brehm Building
232-236 W. State St. c.1850

This Greek Revival structure is so large that it is unlikely that carpenter, Jacob Brehm, built it as a single family residence. Its original use has not been determined, but it appears to have been a hotel or a commercial building. The masonry walls have been covered with stucco, and the cornice is of wood. The one-story wing is a later addition.

831. St. Mary' Cemetery Chapel
W. State St.,
intersection Kendall St. c.1875

This Victorian Gothic chapel has a number of design characteristics not normally found on buildings of this small scale. In addition to fully buttressed side walls, it has a half-octagon apse and Gothic corbelling on the front wall. Over the front door is a cross recessed in the CCB masonry. The bell cupola has a sheet metal roof. Throughout the cemetery, numerous, fine quality, cast and wrought iron crosses can be seen.

832. Pliny M. Perkins Farmhouse
565 W. State St. c.1845

When this house was erected, in the 1840's, Perkins owned 320 acres. Only the front of his dwelling was given the handsome veneer of cobblestones, while the other walls were left in coarse masonry. Unlike most houses of similar construction, the cobblestones here have been graded from the smallest at the bottom to the largest at the top. Lintels are wooden and flush with the surface, and the false quoins are made of CCB. In the basement is a fieldstone room, blackened with greasy smoke, which was probably an indoor smokehouse. John Prasch bought the farm in 1869.

833. St. John the Divine Episcopal Church
148 Edward St. 1893

More roof than building, this Romanesque church is made of CCB set on a coursed limestone rubble foundation. The brick buttresses seem to provide the necessary support for what seems like a great roof weight. The parish was established in 1869 and became an "organized mission" church in 1880. Services were held at various locations until this building was erected on a lot purchased from F.S. Perkins. Edward Brook, a part owner of Burlington Brick & Tile Co., donated the bricks.

834. Cross Evangelical Lutheran Church
232 N. Perkins Blvd. 1883

Originally a German-speaking congregation, Cross Lutheran initiated English services in 1916. This church, which was erected in the year of incorporation (1883), once had a steeple. In 1939, when the congregation moved to another location, this building became a meeting hall and was renamed "Luther Hall". In 1964 the CCB Gothic building became the home of the Burlington Historical Society through the will of its first president, Mrs. Fulton.

835. Three Cobblestone Residences
216, 208, 200 W. Jefferson St. 1852-54

Two German carpenters, J. Heinrich Burhans and J. Heinrich Reuter, bought adjacent lots in 1851, and in the next two years gathered cobblestones while excavating their foundations. Both built their houses together, and they shared a common well on the lot line. These two dwellings (numbers 200 and 208 respectively) were completed in 1854. The Reuter house has its gable end to the street, while the others are set parallel. Little is known about 216.

836. St. Mary's Catholic Church
108 McHenry St.   1890-91

The pride of Burlington, St. Mary's spectacular 186-foot spire dominates the city. For its style and age, this Victorian Gothic church is unusually complex and detailed. Basically CCB, the structure is trimmed in cut limestone and sheet metal. The square tower becomes octagonal at the roofline and has corner buttresses with pinnacles. Above, an octagonal belfry, with eight gables and eight pinnacles, supports the spire. The parish, founded in 1844, first had a frame church and, then (1859) erected the nearby cobblestone structure (see #837).

837. Immaculate Conception Church
500 McHenry St.   1855-59

Perhaps the most ambitious cobblestone building in Wisconsin, this Gothic Revival church was designed by Milwaukee architect, Victor Schulte. From its angle-buttressed tower to the stone belfry, the walls are made with heavily mortared cobblestones. The church once had a tall steeple, but it was eventually judged a safety hazard and had to be removed. All of the Gothic windows still contain their diamond-paned grisaille glass. In 1893 a second floor was built through the nave to convert the building into a school.

838. Bank of Burlington
500 N. Pine St.   1909

In the cornerstone of this bank is a can of condensed milk and one of evaporated cream. Charles B. McCanna, who was president of the bank when this building was erected, also was the president of Wisconsin Condensed Milk Company, which occupied the second floor of the new structure. There was still another tie between the two businesses, since this building was heated by steam piped here from the milk processing plant. The bank, which was organized in 1871 by J.I. Case (see #930) and others, spent $80,000 to build this impressive neoclassical edifice.

839. Western Union Hotel
400 N. Pine St. c.1865

Built by Jacob Steinhoff, this hotel was named for the Western Union Railroad which passed only a block from here. Later it was operated by Fred Jaucke, who subsequently moved to Cedarburg and purchased the Washington House Hotel (see #379). This building once housed the post office, and its third floor was used as a dance hall. One of Racine County's finest Italianate buildings, its windows are all semicircular-arched. These handsome double hung windows still have their original tracery. Note the original side entrance.

840. St. John's Evangelical Lutheran Church
148 N. Pine St. 1874

Organized in 1858, St. John's congregation first purchased a house which served as church, school and parsonage. In March of 1874, this lot was acquired, and the main body of the frame church was erected for $3,958.26. Although it has Gothic windows and arches, the handsome clapboarded structure, with its well-proportioned steeple, is more nearly New England colonial in design. The altar niche and sacristy were added in 1899, and a year later the art glass windows were installed.

841. Jacob Muth Residence
501 E. State St. c.1860

A maltster from Germany, Jacob Muth became a naturalized citizen in 1846. He owned and operated a malting business on the other side of Main Street, and there is a tunnel (now sealed) which leads from the basement of this building to the old malt house. The residence and its eastern wing are made of cobblestone, and the CCB barroom on the west was added at least 60 years ago when the house became a tavern.

842. Stone Residence
508 E. Jefferson St. c.1840

Located in an area once known as "Foxville", this old stone house was built close to the street in a fashion which was typical of the times. Not much is known of its history, but it is one of the oldest houses in Burlington. The basic 1½-story structure is a simple Greek Revival design with a frame lean-to addition on the rear. The well-built stone walls are laid with alternating horizontal courses of cobblestones and thin limestone rubble.

843. Pioneer Log Cabin
Milwaukee Avenue
at Echo Park c.1860

In 1903 Dr. Francis Meinhardt located this cabin and purchased it for his own use. It was moved to his spacious estate (see #826) and rebuilt in a grove of pines. The one-room structure was used for a recreation room and lawn parties. In 1960 his grandnephew donated it to the city of Burlington to be used as an example of pioneer architecture. The building was then moved to its present location on the banks of Echo Lake, which was once a mill pond.

844. Auditorium Hotel
6000 Brown's Lake Drive c.1889

In 1908 this large frame building was even larger, and it had a spacious veranda which ran along its south side and around the back. At this time it was a resort hotel on Brown's Lake, but somewhere, within the many additions, is said to be the farmhouse that once belonged to Michael Cunningham. In 1876 Cunningham owned 374 acres here, including the land across the street where the golf course is today. The remaining shingle and scroll-cut details indicate the original design was Queen Anne.

845. Old Town of Voree Marker
Hwy. 11, S.W. corner
Mormon Rd. 1935

Here, at the place where Highway 11, Mormon Road and the White River cross, at the Walworth County line, was once the old town of Voree. It was settled by a group of Strangite Mormons which had broken away from the original Church of Jesus Christ of the Latter Day Saints. When the founder of that religion, Joseph Smith, was killed by an angry mob in 1844, two men fought to become his successor. Brigham Young took the majority of the 20,000 Mormons living in Nauvoo, Illlinois, and moved to Utah, where they founded Salt Lake City. James Jesse Strang (see #846) convinced a smaller group to come here and founded Voree.

846. James Jesse Strang Residence
154 Highway 11   **1844**

The town of Voree (garden of peace) was founded by Strang, who claimed to be God's chosen successor to Joseph Smith, the founder of Mormonism (see #845). He and his followers built numerous houses and laid the foundation for a huge temple, but by 1850 local pressure forced the colony to move to an island in upper Lake Michigan. There he was crowned King James I, but internal strife resulted in his being shot. He returned here to die in 1856.

CALDWELL

Joseph Caldwell, a native of Hubbardton, Vermont, came here in a wagon in 1835 and staked a claim five miles north of this intersection. His crossroads settlement was first named "Caldwell's Prairie". A brother-in-law, Ira Rice, built a house to the south (See#815). Caldwell also talked two of his neighbors from Vermont into moving here. In the 1830's and 1840's many families arrived from New York and New England (principally Vermont). Most started with log houses and raised sheep. They sold the wool in Milwaukee and saved money until they could afford to build more substantial homes. At this little crossroads are more interesting, and well preserved, buildings than in any other location of its size in the county.

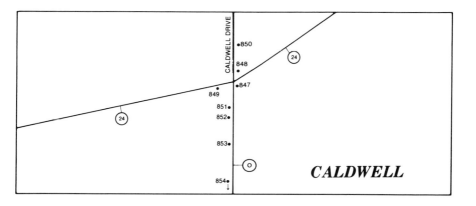

847. Henry Peacock Residence
3365l Highway 24   **1879**

An old handwritten contract between Peacock and his carpenter, C.R. Simmons, survives to tell the story of this house. It is dated March 17, 1879, and states that Simmons will "furnish all materials", including doors, blinds, moldings, etc., and do all of the carpenter and joiner work for $160 and board. Extra drawings or labor were to be done at 15 cents per hour. It also stipulated that Mr. Peacock was to assist the carpenter in moving lumber and putting up the frame. The house was patterned after another the owners had seen between here and Milwaukee. The two-story frame structure is still completely original and has much fine scroll-cut wooden ornament. It was first painted dark green. When the Peacocks first came here from Vermont, in the 1840's, they built a two-story Greek Revival frame dwelling near this house. When the new house was completed, the old one and a large barn on the property were sold and moved to another farm. (A remarkable old photograph shows the original house on runners being pulled across the snow by a dozen horses.) Behind the house is a stable and buggy shed with scroll-cut bargeboards. Still occupied by a great granddaughter of Peacock, the house has retained all of its rich, deeply molded, door and window casings.

848. Caldwell Store
Highway 24, N.E. corner
Highway O   **c.1875 and 1890's**

The first general store on this corner was built before the 1860's. This structure was erected in two stages, with the western segment being the original. Unlike some false front stores, where the square facade extends high enough to have a horizontal cornice, this one extends only part way up, and the angle of the roof ridge becomes a part of the cornice. The east section, built the same way, was added in the 1890's. A long-time resident remembers when children could make purchases here with an egg for payment.

849. Albert Patterson Residence
33725 Highway 24   **c.1879**

The corner on which this house stands was originally claimed by a New Yorker, Josiah H. Utter, who had come here among the first settlers and purchased 152 acres. Patterson, a veteran of the Civil War, married Emma Jean Utter and became owner of half of the quarter section. This well-proportioned frame dwelling, like most buildings in Caldwell, is unspoiled and well preserved. It is set on a fieldstone foundation and still has its original porch and richly molded cornices.

850. Old Congregational Church
Highway O just north of
Highway 24   **c.1855**

Built as a community church, this venerable old structure has been used by many religious groups through the years. It was first occupied by Congregationalists, then Baptists and then Methodists. In its last years as a church the building was used alternately by two groups. When the new church (see #852) was erected, around 1902, this was moved to its present location to become a garage. Originally the two-story Greek Revival structure was painted white and had a louvered belfry with four pinnacles between which were lattice-work railings. The double hung windows had 12 over 12 lights.

851. Farmer's Club Hall
8506 Highway O   **1874**

Built by New England sheep raisers, this frame structure was erected for use during the area's sheep shearing festivals. Farmers came from as far as Milwaukee and Chicago to attend these popular events. An old photograph shows a large crowd in front of the building with a group of musicians standing on the church steps and numerous pieces of farm machinery scattered around. This frame, one-room building is set on a fieldstone foundation and has been used as a village hall for meetings, banquets, dances and graduations.

852. Caldwell United Methodist Church
8504 Highway O   **c.1902**

This well-preserved Gothic church has a number of pleasant and unusual design features. Its informal ell-shaped plan, with a tower set in the corner, provides a double entrance. The windows are all equilateral Gothic-arched, and the nave window has intersected tracery. The tower was once surmounted by a steeple but, being in open country, it was hit by lightning so frequently that the congregation decided to have it removed.

853. Caldwell Grade School
8318 Highway O   **1869**

Nineteenth century graffiti is hard to find today, but here, preserved in masonry, is one of the best remaining examples. It all started when a student, Johnny Stankey, and his schoolmate, Bennie Clark, cut their names and the date into the brick wall. It was then, on February 26, 1898, that it suddenly became popular to record one's name on his school. As the years passed, many other boys carved their names, until finally, the girls got up enough nerve (they preferred the south side of the doorway). One especially interesting entry reads ... "Titanic wreck April 23, 1912." Never, however, did anyone outdo Johnny and Bennie, whose deeply incised names are still the most prominent "guards" around the entrance. One student even inscribed a threat, "I can knock anyone down in this school with my little finger...F.B." (Fred Brach). The school building, beautifully constructed of CCB, is set on a limestone and fieldstone foundation and has a later addition to the rear. The datestone, over the door, reads, "School District No. 6, 1869".

854. Warren Greeley Farmhouse
7624 Highway O   **1882**

The Greeleys were among the early pioneers of Caldwell, and this house once was the center of a 200-acre farm. The two-story CCB dwelling is set on a foundation of multi-colored granite. Its molded wooded cornice boards are exceptionally rich, and the house is dated on a stone located under the main gable peak. Once a long veranda stretched from the front door to the corner of the ell. It was later replaced by the corner canopy which now protects the two facing entrances.

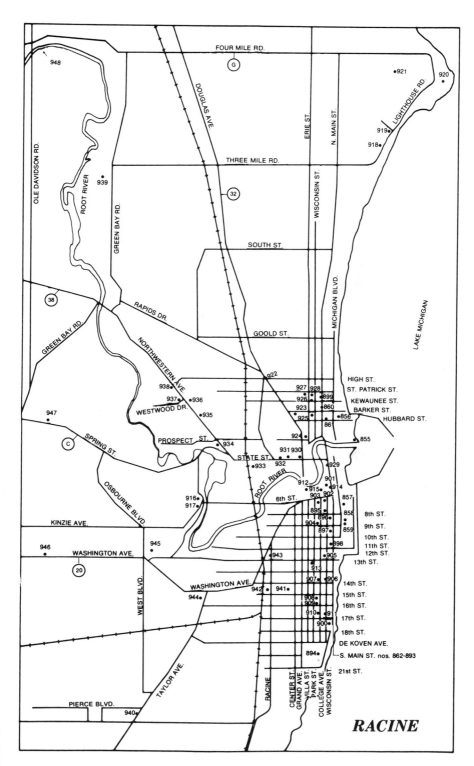

RACINE

RACINE

Once called Port Gilbert after its first permanent settler, Capt. Gilbert Knapp, this city has been called many names through the years. "Belle City of the Lakes" resulted from its beautiful position jutting nearly three miles into Lake Michigan at Wind Point (see #920). "Kringleville" was a more recent nickname taken from the favorite pastry of the city's many Danish residents (the kringle). Racine, the French word for root, was substituted for the less attractive Indian word "Kipikawi" which means the same thing. First a trading port, Racine soon became the county's major industrial center with the J.I. Case Threshing Machine Company being considered its "anchor". In the 1860's Danish immigrants began to arrive in such great numbers that, even today, over one-third of the population is of Danish descent. Architecturally Racine is one of the richest settlements in the Midwest for its size. Here one can see an unusual number of high quality Greek Revival structures built in the 1840's and 1850's. From the picturesque Revival styles of the late 19th century to the "moderne" or art-deco of the early 20th, Racine has a generous supply of well-preserved examples. Here, too, are a number of Frank Lloyd Wright's most important and world-famous works.

NR WRL

855. Racine Harbor Lighthouse
North entrance to Root River   1866
When this brick lighthouse was erected, at the end of the Civil War, it stood like an island in Lake Michigan. Built on a crib made of timber pilings and filled with stone, the structure was then at the end of a 200-foot pier. In 1903 the light, which once shone from its tower, was moved to a new tower located further out in the lake. At that time the Coast Guard station to the west was built. The lighthouse has been somewhat altered, and the Coast Guard discontinued service here in 1973.

856. Racine Water Works
100 Hubbard St.   1931-32
A picturesque complex of Gothic buildings, this facility was built to replace the Racine Water Co. plant of 1886. Once privately owned, the plant now belongs to the city and includes filtration, pumping and service areas. The basic material is pressed, glazed brick, and it is trimmed with cut stone in a decorative manner. The castle-like appearance is created by battlemented parapets, buttresses, hood molds over the windows and the large square tower with its turrets.

857. Memorial Hall
72 7th St. 1924

Conceived as one element of a total lakefront development, the Memorial Hall Commission was created by city ordinance in 1921. This building was intended to be a "symbol of gratitude for those who served in World War I". Meeting rooms were provided for the exclusive use of military veterans of all wars, their organizations and auxiliaries. Chicago architect, Howard Van Doren Shaw, drew the plans for the classically oriented limestone edifice. A monumental, carved stone seal of Wisconsin is flanked by a pair of eagles above the entrance.

858. William W. Dingee Residence
827 Lake Ave. 1867

In its heyday this house sat on a large lot and was surrounded by beautiful outbuildings, all of which are now gone. There was a scroll-cut gingerbread summerhouse, or "gazebo", and an octagonal board-and-batten barn with a louvered cupola. The French "Second Empire" mansion has that styles, characteristic concave mansard roof, but it was much more attractive when the original two-sided porch, with its fancy turned balusters, was still intact. Dingee was a mechanical engineer for the J.I. Case Plow Co.

859. Joseph Schroeder Residence
837 Lake Ave. 1884

This relatively common, eclectic Victorian house is distinguished by a number of refinements and details. Each clapboard has, instead of the usual square cut, a quarter-round molding on its edge which gives the total composition an added touch of quality. The brackets and modillions of the cornice are cut on angles to conform with the triangular peak. Built by a dry goods dealer, the original house cost $16,839.67 (a very sizeable sum in that decade).

860. Lorenzo Janes School
1400 N. Main St. 1896-97

The first schoolhouse on this site, the old Fourth Ward School, was one of three identical buildings, erected in 1855, from the same plans. One of them, the Winslow School (see #907), is still standing, but this building was torn down and replaced by the present structure. Its picturesque shapes are made of CCB and trimmed with ornamental sheet metal. The cylindrical tower, which dominates the building, stands a full story-and-a-half above the roof line.

861. Haumersen Market
1301 N. Main St.   **c.1900**

Built by Fred H., Henry H., and Fred A. Haumersen, this two-story brick commercial structure was originally a grocery and meat market. At the turn of the century, and in a town of this size, Haumersen's must have been the most elaborate establishment of its kind. The cylindrical corner bartizan is covered with sheet metal moldings and ornament which includes the family name of the builders. The old market is still used for its original purpose.

862. Frank J. Mrkvicka Saloon
231 S. Main St.   **c.1890**

The first proprietor of this saloon has not been determined, but the building is believed to have been erected by the Pabst Brewing Co. (see #202). Mrkvicka is the first operator listed at this address, and he apparently took on boarders. The picturesque design, reminiscent of the German New Renaissance style, was useful in the 1920's when Barney Richter opened what was to become a famous German restaurant here. Before that it was variously listed as the "Gem Hotel" and the "Badger Hotel".

863. McClurg Building
245 S. Main St.   **1857**

More history has been made within these handsome Italianate walls than in almost any other building in Racine. Originally the general offices of the Racine, Janesville & Mississippi Railroad, the structure has also been a municipal court, a movie theater, a restaurant, a hotel, the Bijou vaudeville house, Racine's first Turkish bath, and the first public library. The red brick for its walls is said to have come by boat from Buffalo, New York. The exceptional first floor "front" and the large keystones are made of cast iron.

864. Wolff Clothing Store
330 S. Main St.   **c.1882**

An interesting variation on the common Victorian commercial building, this CCB structure has two noteworthy features. The second and third floor fenestration is set in sunken panels which are created by a blind arcade of three bays' width. The cornice, made of sheet metal, is unusually deep and complex, with numerous small scale geometric patterns for ornament. Beginning with Simon Wolff, in 1882, this building remained a clothing store for many decades thereafter.

865. Hall Block
340 Main St. c.1885
This picturesque commercial building, with its Flemish Renaissance-inspired gable, is built with three compatible materials; red brick for the basic wall, red terra-cotta ornament, and red sandstone. The ornamental terra-cotta panels, between the second and third floor windows, are identical to those on the Milwaukee Club (see #37) and were probably purchased from the same catalog. Built by Chauncey Hall (see #889), this building was first occupied as a clothing store.

866. Neisner's Building
422 Main St. c.1930
It is not known when the original building was erected, but this remodelled facade is a good and typical example of the glazed, polychromed, terra-cotta facing of the period. Used as a modernizing cover-up, this superficial treatment features art-deco geometric ornament, polished granite wainscoting, and nickel-plated picture window frames. Also typical of the period is the store's name, "Neisner's", set in the entranceway terrazzo in metal.

867. Manufacturer's National Bank
440 S. Main St. c.1870
In 1871 the first bank to be founded in Racine (1845) merged with another to form the Manufacturer's National. A year later they leased this building and, in 1876, became its owner. Originally a three-story brick, Italianate structure, it was completely refaced in 1919. The present white marble facade, with its carved details, is set on a granite "foundation", and has a pantile roof and cast iron lintels over the first floor windows.

868. Market Square
S. Main St. between 5th & 6th Sts.
When Racine was first platted, this square was set aside for public use. It was first called "Haymarket Square" because it served as a produce-selling area by farmers. Two courthouses, two churches, numerous early commercial buildings and hotels have faced into this block over the years. In 1884 a large stone monument was dedicated "in memory of Racine's loyal and noble sons who enlisted to defend and perpetuate the union of these United States in the War of 1861-1865." The name was then changed to Monument Square.

WRL

869. U.S. Post Office
603 S. Main St. 1930-31

According to the cornerstone on this dignified neoclassical building, A.W. Mellon was then Secretary of the Treasury, and the "acting supervising architect" was James A. Wetmore. The entrance portico is supported by six, fluted, Corinthian columns; and the basic material is limestone, with the steps being made of granite. Earlier Racine post offices were located in various commercial buildings (including the Shoop Building, see #929). An earlier building, erected in 1898, preceded this one on the same lot.

870. St. Luke's Episcopal Church
624 S. Main St. 1866-67

One of Racine's most important Victorian Gothic churches, St. Luke's was designed by Milwaukee's most important architect, Edward Townsend Mix. This stately CCB structure replaced an earlier church (1845), on the east side of Market Square, which was destroyed in an 1866 fire. Especially notable are the heavily molded doors, the broach spire and the tower set on an angle. In 1887 what were described as "the finest tower clock and chime of bells west of New York City" were added.

871. Carnegie Library
701 S. Main St. 1903

St. Louis architect, John L. Mauran, drew the plans for this imposing neoclassical structure. Andrew Carnegie gave Racine $50,000 for this building with the stipulation that the city provide a site and $5,000 per year for support. Set on a Bedford limestone foundation, the buff, pressed brick walls are decorated with horizontal banding and high-relief ornament in terra-cotta of a matching color. The large copper lanterns flanking the entrance come from the old 6th Street bridge. The Racine County Historical Museum has occupied the building since 1961.

872. Dr. Charles F. Shoop Residence
803 S. Main St. 1893

One of Racine's numerous surviving Classical Revival mansions, this commodious structure was the home of the president of a famous patent medicine firm (see#929), who in 1921 gave the land for Shoop Park to the city of Racine. The principal block of his house is rectangular, with a portico supported by four Roman Ionic columns, but the transverse block has a very unusual gambrel roof. Especially notable is the balcony under the portico and the shield-shaped window of the pediment.

873. Harry M. Wallis Residence
820 S. Main St. 1895

The Classical Revival produced highly ornamental designs such as the Carpenter (see #893) and Miller (see #883) houses. This unusual variation, although influenced by the same style, has cleaner, simpler lines and the bold formal composition of the earlier Greek Revival (see #884 and #891). This property was purchased by J.I. Case, in 1887, and given to his daughter Jesse, who married H.M. Wallis. By 1902 Wallis was president of J.I. Case Company.

874. Henry Stephens Residence
827 S. Main St. c.1857

This handsomely proportioned brick Italianate dwelling was built by Henry Stephens (sometimes spelled Stevens) and later owned by Dr. Charles S. Duncombe. The doctor is said to have added the room on the south as an office in the 1870's. Coal and wood merchant, William H. Pugh, bought the house from Duncombe in 1901. The semicircular arches of the second floor windows are repeated in the chimney and in the cornice where it passes over the half-octagon oriel.

875. Thomas Jefferson Emerson Residence
842 S. Main St. c. 1858

This huge, hotel-sized, Italianate mansion was built by a local civic leader whose grandfather was a brother of Ralph Waldo Emerson. T.J. Emerson came to Racine from Maine where he had established a fine reputation as a lawyer. During Lincoln's administration he was an internal revenue collector and he later invested his savings in an oil mill which operated successfully for over 25 years as the "Emerson Linseed Oil Co." His house has been seriously altered; but the original roof line, with its double-bracketed cornice, survives.

876. George Q. Erskine Residence
920 S. Main St. c.1885

This Victorian eclectic design, with its four-story tower, is executed in CCB and trimmed with carved stone lintels, Its owner, George Erskine, lived in a house at this address as early as 1872. At that time he was an internal revenue collector, but later became a vice president of the J.I. Case Plow Co. The original decorative shingle work can still be seen on the tower's pyramidal roof. The front porch is a later addition.

877. Thomas Harvey Residence
929 S. Main St. **1850 and later**

Originally the back section of this house stood at the intersection of 17th and Chatham Streets. Because of bluff erosion the old corner no longer exists, but the house, built by Thomas Harvey, was moved to this site and later enlarged. The front addition, probably erected in the early 1880's, is an excellent example of stick-style or Eastlake design. Especially notable are the grooved framing boards, the recessed porches and their scroll-cut balusters.

878. Lucius S. Blake Residence
936 S. Main St. **c.1870**

Called "The Fanning Mill King", Lucius Blake made his fortune in numerous enterprises including the process by which he separated wheat from chaff, (the fanning mill). His Italian Villa-styled mansion is a handsome CCB structure with a double-bracketed cornice and a full three-story tower with a concave mansard roof. Among his many local projects was the building of the famous Blake Opera House which burned down in 1884.

879. Charles H. Baker Residence
116 10th St. **c.1893**

Contractor Josiah Hocking, who was a neighbor at 106 10th St., built this house for Mr. Baker. Baker was one of the principal owners of the J.I. Case Company. Around 1908 his three-story frame mansion was purchased by Alexander J. Horlick, who was mayor of Racine at the time and vice president of Horlick's Malted Milk Co. In 1952 a civic leader, H.M. Benstead, acquired and renovated the house and gave it to St. Luke's Hospital School of Nursing to become the Henrietta Benstead Residence Hall.

880. Abraham and Mary Todd Lincoln Monument
East Park (S. Main St. between 10th & 11th Sts. **1943**

This is the first statue in the United States which was erected to the memory of a president and his wife. It was executed in grey Georgia granite by Chicago sculptor, Frederick C. Hibbard. The project so enthused Hibbard that he is said to have reduced his usual fee for the work. Both of the Lincolns' noses were once broken off and repaired with special pins, and now vandals have again defaced this historic monument. Previously, East Park was graced with a bandstand and a fountain.

881. Henry S. Durand Residence
1012 S. Main St. 1856

Racine's most important Italianate mansion, this was the home of the banker and insurance man who, with three others, purchased land and laid out La Crosse, Wisconsin. The huge three-story CCB house has handsome front porches, a porte cochere, and a cupola on the roof. The eaves brackets are of exceptional size and quality. In 1920, local Masonic lodges combined resources and purchased this building for a clubhouse. It was later enlarged by the addition of an Egyptian temple (see #898).

882. Joseph Miller Residence
1100 S. Main St. 1893

Built by the founder of the J. Miller Shoe Company, this Victorian eclectic mansion is distinguished by its rich variety of materials and textures. At the top of the cylindrical tower is a band of buff terra-cotta tiles, each of which contains a fleur-de-lis. The ornate original chimneys are capped with decorative terra-cotta tiles and chimney pots. Sandstone belt courses, sheet metal, prism glass windows and a slate roof complement the CCB walls.

883. Henry C. Miller Residence
1110 S. Main St. 1899

Henry was the son of Joseph Miller, who built his mansion next door (see #882). This imposing frame dwelling blends Georgian details with the then-popular Classical Revival style. The plans were drawn by Racine architects Guilbert and Funston. While most homes of this style and vintage (see #893) were all frame construction, here is an unusual variation where the first floor is made of brick, with artificial quoins, and the upper floors are frame.

884. Eli R. Cooley Residence
1135 S. Main St. c.1853

One of the finest Greek Revival temple-style houses in Wisconsin, this beautiful frame residence has been restored and maintained with the respect it deserves. It is believed to have been designed by Racine's foremost architect, Lucas Bradley (see #903), for a local hardware merchant, Eli Cooley. When Racine was only a village, Cooley was president and, in 1850, he became the city's third mayor. His distinguished house has a pedimented portico supported by four fluted Doric columns.

HABS NR WRL

375

885. David Lawton Residence
1136 S. Main St. c.1852

The original owner of this fine CCB dwelling has not been determined, but it was occupied for over a quarter century by the Lawtons, beginning in the early 1870's. Mr. Lawton was president of the Belle City Manufacturing Co., which built seed cutters and sold building materials, seeds, and agricultural implements. Originally a four-room building, the house has been enlarged twice. Its street facade is handsomely framed with four brick pilasters and a full triangular pediment.

886. Thomas Jones Residence
1144 S. Main St. 1868

One of Racine's most important Italianate mansions, this was built by contractor/architect Lucas Bradley for a member of the lumber firm, Jones, Knapp & Co. By 1879, it had become the home of Daniel Alpheus Olin, general superintendent of the Racine and Southwest Division of the C.M. & St. Paul Railroad. The wooden cornice is supported by scroll-cut brackets and modillions and its CCB walls are panelled with brick pilasters. Especially notable are the porch and the double-bracketed cupola.

887. Charles H. Lee Residence
1202 S. Main St. c.1885

If any house in Racine could be said to follow the principles and styling of English tastemaker, Charles Eastlake, this would be the one. At a distance it looks like an ordinary frame eclectic design, but the highly unusual details are what give it character. Each clapboard has a shadow-line groove on its bottom edge, and all of the stick framing is double-grooved. Also note the original gutter troughs and decorative pressed glass in the main window.

888. Thomas D. Pushee Residence
1228 S. Main St. c.1875

This unusually long and narrow house appears to have been drastically remodelled around the turn of the century in the then-popular Classical Revival style. It was probably built by Pushee, who sold groceries, wallpaper, gas fixtures and paint. The sides, which still show the age of the structure, have paired scroll-cut brackets. When the portico was added, two second floor windows were equipped with balconies, and the front facade was faced with smooth, flush siding.

889. Chauncey Hall Residence
1235 S. Main St. **c.1850**

NR WRL

This is a good, typical example of the Gothic Revival residential style promoted by New York landscape architect, Andrew Jackson Downing. Its red-painted CCB construction is accented with lacy scroll-cut bargeboards and deep, rich hood moldings over the windows. Bachelor tailor Hall is said to have made numerous suits for the owner of a local brickyard. That man never paid, and Chauncey finally accepted the bricks, from which this house was built, as his fee.

890. Judd-Freeman Residence
1242 S. Main St. **c.1856 and 1894**

The rear block of this large and picturesque Queen Anne mansion was built before the Civil War by George B. Judd, a lawyer who came to Racine from Connecticut. The extensive front addition is thought to have been built in the 1890's by Charles Freeman, president of S. Freeman & Sons Manufacturing Co. (boilers). The highly complex design includes wooden panels, cut shingles, scroll-cut and spindle ornament. Especially interesting are the wavy clapboards on a south peak and the unusual, bracketed pitched roof over the southeast corner octagon bay.

891. William Hunt Residence
1247 S. Main St. **c.1844**

HABS

Originally this fine Greek Revival house stood on the southeast corner of 9th and Main Streets. Henry Mitchell, a Scottish wagon maker, later moved it to the corner of 9th and Lake Streets to make way for a new house at the original site. In 1912 Mrs. J.W. Knight had the house moved, once again, to the present location. In many ways it resembles the Cooley (see #884) and Collins (see #948) houses, but its portico is only one-story high and the columns are fluted Ionic. Like the Collins house, its facade is made with flush boards.

NR WRL

892. Thomas P. Hardy Residence
1319 S. Main St. 1905

A bachelor attorney, Hardy had once been a schoolmate of Frank Lloyd Wright's at the University of Michigan at Ann Arbor. This important early example of Wright's prairie style has a wood and stucco exterior with his omnipresent geometric leaded glass windows. The symmetry of the street facade is carried throughout the design, which rambles down the lake bluff, creating a three-story house. The living room is two-stories high and has a great expanse of glass facing Lake Michigan.

893. Charles R. Carpenter
Residence
1324 S. Main St. 1896

Built by the cashier of Commercial Savings Bank, this imposing frame structure is one of the city's best examples of the Classical Revival style which followed the lead of the World Columbian Exposition in Chicago in 1893. Its entrance portico is supported by four fluted Ionic columns. The two-story porch has delicately turned wooden balusters on the ground floor and lacy wrought iron on the second. It is now used as a group home for girls by the Taylor Children's Home.

894. Racine College
600 21st St.   1852 and later

This English "collegiate" Gothic building complex is one of the finest examples of its type in the Midwest. Set on a beautiful, wooded, 40-acre tract on the Lake Michigan bluff, these seven CCB buildings are arranged in a loose quadrangle around a chapel and graveyard. At a Milwaukee convention, in 1851, it was decided that southeastern Wisconsin needed an Episcopal college. That institution was then offered to the first city that could contribute six acres and $6,000 toward construction. Racine quickly seized the opportunity with 10 acres and $10,000. The first building, Park Hall, was erected on what is now the northeast corner of the complex in 1852. It was named after the college's first president, Dr. Roswell Park, who was later buried on the grounds. Other buildings followed Kemper Hall (1854), St. John's Chapel (1864), Taylor Hall (1867), dining hall (1871), assembly hall (1872), and finally the gymnasium and swimming pool in 1875. Two subsequently burned and were rebuilt after their fires (Park Hall, 1863; and Taylor Hall, which is pictured here, 1875). Most of the buildings were designed by New York architect J.F. Miller and built by Lucas Bradley (see #903). The design of the chapel, however, has been attributed to Bradley. All structures are CCB on limestone foundations with red-orange brick trim. The complex is now used as the De Koven Foundation for Church Work and takes its name from Rev. James De Koven who served as rector and warden of the college between 1859 and 1879, and is also buried on the grounds.

895. Racine County Courthouse
730 S. Wisconsin Ave.   1930-31

The renowned Chicago architects, Holabird and Root, designed this distinguished example of Moderne, skyscraper architecture. Its Bedford limestone walls are decorated with low-relief carvings created by Swedish sculptor, Carl Milles. The ornamental designs, depicting "the agricultural and industrial life of the county", were first modelled in clay and cast in plaster by Milles. The actual stone carving was done by John Magnus Johnson. This was Milles' first American commission.

896. First Baptist Church
801 S. Wisconsin Ave.   **1876**

The unusual cornerstone, at the base of this church's tower, has two sides with sunken panels. One facet contains the date, in raised numbers, and the other has the word "Centennial," which probably refers to the nation's 100th year. Corner towers are not unusual, but this one is set on an angle like St. Luke's Episcopal Church (see #870). The tower once had a tall steeple which was blown down in a late 19th century "hurricane".

897. Two Family Dwelling
901-03 S. Wisconsin Ave.   **c.1900**

This otherwise ordinary duplex is distinguished by a pair of two-story porches which have survived in almost mint condition. The upper decks, recessed like the entrance porches, give the main gable the apparent function of a pedimented portico. The scroll-sawn fretwork, which decorates and frames the four porch openings, is still crisp and perfect. The first listings here show F.E. Field (a teacher) and W.J. Griffith (a commercial traveler).

898. Masonic Temple
1015 S. Wisconsin Ave.   **1922-23**

Architect Edmond B. Funston, who was a member of Racine Lodge No. 18, drew the plans for this highly unusual "Egyptian" temple. It was attached to the old Durand mansion on Main St. (see #881), which was also used by the Masons. The buff brick building is decorated with glazed polychromed terra-cotta ornament. Flanking the entrance are two columns with open papyrus flower capitals similar to those at Karnac. Other Egyptian decoration includes a scarab beetle, lotus flowers and a frieze of hieroglyphics.

899. Union Methodist Episcopal Church
1529 S. Wisconsin Ave.   **1881**

This little brick church has a cruciform floor plan with two half-octagon transept wings. This feature, common in larger churches and cathedrals, is rare at this small scale. The 4th Ward Union Sabbath School Association erected a building on this corner in 1858. When it burned down, in 1881, this structure was built to replace it. The CCB Gothic church once had an unusual steeple with an open belfry and an octagonal spire. Set above the entrance is a datestone explaining the two buildings on this corner.

900. Samuel Curtis Johnson Residence
1737 S. Wisconsin Ave.   **1903**

This was the first house ever built for the manufacturer of Johnson Wax. Previously the family had lived in rented space on Washington Ave., Main St., and College Ave. (see #911). The design of this house with its scalloped bargeboards and steeply pitched roof, is reminiscent of the earlier Gothic Revival (see #889). Its handsomely proportioned front, featuring an unusual half-octagon porch, was designed by Johnson and built by carpenter Thomas Hay. Johnson came to Racine in the 1880's and first sold parquet floors for the Racine Hardware Co. He later bought the company and finally went into manufacturing wax products. There are two of his parquet floors in this house.

901. Casino Hall
500 College Ave.   **c.1889**

For years the Young Men's German Catholic Society (sometimes listed as the G.C.Y.M.A.) met in this hall. The two-story CCB commercial structure has a false front which hides a functional pitched roof. The pleasantly detailed facade is divided into three bays by brick pilasters and is trimmed with sheet metal and ornamental brickwork. Both materials contribute to the unusually deep and complex cornice.

902. Universalist Church of the Good Shepherd
625 College Ave.   **1895**

This picturesque variation of Romanesque architecture is built with a colorful combination of materials and textures. The CCB walls are set on a red sandstone foundation which is banded with alternating courses of rockfaced and chisel-tooled surfaces. The congregation organized in 1842 and first built on Market Square in 1851, on a site which was later purchased for the Hotel Racine (1891). Olympia Brown Willis, the first ordained woman minister in the country, once served this congregation.

903. First Presbyterian Church
716 College Ave.   **1851-52**

This beautifully proportioned example of Greek Revival architecture is the masterpiece of Racine's most celebrated architect, Lucas Bradley. Flanking the recessed porch, which is supported by two stone Doric columns, are four brick pilasters which support a triglyph frieze, also made of CCB. The spectacular belfry and spire are reminiscent of the English Renaissance designs in London by James Gibbs (1682-1754) and Sir Christopher Wren (1632-1723). The spire has been hit and damaged three times by lightning (see First Congregational Church, #931, which resembles this and once had a similar spire).

904. First Church of Christ Scientist
402 9th St.   **1920-26**

This distinguished neoclassical ediface was designed by the renowned Chicago architect, Solon Spencer Beman, and built by Anton Kratochival. Beman also designed an insurance company office in Milwaukee (see #25) and was the creator of Pullman City on Chicago's south side. Here he executed a formal plan with very refined moldings and a strictly symmetrical composition with eight Ionic columns. The white stucco finish accentuates the simple beauty of moldings and the shadows they cast.

905. Plymouth   Congregational Church
1143 College Ave.   **1912-13**

Organized in 1904, this congregation retained the Racine architectural firm, Chandler and Park, to draw plans for this neoclassical church. Its entrance portico is flanked by a handsome pair of fluted Doric columns, and the octagonal main auditorium is crowned with an octagonal lantern which has a standing seam sheet metal dome. The dark brown tapestry brick walls are trimmed with cut Bedford stone and art-deco-oriented, milk glass windows.

906. St. Luke's Hospital
1310 College Ave.   **1876**

This hospital was established, in 1871, by Rev. E.C. Porter, Rev. James De Koven (see #894), Dr. John G. Meachem and others. W.H. Amos, of Racine College, presented the plans for this Gothic building, which, like the college complex, is built of CCB with red-orange brick trim. This building, now the administrative unit, was followed by a general hospital in 1925 the Alice Horlick Maternity Unit in 1929, and in the 1950's and 1960's grew to the over 3-million dollar complex which surrounds the original structure.

907. Winslow School
1325 College Ave.   **1855-56**

Originally the "Third Ward School", this is among Racine's oldest schoolhouses. It was one of three buildings erected in the same year from the same plan by contractor, Lucas Bradley (the others were 4th Ward Janes and 5th Ward Garfield). In 1897 Racine architect, James Gilbert Chandler, remodelled this structure, adding dormers and the tall entrance pavilions with ornamental sheet metal work. The two-story CCB school was then renamed after Horatio G. Winslow, a well known local educator.

908. August C. Frank Residence
1520 College Ave.   **1895**

This picturesque mansion was used as the Park Place Tea House between 1939 and 1950. Its original owner, August Frank, was the business partner of Ernest Hueffner, who lived next door (see #909). His spacious mansion is so designed that it looks light and delicate for its size. The three-story frame structure is loosely patterned after French chateaux of the Renaissance. Note the fleur-de-lis-style sheet metal fineals, the porch balustrade and the clapboards bent around the north tower.

909. Ernest J. Hueffner Residence
1526 College Ave.   **c.1875**

The words, "I helped build this house", are scratched in the brick of a second floor bedroom wall and signed by the builder, L.S. Jones. Hueffner, the owner, was a vice president of Manufacturer's National Bank (see #867) and a partner in Hueffner & Frank, Leather & Findings. His CCB residence is a fine and well-preserved example of Victorian eclectic design. Among the exceptional original details surviving are the eaves brackets, chimneys, porches, verge boards and carved stone lintels.

910. Randall W. Smith Residence
1610 College Ave.   **c.1864**

Built by a railroad president, this dignified house once deteriorated into a boarding house and had clotheslines in its parlor. It has, since 1939, been restored to much of its original elegance and is now a private residence again. The formal symmetrical plan is centered in a two-story brick block with segmental-arched windows and a hipped roof. Flanking the block are two one-story wings which give the composition a certain grandeur.

911. Residence
1643 College Ave.   **c.1860**

Said to have been built for a headmaster of Racine College, this handsome two-story frame Italianate house has most of its fine, original, ornamental detail. It was later (1894-1897) rented by S.C. Johnson until he built his own house on Wisconsin Ave.(see #900). There is an interesting, diminutive, 2-story "ell" on the north side and a stacked half-octagon bay window on the south. Especially notable are the bold scroll-cut brackets of the front porch and the oversized wooden "keystones" over the windows.

912. Daniel Slauson Parsonage
504 Park Ave.   **1846**

One of the few remaining Federal-style buildings in southeastern Wisconsin, this structure once had five tall chimneys. The central shaft survives, but the other four once rose from the two end walls in a fashion characteristic of that style. The north half of the building was a gift to the Methodist Church for use as a parsonage. It is not known whether Slauson occupied the south half since he also had the Washington Ave. acreage at that time (see #944). Slauson, once called "the father of the Methodist Church in Racine", was also an early preacher.

913. St. Catherine's High School
1200 Park Ave.   **1924**

Originally a day school for young ladies (with boarding), St. Catherine's Female Academy dropped the word "female" in 1888. In 1924, this building was erected as a coeducational offshoot of the Academy. The plans were drawn by Chicago architect, Barry Byrne, who also designed the similar St. Patrick's Church (see #924). Described as "modernized Gothic", this imaginative design is carried out in orange brick with buff terra-cotta trim. A major addition was made on Park Ave. in 1948.

914. Commercial Buildings
218, 216 6th St.   c.1929
These business facades afford an excellent opportunity to compare two variations of the "moderne" art deco style. Number 218 is faced with polychromed and glazed terra-cotta with low relief ornament. It has bronze entrance ornaments and a leaded glass transom. Number 216 is faced with a pink-gray granite into which low-relief floral ornaments have been carved. Framed by this granite mantel is a bronze and glass two-story curtain wall.

915. YMCA
314 6th St.   1886
Before 1884, this site was occupied by the spectacular Blake Building and Opera House (see #878). On December 28 of that year, the Blake was destroyed in one of Racine's most disastrous fires. The Young Men's Christian Association, which had been organized in 1875, erected this building two years after the fire. The picturesque CCB structure is trimmed with red sandstone, red terracotta and sheet metal. Its style leans to the Queen Anne, which was used infrequently for commercial buildings.

916. Martin Luther College
6th St., N.W. corner
Kinzie Ave.   1901-02
Built to serve Danish students of high school age, this college was conceived by the men of the Danish Evangelical Lutheran Emmaus Church. At one time its enrollment averaged 100 students, but the school was discontinued in 1912. The building later served as a boarding-house for J.I. Case workers (see #930) and then as a boarding home for women. Now it is used as a parish house for Holy Communion Church (see #917). The three-story CCB building once had two large verandas across the front, and one wrapped around the southeast corner to become a double-decked porch with a corner gazebo/pavilion.

917. Holy Communion Lutheran Church
6th St. at Clarence Ave. 1928

When this church was organized, in 1898, there were already nine flourishing Lutheran congregations in Racine, but they conducted services in the Danish, Swedish, Norwegian and German languages. This became the first English Lutheran church in town, and it held early services at the YMCA building (see #915). In 1925 the congregation purchased the "Luther Hill" property (see #916) and erected this fine perpendicular Gothic edifice in limestone with a slate roof.

918. The Prairie School
4050 Lighthouse Drive 1965

The Prairie School is an independent, coeducational college preparatory day school located in Wind Point. Designed by Taliesin Associated Architects, the school retains the Frank Lloyd Wright architectural concepts, including elliptical and circular-shaped walls of reddish Streator brick and cypress. One large circular building houses the lower and middle schools. They are joined to another semicircular building which houses the upper, or high school. At one end is the school's circular library. In the circles are open, round courtyards.

919. J.B. Thomas Farmhouse
4226 Lighthouse Dr. 1852 and later

One of the few Gothic Revival houses remaining in southeastern Wisconsin, this humble frame dwelling was built in two stages. Mr. Thomas moved here from Chicago and, by 1852, had purchased a 65-acre tract and built the rear section of the house. The date when the front was added is not known. Especially interesting are the unusual scroll-cut bargeboards, the beautifully proportioned front porch and the lancet window over the porch with its hood molding.

920. Wind Point Lighthouse
4725 Lighthouse Drive   1880

Described as the "oldest and tallest still standing on the Great Lakes", this lighthouse rises 112 feet above Lake Michigan. In the beginning it was equipped with kerosene lanterns, and the keeper had to climb the tower twice a day (284 steps, round trip) carrying two 5-gallon cans of oil. In 1964 the lighthouse was equipped with an automatic 1,000-watt lamp that throws a 2-million-candlepower beam which can be seen 19 miles away. A cast iron lantern, identical to Milwaukee's North Point house (see #132), tops the CCB tower.

NR WRL

921. Herbert F. Johnson Residence
33 Four Mile Rd.   1938

Called "Wingspread" by its architect, Frank Lloyd Wright, this sprawling residence is regarded as the last of his prairie houses. It was designed around a spectacular central room which includes fireplaces, skylights, and a spiral staircase that leads to a rooftop cupola. Radiating from the corners are four wings laid out like a windmill or pinwheel. In 1960, through a gift of Mr. and Mrs. H.F. Johnson, the house became headquarters for the Johnson Foundation and is now an educational conference center.

922. Karel Jonas Monument
Douglas Ave. at High St.   1912

"Erected by his grateful countrymen," this monument is a tribute to a nationally famous Bohemian-American. Jonas (see#925) came to Racine from Prague, in 1863, and published a Bohemian-American dictionary which ran through 16 editions. He edited the first Bohemian language newspaper in America and wrote a treatise on American law for immigrants. This bronze statue, by sculptor Mario Korbel, is set on a 38-ton Carolina granite base. It was moved here from its original site at Michigan Boulevard and Barker Street.

923. Racine Fire Station No. 4
1339 Lincoln St. 1888

One of southeastern Wisconsin's finest remaining, late Victorian fire stations, this Fourth Ward facility still has its spectacular four-story hose-drying and observation tower. Inside, there are still harness rings hanging from the first floor ceiling. The fire bell, which once hung in this building, was removed in 1933 and installed at the St. Francis Friary near Burlington (see #822). The CCB structure is set on a limestone foundation.

924. St. Patrick's Catholic Church
1100 Erie St. 1924-25

Called "Modern Gothic", "American Gothic" and "New Gothic" at the time of its completion, this striking and revolutionary church design was influenced by the art-deco and "moderne" movements. The main construction material is tan brick, and the geometric ornament is executed in buff terra-cotta. The architect, Barry Byrne of Chicago, is said to have symbolized the four Christian evangelists in the corner towers, which have streamlined equivalents of Gothic pinnacles.

925. Karel Jonas Residence
1337 Erie St. 1880

This was the home of one of the country's outstanding Bohemian-Americans. A distinguished diplomat, journalist, author and politican, Jonas was so loved by Racine's Bohemian community that a monument was erected in his honor (see #922). After rising to the post of lieutenant-general in Wisconsin, he was appointed consul to Prague by President Cleveland. Later he became consul general to St. Petersburg. His house appears to have originally been an ell-shaped building with the tower/cupola and its base being later additions.

926. St. John's Evangelical Lutheran Church
1501 Erie St. 1896

Among Racine's Victorian Gothic churches, St. John's stands out as one of the most ornate, with its unusually complex array of lancet arches, pinnacles, finials, and spires. Also uncommon is the use of two cornerstones, each of which has three sides. The CCB structure, set on a limestone foundation, is trimmed with sheet metal. Organized in 1862, the congregation held its last German service in 1958.

927. John Goetz Residence
1518 Erie St.   c.1875
The original owner of this unusual little dwelling was a mason, and he is believed to have designed and built the house himself. The CCB structure is set on a limestone foundation and has an interesting, variegated roofline. Some sections of the roof are pitched, some are hipped, and the front pavilion has a tall mansard roof with dormer windows.

928. St. Joseph's Catholic Church
1533 Erie St.   1875
In 1862, 42 families broke away from St. Mary's congregation and organized this parish. For a while they attended Sunday masses at St. Mary's, but eventually built a school (1870) and used it for services. The CCB, Victorian Gothic edifice, set on a limestone foundation, is trimmed with cut stone and sheet metal. The steeple, three bells and the sacristy were added to the original structure at a later date.

929. Dr. Shoop Family Medicine Co.
215 State St.   1893 and later
Doctor C.F. Shoop established a medical practice in Racine in 1883. He later discovered the profit in patent medicines and established a business which made Racine one of the important centers for such concoctions in the country. By the early 1900's he employed over 300 men to turn out in excess of 2,000 bottles of the "cure" per day. Among his creations, which went to all corners of the United States, was the "restorative", a 12 percent alcohol mixture which claimed to cure nerve, stomach, kidney and heart ailments. He also marketed a "green salve for lips and skin", a catarrh remedy, and a cure for rheumatism. The large Richardsonian Romanesque building, on the corner of State Street and the river, was the factory where medicines were compounded. Built in 1893, this five-story behemoth is made of CCB with red sandstone trim. Behind it, and to the east, is the little jewel of an office building where Shoop's own quarters were located. Probably built a short time after the factory (about 1897), this two-story structure is basically made of buff sandstone with much elaborate ornamental trim. Six arched window transoms are made of costly prism-ground leaded glass, and there is one fine wrought iron grille on the alley side. The Renaissance-inspired design includes four Corinthian columns and three carved heads used as keystones. Shoop's residence, on Main Street, still survives (see #872).

Factory

Office

930. J.I. Case Office Building
700 State St. 1904

Charles McIntosh, treasurer of the J.I. Case Threshing Machine Co., was visiting his son in Boston when he was attracted to the Boston Public Library. Completed in 1895, that library was designed by the famous architect, Chas. F. McKim. According to tradition, McIntosh and Richard Robinson convinced their fellow directors at Case to pattern the company's office building after that landmark. The Boston structure was, in turn, inspired by the Bibliotheque Sainte Genevieve in Paris. Racine architects, Wilson and Guilbert, drew the plans for this classical limestone structure.

931. First Congregational Church
826 State St. 1854

In 1850, a dissident group from the First Presbyterian Church broke away to found this congregation. Their first church, described as "Swiss cottage and Gothic style", burned within one year; and then this Greek Revival-influenced building was erected. The church originally had a beautiful tower, and it looked much like Lucas Bradley's masterpiece (see #903), from which the members had come. Lightning destroyed the spire in 1912 and, after a fire in 1948, the building became The Playdium Dance Hall. It was rededicated as the St. George Serbian Orthodox Church in 1958.

932. Lincoln Block
906 State St. c.1900

One of Racine's most exceptional applications of architectural sheet metal work, the Lincoln Block has two octagonal bartizans, four bay windows and an ornamental "pediment" which contains the building's name. While the great majority of commercial sheet metal work was in zinc or galvanized iron, here the chosen material was copper, the most costly of the common sheets. It is handled, in this application, with a great variety of complex and ornamental shapes.

933. Chicago & Northwestern Railroad Depot
1417 State St. 1901

The original wooden depot on this site, built in 1888, was temporarily moved to the side while this building was being erected, and it was then donated to a church (see #934). The plans for this modern classical facility were drawn by Chicago architects, Frost and Granger. The red brick walls are trimmed with cut limestone, which includes a large slab on the north wall with the initials "C. & N.W.Ry." incised in serif letters. Once 20 passenger trains a day stopped here, but now the depot is used only as a freight office.

934. Old Chicago & Northwestern Railroad Depot
1769 State St. 1888

When the new railroad depot was being built in 1901 (see #933), this earlier structure was moved to the side temporarily. Rev. Robert Hindley, of St. Stephen's Episcopal Church, wrote to the president of the railroad and asked that the old building be donated to his church. The company agreed; and the frame structure, which had cost $3,000 to build in 1888, was trundled to its present site behind the church to become a Sunday school. It is an excellent example of stick-style architecture with neatly chamfered braces and mullions.

935. Horlick's Food Company
2121 Northwestern Ave.
1905 and later

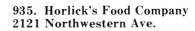

Malt (sprouted barley) and wheat flour were combined with evaporated milk to produce what William Horlick called "malted milk". Originally designed to be a highly digestible food for infants and invalids, it rose to fame and built a fortune at the soda fountains of America. A native of England, Horlick gave to his factory a castle-like appearance. The principal buildings in the complex date from 1905 to 1907. Their CCB walls with turrets, towers, and clock overlooked a pool with swans and a brick driveway and courtyard.

936. James F. Gilmore Junior High School
2201 High St. 1975

This clean, contemporary composition is earth-bermed to reduce its profile and impact on an otherwise low profile neighborhood. The restful exterior design and the related landscaping replace what was an abandoned urban landfill area. Simple geometric masses are creatively related to their function and present a pleasing appearance. The entrance is sheathed in reflecting glass, and the walls are made of prefinished aluminum sandwich panels. The two areas are joined by rounded shafts of glazed brick.

937. William Smieding Residence
2320 Westwood Dr. c.1870

Prussian-born Smieding came to Racine in 1850 and opened a pioneer drug business on Main Street with his brother Henry. After about forty years they sold the business and William retired to his 35-acre estate here, in what was then relatively undeveloped country. The two-story square Italianate house has a fine cupola on its hipped roof. The scroll-cut and spindle front porch, which stretches across the full width of the house, is original.

938. James Walker Residence
2519 Northwestern Ave. 1856

One of Racine's earliest settlers, Walker came here with the city's founder, Gilbert Knapp, in the 1830's. Around 1844 he built a six-room frame house on his quarter section (160 acres). In 1856 the present two-story brick block was added on the front, and the farm became known as "Willow Hall". The beautifully detailed brick block is framed with pilasters like the similar Pierce House (see #940), and it has a cupola on the roof. In 1938, the widow of Charles A. Wustum (the son of the house's second owner) died and gave the building and grounds to the city for an art museum.

939. Riverbend Nature Center
3600 N. Green Bay Road   **1974**

This nature lodge, on 55 acres of property along the Root River, is used for year round nature study activities. The natural beauty of the site includes prairie grasses and wild flowers which make excellent cover for the various species of birds and wild life of all types native to this area. A natural amphitheater is used for lectures, plays, and music, in an outdoor setting. There are hiking and cross-country ski trails and an area for archeological digs.

940. Joshua Pierce Farmhouse
2800 Taylor Ave.   **c.1856**

One of Racine's finest Italianate residences, this 2-story CCB design has excellent proportions and fine detailing. Compare the brick pilasters and the double-bracketed cornice to the very similar Walker residence (see #938). They are almost identical except for the additional refinement of the cornice, which here matches the shape of the second floor window lintels. In the early 1900's this house was converted into the "Highland" apartments. Pierce's house once sat on a 183-acre farm.

941. S.C. Johnson Buildings
1525 Howe St.   **1936 and later**

NR WRL

The administration building (1936-39) and the Research and Development Tower (1947) for S.C. Johnson & Son, Inc., are considered to be among the most important and revolutionary works of architect Frank Lloyd Wright. The "streamlined" walls were built with red brick (many had to be made into custom shapes) with raked-out horizontal mortar joints. Minnesota Kasota stone was used for trim, and 60 miles of Pyrex glass tubing was employed in lieu of windows. These structures, with their custom-designed furniture and many innovations, were dramatically advanced for their time.

942. Racine Fire Station No. 1
1412 Racine St.   **1882**

One of Racine's many picturesque fire stations, this structure is designed like a medieval castle. From it, massive rusticated sandstone blocks to its battlemented parapet, the building resembles a fortress. The CCB walls have false machicolations (the projecting parapet wall through which boiling oil was poured on attackers) and arrow loops (the slits through which bowmen fired). The fire engine door is appropriately framed by a large Romanesque arch.

943. Gillett Building
1123 Washington Ave. 1897

A very unusual Victorian commercial building, this two-story CCB structure contains a number of creative design variations. The two Palladian-inspired second floor windows have flush cut stone lintels which determine the shape of the recessed brick panels in which they are set. The sheet metal frieze follows the same contour. The building may have been erected by Eugene Gillett, who was a dealer in bicycles and supplies.

944. George Murray Residence
2219 Washington Ave. 1874

Originally this was the homestead of Daniel Slauson (see #912), who was one of Racine's earliest settlers. He farmed this land, beginning in 1837, cut timber here and established the city's first lumber-yard. His daughter, Mary, married his business partner, George Murray, and they are believed to have built this house. The spectacular Italianate mansion, one of the largest in Wisconsin, was erected by Joseph Moon of the firm Corse, Moon & Davis. The CCB walls rest on an unusual foundation with 4-foot-high slabs of limestone facing.

945. Mound Cemetery
1147 West Blvd. 1851

Racine's oldest, largest, and most beautiful cemetery is named for the fourteen prehistoric Indian mounds which are preserved here. It was mainly at the instigation of Dr. Philo R. Hoy that these thirty- to forty-foot-diameter burial mounds were saved. A pioneer Wisconsin archaeologist, Hoy personally laid out the cemetery roads to wind around and avoid disturbing these ancient earthworks of the Potawatomi Indians.

WRL

946. Robert Mosley Walker Residence
4310 Washington Ave. c.1865

Only two families have owned this well-proportioned Italianate dwelling. When the two-story CCB house, with its half-octagon bay, was new, it sat on an 80-acre tract. Inside is a rarity in the art of wood graining. On the jambs of a dining room doorway the artisan entwined the names of the three Walker children (Mort, Nelson and Mable) in the pattern of wood grain. The daughter, Mable, eventually married William Tallman, who built the famous mansion in Janesville. A spectacular walnut bedroom set from her mansion is now in this house.

947. Breese Farmhouse
4510 Spring St.   **c.1860**

Now set on two acres, this house once surveyed a 140-acre farm owned by "Jones and Breese". In the early days this handsome brick Italianate dwelling was crowned by a cupola. The most interesting feature in its design is the eastern ell-wing, which is recessed and surrounded by porches. This was accomplished by squaring off the hipped roof and its bracketed cornice, thus creating a two-story, two-sided veranda. Much of the old farm was turned into a country club.

948. Henry Collins Residence
6419 Nicholson Rd.   **c.1853**

An exceptionally fine example of Greek Revival temple-style architecture, this house closely resembles the Cooley house on Main St. (see #884). Their Doric tetraprostyle porticos are almost identical, but this house lacks the matching north wing. While the rest of the building is covered with overlapping clapboards, the formal front has the added refinement of matched flush boards, which creates a smooth facade. Inside much of the original ornamental plaster remains.

NR WRL

ROCHESTER

There was an early attempt to call this town "Waukeeshah." That Pottowatomie Indian word, meaning "fox," was cut into an oak tree on this site by Joshua Hathaway. It even appeared on the earliest sectional maps, but as settlers began to move into the area, the name "Rochester" took hold. Since many of the first arrivals were from New York and New England, it is believed that the town was named after Rochester, New York — "honoring associations of some of the earliest settlers." Numerous industrious men set up shops here and the community quickly became a commercial center. Among the early industries were the Fanning Mill and wagon and carriage businesses of R.E. Ela (see #950). Jerome I. Case came here with a threshing machine and labored to improve its operation. Up to this time an additional step was required to separate wheat from chaff after the threshing operation. He developed, in a small house on the southeast corner of Main and State Streets, a successful machine that combined both threshing and separation functions. J.I. Case took his invention to Racine where he founded the widely-known business which made him a fortune. The railroads and major highways bypassed Rochester and, lacking the transportation incentive for growth, the community has remained small until the present day.

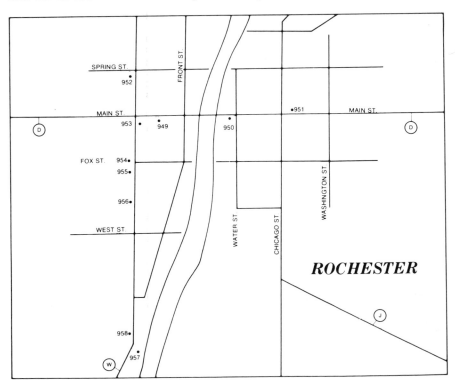

949. Union House Hotel
Main St. between
Front and State Sts. 1843

Levi Brown Godfrey, generally considered to be the founder of Rochester, erected the first frame building on this property in the 1830's. Used as a hotel, that pioneer structure also housed the first post office established here. In 1843 Peter Campbell bought the frame hotel and built this two-story Greek Revival brick addition on the front. Later the old building was removed, and the present rear wing was built in its place. Campbell sold the business in 1856 and, before the Civil War, it passed through the hands of Edward Reynolds, Peter Silvernale, and James Gibson.

950. Richard Emerson Ela
Residence
Water St., S.W. corner Main St. 1839

A native of Lebanon, New Hampshire, Mr. Ela came to Rochester, in 1839, and erected a small frame house which still exists as a part of the present structure. In its cellar he built fanning mills, which he sold in the nearby country. After that business had assumed sizeable proportions, he engaged in the manufacture of wagons, carriages, safes and plows and later became the largest landowner in the vicinity. As his fortunes grew, so did his house. The two-story, frame, Greek Revival building has an interesting, pedimented doorway and a denticulated cornice.

951. W.R. O'Berry Residence
302 Main St. c.1855

When it was new, this pleasant, orange brick house was of simple Greek Revival design. Later the end gable cornice returns, which are an important characteristic of the style, were removed and the two-story porch was added. In that remodelling (perhaps 1885) a window was cut deeper to make the upper doorway. Inside, hewn beams, two-panel doors and cast iron latches belie the true age of the house, built by local produce dealer, O'Berry.

952. Abial Whitman Residence
State St. at Spring St.   c. 1847

One of Rochester's earliest settlers, Whitman came here, with his bride, in 1843. He began building this house in the 1840's and then, with his brother-in-law, went to California. He made a "fortune" there in the grocery business but died on the return trip and never saw the house completed. His widow returned to Vermont and married Ezra Brown. They later settled in this house, and one of their daughters married the son of Philo Belden, the land speculator who had sold this property to Whitman. It is still occupied by the Belden family. The Greek Revival residence has six fluted Doric columns and flush board siding under the porch.

953. Grace Universalist Church
103 State St.   c.1869

The principal, one-room section of the present structure was built by the First Universalist Society of Rochester between 1868 and 1870. In 1901 an older (1840's) church organization, the Congregationalists, purchased this building with the promise that it would be repaired and become "a house of worship for the people of Rochester, and that this will be done as speedily as our finances, and the extent of the repairs needed, permit." As the years passed, several denominations have shared this true community church. The CCB Gothic edifice has two octagonal belfry drums and one steeple.

954. Hiram Cahoon Residence
104 State Street   c.1851

On the 1858 map of Rochester there is only one residence shown between Fox Street and Main Street, and the name attached to it is "H. Cahoon." This property, like most of the early village, was originally owned by Levi Godfrey. In 1846 it began changing hands almost yearly until Cahoon bought it in 1851. The frame, Greek Revival dwelling has a symmetrical facade with a central door. The scroll-cut bargeboard and roof edging are common on Gothic Revival buildings, but rare with this style.

955. Anthony Thompson Residence
108 State Street   **c.1858**

Althought built by Thompson, this house has long been associated with Rochester's first cabinet maker, Orlin Wright, who had come to this vicinity with his family in 1840. He established a shop on Muskego Creek near the sawmill to utilize the water power. This house, and two others of the same basic style and size, afford an opportunity to compare design variations on one street. Unlike the Cahoon house (see #954), this has a less formal, off-center entrance and no bargeboards.

956. Joseph Jackson Residence
208 State Street   **c.1855**

A family of merchants, the Jacksons came here from Poughkeepsie, New York, in 1842, and opened a store. The father died, in 1846, and brothers Joseph and Abraham eventually operated separate stores. In 1876 Joseph was listed as a boot and shoe dealer. His two-story, red brick, Greek Revival house is still another variation of the size and style seen in other dwellings on this block (see # 954 and #955). Here, the entrance is offset to the right, and the roof is edged with scroll-cut bargeboards.

957. Rochester Mill
605 Front St.   **1884**

The first mill on this site, built in the early 1840's, burned down and was rebuilt in 1858. During the Civil War, A.J. Russell (see #958) and James Jones purchased the business. By 1884 it was wholly owned by Russell, who then built the present four-story frame structure. Immediately behind the building are a mill race and dam across the Fox River. The "new" mill was equipped with all of the latest equipment, including a "full roller process system." The mill is set on a substantial limestone foundation.

958. Andrew J. Russell Residence
602 Front St.   **1865**

One of southeastern Wisconsin's finest examples of the rural Italianate villa, this was the home of the proprietor of the Rochester Mill across the road (see #957). This house has fine limestone walls, with raised pointing, and quoins. Paired brackets and a richly molded cornice support the hipped roof. The cupola, which is embellished with oversized scroll-cut corner brackets, is exceptionally large. A 1½-story frame wing is attached on the rear.

WATERFORD

Indians living in this area had established, at this location on the Fox River, a regular place to ford the stream. This is believed to be the origin of the name "Water-Ford". The first settlers, Samuel **Chapman** (see #962) and Levi Barnes, came here in 1836 and established first a sawmill and then a grist mill. The early development of the village was seriously interrupted, in 1898, when a disastrous fire swept through the east side destroying twenty-two buildings. As a result, the volunteer fire department was organized that year. In 1906 Waterford was incorporated with William Shenkenberg as the first village president.

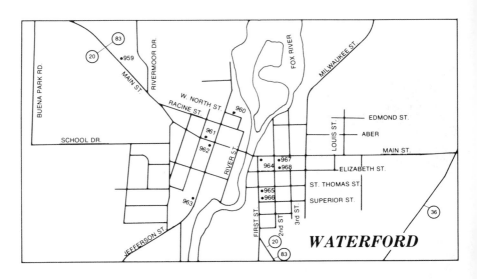

WATERFORD

959. Caley Residence
4017 Highway 83   **c.1870**
The farm, on which this house stood once extended from Buena Park Road to the river in Waterford. The two-story main block has a hipped roof, while a pitched roof was used on the ell wing. The house derives its character from the original paired brackets, the richly molded cornices, and the front porch which still retains all of its fine scroll-cut ornament.

960. John Thomas Residence
304 W. North St.   c.1880

Basically an ordinary 2½-story frame dwelling, this Victorian eclectic design is distinguished by a number of unusual decorative details. The main gable triangle has a pair of unusual pointed windows with pinwheels in their tracery. Around these are fancy cut shingles, moldings, lathe-turned "buttons" and brackets with drop finials. A number of windows are paired under a common lintel. This was later the home of Walker Whitley, first president of the State Bank of Waterford.

961. Moe Residence
310 W. Main St.   1853

This handsome Greek Revival house is believed to have been built by the owner of a local dry goods store. Its painted brick walls are set on a cobblestone foundation, and the corners are designed with brick pilasters which support a slightly projecting brick cornice. For years the house was associated with the name of a subsequent owner, the Knudtsen (or Knutson) family.

962. Samuel E. Chapman Residence
S. Jefferson St. near Main St.   1837

Built by one of the founders of Waterford, this humble residence began as a small Greek Revival frame house, and its front door opened to Main Street. It was enlarged later, and the scroll-cut gingerbread porch was added. Now it has been covered with aluminum siding. Chapman and Levi Barnes are said to have come from the East on horseback and between them claimed the majority of what is now Waterford.

963. Peter Hattlestad Residence
218 S. Jefferson St.   c. 1848

This painted red brick house is said to have been built by an early Mormon settler. The two-story Greek Revival design is executed in red brick which is now painted. The otherwise common design is distinguished by two unusual features. The foundation is made of limestone rubble, but it is faced, on the front only, with cobblestones laid with raised mortar joints. The walls are framed with pilasters, sunken panels and moldings, all made of brick.

964. Henry J. Kortendick Block
Main St., S.E. corner 1st St. 1898

The first buildings on this historic corner were a stone house, a cooper's shop and a barn. In 1890 Kortendick bought the property and replaced the house with a large frame building which served as a residence, meat market and hotel. A major downtown fire, in 1898, destroyed all of the buildings owned by Kortendick, and he immediately erected this two-story CCB commercial structure. On the corner, over the datestone, is an unusual sheet metal construction to match the cornice of the same material.

965. St. Thomas Aquinas Catholic Church
**S. 1st St., corner
St. Thomas St.** 1880-81

This fine stone Gothic structure was built to replace the parish's first church, which had served since 1851. The cornerstone was laid on May 9, 1880, and it, along with all of the quoins and cut stone trim, was hauled here from Waukesha. The limestone for most of the construction was quarried locally. About half of the building's $20,000 cost was in labor donated by the parishioners. An unusually tall lancet arch encloses both a window and the main entrance.

966. St. Thomas Aquinas Parochial School
Superior St., N.E. corner 1st St. 1864

The School Sisters of Notre Dame arrived here in September of 1864, and this fine Italianate school was built, partly by the labor of the parishioners. A carpenter, B. Giesing, was paid $300 for his work, and the mason, who laid the fine limestone walls, made $510. The two-story structure is trimmed with quoins and a fine cornice with scroll-cut brackets. The window lintels are made with brick-sized limestone blocks. The last classes were held in the building in 1966, and it is now used for storage.

967. Louis Noll Block
107 2nd St. 1898 & 1906

In 1863 Louis Noll opened a store here and lived on the premises. The fire of 1898 (see #964) destroyed his first building, and this large structure was erected immediately to replace it. The central section, below his name on the cornice, was a general store, while the north third was a drugstore and the south a saloon. The two-story frame structure has a sheet metal cornice. In 1906 the slightly shorter addition on the north was built to accommodate Noll's bank, which received its charter the following year.

968. Louis Noll Co. Warehouse
119 2nd St. c.1912

This is one of the rare surviving examples of sheet metal architecture in Wisconsin. Cornices and trim made of sheet metal were common, but here the entire facade is sheathed in the material. The stone-block texture was stamped into large sheets of galvanized iron, and they were then nailed to a frame building. After the fire (see #964), much of Waterford was rebuilt with this material. Originally this was a warehouse for Noll's store (see #967), but later it became an agricultural implement store.

ACKNOWLEDGEMENTS

The author wishes to thank the many individuals, public officials, and institutions without whose generous assistance this book would have been impossible. Although it would not be practical to publish a complete list, he wishes especially to recognize the following:

MILWAUKEE COUNTY

Milwaukee Public Library
  Orville Liljequist
  Paul Woehrmann
Milwaukee County Historical Society
  Harry Anderson
Historic Walker's Point Inc.
  Bruce Kriviskey
Marion G.Ogden

OZAUKEE COUNTY

Ozaukee County Historical Society
  Alice Wendt
John Armbruster — Clerk & Treasurer, City of Cedarburg
Cedarburg Public Library
Barbara Hulka
James B. Pape
Edward Rappold
Donald Miller
Anna Ubbink
Viola Ubbink
Port Washington Public Library

WASHINGTON COUNTY

Washington County Historical Museum
  Margaret Hawig
  Edith Heidner
West Bend Community Historical Library
  John C. Reid
West Bend Chamber of Commerce
  Dianne Bliss
Mary Beth Winkowski
Elmer Plaum
Wilmer Wendel
Orville Radke
Hartford City Hall
Jerry Gundrum

WAUKESHA COUNTY

Waukesha County Historical Museum
Jean Penn Loerke
The State Historical Society of Wisconsin
Alan C. Pape
Carroll College
Genevieve Caspari
Willard Griswold
Don Mericle
Oconomowoc Public Library
Josephine Machus
Jean Johnson
Rae Kinn
Betty Duerson
Mae Mahoney
Mrs. Paul Van Valin

RACINE COUNTY

Racine County Historical Museum
Gilbert Steig
Racine Public Library
Irma Deck
Joan Hamilton
Racine Urban Aesthetics Commission
Suzanne Foreman
S. C. Johnson & Sons Inc.
Sister Mary Letitia — Superior,
DeKoven Foundation for Church Work
Nelson Peter Ross — History Dept. Chairman, Carthage College
Dorothy Osborne
Burlington Historical Society
Henrietta Vande Sand
Francis Meurer
Burlington Public Library
Grace Lofgrem
Cathryn Smith
Mary Ela
Waterford Public Library
Virginia Zoelle
Oliver J. Noll

GENERAL

Heritage Financial Council
Gerritt W. Holgerson
Marion D. Holgerson
Maurice W. Holgerson
Georgianne S. Zimmermann
Quincy R. Zimmermann

LANDMARK INDEX

MILWAUKEE COUNTY

A

	Page
A.O. Smith Corp.	153
Abbot Row	66
Adelman Laundry Building	98
Adler, E.D. residence	73
Airport, Milwaukee County's First — Currie Park	154
Akin, William W. residence	82
All Saints Episcopal Cathedral	58
Allen Bradley Co.	156
Allis, Charles residence	73
Annason Apartment Building	95
Annunciation Greek Orthodox Church	154
Armory Courts Building	95
Artesian Well	173
Astor Hotel	56

B

Badger Mutual Fire Insurance Co.	167
Bahr, Frederick M. grocery store	156
Bank of Milwaukee Bldg.	46
Bankers Building	38
Basilica see St. Josaphat Basillica	
Baumbach, Ludwig von residence	151
Baumbach Building	49
Baumgarten, Francis M. residence	57
Bennett, Russell residence	175
Bergh, Henry Monument see Henry Bergh Monument	
Bertelson Building	74
Beth Israel Synagogue	128
Biltmore Grand Apartment Hotel	132
Birchard's and Follansbee's Block	44
Black, Elizabeth residence	72
Blatz (Val) Brewing Co. office building	65
"Boat House" see Gustorf, Edmund B. Boat House	
Bodamer log cabin see Finen/Bodamer log cabin	
Bogk, F.C. residence	85
Bours, Dr. Thomas R. residence	81
Bow Street Swamp	163
Breakwater light	50
Bridge, Swing, S. 11th St.	162
Bridge, Wisconsin Ave. see Wisconsin Ave. Bridge	
Brown, James S. residence	57
Brown, Victor L. residence	87

Buemming, Herman W. residence	66
Burns, Robert statue see Robert Burns statue	
Button, Dr. Henry Harrison residence	55
Button Block	48

C

Calvary Cemetery Chapel	145
Calvary Presbyterian Church	111
Chamber of Commerce Bldg.	46
Chapman, T.A., Co. Inc.	44
Charles Allis residence see Allis, Charles residence	
Church, Benjamin residence	96
Church of the Immaculate Conception	174
City Hall see Milwaukee City Hall	
Clapp, Rev. Luther residence	148
Colby and Abbot Building	63
Collins/Elwell residence	71
Commerce and Arts Statue	179
Commerce Street	121
Commercial Building (S. 5th)	160
Congregational Church Annex	293
Continental Plaza	109
Cotzhausen, Frederick W. von residence	124
Court of Honor	109
Courthouse Square	61
Cowdery, Edward G. residence	81
Cross Keys Hotel	48
Cudahy Tower and Apartment Building	54
Currie Park Airport see Airport, Milwaukee County's First — Currie Park	
Curtin, Jeremiah residence see Jeremiah Curtin residence	

D

Damon, Lowell House see Lowell Damon House	
Daniel Webster Hoan Bridge see Harbor Entrance Bridge	
Day, Dr. Fiske Holbrook residence	149
Dearholt residence	89
Decker, Abel residence	157
Deutsche Evangelische Zions Kirche	179
Diedrichs, Edward residence	69
Dittmar Building	147
Douglass, George residence	82
Downer, Jason residence	68
Downer College Buildings see Milwaukee—Downer College Buildings	

Drott Tractor Co. Building 136
Durr, Emil residence 158

E

Eagle Mill 122
Eagles Club 135
Estabrook Park Benjamin Church
  residence see
  Church, Benjamin residence
Evan and Marion Helfaer Jewish
  Federation 71
Evan P. and Marion Helfaer
  Theater 131
Excelsior Block 43

F

Faries, Dr. Robert J. residence 139
Federal Building 45
Field, Samuel A. residence 91
5th District Schoolhouse 178
Finen/Bodamer log cabin 180
First Baptist Church of Wauwatosa. 150
First Church of Christ Scientist 71
First Congregational Church of
  Wauwatosa 147
First Milwaukee Cargo Pier
  Marker 49
First National Bank Building 39
First Unitarian Church 66
First Wisconsin Center 45
First Wisconsin Garage Building 39
Fitzgerald, Robert Patrick
  residence 58
Fitzgerald, William E. residence.... 76
Florida Street Double Townhouse. 157
Flushing Station 76
Forest Home Cemetery Chapel 164
Forest Home Neighborhood
  Library see
  Milwaukee Public Library, Forest
  Home Branch
Forst Keller 120
Fourth Church of Christ
  Scientist 101
Fourth Street School 117
Fred Loock Engineering Center 64
Frederick William von Steuben
  Monument 152

G

Gallun, A.F. residence 80
Garden Homes Housing Project 99
General Thaddeus Kosciuszko
  Monument 161
German English Academy 65
German Y.M.C.A. 124
Germania Building 113
Gesu Church 131

Gettleman's Menomonee
  Brewery 144
Gimbels Department Store 104
Gipfel Brewery 118
  see also Cross Keys Hotel
Globe Tavern 172
Goethe & Schiller Monument
  Washington Park 150
Goldberg, B.M. residence 80
Goldsmith Building 45
Goll, Fred T. residence 72
Goodrich, William O. residence 78
Grace Lutheran Church 65
Grand Avenue Congregational
  Church 134

Grand Avenue Viaduct 137
Greek Orthodox Church
  (Wauwatosa) see
  Annunciation Greek Orthodox
  Church
Greendale, village of see
  Village of Greendale
Greene, Howard residence 76
Gustorf, Edmund B. Boat House ... 101

H

Harbor Entrance Bridge 49
Harms, Charles Grocery Store 159
Harnischfeger, Henry residence 136
Hart, Thomas B. residence 148
Harrison, Stephen A. residence 68
Hathaway Apartments 75
Hawley-Bloodgood residences 69
Helfaer, Evan and Marion Jewish
  Federation see
  Evan and Marion Helfaer Jewish
  Federation
Helfaer, Evan P. & Marion Theater
  see Evan P. & Marion Helfaer
  Theater
Henni Hall — St. Francis
  Catholic Seminary see
  St. Francis Catholic Seminary
  Henni Hall
Henry Bergh Monument 98
Highland Avenue Methodist
  Church 126
Hilbert, Heliodore residence 158
Hinkel, John Saloon 114
Hinton, Francis residence 69
Hoan Bridge see
  Harbor Entrance Bridge
Holy Rosary Catholic Church 100
Holy Trinity Roman Catholic
  Church 158
Holy Trinity School 159
Homrighausen Flats 126
Honey Creek Settlement 178
Horse Watering Trough
  (Richard Whitehead, S. 16th St.) 163

Hotel Wisconsin 107
Humphrey, Jasper residence 157

I

Ilsley, James K. residence 56
Immanuel Presbyterian Church 57
Inbusch, John Dietrich residence.. 59
Iron Block see
    Excelsior Block
Irvington Hotel 146

J

J.P. Kissinger Block   see
    Kissinger Block
Jacobus, Charles saloon 147
Joan of Arc Chapel see
    St. Joan of Arc Chapel ....
Johnson Service Co. Bldg. 47
Johnston Hall 130
Jones Island 171
Juneau, Joseph farmhouse 178
Juneau, Peter residence 177
Juneau Park 54

K

Kalvelage, Joseph B. residence 141
Kane, Sanford residence 73
Kasten, Walter residence 85
Keenan, Matthew residence 62
Kenwood Masonic Temple 85
Kern, John F. residence 87
Kissinger Block 48
Knickerbocker Hotel 56
Koch, George J. residence 140
Koenig, Frederick residence 151
Kosciuszko, Genl. Thaddeus
    Monument see
    General Thaddeus Kosciuszko
    Monument

Kresge Building 106
Kunckell, Carl residence 164

L

Lake Park 88
Layton House Hotel 164
Liberace Museum (proposed) see
    Day, Dr. Fiske Holbrook
    residence
Lime Kilns see
    Trimborn, Werner farm and lime
    kilns
Lincoln, Abraham speech site 130
Linwood Avenue filtration plant.. 92
Lipps Hall 115
Log Cabin, W. Layton Ave. see
    Finen/Bodamer Log Cabin
Loock, (Fred) Engineering Center
    see Fred Loock Engineering Center

Lou Fritzel 63
Lowell Damon House 149
Loyalty Block see
    Northwestern Mutual Life
    Insurance Bldg. (old)
Luick, William F. residence 86
Luscombe, Samuel D. residence ... 152

M

MGIC Plaza 40
McGeoch Building 47
McGovern, Francis residence 60
Machek, Robert residence 125
McIntosh, Charles L. residence 72
Mackie Building see
    Chamber of Commerce Building
MacLaren, Myron T. residence 89
Majestic Building 106
Marc Plaza Hotel see
    Schroeder Hotel
Marine Plaza 43
Mariner (John) Building 63
Mariner Tower see
    Wisconsin Tower Building
Marquette, Fr. Jacques Camp 113
Marquette University — Johnston
    Hall see
    Johnston Hall
Marquette University — St. Joan of
    Arc Chapel see
    St. Joan of Arc Chapel
Marshall & Ilsley Bank 39
Matthews Building 106
Meinecke Toy Co. Building 40
Metcalf, William H. residence 60
Miller, Carl A. residence 80
Miller, Fred Brewing Co. 144
Miller, Frederick residence 143
Miller, George P. residence 55
Milwaukee Area Technical
    College see
    Milwaukee Vocational School
Milwaukee Art Museum see
    Milwaukee County War
    Memorial Center
Milwaukee Auditorium 118
Milwaukee City Hall 37
Milwaukee Club 52
Milwaukee County Center for
    the Performing Arts see
    Performing Arts Center
Milwaukee County Courthouse 119
Milwaukee County Historical
    Society see
    Second Ward Savings Bank
Milwaukee County War Memorial
    Center 41
Milwaukee — Downer College
    Buildings 102
Milwaukee Gas Light Co. 53

Milwaukee Journal Co. Building ... 114
Milwaukee Public Library 109
Milwaukee Public Library—Forest
Home Branch 165
Milwaukee Road Passenger
Station (1965) 111
Milwaukee School of Engineering
Fred Loock Engineering
Center see
Fred Loock Engineering Center
Milwaukee State Normal School ... 133
Milwaukee Tower see
Wisconsin Tower Building
Milwaukee Vocational School 119
Mitchell, Alexander residence 110
Mitchell, John Lendrum
residence 180
Mitchell Building 46
Mitchell Park Horticultural
Conservatory 168

N

Natatorium (S. 4th St.) 159
National Soldiers Home
(Wood, Wis.) 145
North Avenue Dam 121
North Point Lighthouse 88
North Point Water Tower 84
North Presbyterian Church 64
North Shore Apartments see
Armory Courts Building
North Shore Bank see
Armory Courts Building
Northwestern Hannan Fuel Co.
Bldg. 75
Northwestern Mutual Life
Insurance Co. 53
Northwestern Mutual Life
Insurance Co. Bldg. (old) 47
Northwestern National
Insurance Co. 53
Nunnemacher, Robert residence.. 87

O

Octagon House 127
Oldest Building, Milwaukee see
Cross Keys Hotel and
Gipfel Brewery
Oneida Street Station 40
Oriental Theater 75
Ott, Emil H. residence 77

P

Pabst, Capt. Frederick residence ... 133
Pabst, Frederick Jr. residence 140
Pabst, Gustav G. residence 78
Pabst Brewing Co. 120
Pabst Building 38

Pabst Theater 38
Pabst Whitefish Bay Resort Site 94
Paetzold, Lorenz residence 163
Paine, Halbert E. residence 77
Painesville Cemetery & Chapel 177
Park Lane Apartments 74
Peck, James S. residence 55
Peckham, George W. residence 58
Performing Arts Center 41
Pettibone, Sylvester residence 134
Pettibone Place 134
Pfister Hotel 52
Pickle Alley (Yale pl.) 146
Piggsville 144
Plankinton, Elizabeth residence .. 132
Plankinton Arcade Building 105
Post Office (Main) see
United States Post Office
Pritzlaff Hardware Building 112
Public Service Building 112
Pythian Castle Lodge Building 167
Puddler's Hall 173

R

Radio City 99
Railway Exchange Building 44
Rawson, Edward residence 177
Richards, Arthur L. residence 169
Richards, Daniel H. 128
Richardson Place 139
Rische, C.H. Flats 135
Riverside High School 101
Robert Burns Statue 70
Robertson, Orrin W. residence 89
Ross, Randall Austin residence ... 91

S

Sacred Heart Sanitarium 169
St. Cyril and Methodius
Catholic Church 166
St. Francis Catholic Seminary
Henni Hall 175
St. Francis of Assisi Roman
Catholic Church 125
St. George Syrian Catholic
Church 125
St. Hyacinth Roman Catholic
Church 166
St. Jacobi Evangelical Lutheran
Church 165
St. James Episcopal Church 110
St. Joan of Arc Chapel 131
St. John deNepomuc Rectory 117
St. John's Cathedral 61
St. John's Evangelical Lutheran
Church 179
St. John's Infirmary Marker 84
St. Josaphat Basilica 161
St. Joseph's Convent Chapel 168
St. Lawrence Catholic Church 168

St. Lucas Evangelical Lutheran
Church 174
St. Mary's Church 64
St. Mary's Hospital 84
St. Michael's Roman Catholic
Church 126
St. Patrick's Roman Catholic
Church 162
St. Paul's Episcopal Church 59
St. Robert Catholic Church 95
St. Sava Serbian Orthodox
Cathedral 180
St. Stanislaus Roman Catholic
Church 161
St. Stephen's Evangelical Lutheran
Church 160
St. Vincent de Paul Catholic
Church 166
Sandburg, Carl residence 127
Sanger, Casper Melchior residence 124
Sawyer, James residence 81
Scandinavian Evangelical
Lutheran Church 156
Schlesinger, Armin A. residence ... 90
Schlitz, Joseph Brewing Co. 117
Schlitz Audubon Center 98
Schneider, Emil residence 158
Schroeder Hotel 107
Schuster, George J. residence 136
Second Church of Christ
Scientist 139
Second Ward Savings Bank 113
Senn (Nicholas) Block 116
Serbian Orthodox Church see
St. Sava Serbian Orthodox
Church
Sheriff, James residence 157
Shorecrest Hotel 74
611 N. Broadway Building see
Northwestern Mutual Life
Insurance Building (old)
Slocum, A. Lester residence 86
Smith, A.O. Corp. see
A.O. Smith Corp.
Smith, Lloyd Raymond residence . 77
Soldiers Home see
National Soldiers Home
South Division High School 165
South Shore Yacht Club 171
Sovereign Apartment 132
Spite House 102
Spring Water see
Artesian Well
Starkey, Joseph A. residence 172
Steinmeyer Building 115
Sternemann, Theodore residence.. 140
Steuben, Frederick William von
Monument see
Frederick William von
Steuben Monument

Stone, J. Stanley residence 91
Story School 143

T

Third Church of Christ Scientist ... 153
Thompson, Henry M. residence ... 90
Time Insurance Co. Building 108
Tivoli Palm Garden 160
Trimborn, Werner farm and lime
kilns 182
Trinity Lutheran Church 120
Tripoli Temple Shrine Mosque 135
Trostel, Gustav J.A. building 86
Tullgren, Herbert W. building 152
Turnverein Milwaukee Hall 116
1260 Apartment (1260 N.
Prospect) 70
Typewriter (Invention)
Historical Marker 118

U

UWM Library Building 102
Uhrig, Franz Joseph residence 151
Uihlein, Herman residence 94
Uihlein, Paula and Erwin
residence 90
United States Post Office —
Milwaukee (Main) 111
United States Post Office —
Wauwatosa (old) 146
University Club 54
University of Wisconsin-Milwaukee
Library see
UWM Library Building

V

Van Ellis Building 128
Viaduct, Wisconsin Ave. see
Grand Avenue Viaduct
Vieau, Jacque Cabin Site 167
Villa Terrace see
Smith, Lloyd Raymond residence
Village of Greendale 181
Vogel, Fred Jr. residence 94

W

Walker Square 162
War Memorial Center see
Milwaukee County War
Memorial Center
Warner Building 105
Washington High School 153
Washington Highlands 145
Watts Building 61
Wauwatosa Cemetery see
First Baptist Church of
Wauwatosa

Wauwatosa Post Office, old see
United States Post Office
Wauwatosa (old)
Wauwatosa Womans Club 148
Weaver, James residence 320
Well, Artesian see
Artesian Well
Wells Building 52
Welsh Congregational Church 173
Whitnall, Charles residence 127
Whitnall Park 182
Williams, Joseph residence 174
Wisconsin Ave. Bridge 43
Wisconsin Club see
Mitchell, Alexander residence
Wisconsin Consistory 60
Wisconsin Hotel see
Hotel Wisconsin
Wisconsin Telephone Co. 108
Wisconsin Telephone Co.
Branch Exchange (W.
Washington St.) 158
Wisconsin Tower Building 108
Woman's Club of Wisconsin
Clubhouse 59
Wood Wisconsin see
National Soldiers Home

Y

Yale Place see
Pickle Alley
Yates, Col. Theodore residence ... 138

Z

Zielsdorf residence 82

OZAUKEE COUNTY

A

Anchor from Steamer Toledo 225
Anschuetz, Peter residence 205
Armbruster, John jewelry store.... 195

B

Bach, Frank residence 187
Band Concert Shell 224
Becker, Jacob saloon (#380) 194
Beger, Herman farmhouse 189
Bidinger residence 232
Binc's Block 219
Bodendoerfer farm 212
Boehme, Adolph Martin residence 199
Bohan, John residence 217

Bohan (Teed) residence see
Teed-Bohan residence
Borchardt T. residence and shop .. 234
Brabender, John residence 223
Bridge, Iron (Grafton) 207

C

Callahan, Daniel residence 211
Cedar Creek Marker 205
Cedarburg City Hall 202
Cedarburg Firehouse 202
Cedarburg Grade School 196
Cedarburg High School 196
Cedarburg Jail 202
Cedarburg Mill 203
Cedarburg State Bank 193
Cedarburg Woolen Mill 198
Cedarburg Woolen Mill office 198
Central House Hotel 192
Clark, Jonathan Morrell residence 214
Cooley, Warren residence 234
Columbia Mill remains 204
Columbia Park 221
Concordia Mill 212
Covered Bridge 187

D

Deckers Corners Tavern 187
Dobberpuhl, Carl residence 200
Dodge, Edward residence 221
Dundlinger farmhouse 188

E

Eagle Hotel (Saukville) 227
Eagle Hotel and Dance Hall
(Waubeka) 233
Engels and Schaefer Brewery 201
Evangelical Friedens Kirche 224
Excelsior Mill and residence 204

F

First Immanuel Lutheran Church.. 201
First National Bank 218
Fischbach farmhouse 222
Fischer, George residence 196
Flag Day, Birthplace 234
Founders Monument 200
Friedrich, Charles Gottlieb
residence 197

G

German Free School 195
Gleitzmann, Adam residence 203
Glunz, Louis Dance Hall see
Louis Glunz Dance Hall
Grafton Flouring Mill 208
Grafton Hotel 209

Grafton Woolen Mill 208
Groth family store 198
Grundke, John residence 193
Guiteau, Luther residence 186

H

Hand, Valentine residence 211
Hennings, Johann Friedrich
  farmhouse 185
Hentschel, Henry general store 211
Hilgen residence 206
Hilgen, E. residence 204
Hilgen, Frederick residence 205
Hilgen, Richard residence 206
Hilgen-Schroeder Mill store 203
Hoehn, Louis residence 194
Hoffmann House Hotel 218
Hovener, Louis farmhouse 185

I

Immaculate Conception Catholic
  Church 227
Immanuel Evangelical Lutheran
  Church 192
Irwin, Thomas farmhouse 188

J

Janssen, Edward residence 210
Jochem, L.E. general merchandise
  store (#380) 194
Jochem, Leopold residence 197

K

Kafehl, Ernst F. residence 201
Klessig, Heinrich store 233
Kohlwey, Frederick residence 208
Kohlwey Blacksmith shop 208

L

Labahn, Herbert residence 222
Lau, Eggert residence 212
Lauterbach, J. building 192
Lehmann, C.W. hardware store ... 194
Lighthouse (Port Washington) see
  U.S. Coast Guard Lighthouse ... 213
Log Slaughterhouse 213
Louis Glunz Dance Hall 189
Luening, Dr. Fred A. residence 199

M

Mamer, M. residence 223
Methodist Episcopal Church 205
Mielke, E. residence 202
Mike Binc's Block see
  Binc's Block
Milwaukee Northern Bridge
  Cedar Creek 202

Milwaukee Northern substation .. 200
Moeqenburg, F. residence 200
Mueller, Heinrich residence 224

O

O'Brien, John farmhouse 214
Octagonal Barn (Mequon) 215
Ozaukee County Courthouse 223

P

Pagoda filling station see
  Wadhams Pagoda filling station
Pierron, Peter farmhouse 222
Pioneer Village 188
Poggenburg, Christian farmhouse.. 186
Port Washington Harbor 218
Port Washington High School 221
Port Washington Power Plant 220
Pulaski Hotel 226

R

Reichert, John farmhouse 214
Residence (Port Washington) 217
Residence (Saukville) 227
Riveredge Nature Center 188
Roth, Henry residence 196
Roth, Henry rooming house 198
Roth, John residence 197

S

St. Francis Borgia Roman
  Catholic Church 191
St. John's Catholic Church 234
St. Johns Evangelical Lutheran
  Church 185
St. Mary's Catholic Church 220
St. Mary's Cemetery 225
St. Mary's Cemetery Chapel 228
St. Peter's Evangelical Church 227
Schnabel, E. farmhouse 186
Schroeder, Jurgen general store
  (#380) 194
Schroeder, Juergen residence 194
Schroeder, William H. residence ... 195
Schuette, John Sr. residence 191
Schumacher, Jacob residence 224
Schumacher Monument Co. 219
Seegers, W.H. farmhouse 186
Slaughterhouse (Mequon) see
  Log Slaughterhouse ....
Stallman, Eilert residence 204
Sullivan, Michael farmhouse 199

T

Teed, Byron residence 218
Teed-Bohan residence 217

Thiensville Mill Stable 230
Thiensville Mills 230
Thiensville State Bank 230
Thiensville Village Hall and
    Fire Department 229
Thill's Hotel 222
Thoreau School 215
Trinity Evangelical Lutheran
    Church (Cedarburg) 203
Trinity Evangelical Lutheran
    Church (Mequon) 215
Turner Hall 211

U

Union House Hotel 193
U.S. Coast Guard Lighthouse 220

V

Vail, James residence 220

Van Buren School 231

W

Wadewitz Butcher Shop 233
Wadhams Pagoda filling station 202
Washington House Hotel 193
Waubeka firehouse 233
Weber, August residence 197
Weber, John residence 201
Wilson Hotel 219
Wirth Building 192
Wisconsin House Hotel 219
Wisconsin Lutheran Seminary 215
Wittenberg, Diedrich residence 199
Wollner, Martin farmhouse 187
Wurthmann, E.G. store 195
Wurthmann, Erhardt residence 191

Z

Zaun, Jacob farmhouse 214

RACINE COUNTY

A

Abraham and Mary Todd
    Lincoln Monument 374
Auditorium Hotel 361

B

Baker, Charles H. residence 374
Bank of Burlington 359
Beardsley, Elam farmhouse 350
Blackburn, Matthew farmhouse... 351
Blake, Lucius S. residence 374
Breese farmhouse 395
Brehm, Jacob building 357
Buchholtz, Charles farmhouse 350
Burlington Bank see
    Bank of Burlington
Burlington Cobblestone residences
    see Cobblestone residences
    (Burlington)
Burlington Settlers Monument 357

C

Cahoon, Hiram residence 398
Caldwell Grade School 366
Caldwell Store 364
Caldwell United Methodist
    Church 366
Caley residence 400
Carnegie Library (Racine) 372
Carpenter, Charles R. residence ... 378
Case, J. I. see
    J. I. Case
Casino Hall 381
Chandler, Oliver W. residence 355
Chapman, Samuel E. residence 401
Chicago and Northwestern Rr.
    Depot 391
Chicago and Northwestern Rd.
    Depot (old) 391
Cobblestone residences
    (Burlington) 358
Collins, Henry residence 395
Colonel Heg Memorial Park 349
Commercial Buildings (Racine) ... 385
Congregational Church, old,
    Caldwell 365
Cooley, Eli R. residence 375
Corliss Hotel 347
Cross Evangelical Lutheran
    Church 358

D

Dingee, William W. residence 369
District no. 3 Schoolhouse
    (Racine) 351

Dr. Shoop Family Medicine Co. ... 389
Durand, Henry S. residence 375
Durgin, Deacon T.W. residence ... 357

E

Ela, Richard Emerson residence .. 397
Ellertson, Hans farmhouse 348
Emerson, Thomas Jefferson
   residence 373
Erskine, George Q. residence 373

F

Farmer's Club Hall 365
First Baptist Church 380
First Church of Christ Scientist 382
First Congregational Church 390
First Presbyterian Church 382
Frank, August C. residence 383

G

Gillett Building 394
Goetz, John residence 389
Grace Universalist Church 398
Greeley, Warren farmhouse 366
Green Bay Road Marker 346

H

Hall, Chauncey residence 377
Hall Block 371
Hardy, Thomas P. residence 378
Harvey, Thomas residence 374
Hattlestad, Peter residence 401
Haumersen Market 370
Heg Memorial Park see
   Colonel Heg Memorial Park
Henry J. Kortendick Block see
   Kortendick Block
Holy Communion Lutheran
   Church 386
Horlicks Food Co. 391
Hoyt, Franklin E. residence 352
Hoyt residence 352
Hueffner, Ernest J. residence 383
Hunt, William residence 377

I

Immaculate Conception Church ... 359

J

J.I. Case Office Building 390
Jackson, Joseph residence 399
James F. Gilmore Jr. High
   School 392
Johnson, Herbert F. residence 387

Johnson, Samuel Curtis
   residence 381
Johnson Wax buildings see
   S.C. Johnson Buildings .
Jonas, Karel Monument see
   Karel Jonas Monument
Jonas, Karel residence 388
Jones, Charles A. residence 354
Jones, Thomas residence 376
Judd-Freeman residence 377

K

Karel Jonas Monument 387
Kortendick Block 402

L

Lawton, David residence 376
Lee, Charles H. residence 376
Lighthouse (Racine) see
   Racine Harbor Lighthouse
Lighthouse (Wind Point) see
   Wind Point Lighthouse
Lincoln Block 390
Lincoln Monument (Racine) see
   Abraham and Mary Todd
   Lincoln Monument
Lorenzo Janes School 369
Louis Noll Block see
   Noll Block

M

McClurg Building 370
Manufacturer's National Bank 371
Market Square 371
Martin Luther College 385
Masonic Temple (Racine) 380
Meinhardt, Anthony residence 356
Memorial Hall (Racine) 369
Merrill, Lewis residence 351
Miller, Henry C. residence 375
Miller, Joseph residence 375
Moe residence 401
Mound Cemetery 394
Mrkvicka, Frank J. saloon 370
Murray, George residence 394
Muth, Jacob residence 360
Mygatt farmhouse 350

N

Neisner's Building 371
Noll Block 403
Noll, Louis warehouse 403
Norway Lutheran Church 349

O

O'Berry, W.R. residence 397
Old Muskego Marker 349

P

Patterson, Albert residence 365
Peacock, Henry residence 364
Perkins, Origen residence 356
Perkins, Pliny farmhouse 358
Pierce, Joshua farmhouse 393
Pioneer Log Cabin 361
Plymouth Congregational Church.. 382
Prairie School 386
Pushee, Thomas D. residence 376

R

Racine College 379
Racine County Courthouse 379
Racine Fire Station no. 1 393
Racine Fire Station no. 4 388
Racine Harbor Lighthouse 368
Racine Water Works 368
Residence (Italianate)
(Burlington) 355
Residence (Racine) 384
Residence (Two family) (Racine).. 380
Rice, Ira A. residence 350
Riverbend Nature Center 393
Rochester Mill 399
Rowe, William farmhouse 353
Russell, Andrew J. residence 399

S

S.C. Johnson buildings 393
St. Catherine's High School 384
St. Francis Friary 353
St. John the Divine Episcopal
Church 358
St. John's Evangelical Lutheran
Church (Burlington) 360
St. John's Evangelical Lutheran
Church (Racine) 388
St. Joseph's Catholic Church 389
St. Louis Catholic Church 346
St. Luke's Epicopal Church 372
St. Luke's Hospital 383
St. Mary's Catholic Church 359
St. Mary's Cemetery Chapel 357
St. Patrick's Catholic Church 388
St. Thomas Aquinas Catholic
Church 402
St. Thomas Aquinas Parochial
School 402
Schoolhouse, District no. 3 Racine
see District no. 3 Schoolhouse
Schroeder, Joseph residence 369
Shoop, Dr. Charles residence 372
Shoop Family Medicine Co. see
Dr. Shoop Family Medicine Co.
Skunk Grove Marker 348
Slauson, Daniel Parsonage 384
Smieding, William residence 392

Smith, Randall W. residence 384
Stephens, Henry residence 373
Stone residence (Burlington) 360
Strang, James Jesse residence 362

T

32nd Division Memorial Highway
Marker 346
Thomas, J.B. farmhouse 386
Thomas, John residence 401
Thompson, Anthony residence 399

U

Union Grove Congregational
Church 347
Union Grove School 348
Union House Hotel 397
Union Methodist Episcopal
Church 380
U.S. Post Office (Racine) 372
Universalist Church of the Good
Shepherd 381
University of Lawsonomy 347

V

Voree, Old Town Marker 361

W

Walker, James residence 392
Walker, Robert Mosely residence .. 394
Wallis, Harry residence 373
Western Union Hotel 360
Whitman, Abial residence 398
Winslow School 383
Wind Point Lighthouse 387
Wingspread see
Johnson, Herbert F. residence
Wolff Clothing Store 370

Y

YMCA (Racine) 385

A

Adam Maurer Hotel 239
Amity Leather Products Co. 264

B

Backhaus, Otto farmhouse 256
Baptist Church 268
Barton Roller Mill 270
Bloor, Fred residence 251
Braatz-Foley barn 244

C

Christ Evangelical Church 249
Courthouse Square 267

D

David's Star Church 245
Demmon, Walter farmhouse 238
Diefenthaler & Co. store &
    saloon 249

E

Eagle Brewery 266
Everly, Francis log home 237

F

Falkenstein, Gottfried residence .. 253
First Congregational Church 251
Fischer's General Store 257
Frankin Grist Mill office 237
Frisby, Leander residence 264

G

Gehl, Mike general store 242
German Evangelical and
    Reformed Salem's Church 242
Germantown Mutual Insurance
    Co. 249
Germantown Mutual Insurance
    Co. Marker 248

H

Hartford City Hall 252
Hausmann, Dr. residence 255
Hoffmann, Peter farmhouse 237
Holy Angels Catholic School 268
Holy Hill 246
Holy Trinity Catholic Church
    (Kewaskum) 255
Holy Trinity Catholic Church
    (Newburg) 259

K

Karsten, Fred residence 269
Kessel, Peter farmhouse 245
Kissel Motor Car Co. Marker 251
Kreutz, P. Block 252
Krohn, Herman shop 254

L

Leonhardt, Henry farmhouse 247
Lizard Mound State Park 238
Log home, Francis Everly see
    Everly, Francis log home

M

Maas, Nicholas Cobbler shop 258
McLane School 266
Masonic Temple 265
Maurer, A. hotel see
    Adam Maurer Hotel
Mayer, Carl residence 266
Mayer, Charles M. residence 269
Mike Gehl general store see
    Gehl, Mike general store
Miller, Charles residence 256
Mueller, J.M. residence 255

N

Newburg Fire Station 258
Newburg Grade School 258

O

Odd Fellows Hall
    (Scenic Dr. and Bolton Dr.) 242
Odd Fellows Hall
    (Slinger) 261
Old Settlers Triangle Marker 265

P

Penoske, E. residence 261
Petri, Wendel barn 242

R

Reichert, Dr. J.E. residence 261
Residence (Hartford) 252
Residence (West Bend (Barton)).. 271
Riley, William farmhouse 243
Rogge, Henry farmhouse 238
Rosenheimer, Lehman
    general store 262
Rosenheimer Family Cemetery 262
Roth's Hotel barn 260

S

Sachse, Dr. Fred'k W. residence ... 251

St. Agnes Convent 271
St. Augustine Roman Catholic
    Church 245
St. Johannes Evangelical
    Lutheran Church 267
St. John of God Catholic Church.. 243
St. John's Evangelical Church 248
St. Lawrence Catholic Church 239
St. Mary's Immaculate
    Conception Catholic Church 271
St. Mary's School 271
St. Paul's Lutheran Church 261
St. Peter's Church (E. Newark
    Dr.) 245
St. Peters' Roman Catholic
    Church (Slinger) 262
S.S. Peter and Paul's Catholic
    Church, Rectory and School 241
Saxonia House 244
Schlegel, Gottlieb Bakery 264
Schroeder, Albert farmhouse 253
Schroeder, F.W. farmhouse 238
Schuler, Fred C. residence 243
Schumacher, John farmhouse 240
Schunk, Jacob farmhouse 248
Schwin, Peter farmhouse 244
Seeley, Smith M. residence 252
Sell, John farmhouse 239
6th District Grade School 262
Spaeth, J. farmhouse 237
Staats Brewery House 249

T

Templar Hall 255
Treverani's Hotel and Saloon 265

W

Washington Co. Courthouse 267
Washington County Jail 267
Washington House Hotel 265
Webster House Hotel 257
Weil, B. Schlesinger residence 268
Weinand, Max saloon 258
Weninger, Jacob farmhouse 240
West Bend City Hall 268

Z

Ziegelbauer residence &
    blacksmith shop 239

WAUKESHA COUNTY

A

Allen, Frank E. residence 340
Andrews, Laurel residence 301
Andrews, Sewall residence 301
Angrave-Waite Block 329

B

Baer, Albert residence 296
Baptist Church (Mukwonago) 301
Bark River Hotel 299
Barnard, E.W. residence 322
Barnes block 329
Barney, Sebina residence 283
Blair, William residence 335
Brookins, H.J. 307
Buchner, John P. residence 336
Burr Oak House Hotel 294

C

Campbell, Albert farmhouse 280
Carroll College 339
Chandler, Walter Seymour
    residence 338
Chesney, Rev. Rufus residence ... 283
Clark, John J. dry good store 328
Clark residence 309
Cook, Alexander residence 337
Cordie, Joe store and residence ... 278
Craig, Perry farmhouse 287
Craig, Randall V. farmhouse 286
Crummy, J.M. residence 322
Cushing Memorial Park 291
Cutler Park 332

D

Davidson, Andrew residence 319
Delafield Presbyterian Church 289
Dousman, Michael residence 281
Dunbar Oak Marker 325

E

Edgerton, Elisha farm 279
Edwards, David residence 304
Enterprise Roller Mill 296

F

Fabacher residence 335
Field, Judge Martin residence 301
First Baptist Church (Merton) 298
First Baptist Church (Waukesha)... 330
First Congregational Church
    (Oconomowoc) 313
First Congregational Church
    (Waukesha) 340

First German Reformed Church
(Waukesha) 331
First Methodist Church
(Waukesha) 330
Fish Hatchery, Wisconsin State
see Wisconsin State Fish
Hatchery
Foster/Rockwell residence 309
Fountain Spring House (site) 333
Frame, Andrew residence 333
Freewill Baptist Church 283
Fuller, Mrs. H.G. residence 308

G

George, Henry Carl residence 335
Gould, David residence 306
Greaves, William farmhouse 278
Griswold, Amos farmhouse 280

H

Hadfield, Abram H. residence 340
Hadfield, Joseph Jackson
residence 340
Hadfield, Samuel guesthouse 331
Hall, John M. farmhouse 277
Hawks Inn 288
Hawks Inn Dance Hall 289
Heath, John grist mill 290
Hemlock, Daniel J. residence 337
Henshall, Dr. James A. coach-
house 312
Hewitt, Dr. Edward Harvey
residence 311
Hinkley, Ahira Rockwell
residence 285
Hinkley, P. farmhouse 285
Hitchcock, James C. residence 307
Hodgson, John residence 281
Hubbell, Capt. Stephen A.
residence 323

J

Jackson Block 328
Jackson residence 341
James, Samuel D. residence 341
Jameson and James Block 329
Jones, Robert residence 338
Justice Statue 327

K

Kellogg Drug Store 305
Kemper, (Bp.) Jackson
residence 290
Kiekhefer, Robert J. residence 281
Kline's Hotel 292
Klos, Peter saloon 305
Koehler, Frank residence 296

L

Lain, Isaac residence 330
Lapham Peak-Kettle Moraine Dr. .. 280
Log house (Menomonee Falls) 297

M

Maas, Gottlieb residence 313
McCurlie, George residence 293
Mann, William G. residence 332
Mann block 304
Masonic Temple (Waukesha) 334
Medbury residence 308
Meidenbauer, John Konrad
residence 283
Methodist District Parsonage 338
Meyer, Dr. Louis A. residence 311
Miller, Dr. McL. residence 306
Mills, John general store 321
Milwaukee & Madison Railroad
Depot (Waukesha) 339
Milwaukee Road Depot
(Oconomowoc) 314
Mineral Spring (Waukesha) see
Silurian Mineral Spring
Mitchell, John residence 299
Moore, Dr. Volney L.
residence 326
Mukwonago House Hotel 300

N

Nashotah House-Chapel 279
Nashotah House Episcopal
Seminary 279
National Hotel 327
Neff, Charles Morgan residence ... 322
Nickell Block 329
Notbohm Block 310

O

Oak Hill Cemetery 281
Oconomowoc City Hall 310
Oconomowoc National Bank 310
Oconomowoc Public Library 305
Oconomowoc Public Library
Griffins 306
Octagon House (Merton) 298
Odd Fellows Hall (Pewaukee) 315
Okauchee House 277
Old Falls Village 297
Old Waukesha County
Courthouse 327
Old World Wisconsin 284
Orient Block 328
Ottowa Town Hall 282
Our Saviour's Evangelical
Lutheran Church 313

P

Palestine School 285
Parsons, Jonathan residence 284
Pearmain residence 289
Peck, Harold residence 307
Powrie, William residence 338
Presbyterian Parsonage
  (Waukesha) 341
Proudfit, Andrew residence 289
Putman, Pliny residence 313
Putney Block 328
Putney, Aaron residence 331
Putney Block #2 327

R

Railroad Depot - Waukesha see
  Milwaukee and Madison
  Railroad Depot
Rector, Joseph residence 314
Reed residence 322
Reformed Presbyterian Church
  of Vernon 286
Residence (210 W. Laflin,
  Waukesha) 336
Residence Greekrevival
  (403 McCall St., Waukesha) 336
Residence (603 N. West Ave.,
  Waukesha) 335
Resthaven Sanitarium 326
Richard Street residence
  (Waukesha) 331
Robinson Block 330
Rosenkranz, O.L. residence 311

S

St. Albans Episcopal Church 320
St. Anthony Catholic Church 297
St. Catherine's Catholic Church ... 276
St. James Catholic Church 278
St. Jerome Catholic Church 304
St. John Chrysostom Church 290
St. John's Military Academy 290
St. Joseph's Catholic Church 341
St. Mary Church
  (Menomonee Falls) 297
St. Mary's Catholic Church ....
  (Pewaukee) 316
St. Matthias Episcopal Church 326
St. Paul Catholic Church 282
St. Paul's Evangelical Lutheran
  Church 287
St. Paul's United Evangelical
  Congregation Church 296
St. Theresas Catholic Church 292
Saloon (Lannon Road) 278
Sanger Casper Melchior
  residence 337
Schneider, Jacob residence 299

Schneider, Phillip residence 299
Schreiber, Henry barn 284
Schuttler, Henry residence 309
Scudder, Captain residence 307
Silurian Mineral Spring 326
Sloan, William P. residence 337
Smith, Jesse Inn 286
Stockman House Tavern 302
Stone farmhouse
  (old Village Road) 282

T

Totten, Henry residence 333
Townsend, Dr. Hosea residence ... 308
Townsend House (site) 312
Trevor R.R. Depot North Lake 277

U

Union House Hotel 282
Unitarian and Universalist
  Church (Mukwonago) 302
United States Post Office
  (Waukesha) 334

V

Vernon United Presbyterian
  Church 286

W

Wallman & Lotz furniture store ... 302
Ward, Marjorie residence 309
Warren, Stephen residence 294
Water Utility, Waukesha see
  Waukesha Water Utility
Waukesha County Courthouse
  (old) see
  Old Waukesha County Courthouse
Waukesha Water Utility 334
Weeks, Moses residence 336
West, Deacon residence 315
Westover, George residence 304
Wintermute, Dr. Charles E.
  residence 320
Wisconsin Central Car Shops 329
Wisconsin Masonic Home 280
Wisconsin State Fish Hatchery 291
Woodlands Hotel 312
Worthington, Theo. residence 310

Y

Yanke, Louis saloon 334

Z

Zion Episcopal Church 306

MILWAUKEE COUNTY ADDRESS INDEX

*There are 46 entries in The Heritage Guidebook which do not
appear in the address index because they did not have house numbers.*

ASTOR ST. (North)
1037 56
1100 57
1122 57

BECHER ST. (West)
1414 166

BELOIT RD. (West)
6014 178

BLUEMOUND RD. (West)
5503 145

BROADWAY (North)
302 49
611 47
836 64
1020 65
1120 65
1209 65

BROWN DEER RD. (East)
1111 98

BURNHAM ST. (West)
2714-34 169

CAMBRIDGE AVE. (North)
3138 101

CAPITOL DR. (East)
709-33 98
720 99
2121 95
2214 95

CASS ST. (North)
1135 59
1219 60

CHURCH ST.
1511 147
1609 148

COMMERCE ST
.... 121

CONGRESS ST. (West)
9400 154

DOWNER AVE. (North)
2705 102

FARWELL ST. (North)
2230 75

FLORIDA ST. (West)
329-331 157

FOND DU LAC AVE. (West)
2654 128

FOREST HOME AVE. (West)
1432 165
2405 164
2504 164
6802 179

FRANKLIN PL. (North)
1241 69
1249 69

GALENA ST. (West)
235 117

GORDON PL. (North)
2443 127

GRANGE AVE. (West)
8685 181
8881 182

HACKETT ST. (North)
2648 85

HARTFORD AVE. (East)
2311 102

HARWOOD AVE. (West)
7335 146
7720 146

HIGHLAND AVE. (West)
2026 126
2722 139
3112 140
3209 140

HOMER ST. (East)
606 174

HUMBOLDT AVE. (North)
4151 98

JACKSON ST. (North)
802 61

JEFFERSON ST. (North)
706 52
761 61
777 62

JUNEAU AVE. (East)
828 58
924 56
1028 56
1060 55
1228-36 68

JUNEAU AVE. (West)
300 116
423 118
917 120
1037 120

KANE PL. (East)
1830 75

KENWOOD AVE. (East)
2519 101
3230 89

KILBOURN ST. (East)
250 40
432 64
813 59

KILBOURN ST. (West)
500-90 118
2432 141
3815 143

KINNICKINNIC AVE. (South)
2605 174
3317 175

KNAPP ST. (East)
914 59
1139 69

LAFAYETTE PL. (East)
2022 76
2127 77

LAKE DR. (North)
2025 76
2320 84
2743 81
3201 89
3266 89
3288 90
3319 90
3432 91
3474 91
3510 94
5270 94

LAKE DR. (South)
3257 175

LAPHAM ST. (West)
1321 165

LAYTON BLVD. (South)
550 168
550 167
1434 168
1501 168
1545 169

LINCOLN AVE. (West)
601 161
5301 180
6014 177

LINCOLN MEMORIAL DR. (North)
750 41
1701 76
3000 92

LISBON AVE. (West)
7709 152

LOCUST ST. (East)
1208 127
1615 101

McKINLEY AVE. (West)
3112 140
3238 141

MARIETTA AVE. (North)
2931 82
3270 90

MARSHALL AVE. (North)
817-9 57
1029 58
1119 58

MASON ST. (East)
411 63

MICHIGAN ST. (East)
207 46
210 46
225 46
322 47
507 47

MICHIGAN ST. (West)
231 112

MILLER LN. (West)
3713 143

MILWAUKEE AVE. (West)
8000 149

MILWAUKEE ST. (North)
700 62
727 62
733 63
759 63
1001 64

MITCHELL AVE. (West)
1321 165

MUSKEGO AVE. (South)
1942 163

NATIONAL AVE. (West)
1635 167
1925 167
8405 178

NEWBERRY BLVD. (East)
2430 81
2727 80
2909 80
3000 80

NEWPORT AVE. (East)
2933 91

NORTH AVE. (West)
5919-27 152

OAKLAND AVE (North)
2011 100
4001-15 95

OGDEN AVE. (East)
1009 66
1019-43 66

PALMER ST. (North)
1823 124

PETTIBONE PL.
.... 134

PLANKINTON AVE. (North)
305 112

PLEASANT ST. (East)
1012 66

PROSPECT AVE. (North)
1201 68
1229-31 69
1216 68
1260 70
1360 71
1363 71
1451 71
1537 72
1550 72
1584 72
1681 73
1841 73
1930 74
1962 74
2101-05 74
2150 75

RAWSON AVE.
1020 177

RICHARDSON PL. (West)
.... 139

ROYALL PL. (East)
1630 73

RUSSELL AVE. (East)
1023 174

RYAN RD.
2740 177

ST. CLAIR ST. (South)
2414 172
2463 173

ST. PAUL AVE. (West)
341 111
433 111

SCOTT ST. (West)
202 156

SHEPARD AVE. (North)
2704 82
2705 81

SHERMAN BLVD. (North)
2525 153
2915 153

SOUTH SHORE DR.
2582 172

STATE ST. (East)
1024 55

STATE ST. (West)
333 114
1617 125
2710 138
3011 139

4000 144
4400 144
7616 147

SUMMIT AVE. (North)
3043 82

SUPERIOR ST. (South)
2590 172
2739 173

TERRACE AVE. (North)
2214 77
2220 77
2230 78
2234 78
2420 85
2550 85
2611 86
2675 86

TEUTONIA AVE. (North)
2432 128

UNDERWOOD AVE.
1417 147

VAN BUREN ST. (North)
790 60

WAHL AVE. (North)
2409 87
2569 87
2601 86
2691 87

WASHINGTON ST. (West)
239 158

WATER ST. (North)
330-2 48
402 48
500 48
710 38
721 39
735 39
746 39
929 41

WAUWATOSA AVE. (North)
1626 148
1828 148
2107 149

WAVERLY PL. (North)
1105 55

WELLS ST. (East)
108 40
125 40
144 38
200 37
718 60
924 54
925 54

WELLS ST. (West)
135 113
515 108

1820 133	640 157
3205 136	803 158
	813 158
WISCONSIN AVE. (East)	821 158
110 38	**FOURTH (North)**
111 43	1034 116
205 43	1542 117
229 44	1702 124
323-31 44	1927 125
324 52	
407 44	**FOURTH (South)**
424 52	605 158
425 45	621 159
517 45	1646 159
526 53	
626 53	**FIFTH (North)**
720 53	735 108
777 45	**FIFTH (South)**
	639 159
WISCONSIN AVE. (West)	729 160
101 104	1037 160
161 105	1136 160
212 105	1681 161
215 106	
231 106	**SIXTH (North)**
301 106	1015 119
509 107	**SEVENTH (South)**
606 108	1105 162
735 109	
814 109	**NINTH (North)**
833 110	901 119
900 110	1046 120
935 111	
1131 130	**THIRTEENTH (North)**
1145 131	525 131
1341 132	
1492 132	**FIFTEENTH (South)**
1810 132	2427 166
2000 133	**SIXTEENTH (South)**
2051 134	2221 164
2133 134	
2401 135	**EIGHTEENTH (North)**
3000 135	2469 127
3424 136	**NINETEENTH (North)**
3841 136	950-960 126
	1305 125
FIRST (North)	
2863 128	**TWENTY-THIRD (North)**
	626-30 135
SECOND (North)	
1825 124	**TWENTY-FOURTH (North)**
	1453 126
SECOND (South)	
801-5 156	**TWENTY-SEVENTH (North)**
1201 156	3533 153
THIRD (North)	**THIRTY-SECOND (North)**
720 107	1731 151
910 113	**THIRTY-FOURTH (North)**
1001 114	1727 151
1050 115	
1101 115	**FORTIETH (North)**
	1440 151
THIRD (South)	**FIFTY-FIRST (South)**
408-410 157	3201 180
634 157